TALES MY
FATHER TAUGHT ME

BY SIR OSBERT SITWELL

The Author at Home

TALES MY

FATHER TAUGHT ME

An Evocation of Extravagant Episodes

Sir Osbert Sitwell

WITH ILLUSTRATIONS

An Atlantic Monthly Press Book

LITTLE, BROWN AND COMPANY
Boston   Toronto

ACKNOWLEDGMENTS

My acknowledgments are due to the Dropmore Press and to Messrs Gerald Duckworth & Co. Ltd, under whose auspices 'Hortus Conclusus' appeared as a preface to my father's book *On the Making of Gardens*; to the Editor of *Lilliput* in whose magazine 'Making a Bolt for It' first appeared (to Messrs Macmillan & Co. Ltd, under whose auspices it appeared in my book *The Four Continents*); to Mr John Lehmann, who first published, in the *London Magazine*, 'Recollections of An Awkward Afternoon in Knightsbridge', and to the Editor of *The Reporter*, where 'Unusual Holidays' appeared under the title 'My Father's Excursions and Alarms'.

I thank Mr Thomas Mark for his help with the proofs and Miss Andrade for her work on them.

I wish to thank the *Atlantic Monthly* for permission to reprint the following chapters: Chapter 9 'The Adventure of the Phantom Tax-inspector', Chapter 14 'Unforgotten Feasts', Chapter 18 'Creating', Chapter 19 'A Rap Over the Knuckles', Chapter 24 'Magic', and Chapter 28 'The New Jerusalem'.

I also wish to thank *Vogue* for permission to reprint the following chapters: Chapter 12 'Ideas from the Bureau', Chapter 15 'By Rail and Boat', and Chapter 20 'Popularity'.

CONTENTS

CONTENTS

ILLUSTRATIONS

The author wishes to thank Hans Wild for the photographs in this book. The credit due him was inadvertently omitted.

INTRODUCTION

THE chief object of a preface or introduction is to give an author the chance of tilting his book at the correct angle for the reader, and sometimes to explain how it came to be of a certain form and why it developed as it did. Thus, the origin of this book is comparable to that of jewels. When a large gem has been detached from its matrix to be cut and polished there inevitably remain fragments of precious stone. To these the expert artificer then turns his attention, proceeding to fashion them, however small they may be, into separate ornaments, or parts of them. Similarly, after the life-size portraits of my father and myself emerged from the five volumes of my autobiography, *Left Hand, Right Hand!* many memories of him that I had been compelled to omit, for reasons of the general design and by the laws immanent in every individual structure, seemed to claim my attention with a vivacity of their own. This book came into being in this way, and has been written with no other object than to engage the interest of the reader: but I hope that because I have, after this fashion, declared my purpose, he will not accuse me of levity or assume that I do not realize the tragic implications under the smiling lawns, or perceive the flames and fury of great catastrophes veiled behind flimsy screens. Nor should it be taken for granted that it was easy to write. It was not. Indeed, I experienced the same feelings as must have afflicted Sir Arthur Conan Doyle when confronted with the composition of *The Return of Sherlock Holmes.*

My father had become more finely drawn with the years, and the gothic age in which he had for so long chosen to immure himself had left its mark on his appearance, so that from the elegant young man of the eighties, who was depicted by Frank Miles and by Du Maurier in pencil drawings, he had come to resemble a bearded medieval effigy stridden down from a tomb. His energy, however, even when he was resting in bed, remained undiminished, and he still threw himself—and any other person he could find within range—into every activity in which he was interested. The only other sign of age that he showed as he grew older was that he appeared at times to suffer from what Bernard Shaw, inventing a name for it, and thus isolating and focussing a widely prevalent condition, called a *time lag.* For instance, when my elder nephew was two years old my father looked down one day at the innocent infant lying peacefully asleep in his perambulator and remarked to me in a sentimental voice:

'I do hope that they won't forget to teach the little man to sing after dinner. Nothing makes a man so popular.'

When I made an effort to explain to him that if today a man tried to sing after dinner he would be more likely to be lynched than applauded, he became annoyed and reiterated:

'Nonsense! Nothing makes a man so popular!'

Another figure must be mentioned who comes back into these pages. The reader of *Left Hand, Right Hand!* will recall Henry Moat, now family butler and formerly my father's foil on so many trips in search of the wildest geese. His return to the household after several years was the most welcome event.

It only remains for me to explain that the papers which follow are treated singly. I do not attempt to arrange them in strict chronological sequence: albeit they have their own inherent order, so that each episode is essential to the book of which it forms a chapter. I trust that in perusing it the reader will become further acquainted with the ways of an exceptional man and an exceptional parent, and that when he speaks in these pages the reader may catch momentarily the very run and intonation of his voice. . . . Now let us embark for the Sweet South in the early nineteen-hundreds.

I

HORTUS CONCLUSUS
MY FATHER AND THE GARDEN

In the happy days of the far-off first decade of the nineteen-hundreds, about the time that Princess Ena became engaged to King Alfonso, that Melba was singing in *Madame Butterfly*, that Miss Lily Elsie was appearing in *The Merry Widow*, in short, in the golden days of good King Edward, a visitor in the spring or autumn to any of the great Italian or remarkable Sicilian gardens, especially those that were more remote, might have chanced to see a tall, distinguished-looking Englishman with a high-bridged nose, and with fair, fine hair and a slightly darker golden moustache, flourished upwards a little in the manner of Kaiser Wilhelm's, seated on a bench, regarding his surroundings with analytic concentration. He would be wearing a grey suit and a wide-brimmed hat, a striped linen shirt with a stiff white winged collar, and starched cuffs fastened by large carbuncle links; probably he would be sitting on a circular rubber air-cushion shaped like a lifebuoy, so well known a seat-mark in the daily life of the Reading

Room of the British Museum, while slung round his body as if he were at a race meeting would be a leather case containing a pair of binoculars, and beside him—for he took care to sit in the shade—a sun-umbrella lined with green. Not far off, within the carrying of a voice, from the thick blackness of an ilex grove would peer a ponderous figure, watchful, but with an eye for those who passed as well as for the safety of the rectangular, varnished wicker box in his custody, which each day contained a cold chicken. Over one arm would be folded a thick coat. . . . As he stood there he had something of an air of a night watch on a ship, and his appearance, though his skin was bronzed, or indeed copper-coloured, was as northern and national as that of the gentleman on the bench. He, meanwhile, had taken an envelope out of his pocket and was scratching on it with the stub-end of a pencil remarks angry or meditative; crossly, how a gardener had removed the patina or the lichen from a stone moulding since last he was here, or, reflectively, comparing the merits, where an effect of mystery was desired, of broad shaded ilex with thin-spired cypress, or of the different hues, textures, and sounds of varying kinds and speeds of falling water, and the sense of coolness and peace thereby induced. . . .

The visitors might perhaps enquire—as often they did when they got back to the hotel—who the English gentleman might be, and who the nautical figure hovering so heavily in the background—and the answer would come, Sir George Reresby Sitwell and his servant, Henry Moat. For in those years my father was busy collecting material for the book he planned on gardens.

In 1900 he had suffered a bad nervous breakdown and had decided in consequence to give up politics. In the ensuing years he travelled much in Italy, and of his recovery there the book was the fruit. He had already written several works of an historical nature, or illustrative of the manners of some particular period, but had issued them from his own printing-press. They had not been for sale. But this new volume was to be published by Murray's and its aim was high, for I recollect his saying to me that he hoped it would rank in the future with Bacon's essay, *Of Gardens*.

On the Making of Gardens, as it is called, certainly stands as the most complete expression in my father's writings of one facet of his personality, of one concentration of his interests—but there were hundreds of others. Though he worked so hard at all the innumerable matters on which he was engaged, the truth is that he found it difficult to finish anything. The garden at Renishaw remains—and is now likely to remain—uncompleted in its detail. And the family-history, at which he had worked for two decades, was found after his death with still one chapter lacking.

Time seems to have been too short for him in his span of eighty-three years, and only this one book is an idea of his conceived, attempted, and completely achieved—whatever may be judged of the achievement—wholly realized down to the last comma and the final full-stop. Moreover, when setting himself to anything he spared no pain, either to himself or to others—it would often have been, in result, better if he had. Thus, before beginning to write the book, he spent endless hours mastering the full intricacies of English grammar, under the tuition of Major Viburne, who appears as a fitful—in every sense—shadow in the pages of my autobiography, and who knew much less about syntactic matters than did his pupil. In brief, my father took too much trouble. In order to write a sentence on the psychology of garden-making he would read a hundred slightly obsolete technical volumes, nor would he always afford his imagination sufficient room for its full sweep, since he relied overmuch on notes. (One difference between the journalist and the writer resides in this, that the first makes jottings and directly transcribes from them, while the second allows—or should allow—the subject matter of his book to grow organically, like a plant, in the mind and on the paper.) Thus, in illustration of what I mean, I once saw my father setting off from the door at Renishaw in a very old carriage, about eleven on a September night. As usually he went to bed at ten, I was surprised, and enquired what he was doing. 'Just driving down to Eckington Church to observe the effect of moonlight on the tower,' he replied with a flutter of his hand, as if conferring a favour upon the edifice; 'I want it for my chapter "Eckington Church in the Thirteenth Century" in *Tales of My Native Village.*'

Howbeit, never was any book more pondered upon at every stage than were his garden essays. For hours the author would lie on his bed wrestling with each current problem, and if Henry's footstep was heard in the passage, or a hotel housemaid dared to wipe and rattle surreptitiously the door handle—a favourite trick when a writer is at work—he would dart out of bed, clearing his mosquito net as if by magic, open the door with a snap, and look out blandly, while making at the same time a humming noise which held in it—if you listened carefully—an icy-cold but terrible menace. (Strangers, however, were apt to mistake this sound for one engendered by happiness, and in consequence often received surprises.)

Unfortunately, then, as I have said, his energies were dissipated over a field too broad for their employment. But though he was adept at taking hold of the wrong end of a thousand sticks, yet when by chance he seized the right end his grasp of it was remarkable, because of the intellectual power and application, as well as the learning, which he brought to his task. And in the book I have mentioned, *On the Making of Gardens*, we have a complete work containing a great deal of thought and couched in phrases often of stilted beauty, and even if the whole volume from its opening 'Time is a wayward traveller' down to the closing sentence which begins 'Flying shafts of silvery splendour . . .' carries for us the haunting and mocking echo of Sir Austin Feverel's *The Pilgrim's Scrip*, even if fountains are throughout inclined to 'plash', and the 'goat-herd' to figure overmuch in a landscape not untouched by Alma-Tadema, still, it is none the worse for that, being a genuine period-piece, instilled with considerable imagination, influenced by the philosophies current ten years earlier, and with, not far behind each page, those crepuscular sensations made fashionable by Maeterlinck, together with a reverbera-tion of the august, if far-fetched, rotundities of Walter Pater. Moreover—and this is where he took the *right* end of the stick—the principles he enunciated (so my gardening friends, whose judgment I trust, have told me) are invaluable in the practical design of gardens, in the counterpoint of light and shade, and the correct employment of water as a device for variation.

In short, he knew what he was talking about, having observed, noted, and practised. His knowledge of gardens—Italian, in particular—was unrivalled (several later writers have had recourse to the lists obtained from him), but not, I hasten to add, of flowers, about which, paradoxically to English ideas of the present day, no man knew or cared less, for he had early imbibed the Mediterranean conception, imposed by brightness of climate, that a garden is a place of rest and peace, and in no way intended for a display of blossoms (for that, you had 'a flower garden' away from the house, and hidden). Such flowers as might be permitted, had, like all else in good taste, to be unobtrusive, not to call attention to themselves by hue or scent, but to form vague pointillist clouds of misty colour that could never detract from the view, and to infuse into the air a general sweetness never to be identified. The pastel-shade sweet peas and stocks of the nineteen-hundreds, love-in-the-mist, a few washed-out roses, and a kind of reed with a blue flower—these passed muster: but even they were sacrifices to my mother's insistent though contrary demands for scent and colour. 'Horticulturists' blossoms' were what he most detested, and, to make a personal confession, I remember that as a schoolboy on holiday, when my father had been particularly disagreeable, I used always to go into the garden to tend a rhododendron that carried a purple blossom of a peculiarly obtrusive and fiery appearance which he could see from his study window, and which greatly offended his eye, although for some reason or other he never eradicated the shrub in question. This I did because I had been told by someone that if you removed the dead racemes from a branch it would flower again, only more flagrantly, the following spring.

To return to his book on gardens, I remember well the initial stages of its first publication, for I had never before seen galley proofs, and my father gave them to me—I was sixteen—to read, with his corrections marked on them (I little knew, then, how such flat paper serpents were to entangle and devour my life, as if I were Laocoön). And I used to take them into a corner of the small apartment which we had rented that year in Florence, to revel in the sense of importance which this new acquaintance with the technical ways of the literary world conferred upon me. . . . Not only were these the first corrected proofs I had seen, they were, alas, also the first I ever lost! . . . Eventually, after a week of utter ignominy and disgrace, they were found in a cupboard in my room where, of course, I had placed them for safe keeping. Later in the year—for publishing was then a quicker business altogether—my father's great moment arrived, and the book came out—I think in August

1909. But, it is sad to recall, little more happened. One or two appreciative essays such as were written in those more leisurely days appeared in the weekly papers. He, and I, waited . . . but the rest was silence. Naturally he was disappointed, and blame was distributed impartially, some of it no doubt coming to me, but a good deal being placed to my mother's account.

I remember, too, his remarking of the top cover of his book, which was concealed under an azure dust-jacket, but displayed in bright colours the hardest and most stilted of garden vistas, that 'Murray's have managed to contradict by the design on the outside of the book every rule I have formulated inside it.' . . . However, he was pleased with the printing, if not with the reception. And I think that the actual moment of the appearance of the book was most pleasant for him. He had been ill, as the reader knows, and the process of study in gardens had healed him. The publishing of his work had constituted, moreover, a declaration of independence, and an affirmation of faith. It must have brought back to him lovely sunny days spent in his own company, which he always greatly enjoyed, with Henry and the luncheon-basket discreetly within call. Sometimes he took me with him, and on these occasions he was at his most amiable. There were, as well, adventures, such as that of which I heard subsequently from Henry, though I was not myself present. My father was meditating, just before the hour when the garden was to be closed, at the very bottom of the terraced slopes of the Villa d'Este, between the giant cypresses. He was deep in thought when four ancient *custodi* advanced on him from the four different quarters of the compass. Immediately concluding that the old men were brigands (for he always lived at least a hundred years before his time), he, as Henry put it, 'fair biffed 'em with his umbrella. You could hear 'em squawk half a mile away! But Sir George

[21]

was as cool as a cucumber and called me, saying: "Henry, the weather has changed. I had better put on my coat." ' . . . From such escapades, he, alone of living men, seemed qualified always to emerge victorious and scot-free. It was enough in those days for Henry to explain that his master was an English *signore*.

The effect, however, on my father of the lack of success of his book was considerable. He had, he told me, hoped to earn by it, now that his world was threatened by Lloyd George's Budget, something to leave to my brother Sacheverell. This hope was disappointed. And then there was another side to it. Many of my mother's friends, violently opposed to books in general, now regarded him as a traitor who had placed himself on the wrong side of the fence. Only the Bevy, which I have described elsewhere, sent up at his approach somewhat mildewed hosannahs of faint artistic praise. Meanwhile, he set himself to problems that were more immediate and practical than the theories of garden design. He arranged to send me to an army-crammer's, from which I was seldom allowed to escape—and when I did make a sortie and go home was rarely greeted with rapture. Then he had long been at work on an invention—a stick which would discharge vitriol at mad dogs and thus dispose of them. (There had been an epidemic of hydrophobia in England some twenty years before, but he had never as yet completed or patented his idea.) To this matter he now gave his mind. In addition, he made more miscellaneous notes: *Rotherham under Cromwell, Sheffield in the Wars of the Roses, Court Formalities at Constantinople, Marriage Chests of the Middle Ages, How to Preserve Fruit, The Correct Use of Seaweed as an Article of Diet, Sacheverell Pedigrees, My Views on Democracy*; each of these, and of a thousand other subjects, had a box devoted to it. These boxes were specially made for him, to contain half-pages of foolscap, and were fashioned of a material the colour of an aubergine, and in texture like a skin with goose-flesh. . . . Indeed, in everything connected with writing he had his own ways. His pens were of a fine, scratchy variety, composed of three long nibs and holders, each made entirely of one piece of metal. Three of these fitted together made a small metal rod which he could carry in his pocket without danger, but they were so thin as to render his handwriting even lighter and more spidery than it would have been in any case. For the rest, if he could not write about gardens with success, at least he could make them in the world of actuality. He abolished small hills, created lakes, and particularly liked now to alter the levels at which full-grown trees were standing. Two old yew trees in front of the dining-room windows at Renishaw were regularly heightened and lowered; a process which I then believed could have been shown to chart, like a thermometer, the temperature of his mood, and to which he always referred as 'pulling and dragging'. ('That oak tree needs to be pulled and dragged!') From the wooden towers constructed for the purpose in the lake and on the hill he would measure and survey. His head throbbed with ideas, the majority of them never to be put into practice. Glass fountains, aqueducts in rubble, gigantic figures, cascades through the woods, stone boats and dragons in the water of lake and pool, blue-stencilled white cows 'to give distinction to the landscape', many of these schemes, alas, remained where they were born. But they were a fine exercise for him, and a diversion. And it must be remembered that he would be occupied, too, every day in instructing all those about him in whatever was their speciality, while at the same time he was, besides, ferociously engaged in combat over his own affairs; for, as he rather piteously remarked to me, 'One has to think of *oneself a little.*'

[23]

2

ALL ON A SUMMER'S AFTERNOON

ANY attempt to halt the flight of time and to hover for a moment above selected incidents is always far from easy for a writer—especially when the method of dating prevalent in the family circle and household is a private system; as in my home where everything was dated by my father's beard. That was the Great Divide. 'It happened the year after Sir George grew his beard,' the gardener would say, or my mother would remark: 'That was not long before your father grew his beard.' The afternoon of which I am writing, however, is easy to place. It was in the year 1909 (before my father grew his beard) when I was sixteen—one of many awkward ages—that my mother administered to my father a severe esthetic shock.

It occurred at the beginning of the summer holiday, and my father had not paid a visit to Renishaw for nearly twelve months. He had been travelling in Italy and it was in the autumn of the same year that he was to buy Montegufoni.

Now, however, the family was gathered together again at Renishaw, and I remember most vividly this particular day there, because, among its other memorable features, it was on the same afternoon that I experimented first with tobacco— or rather that tobacco first experimented with me, for it was a one-sided tussle. I had appropriated from my father's study one of the very strong Egyptian cigarettes that he then smoked, and took it to the end of the garden, where there were some chairs put out. I sat down and lighted it. I had for a long while noticed the delicious aromatic fragrance of these cigarettes, and how blue was their smoke, as it lay on the air in layers in my father's study. So now I inhaled deeply once or twice—and within a few minutes felt ill beyond the reach of human aid. I am convinced that not even the first pipe of opium can have more effect on a neophyte than does the first cigarette of a lifetime. Why on this single occasion should a cigarette produce such consequences and never again? Though some factor must be present to account for the deadly malaise that ensues, I have never heard an explanation given that was satisfactory. Be that as it may, there I was immobilized, in a chair at the end of the garden in a trance-like condition for an hour or more; a state rendered not less alarming by the fear, indeed almost the certainty, that my father would come out, find me, and ask me to accompany him on a tour of the garden. It would be impossible for me to refuse, though I could, for that period, only have accomplished it by crawling on all-fours, an innovation I could not imagine would win his favour or even approval. Fortunately, however, he did not appear for a long time—perhaps the Sacheverell pedigree was giving him trouble—and I was able to walk about again by then and had decently interred the cigarette which I had been obliged to throw down on the ground in a hurry.

[25]

My mother, contrary to habit, was the first to appear—but she, too, had suffered a shock. . . . In those days of courtesy to employers it was unusual for them to hear anything but good of themselves, nor were they accustomed as yet to Lady Chatterley's language, or to be addressed except politely and formally—none of that free and easy manner that pertains today to the new equality; no such greetings as: ' 'Morning, chum! I'm taking a day off today.' No, things were different. . . . My mother, then, was walking down the long stone corridor to speak to the housekeeper, when she saw a very small child strapped into a perambulator just outside the door of the Housekeeper's Room. My mother, who was devoted to children, stopped for a moment to speak to the infant, though she was too young, my mother thought, to talk much. Imagine her astonishment and consternation when the little girl—for such she was—wagged a fat, warning finger at her and pronounced, with a diction so exquisite that it would have done credit to a great actress, and without a trace of the local rough northern dialect, the unexpected words:

'You jigger off, m'lady.'

The child's mother, a former housemaid who had married a miner, heard the words of her offspring and rushed out and apologized, adding: 'I'm sure I don't know where she picks up such expressions. Certainly not at home. Her father is always on to her about it. He says she swears worse than any man in the pit.'

This my mother was relating to me in the garden when my father arrived on the scene, in his usual summer rig, with his binoculars slung round him, ready for the distant views. For a moment he surveyed the prospect and for the first time suddenly perceived a construction of, apparently, lattice and flimsy twigs, with some very ostentatious roses trailing about on it.

[26]

It only escaped being a pergola by its plainly very temporary nature, just as the rambler roses on it only just escaped being Dorothy Perkins. That was the most that could be said for it. It—the near-pergola—stood in a conspicuous position, technically beyond the confines of the garden but in the direct line of view. As the full enormity of this skimpy ornament dawned on him, my father gave what is so seldom encountered in real life, though it abounds in mid-Victorian novels, 'a hollow groan'. His rules for the formal garden were, as I have explained, that nothing in it should look temporary and, further, that the flowers should be kept in their place and not permitted to challenge with high colour the prospect of lake and hill and woodland. No flowers should in fact be brighter than a love-in-the-mist, its pale blue petals obscured by green veils; that was the most gaudy blossom allowed. . . . Therefore, at first, he could hardly believe his eyes.

'Ida, what on earth is that extraordinary thing over there?' he called to my mother, pointing at the object.

'I like colour in the garden, George,' she replied, 'and I can see it from my bedroom windows, so I told Betts to have the roses planted there as a surprise for you. . . .'

'It certainly has been a surprise! It must be taken down at once. It ruins the whole effect of the garden and, besides, it's just where the wooden tower is to be put up so that I shall be able to see clearly the distant views from the level of the proposed new terrace.'

Not much could be seen from my mother's bedroom windows, since she had obscured the view with high window-boxes, which were planted with different kinds of sweet geranium. The more these flourished, the less you could see. My father, however, did not so much object to them because their desultory flowers were sparse and noncommittal in hue.

Now my mother's dog began to chase busily a non-existent rabbit through such flower-beds as were allowed, leaving behind him on the air a series of excited little barks and on the ground a trail of broken flower heads, the result of his impetuosity—the dog only noticed a rabbit when there was not one there. My father watched him patiently. He commented: 'I must say *I* don't see anything for him to chase—but probably there is,' and with a note of despair in his voice he added: 'Ernest Betts and Hollingworth between them have let the rabbits into the garden and goodness knows when they will be got out!'

Indeed, they were quite tame and at certain hours could be seen playing some game they had apparently invented, running and jumping in and out of the croquet hoops. In the early morning and late in the evening was the time to see them, and if you looked out of window from an upper storey then, you could discern them turned to gold by the lateral rays of the sun; though among them was a black rabbit, usually, I thought, the victor in the games; while the presence of several young black rabbits bore witness that no colour prejudice existed in the rabbit world as yet. Sometimes, too, you would see the mother rabbit setting out with her young for a picnic in one of the beds of lilies—plants which always ranked as a great delicacy with them. . . . Certainly, from what one could see of them, one would have presumed that they belonged to a privileged species, and it was somewhat of a shock to find them classified as vermin.

My father, as I had expected, asked me to accompany him, and we set off at a great pace, so that I had almost to run to keep up with him. Fortunately I had by now fully recovered from my cigarette-smoking. He began at once explaining to me his revised plans for altering the north front and as he outlined the scheme his walking grew faster and faster, as always when he became excited about alterations to house and garden. From the brow of the hill he suddenly swung round, undid the binocular-case and clapped the glasses to his eyes. After examining the vast stone bulk of the house, he stabbed the air with his forefinger and said:

'There I propose to have two great erections. . . . What are you laughing at?'

Then he turned round again, examining the park through his binoculars, and the land beyond it, until, concentrating eventually upon a plantation of trees on the hill opposite, he remarked to me:

'To get the full effect of distance I'm afraid I shall have to fell old Taylor's clump over there.'

'But won't he object?' I enquired nervously.

'Really, I can't be expected to ruin all my plans just because an obstinate old man won't cut down a few trees. He'll be lucky, if only he'd realize it, because our woodsman will do it for him—I shall charge him nothing for the labour—and he can sell the timber.'

As we turned round to walk back to the house, the north front was suddenly illumined by the sunlight, which only reaches it in the late afternoon, and, even then, shines on it sideways, as it were. Nevertheless, its strength dispersed the tents of mist that still lingered on here, like gigantic mush-rooms. Suddenly a breeze came and the great branches of the trees, oak, beech, and elm, fluttered their leaves on the air. Now the farmer's boy could be heard summoning the cattle to be milked, with a call that suggested a local adaptation of yodelling, and carried to a considerable distance. Soon he could be seen leading a line of cattle across the park to the home farm. The glory in the grass and in the trees would only last for a short while and then mists would come back to settle like great birds in the branches of the trees. We entered the house and crossed the hall towards the small garden door. The south front was as welcoming as the north was forbidding. Every object here glowed and the fragrance of stock, tobacco plant, and mignonette lay like a benison on the air.

3

CIGARETTE ENDS

I T W A S two years later and I was eighteen, before my father
discovered that I smoked; he confined himself to delivering
a lecture to me every day for several weeks running upon the
perils of throwing away cigarette ends without first taking the
trouble to see that they were properly put out. From this he
went on to a dissertation about fireplaces. Such a pity, he
considered, that we did not still have a central hearth as they
did in medieval times, no chimneys to worry about, just a hole
in the roof, and no glass in the windows so as to give you
plenty of fresh air. . . . This advice—about taking trouble to
see that cigarette ends were put out—seemed unusually sensible.
Accordingly, I was very careful—more careful even than
customarily—on the occasion when my father first took me
for a day or two to stay at Weston. Its lately deceased owner,
my great-aunt Lady Hanmer, had left my father as executor
of her will, and he had come here to discuss with a government
assessor the approximate values it was proposed to place on

certain objects in the house for the purpose of death duties. There was a heat-wave prevailing, a weather condition which seldom improves the temper, especially of Englishmen: but both men remained remarkably cool, when it is remembered that even in 1911, long before death duties had reached their present scale, they were regarded as iniquitous by those who had to submit to paying them.

My father at first took the assessor to be a rather rustic character, who would not be able to stand up to the full repertory of tricks, quirks, and tireless ingenuity to which he would be exposed, but he was soon forced to recognize that a worthy antagonist faced him. For example, when my father passed him a miniature to be catalogued, and suggested that the entry for it should read: 'Portrait miniature of old gentleman in white wig, wearing a blue ribbon', he examined it and said: 'I prefer to put: "Miniature on ivory of Lord North in wig, wearing the Order of the Garter."'

This was the first time I had stayed at Weston, which for a long while had been shut up, though I had once visited the house for the afternoon some six years before. That expedition remains unforgettable for several reasons—among them because it was the last horse-drawn jaunt in which I took part, albeit I was shortly to move more than ever before or since in equine society: but then my experiences could only be described as single-handed encounters with the brutes. (I was attached to a cavalry regiment and practised in the Riding School at five o'clock every morning all kinds of fancy-riding and still more obsolete Cossack tricks.) These encounters may have ranked as jaunts from the horse's point of view, but for myself could not be so described. No, this expedition was my last horse-drawn jaunt. . . . I was staying with two cousins at Bloxham some fifteen miles away, and when they heard that

View of Renishaw from the Steps of the Two Giants

I had never been to Weston, though it had been in my grandmother's family for over two hundred years, having always
passed from mother to daughter or from aunt to niece, they
decided I ought to see it. To reach Weston, which then seemed
remote from anywhere, necessitated that I should make the
journey in a hired wagonette, driven by the local carrier, with
a face by Roger van der Weyden and bearing a name with a
curious literary rhythm, for he was called Oliver Tendell
Soames, which gave out a distorted echo of the name of one of
my father's favourite authors. For what seemed long hours,
we rolled down leafy lanes, the hedges in their first shrill
unfolding forming almost a green tunnel. It must have been in
late April 1905, and no drive could have been more delightfully
out of its century. The houses in the villages all had thatched
roofs and seemed to have remained in the late sixteenth century
or even earlier, in the time of Brueghel the Elder. When at
last we reached our goal it was nearly time to return, but not
before we had seen some of the beautiful objects in the house,
or walked in the garden which was then more full of wild
flowers than of cultivated. There was a hollow at one side
bordered by very old trees which was full of most fragrant
white violets, and white, as well as speckled, maroon-coloured
fritillaries, looking as if made of dyed shark-skin.

I had arrived there this second time in the month of May
1911. This visit was remarkable to me for different reasons from
those which had governed my first glimpse of the house. My
father sent Henry Moat down to the cellar to fetch one of the
rugged, hand-made bottles of very old sherry. Henry soon
returned with a dusty, cobwebby bottle which he had opened.
My father said to him: 'Just pour yourself out a little and tell
me if it is corked.' Henry accordingly sipped it; but his face,
which at first registered a look of joyous expectation, changed

to one of raging disgust as he realized that he had carried up a bottle of home-made cowslip wine.

Impressed by the contents of the house, which seemed in a trance-like slumber undisturbed for centuries, I felt it was my duty to be more than ever careful about cigarette ends. One morning, however, my caution slackened and I threw a cigarette end on to the hearth. Then, realizing what I had done, I rushed across the room and stamped on the stump, still glowing, so as to be sure that it was quite dead, and placed it in a bronze mortar. My father watched me closely, but all I got for my trouble was the remark:

'So like your Uncle Francis!'

The tone of his voice made it quite clear that he was in no whit intending to express commendation. Both my father and mother always thus sought to place the blame on their children by referring to 'Your uncle' or 'Your aunt'. My father had always made it quite plain that he considered I ought only to inherit characteristics from his side of the family, while that any should come down to me from my mother's side ranked as Original Sin. . . . So I took refuge from reproach for an hour or so in the two fields beyond the garden. They were out of bounds for my father owing to his fear of hay-fever, which would certainly preclude him from following me, because these fields at this moment of the year were a paradise of flowers and flowering grasses; among these a profusion of cowslips and great clumps of various kinds of orchis with their leaves of moss-agate or green jade and their spikes of purple and gold and green and gold. . . . But now these flowers no longer appear because modern methods of farming have extirpated them as useless, in the same way that they have also banished the mushrooms which on September mornings used to be found here in such quantities.

[34]

4

GOING FOR A DRIVE

'GOING for a drive' must not be confounded with and is a very different matter from a modern phrase with a certain similarity to it, 'being taken for a ride.' Indeed, it signifies its very opposite. . . . My first instinct when worried or unwell is still to go for a drive: a habit formed long ago in my childhood; though during the time that has elapsed since those days the actual process itself has changed almost beyond recognition owing to the supplanting of the horse by the motor-car, a development which has contracted the country-side. To drive ten miles then occupied the same time as it takes to travel sixty miles by motor-car today, so that all the points of pilgrimage in country I know well have had substituted for them other more distant attractions. The length of the drive was formerly one of its pleasures: to see over Hardwick, driving there from Renishaw some twelve miles away, made of the outing a day's excursion; whereas now it is just a jaunt of an hour or two. Moreover, when you have reached that splendid mansion you realize that its intense personality and beauty have similarly contracted and been spread thin. . . . To be 'taken for a drive' had a further significance. It often spelt convalescence from some childish complaint. . . .

We children were paying a spring visit to my grandmother Sitwell when a bout of whooping-cough was identified —albeit our involuntary Indian war-cries must, one would have thought, have made its nature unmistakable. (Meanwhile, during and after this bout, my father, I recollect, confident that he, too, had caught the infection from passing us children in the garden, could be heard defiantly whooping to—or at—the world from the seclusion of his study, though in the end the illness never developed and even at that time the sounds he made betrayed an air of artificiality and make-believe.)

When we, my sister and I, had sufficiently recovered, my grandmother would send us, attended by a governess, for a drive in the vivid and warm April of those days, through the deep, steep, leafy lanes, the hedges beginning to sing their first green canticles under the warmth of the sun and to show their first furry buds, or we would pass by marshy ground, at this time shimmering with white anemones or showing clusters of kingcups, their substantial knobs just breaking into glazed yellow flowers. We would roll along in the victoria driven by old Hill, my grandmother's coachman, through the heavy springtime, continually finding, it seemed, new roads to explore. Hill was celebrated for the slowness of his driving, and prided himself on a gift for carpentry and painting, and for his surly insistence on personally spoiling in odd hours my grandmother's finest pieces of furniture, however often he had been forbidden to touch them. He liked to cut down the measurements and proportions to suit his own rules of taste and what he had decided was correct, and to paint what passed his rigid censorship in the colours in which he considered they should have been painted. . . . Sometimes for a change we would be taken along the chalk-white nudity of the Hog's Back to see Old Compton and the Watts Chapel, or to the church of St Martha, then we would return to Gosden, watching, as it grew darker, the golden and scarlet battles in the sky which heralded sunset and turned all objects, even the glittering white chalk churches, to a tone of gold.

'Going for a drive' in this slow fashion, however, hardly deserved its name and was more applicable to three other and more exciting occasions. One was confined to those weeks in the year which my grandfather Londesborough spent in Scarborough. The telephone had not yet come into its own, and a footman would come over with a message for my mother to say that 'His Lordship is going for a drive and would like to take the children with him.' So Edith and I, or one of us, would be waiting for him. He would soon arrive in his buckboard, which he drove himself—he was a celebrated whip, and his equipages were known for their elegance—and we jumped up beside him and started off. It seemed to take only a few minutes to be out of the town and bounding across the country-side to some prearranged spot on the moors, in Raincliffe Woods or Forge Valley, renowned locally for their beauty. In theory a groom should have been waiting three-quarters of an hour later at a particular place selected beforehand, to take the reins from my grandfather and enable the three of us to walk down through the woods to meet the buckboard again at a chosen spot. Usually we would reach it by way of one of the walks bearing the name of my mother or of one of her three sisters. The paths would be steep and full of damp green fern between the trees, while occasionally in this private part of the

woods we would find a rare wild flower, for example a
burnet-coloured columbine. In time we would emerge out of
the wood into the valley, as arranged, often to find that the
groom had misunderstood his directions and had gone to the
wrong place. Eventually, by some process of elimination, he
would come upon us, but not before my grandfather had been
given time in which to swear most imaginatively. His figure
and his great height, as he walked up and down furiously,
were most impressive and his beard imparted a certain iconic
air to his appearance. However, as always, he was soon
restored to good humour. . . . At another time he would take
us through the bitter temples of the east wind to the cliffs. The
few trees there were on this coast seemed to have been petrified
in their flight away from the sea, albeit, to the contrary, the
first indication of the spring was to be found here when in
March the golden coltsfoot and celandines flourished in the
rocky meadows.

The second exciting form of 'going for a drive' was when
my mother would take us with her in a hired cab. She would
be wearing her perfect country clothes which suited her simple
beauty, and a bunch of sweet rose-geranium pinned at her
waist. The cab would trundle us round down by way of the
foreshore and the Marine Drive, then in course of being built.
Great white wings of water, as if belonging to some extinct
mammoth race of seagull, would swing up and fall with the
thud of thunder on the huge squares of concrete that had been
placed there as breakwaters, but which, against this background, nevertheless looked as small as a child's bricks. . . .

Most of all, 'going for a drive' meant to drive with my
father round the twelve miles of green road he had made,
doubling and redoubling round the hillsides of the Eckington
Woods. After an early luncheon, we would set out in a

pony cart, painted green and yellow, drawn by a piebald pony of smart appearance but uncertain age. It was common knowledge that he had spent several years in a circus, and he would still, if he heard a certain tune played, begin to prance in circles till it stopped. Even when passing through the territories of the bluebell it was easy to imagine a spangled sylph on his broad back, having alighted thereon from a trapeze. I have mentioned bluebells. To my knowledge their beauty has no rival elsewhere. The beginning of May was here the best season for them: then the whole ground became brighter and more blue than the sky, and they filled the azure perspectives of the woods with a delicate aroma which had in it, as well, a yeasty odour as of newly baked bread. These ebullient groves and glades seemed at first strange in country of such restraint, though in truth it would reveal at other times, too, many dramatic vistas of green precipice and sheer hillside.

My father would not himself drive, which, perhaps, owing to the breakneck character of the woods, was just as well: this drive was plainly one for a professional. . . . The bank on one side was covered with mountain grass, growing like the hair of nereids: on the other, you might obtain a brief glimpse of the top of the dome of trees, now coming into their first green splendour, or drive through a fragrant bower of wild cherry in full flower. My father would not talk: his look was abstracted—more than usually. Wearing a light overcoat and a bowler hat, and sitting on his air-cushion, and with his binoculars pressed to his eyes, he was surveying the prospect which, as you went, unrolled a view of the hills opposite, as when you are shown a Chinese or Japanese scroll. In his own mind he filled these hills and valleys with architectural fantasies: there were temples and waterfalls and huge stone masks from the antique world, through the mouths of which issued the streams, stone boats on dams, and statues and smaller versions—pocket editions, as it were—of the Palazzo del Tè in Mantua, and canals which would lead from the lake to these valleys, so that coming here by boat you would avoid having to pass through the large village of Eckington and ignore the very existence of coal-mines in the neighbourhood. Indeed, as we drove round the woods, new ideas could be seen gliding like fish behind his rather pale eyes (though this was not how he saw his eyes himself, for it was during one of these expeditions, when we were returning and it was nearly dark, that a daddy-long-legs flew up into his eye, and he remarked: 'This has happened to me before. They mistake my eyes for stars.'). Though he had not yet grown his beard, his appearance was gothic and of the north. It matched this country, through which Robin Hood and his band had often roamed, no doubt, since these woods had once been part of Sherwood Forest, at that time of much greater extent than now. It was easy to picture him and his men, dressed in Lincoln green as a kind of protection, forerunner of camouflage, dodging from glade to glade. My father, however, felt little sympathy for them. Indeed, it was while we were driving through these same woods some years later that he had given me his opinion of the famous outlaw and his company. It was a very bad set for any young man to frequent, he warned me. Robin Hood—if he really existed at all—was always on the wrong side.

'I don't object so much to his robbing monks, who were no doubt bigoted and self-indulgent and thoroughly deserved it,' he explained, 'but he should have kept the money for the rich. Of course, it is true that there was no income tax in those days, still it was such a mistake to give the money to the poor, whereas the rich were the only people who knew how to spend it. They could always have found a use for it. Most selfish of Robin Hood not to have grasped that! You couldn't trust him. No, they were a very unpleasant set, I'm afraid,' he proceeded, 'and Friar Tuck and Little John were two of the worst in it, selfish and disreputable. I hope, dear boy, that you'll be careful to avoid the company of people like that.'

'Where should I find it?' I asked.

He ignored my question.

'Every young man,' he went on, 'should beware of joining up with such a party of crack-brained socialists. . . . As for Maid Marian, the less said about her, the better. She was obviously a bad lot. "Queen of the May", indeed! There can be no doubt that she blackmailed Robin Hood.'

'That's interesting. How did you discover it?' I asked. 'Where can I find an account of it?'

'We happen to know,' he replied, with a happy air of 'That's got you.' And he continued inexorably: 'I implore you to be careful not to mix with such people.'

5

RECOLLECTIONS OF AN AWKWARD
AFTERNOON IN KNIGHTSBRIDGE

THE air was—as indeed it should have been—Octobrine in its crispness and sweet odour, and brought the rustic smell of bonfires which could be seen burning brightly in smoky columns. But there was little to see of the flames at their centre, pallid in the sunshine. On the other side the window of the taxicab revealed the usual vista of bricks and mortar and at one point a cloud of dust swirling up in the near distance. For a moment the meaning of this eluded me, but I soon grasped its significance: it must mark the jubilant destruction of yet another of London's fine mansions—jubilant in intention, and no doubt in the expressive movements of the gang demolishing it, though the visual effect of the dust ascending to heaven was, to the contrary, depressing, as of smoke wafted from some biblical offering burnt in a clumsy attempt to propitiate an almost implacable deity. I paid off the cab and entered the dust-storm to find out exactly what was happening. . . . The diagnosis proved correct: Osnaburgh House with all its spacious, richly decorated rooms was in course of being pulverized to make way for office buildings and provide one more functional background in cement and plastic for the horde of bureaucratic typists who in the mysterious evolutionary workings of the twentieth century are plainly today the world's wonder and delight. Nearly asphyxiated, and at the same time turned to stone, I fought my way back to daylight, but not before I had recalled Osnaburgh House as it had looked for a ball given in June 1914.

At the very heart of that hot and dooming summer the guests had danced there to the rhythm of the famous waltz from the *Rosenkavalier*, the strains of which sounded in every London ballroom and were to return to many of the young men dancing that night as they lay a few months later dying of wounds in the barbed-wire thickets and rusty groves of No Man's Land. . . . By this time, the waltz, projected from so long ago—nearly two generations—was playing itself over and over again in my head as I walked away, until, growing tired of it, I experimented with the various remedies recommended to defeat this well-known affliction; curative measures such as deliberately substituting for the repetitive melody a verse or two of the National Anthem, thereby, as it were, indicating to the management that the concert was ended and the music must stop. But, in no degree discouraged, the waltz continued its beat unimpeded. . . . Then suddenly I forgot about it, as a memory of a different sort, but also connected with Osnaburgh House, asserted itself and took possession: those recollections of an awkward afternoon in Knightsbridge which give the title to these few pages—in brief, the incident I am shortly going to relate, the scene for which must have been pitched in the early autumn of 1917. . . . First, a few preliminary explanations are due to the reader.

When before the First World War my father came to London by himself for a few days at a time, his arrival evoked different responses from different people—for example, a member of one of the numerous firms of family solicitors he employed told me in later years that during the period of the visit, or, as he termed it, visitation, he would sit up the whole night through, with a cold-water bandage round his forehead, working out answers to some of the many legal conundrums that would soon undoubtedly shower upon him. . . . For my part, however, I would always in those early years try to find some entertainment or activity which might amuse or engross my father and thus leave him with less time in which to discuss with me my more salient faults and failings. This attempt at diversion was perhaps foolish since, as readers of my auto-biography may remember, my father regarded all save purely esthetic pleasures as sinful (though, to boot, he would as wholeheartedly have rejected as sinful the conception of *sin* itself). But while he condemned amusement of any kind as dangerously self-indulgent, yet if in consequence no effort were made to provide it for him, he was inclined to be resentful. Moreover, the matter was difficult in other respects, too, because he would always refuse to see a serious play or a straight comedy, circuses were not in his line, and musical comedies did not appeal to him—though to this last there were exceptions, for he would exhibit something near enthusiasm for *The Belle of New York* and especially for the sweet singing in it of Miss Edna May. Miss Gertie Millar in certain roles had also been fortunate enough to win his approval. For the rest, *The Miracle* had interested him in 1911, and in 1880 he had enjoyed seeing on exhibition the giant, Chang. . . . Of him my father would often talk, telling us of how the Chinese colossus had been obliged to have a special Brobdingnagian chair made

[44]

for him and that, though he measured eight foot two inches in height, he was so perfectly proportioned that himself did not so much appear gigantic, as cause those who had come to see him to look small, and my father would grow annoyed when I would protest that I liked a giant to be a giant, and that, withal, eight feet two inches did not seem so enormous: no, I was more interested in the idea of Og, King of Bashan, because not only did his height compel him to order a bed to be built measuring nine cubits by four, but tradition maintained also that he walked beside the Ark during the Deluge, that he lived to be three thousand years of age, and that when at last he died one of his bones was used as a bridge over a river. . . . Then there was, in addition, Anak to be considered, of whom the Hebrew spies reported that, compared with him in stature, they were but grasshoppers. . . . To my mind he was a more impressive mammoth, but he deserved special attention as the progenitor of a whole race of giants. Then, too, the claims of the monster Polyphemus must also be borne in mind. His skeleton had been dug up at Trapani in Sicily in the fourteenth century, so it was said, and showed him to have been some three hundred feet in height—there was a real giant for you! . . . All this, however, as my father did not hesitate to suggest to me, was beside the point, since there were nowhere any such giants on show today. . . . For the rest, it was useless to take him to a concert, since music—except his own singing, to which my mother had put a stop long ago—did not please him.

It was difficult: for example on one occasion in 1913 I had made a brave effort to amuse him. He dined with me first at the Marlborough, and appeared to be in tolerably good humour; thence I lugged him to the Hippodrome, to see the current revue, for which I had booked two stalls. No sooner

[45]

had we settled ourselves in them than he began to entertain an aversion—no, that is too cordial a term—more accurately to form an instantaneous but abiding *loathing* for the principal members of the cast; a sentiment which he in no way sought to hide, or even to disguise. Whenever a single one of them appeared on the stage he would rock in his stall, move his feet about, fidget, fume, fuss, look up at the ceiling, sigh loudly, puff, and generally make moan. I suggested that we should leave, but he would not even quit his seat in the interval—when, I remember, he complained to me that the stars 'had no natural dignity or grace'—but insisted on enduring fretfully to the end. . . . The next morning he departed unexpectedly for Scarborough, where a day or two later he slipped the cartilage in his knee, had it operated on, but refused to be given any kind of anesthetic ('No one ever dreamt of taking an anesthetic in the Middle Ages. It is most self-indulgent'). And on being subsequently told by the surgeon not to move, but to lie still, he treated this injunction in so conscientious a manner that as a result he developed pleurisy and was confined to his bed for three weeks.

During this period he alleged that he suffered from insomnia; which led Henry Moat to remark:

'Naturally Sir George can't sleep all night as well as all day.'

But my father had determined to make use of valuable time that would otherwise be wasted, and explained, when I came on leave, and went to visit him in a nursing home, that he had spent the previous nights in experimenting with the various unusual positions in bed that he had found to be the most conducive to sleep. Of what might prove to be this valuable addition to human knowledge he had no intention of depriving the world. He sent for me the next morning and, when he heard my footsteps, called out to me:

[46]

'Come in at once, and shut the door. I've had an idea.'

'About sleeping?' I enquired.

'Yes. . . . The descriptions of my attitudes are difficult to follow in words alone, so I have decided to issue an illustrated pamphlet. I propose to call it *The Twenty-seven Postures of Sir George R. Sitwell*. Do you think that is a good title: will it sell the book, and whom shall I get to illustrate it?'

'Undoubtedly it will sell the book,' I replied, my mind first flying to the famous *Postures* of Aretino, then, more innocently, to the book of Lady Hamilton's Attitudes, and also to the parodying volume of caricatures which followed its publication. 'I will try to think of a suitable artist,' I went on, 'but there's so little of that kind of work being done at present. It's a pity Aubrey Beardsley is dead. It would just have appealed to him.'

My father looked pleased.

'By the way,' I continued, 'I tried one of your positions last night. It certainly helped me to sleep.'

'Which one?' he demanded.

'The one you told me about, where you lie with your nose over the edge of the bed. It's easier to remember than most of the postures.'

'That's *not meant* to make you sleep,' he snapped angrily. 'It's just to pass the time.'

In the end the book was never printed, though I did my best to encourage the idea. . . . At least, however, he found no difficulty in assigning the blame for the several misfortunes that had befallen him. 'It's all Osbert's fault for insisting on taking me to the Hippodrome and obliging me to sit through the whole performance.'

It had been an experiment plainly not to be repeated, and,

[47]

after war broke out, my endeavours to entertain him perforce stopped, until April 1916 when I returned to England and was posted to the Reserve Battalion at Chelsea Barracks, and then when from time to time my father, fresh from the ballistic dangers of Scarborough or the rigours of Renishaw, came to London, again I had to make some attempt to interest and amuse him. . . . No more theatres, and there were few private houses open—then I remembered the wall paintings by J. M. Sert in Osnaburgh House, and recollecting, too, my father's interest in the decorative arts, I wrote accordingly and asked if one afternoon I could bring him to see them. In reply, we were invited to tea the following Sunday.

We arrived together at four-thirty and found already gathered there a small party consisting of our kind hostess and a Mrs Brooke, to whom we were introduced in the customary English mode, rather vague and perfunctory, as well as to a few pieces of ordinary drawing-room furniture who remain nameless and faceless to this hour. Mrs Brooke, on the other hand, was definite in style, if rather tough-looking in a clerical manner—and moreover her face, under the accretions of time and of life at the Rectory in conjunction, seemed familiar, or at least put me in mind of someone with whose appearance I was familiar but of whom I could not for the moment seize the identity. . . . First our hostess conducted us into the Sert room, so that we could examine by ourselves the enormous wall paintings in sepia and gold of elephants, turbaned figures, and palm trees. . . . Sert, albeit not a great artist, certainly knew how to cover large stretches, and could be relied on to provide a sumptuous, smouldering background. Altogether in his span he must have painted acres and acres, nearly a square mile, of wall space. He was an artist who stood by himself in his century, having no rival and no one who

Great Drawing-Room. Family Group by Sargent and
the Renishaw Commode by Adam and Chippendale

The Ballroom at Renishaw. Brussels Tapestries designed by Leyniers
and executed by de Vos

wished to rival him. Since painting had moved away from drawing-room walls, he was now alone in his immense, two-dimensional, half-empty world of a lost Orient, fused of nostalgic, paranoiac visions of grandeur emanating from fancy-dress recollections of India, China, and Persia.

The others soon joined us in this room. . . . My father had been delighted with it from the first sight, and enchanted to find something new yet in no respect modern. Though by nature shy, he was on this occasion so greatly exhilarated that he talked freely. Directly he was in his place at tea he began a furious all-out attack on modern art, delivered with more gusto than he generally allowed himself. From painting he surprised me by divagating into the pastures of modern poetry —surprised me because he had never hitherto shown the slightest interest in that art or even a consciousness that it existed: but on the afternoon in question some magnet seemed to draw him relentlessly towards it. . . . He was just saying: 'Then there was that young man who died in the Dardanelles —I forget his name—they try to make out that he was a genius, but no good, no good, I can assure you,' when with a startling suddenness I realized *why* Mrs Brooke's face was so familiar— from photographs in the Press of Rupert Brooke: the resemblance was very marked; she must be his mother. I gave my father a good kick under the tea-table, but he did not even pause; only the as yet undreamt-of H-bomb could have stopped him. He went on: 'His poems were grossly over-praised in the Press.' . . . I could hardly believe my ears. Could it be true that this was really happening, or was it just a nightmare instalment of an instant in hell? Before, however, his memory could supply the missing name, the crowning horror was skilfully averted—but not before for myself, and no doubt for others, the sepia and gold elephants had begun to

[49]

climb the walls in earnest, and the palm trees wildly to wave their leaves in alarm.

'Sir George,' our hostess bravely intervened, 'you are sitting next Mrs Brooke, the mother of that wonderful young poet, Rupert Brooke. I *must* tell you, because,' she proceeded, drawing on her imagination, 'before tea you were just saying to me—but we were interrupted—how much you admired his work,' and continued, 'how different it is from the work of that other young poet—I, too, forget his name for the moment —of whom you were speaking.'

My father looked puzzled but said no more.

6

CATCHING THE BUS

DEMOLITION has its triumphs no less than construction. The pulling down of Chelsea Barracks removes from London one of its most hideous buildings. Gone for ever is that dingy mass of dirty yellow brick with its air of solidity and its Byzantine or Romanesque arches, windows, and string courses of dull plum colour, gone for ever with its lost echoes of trumpet and drum and of the bugles that crowed the hours for one unpleasant task or another. All that remains of the colossal structure is an additional film of dust, such as that which fell at first on the doomed pleasure resort of Pompeii; a layer that covers the buildings in the vicinity and everything in them. . . . I was quartered at Chelsea during the first weeks of the war, from early August until the middle of December, when I went to the Front. Contemplating that time, the London scene seems effervescent though comparatively peaceful; but the chief impression which remains with one is that of the climate. It appears as if England always reserved a

[51]

special kind of weather to serve as background for public catastrophes, and certainly there never was a finer summer or autumn than in 1914.

Examining the horrors of the Second World War, and before the coming of the Third now so plainly in preparation, the First World War has at its beginning the semblance of an old-fashioned panache about it. When you reached the Front, however, all ideas of chivalry and the like were swiftly dismissed by the universal stench, and by the sight of the pools of mud where whole companies of fat rats played at dusk.

Some incidents of that time remain in memory, and may be worth recording. . . . The war had swept down with great speed; but after a few weeks trench warfare had begun, and advance and retreat equally slowed down. Henceforth, for three years, an advance of a mere hundred yards was to cost thousands of lives, but this cessation of movement led many —why, no one will ever know—to believe that the war was ending. So many years had elapsed since the last European war had broken out—Balkan wars were endemic and not to be counted—that nobody knew quite how to behave or what to do. As a result, everybody recommended alternative and indeed opposite routes as the sole true road to victory. At one moment, for example, those who liked to talk about war with a pretension to strategic and tactical infallibility would advocate the immediate enrolment of every man and woman in the armed forces of the country, and the next, the same people would be advocating 'Business as Usual'. White Feather Trouble, too, had already begun though it was not to reach its apogee until about two years later. Meanwhile, these innocent-looking insults were nearly always offered to officers in plain clothes, or to young men under the age of enlistment. Some of the most ardent and frenetic of these donors—in almost every case a woman—had already begun to lay in a stock of white feathers for future distribution, but then came the difficulty of how to keep them in their original dazzling condition, since in the climate of London they were apt to turn buff in ten days, and black in a month, and somehow to present a buff feather did not seem quite the same thing as to offer a snowy-white plume. . . . Then there was the question of obtaining fresh supplies. Swans were too well able to break the arm or leg of anyone attempting to interfere with them; they must be ruled out absolutely. No, the only sure fresh supply was that to be obtained from the various kinds of seagull that in the winter gathered on the Serpentine, but even on a mild November day, if such came, nobody would wish to plunge into the water in order to pluck from the birds some white feathers. Moreover, if you attempted it, you were likely to get as good as you gave, for their cruel-looking beaks could inflict quite serious injuries. . . . The self-appointed distributors, too, wrote confusing letters to the papers, full of muddled advice and urging the joy and necessity of doing everything possible—including presumably the presentation of white feathers—for the lads who had joined up.

Shortly after the outbreak of the First World War I was sent down to the London Docks in command of the guard to be posted in various spots considered to be of some importance. I imagine we went to Tilbury, or perhaps Limehouse, for I remember long corridors between brick walls, with an occasional Chinese prowling or lounging about in the dark near-distance, for a black-out prevailed. I was also in charge of a large unused warehouse, used as an internment camp for—I was told—prominent enemy aliens who might prove dangerous. I was billeted in this building, which contained many chambers of little splendour but great size, and on arrival I went round these halls to the accompaniment of stamping feet and salutes from the armed guard. The rooms were crammed, and the faces of some of the internees seemed familiar in a vague sort of way. Out of their context, however, I could not recognize them, until one man, who looked cheerful in spite of the prevalent gloom and squalor, greeted me airily with the words: 'Which table would you like tonight, sir?' Then, suddenly, I understood. I was in charge of waiters of enemy nationalities. It was terrible to be obliged to glare at them. Already I had been shocked on the outbreak of war to hear of the suicide of Max, the German hall-porter of the hotel in which my father and mother always stayed when they came to London. I had known him since I was a child. . . . But to return to the warehouse—owing to the conditions in which they were compelled to live, similar to those that had prevailed in eighteenth-century Newgate—it was not long before epidemics of impetigo and the itch, followed by many other and no less attractive diseases, broke out, so that the formal and rhetorical question which the officer going his rounds during these men's dinners was obliged to put to them: 'Any complaints?' came to have a new connotation, and one dreaded the possible replies, giving in full detail the infections from which they were suffering.

When after a few days the moment came for us to be relieved we were relieved in more than one sense. Our footsore successors arrived from Chelsea looking far from happy. I recall that our march—or walk, as I preferred to call it in military circles—had been long, hot, and dusty. Before starting for home, I had just been reading several letters in the morning paper from members of the civilian public who longed, they averred, to make some sacrifice 'for the lads'. I was determined to give them a chance of satisfying, even if vicariously, their so patriotic craving. When, therefore, I saw a motor-bus approaching, I drew my sword, stood in the middle of the road, and stopped it. I then climbed aboard and explained to the driver and the conductor that I was commandeering the vehicle, that they were now to evacuate their present passengers and instead take my party back to Chelsea Barracks. They appeared to face the change with a certain happy insouciance. Not so the passengers. Though I pointed out that they now were afforded the opportunity of personally experiencing that which civilians were always writing to the papers to demand as a right, i.e. to make a sacrifice for the boys in khaki, they went with a bad grace. . . . My platoon was, of course, enchanted, and it was nice to look back as we went rushing on, and see the former passengers dragging along, mumbling to themselves or grumbling to one another.

When I arrived at Chelsea Barracks I found that in the few days in which I had been away a whole gang of senior officers, wearing on their tunics decorations which I at first mistakenly concluded had been the awards for bravery in the Crimean War, had materialized in the Anteroom. When the story of our exploit reached the Orderly Room these higher powers, of whom nothing had hitherto been heard in my lifetime, became much inflamed in their feelings, but they did not want to say too much about it for fear that other young officers would follow suit.

On returning, I found waiting for me, as so often, a letter of advice and discouragement from my father at Renishaw. He had remained there for some time and was still in a pacific —no, not pacific, but anti-the-current-war mood. In this letter he first took a whisk round the shops at which I dealt and emphasized the necessity for economy, so that if I were killed the next heir would not be too badly affected. He then proceeded to remind me of how the visiting General of whom he had often told me had come down from London to look at my father's regiment of Volunteers and had commended him in the warmest terms. The War Office had made a great blunder in disbanding that body, and the point was, could they ever recover what they had lost? The Territorials were not a patch on them, and Lord Kitchener's Army would also prove to be far inferior to these helmeted paragons. As for the statesmanship of politicians, it had been deplorable. 'Such a pity not to consult *me*.' The Emperor William was of a peace-loving disposition (my father felt some affinity to the Emperor William; they shared the same birthday, took the same interest in genealogy, the Middle Ages, and the gothic methods of torture, such as the Iron Maiden, the thumbscrew, and the iron boot). The German generals, most of them, were good fellows, more at home on the golf links than on the battlefield. . . . What had happened was that the Emperor William had suddenly found himself faced with the unexpected mobilization of Russian troops by a bloodthirsty Czar. Meanwhile the German blood was up. Nobody could wonder at it. The only certainty was that we could expect an invasion at any moment. Hollingworth was told to look out for suitable and remote retreats in which, when the Germans arrived, my father and his family could hide safely. Naturally they must want to capture him. When we moved at last to our house in Scarborough the raid on that town by the German fleet quickly followed and confirmed his worst suspicions. They must have been informed of his change of residence and were evidently determined to kidnap him, if only to obtain the benefit of his advice.

7

HENRY MOAT

THE letters from Henry Moat that follow were addressed to Maynard Hollingworth, then sub-agent at Renishaw. Henry spelt his name in three different ways; in these letters he signs himself 'Mouat', otherwise I have retained his original spelling and punctuation. . . . Only three of these five letters are dated. I have therefore placed them in the order in which I presume from internal evidence they were sent. They all clearly belong to his middle period of service before he left in 1913 to be away for several years. The letter I print below is dated July 7th 1905 and is certainly the first of the five in a chronological sense:

Wood End, Scarborough.
I am much obliged to you for sending the boots so promply they just arrived in nice time

I was much amused about the Old Clog he wants to shift out of all business where a little expense is likely to occur but wants to

[57]

shine by keeping his accounts down and let everything go to pot but if it is not done he will have to sit up when we arrive I have a bomb or two. . . .

I should be much obliged if you would put a bed for Mr Pare in my bedroom over the pantry as otherwise the poor fellow will have (probably) to sleep in the barracks and as I always take care he has his food in the Housekeepers room and not in the servants Hall it would look out of place if he slept in the Barracks and had food in the Room

We had a fairly good camp the Sergt cook hung himself and three men got drownded

Trusting you keep well

I remain yours faithfully,

The Old Clog to whom Henry alludes was Charles Betts, who filled several posts at Renishaw, being responsible for the gardens and the woods. My father had at that time wanted some special trees planted and told Hollingworth to hand over the order to Betts. Betts planted something different and when my father complained, tried to throw the blame on Hollingworth.

Henry, as the reader will have grasped, had accompanied my father, who at that time commanded the local Volunteers, to camp. This body generally pitched its tents for a fortnight or so on the disused race-course above the town of Scarborough. If it were to rain, my father and Henry would always return for the night to Wood End. . . . My father was fond of relating how the General, sent down at the bidding of the War Office to inspect the Volunteers when they were carrying out an exercise—and when this hero was no doubt more or less fresh from the mixed bays and thistle-heads of the Boer War —had congratulated my father on his knowledge of strategy and tactics and had gone so far as to tell him that if only he had adopted the Army as a career, England might have had its own Napoleon.

The passage about Pare shows Henry's kind heart. Stephen Pare had been all but totally blinded by being struck by lightning and could only distinguish the difference between light and darkness. He had been with us for many years as odd man, employed at a pitifully small wage. Henry was anxious that he should be given his proper place in the very strict social hierarchy of the servants.

The Barracks was the dormitory in which the younger and less important menservants slept, a survival from the eighteenth century.

The second letter is not dated in full and I can find no clue to the year in which it was written.

> Wood End, Scarborough,
> Nov. 30th.

For the love of Jasus stop sending anymore rotten apples the hampers cost 2/- coming the apples worth no more than 9d and a box arrived thursday I think and 6/- to pay Sir George was furious and wanted to know who ordered them to be sent perhaps you would find out

Well we have Sir George laid up so I dont think he will be able to come to Renishaw for some time

We are having ructions here I shake hands with myself when I find myself alive morn and even. I trust you are keeping well and having plenty of sport

Well the best of good luck to you from your faithfully

The third letter is similarly dated by the month, May 18th only and no year is given, but it carries its own date in the last sentence. My father joined the Liberal Party in 1907.

Hotel Royal Danieli, Venise,

just a blast to say Sir Geo Lady Ida and Mr and Mrs Gray will
be moored at Renishaw for a week from the 27th inst please inform
Mrs Westby

an Italian chef will turn up about the 26th dont shoot him for
Gods sake we want him I hope you are in the highest enjoyment of
existence please have a good rest before we come because he gets up
a(t) 5 o/c in the morning now my kindest regards to you. Sir Geo
has turned a damned old radical good bye

The next letter is dated February 9th 1908.

Wood End, Scarborough.

I am all excitement and jumping about the gambols of a skittish
young hippipotamas Well on friday next there is going to be a
Grand Fancy Dress Ball and there is some young ladies going who
I know are wearing skirts just long enough to cover their tea
things

Well I should like to go but I have not got a fancy costume and
suddenly thought if you would kindly take the great trouble
to send me the coachman's (High Sheriff's) Livery Stockings and
shoes not the overcoat hat or gaiters I should be so extremely
grateful neither of the footman's would fit me but if you would
kindly send the three pairs of shoes as I think the coachmans
would be too big but I am not sure and it would be a pity if you
only sent one pair I promise you on my word of honour I would
send them back next monday Now do be a good fellow and send
them

I hope you are in the pink of condition kindest regards

From yours faithfully

Readers of my autobiography may remember that Henry
went to the ball in this livery and a white wig, representing, so
he stated, Leonardo da Vinci. Indeed, a photograph of him in

[60]

this fancy dress appeared in the pages of *Laughter in the Next Room*.[1]

The next and last letter lists the provisions that my father was taking to Renishaw for a flying visit (I can hear his voice announcing: 'I am going to run over to Renishaw for a few days' picnicking'). In preparation for this sprint, Henry writes to Maynard Hollingworth in January 1909:

> Wood End, Scarborough.
>
> Dear Maynard,
>
> All been well Sir George and I will arrive at the——??? Hall tomorrow evening the train arrives GC 8.32 please send to meet us Brougham and heavy cart Sir George would like Hot Milk and bread the moment he crosses the threshold (please tell Mrs Westby Hot water bottle in his bed) Sir Geo will dine in the train
>
> I am bringing 2 Chickens 2 Soles caviar Bacon plum Jam coffee apples Biscuits Rice Loin of Mutton Blanc Mange Flour tea and Mustard so will you please ask the good lady to order in the other things that she thinks is necessary
>
> Trusting you are well
>
> > Yours faithfully
> > Henry Mouat
>
> P.S. Look out for a wire cancelling everything I will wire Mrs Westby if so. H.M.

Henry had devised through the years several techniques for dealing with my father. One—that of Infinite Patience—he used on this trip, when the following dialogue took place.

'Henry, the coffee wasn't properly made at lunchtime. It should be made in an earthenware pot and should be well stirred.'

'Sir George, it *was* made in an earthenware pot, and it *was* well stirred.'

[1] Page 41.

The point in the antecedent letter, however, which arouses the greatest curiosity is that my father should want 'hot milk and bread the moment he crosses the threshold'. It sounds as if it were a rite culled from the pages of *The Golden Bough* and referred perhaps to some obligation incumbent on the Priest-King in his last days of life before a knife of obsidian put an end to his term of office.

Maynard Hollingworth recently recalled to me some remarks Henry made to him about Major Viburne, for whom Henry cherished little regard. This paladin was disinterred from time to time and chartered by my father to oversee the household, muddle the accounts, and misorder the food. Major Viburne posed as a warrior and a gourmet, but in both instances his experience was limited. During the days of which I am speaking, for example, he was confined, by his own digestion, to a diet of dry biscuits, and he certainly never got nearer than Scarborough to any Front Line in the whole course of his long life. Maynard Hollingworth, then, said one morning to Henry:

'Is Major Viburne coming here this year, Henry?'

Henry looked round and said:

'I rather thought the gale last night would have swept him in, but I don't see him anywhere.'

On another occasion Hollingworth asked him:

'Did Major Viburne see much active service?' To which Henry replied:

'Yes, he fought right through the Canteen Campaign from beginning to end.'

Henry's talk was as uninhibited and as full of humour as were his letters. In his last period of service, many years after the foregoing letters were written, my father's restoration of Montegufoni was in full swing, and none of those who worked in the house could speak English. But Henry's sense of fun triumphed over lingual difficulties. Roars of laughter would come rolling up the stairs from the servants' quarters. The same outrageous robustness of expression still marked his conversation in his broken Italian, no doubt as much as in English. Nothing about him was much changed. Only the sound of his footsteps had grown a little heavier, indeed everything about him had grown a little heavier than in earlier years. In short, he had remained essentially himself, but an expanded self.

Other characteristics marked his talk as well as individual humour. He proved, withal, to be a repository of rough wisdom and of local—as will be seen in a moment, of more than local—lore and was apt to use phrases and turns of speech of forgotten derivation. . . . Thus, in *The Scarlet Tree*, I mention that, looking up at a blue sky with huge white clouds moving in stately progress across it, Henry referred to them as 'them great big Norwegian Bishops'. . . . A few weeks later I received a letter from Australia in which my correspondent, who had just read the book, wrote of the phrase suggesting that the epithet *Norwegian* afforded an ineluctable clue. In Norse mythology, he went on to say, the souls of the dead are represented as bees and were supposed to traverse the sky in what was specifically termed a 'beeship' (*bÿskip*): of which *Bishop* was clearly a corruption. He added that to find the phrase still lingering even in a mutilated form in popular speech constituted a survival of considerable romantic interest. Whitby, which always had many dealings with the Scandinavian countries opposite, remained the centre of Henry's universe, and he always bore with him a blast of nautical air, with the particular tang of the North Sea in it.

8

JEZEBEL HOUSE AND A GRAND PIANO

AT SCARBOROUGH in the winter the incessant roar of the sea, the salt spray that stung the face far inland, the bitter cries of wheeling and pouncing gulls, the attitudes of the bare trees, caught, as it were, in the very act of flight, all seemed designed to create and maintain an atmosphere of power, tension, and of actual terror. For weeks together there would be no break in the tragic estimate thus presented. Howbeit, in the spring and summer months the prim, trim terraces, crescents, and gardens, full of dogs and flowers, appeared to offer a setting for comedy and even for farce rather than for tragedy. In summer tragic events were nevertheless apt to occur, and the mysterious happening which follows I relate here in example of them—though I write of the episode as my memory records it and not from any recent studying of the columns of contemporary newspapers.

My grandmother Sitwell, a delicate old lady of determined and active philanthropy, had many years before, with the aid,

I think, of the Bishop of Hull, established a Home for 'girls of a certain class'. In the repulsive refuge to which these sad Dickensian creatures were consigned, Jezebel House, the matron gave them boots and dresses that served for a prison in themselves and further, as a perpetual corvée, they were compelled to do laundry work. Their resentment at the ungracious way of living they were obliged to follow found easy expression in many a shredded shirt and ripped chemise. . . . Jezebel House itself was a square, red-brick building, doubly fenced and set back behind an inappropriate palisade of thick wood—inappropriate because it seemed unnecessary from the look of it to enforce any more the sense of restriction. Yet, in spite of its plainness, the atmosphere of the building, with its windows glaring coldly above the fence, was not so much gloomy—that was to be expected—as sinister, and I used to notice how often this house associated itself in my mind as the background for any story of crime or mystery which I might be reading: *Dr Jekyll and Mr Hyde*, for example.

At some time during the First World War Jezebel House was shut—shut perforce, since the professional had now begun to make way for the amateur, and in consequence the former kind of occupant was no longer so easily to be found. For the later long years of war, and even for a few years of the peace that followed, the square building stood deserted and dusty. The agent in whose hands the sale of the property rested was a man prosperous, well known and respected in the town, and very regular in his habits and hours of work. Therefore, one day, when he did not return at the usual hour to his home—his house was in the centre of the borough—it seemed so very unlike him that after a little while his wife rang up the office, only to be told that he had left it some hours before. The family began to grow more and more alarmed as the minutes

[65]

went by without any sign of him, and at about nine o'clock his sons went out to start a search. The evening was still light and clear with that very logical, hard summer-evening light of the north. First they visited several empty houses included in their father's lists, thinking he might have taken a client to inspect them, and last among them they called at Jezebel House. They penetrated the wooden barrier, the gate of which they found unfastened, though the front door of the house was locked. Its windows were shuttered and all was quiet, so they decided not to enter but to return home.

From the first his family had been afflicted with an indefinable, irrational sense of disaster, and now, knowing that sleep was impossible, they determined all of them, mother and sons, to stay up. So they remained in the sitting-room which faced the street, waiting hour after hour in absolute silence, for they were too perturbed to talk, and in English seaside towns life used to die early in the evening. Indeed, they sat there until at last the blackness of the sky began to lift a little and the electric-light globes still burning in the room called out beyond the square window-panes an indescribably pure and luminous tone of blue. . . . In these noiseless and innocuous moments before the dawn, at last a curious sound reached them—the sound, it seemed, of something being dragged along outside —and there followed a distinct scratching at the door. All of them rushed to open it, and a heavy, dark body crawled over the step into the lighted room, creeping along on all-fours like an animal. He was charred almost beyond recognition—so badly injured that not even the members of his own family could understand what he said. He had no coat on, but in the hospital to which he was at once taken they found his gold watch, which he usually wore in his breast-pocket, in one of his trouser-pockets. . . . During the few days he lived he tried many times to make himself understood, framing the same words over and over again. At last, only just before he died, they seized the purport of them: '*Jezebel House*'.

The police acted immediately and had the house searched. They found the door still locked on the inside. All the windows were shuttered and bolted. Finally they broke the door open and in a room on the ground floor at the back found the electric light burning. The dead man's coat was hanging on a chair, but they could find no sign of violence, nor of anything having caught fire. The nature of the crime which must have occurred there defied every subsequent attempt at elucidation.

. . . . .

At Scarborough the trim, prim terraces, crescents, and gardens, I was maintaining, seemed in the springtime and summer months to offer a field for comedy and even for farce rather than for tragedy. Singular incidents were always liable to occur there—for example, a few years earlier there had been the episode of the bath and my great-aunt Lady Hanmer, an octogenarian widow whom I have described at greater length[1] elsewhere, so that all I need say about her now is that she lived —had elected to live—near the station in a house built of ugly yellow brick, that she had a genial and ample presence, and to remind the reader of her many shawls, of her eyebrows, or sometimes of just one, lightly painted in—like a sketch for an eyebrow rather than an eyebrow itself—and of the accompanying painted fringe above her forehead, over which was balanced an elaborate cap of lace and ribbons of baby pink and blue. We—my brother and I—had always seen her in one position, seated in an armchair near the fire, in a drawing-room

[1] *Left Hand, Right Hand!*, Vol. I, pages 167-9.

filled incongruously with eighteenth-century French furniture. For us, in memory, she seems to float, very fully swathed, above the smoke from passing trains, as, in an earlier age, patrons were portrayed posturing in apotheosis on rosy clouds on ceilings.

After the manner of the lives of all other human beings, however, Lady Hanmer's life knew more intimate moments, and it was in one of these that she found herself tightly wedged into her bath, and quite unable to rise from it unaided. The door, of course, was locked. . . . She managed by shouting, after half an hour or so, to attract the wandering attention of a young housemaid, who at once ran to inform her superior of their mistress's plight; together, they proceeded to force the door. When they had entered, each took one hand, and pulled and yanked, but all of no avail: Lady Hanmer remained recumbent in the bath, nor, though they tried by pouring in more water, could they float her. They hauled again, but there was no sign of getting her loose—in short, the old lady was too heavy for them. Consulting together, they agreed that it was a man's job to extricate her—but how could a male be introduced into the room without indecency? This constituted indeed a problem; a choice between a breach of the prevailing moral code and a life occupancy of the bath. It was decided that at all costs Lady Hanmer must be restored to circulation. . . . Presently, Wilkins, the head housemaid, had a startling and ingenious idea. She and Emily sought Gimlet, the butler, who had been in Lady Hanmer's service for fifty years, and explained the predicament. Then, no doubt with some vague echo of the Judgment of Paris in their heads, they blindfolded him, tying a black bandage across his eyes, lest perhaps he should cry 'Mine eyes dazzle!' as did the Duke at sight of his sister in Webster's *Duchess of Malfi*. Together the two women led him into the bathroom, where the old lady, placing one hand delicately in his, was drawn to her feet. He was then ceremoniously conducted down to the hall, where sight was restored to him. . . .

But this was only one unusual incident: while the fact that my father had seven times been a parliamentary candidate for the borough, and had in consequence called on every voter on at least seven different occasions—for those were the days of a more limited franchise and a personal visit was expected from each of the candidates—provided still more and wider opportunities for comedy; because in consequence we possessed innumerable friends and acquaintances of every sort in the town, and among them are two I must describe for the unfolding of this episode. . . . One of them, Sister Dorothy, was an acquaintance more than a friend, though circumstances forced us to see her often. For several years she had been in charge of Jezebel House and when that establishment shut she settled herself comfortably on my religious Aunt Florence, who had, most conveniently, just become a permanent invalid. Sister Dorothy was middle-aged and buoyant. In appearance she seemed positively bursting with ill-health, though she contrived in the end to live to be eighty; except for the tea-fiend's protruding teeth, her face looked as if it had been roughly thumbed into shape out of an overripe tomato. Perhaps because she was a member of some Sisterhood vaguely affiliated with the Church of England, and in order to stress her almost official status, she always dressed after the pattern of a travestied nun.

Miss Susan Tugworth, the other person I have to describe for the purpose of what follows, was a real friend, whom I can remember from a very early age. My mother and the rest of the family were very fond of her and she had become a figure in the house, my mother often employing her on various errands in which tact, trustworthiness, and a knowledge of people in the neighbourhood were required. . . . I first recollect the figure of Miss Tugworth when she came to teach me how to write the letter 'S', pointing out to me that it was shaped like a swan. I still recall my efforts to make it look like one, and how the view outside was, appropriately, everywhere of swan's-down, because snow was falling and covered everything, even the trees, with white, soft feathers. Miss Susan, the eldest of her family, was kind and sad and overworked, never from the weight of any particular job, but from the drift and variety of the small burdens which she had assumed, the different kinds of task which she had been obliged to undertake in order to earn a living for herself and her drove of sisters. They were in a genteel way bitterly poor, and lived in a small white house which had belonged to their father, an artist of some repute, known in his day for his pictures of tall, slender, and beautiful women, carrying on their shoulders Grecian water jars or posed among almond blossom and peach. By a mysterious decree of fate, however, he had drawn as his allotted share of children only the very opposite of the type he liked to paint. These sisters, stunted, short-legged, long-bodied, their drawn-out, dog-like faces blue with cold, were all of them charming in their own way—that is to say they had charm, but not of the sort which he would have appreciated. Now he was dead, some of the daughters had married, and others had settled down to being invalids. It had devolved, therefore, on Miss Susan to support the afflicted. She remained patient, with an air of almost amused resignation and humility before the successive tricks of destiny. . . .

At the time of which I am writing, the First World War was over and my father was again filling our Scarborough house with miscellaneous objects he had bought in Italy, and was pouring them into Renishaw as well: which, however, was large enough to absorb the contents of many vans. Not everyone appreciated their esthetic effect, for the English taste is both more sober and less funereal. Thus Henry Moat plainly felt a distaste for these gimcrack but imaginative pieces. He was wont to say of them—as he did, too, of my father's alterations and decoration of rooms—'Everything for show, and nothing for convenience.' If it had been left to him, all would have been of good, sound oak.

In a letter to Hollingworth he writes:

. . . Sir Geo arrives monday at 2 oclock and would like you to have the cases unpacked in the morning already for him to go through I am going to ask him if he will allow me to go through them after him with a huge hammer.

My father used to get very worked up about the disposition of the objects, and it tempted him to rope other people in and obtain their opinion. During one of these expeditions, he was in the drawing-room at Renishaw supervising the unpacking and instructing two workmen, telling them how to convert two altar vases of gilded wood into paraffin lamps. Henry walked in, carrying something for the rooms beyond, and my father called out to him:

'Henry, don't you think these will make excellent paraffin lamps?'

'No, Sir George, I don't,' was the answer.

My father added: 'Then you're quite mistaken. They will.'

Whatever may be the true estimate of the objects, they continued to arrive for some twenty years, except between 1914 and 1918. Fresh loads of gaily ramshackle furniture, painted and gilded chests, tables and chairs, or cabinets gone to the other extreme and blacker than black would come from Naples, Palermo, Florence, Rome, and Venice, bringing with them more than their fair portion of woodworm and death-watch beetle. A few years later, it is true, my father sent back most of these pieces of furniture to Italy: but at the moment they led to Wood End being very crowded. A consequence of this was that one morning my mother sent for me to her room and said:

'The lumber-rooms, as usual, are getting much too full and I think I shall sell the contents of the first of them at the top of the stairs; not that there's much in it that will fetch anything —though there's an old piano that might sell.' After a moment's pause, she added: 'It's curious, I don't remember seeing it before. Don't say a word to your father or he'll only make a fuss. . . . I'll let the auctioneer know and he can perhaps take the things away next week when your father goes to Renishaw for a few days.' . . .

They were duly moved, and in time the auction took place, bringing in some seventy pounds odd, of which the piano accounted for six guineas. (It was one of those recurrent moments when to sell a piano brings in little, while to buy one costs a fortune.)

What my mother had *not* known was that Sister Dorothy had, a short time before, received as a legacy a piano which proved too big for her to house, and that she had therefore asked my father to shelter it for her until she could contrive to find for it a permanent home. My father, who liked her for her practical common sense, as he termed her lack of imagination, and also, perhaps, to be different, had consented. The instrument had duly arrived and had been carried straight up to the lumber-room while my mother was out.

At some moment within the following fortnight my father

must have received a letter from Sister Dorothy to say that she had at last bought a house in which her brother would live and where she could join him on her retirement. She could, there-fore, now have the piano—on which I may add that neither of them could, perhaps fortunately, play a note—and accordingly a van would call for it. My father did not mention the matter to anyone—he saw no need to—but when the van arrived and the men were sent upstairs to the lumber-room to remove the piano and found nothing there he rushed into my mother's room and said without a previous explanation:

'Where is Sister Dorothy's piano?'

Though this was the first my mother had heard of its ownership, she immediately grasped the situation. Not, how-ever, realizing that the van men were in the house, she said, in order to gain time and because the kindly Miss Tugworth had always solved so many difficulties for her: 'I think Miss Tugworth must have got it.'

My father tore out of the room, saying:

'I never heard of such impertinence—to remove a piano without even consulting *me*!'

He then rushed downstairs, spinning like a tornado, and directed the van men to Miss Tugworth's house. . . . The door was opened by one of her sisters, and before she had time to reply four men in green-baize aprons had entered. They strode by instinct straight into the drawing-room where poor Miss Susan Tugworth was sitting alone in a heavy coat, enjoying its brittle, cold splendour. This room was one of the few posses-sions of which the whole family felt proud. It had stayed as it had been left by their mother, full of spindly bamboo tables and useless knick-knacks, small shoes in silver, and heavily cut glass scent-bottles with silver stoppers. It also exhibited a grand piano, which had not been played upon since their mother's

[73]

decease. . . . Going up to the piano, the apparent chief of the gang playfully struck a note and said: "E told us to take it away.' (Obviously the van men had been impressed by my father's considerable personality, for not one of them ever referred to him directly, but as though his name were taboo, because sacred, alluded to him as "E' or "Im'.) The other three men now advanced inexorably on the piano, and together they whisked the heavy instrument out of the room. It was a scene which, to look back on, might have been invented by the contemporary Kafka. Miss Tugworth kept on saying weakly, over and over again: 'You can't do that,' to which they would reply:

'Oh yes, we can. 'E told us to take it away.'

'But it's *my* piano.'

'That's not what 'E says. It's by 'Is orders.'

'Who is "He"? '

"E said you'd know 'oo 'E was.'

Poor Miss Tugworth, so kind and pliant! The van started and carried away her piano to embellish and make genteel Sister Dorothy's new house. Several days passed before Miss Tugworth could even find out where the instrument had gone, or who had given the order for its removal. Whether she ever received it back again I cannot recall: only that she laid no blame on anyone. My mother, on the other hand, was furious with Sister Dorothy and retired to bed for a week, and no one for many years was allowed to mention the word *piano* in her presence.

9

THE ADVENTURE OF THE PHANTOM
TAX-INSPECTOR

IN THE dining-room at Renishaw there hangs among the assembled portraits one which was not there when I was a child. It is not a work of art: in fact the tortoiseshell frame which contains it is responsible for any effect that it contrives to make; nevertheless it is plainly—I fear *plainly* is the precise and operative word—a painstaking, and a painsgiving, likeness. It represents a young girl, who carries perched on the crook of her left arm a rather mean-looking and curiously undecorative green parrot. The girl herself wears on her slightly smug, round face an expression of insipid, innocent surprise; I apprehend that she would look even more astonished could she be aware of the circumstances attendant on the last purchase of her portrait and its reappearance in this house. . . .

We must, since one thing leads to another, begin at the beginning, or even before it, and touch on matters seemingly unconnected with it, but which in reality shaped the course of small events which led to its acquisition—events which though minute in themselves are part of the chains and fetters of the inexorable law of cause and effect. . . . During the winter of 1920–1, then, the door of the house in which my brother and I lived in London could be seen to lack its knocker for a period of some three months, and any friends of ours passing would have been able to interpret the message which its removal carried; for in the same way that the presence of the Sovereign in a city is made evident by the flying of a Royal Standard over his palace there, so, albeit obversely, the taking down of the knocker from the door of his sons' house signalled to those in the know that my father was in London. In addition, if they went by frequently, they would have comprehended that he was paying a longer visit than was his wont. The explanation of the periodic disappearances of this object was that I had found it in a lumber-room at Renishaw, where it had reposed for years: it must have come from Italy, is made of bronze, and its shape—that of a ring slightly pulled out at the sides—is formed by two dolphins, face to face, fin to fin, their entwined tails closing the circle. Seeing it, I at once grasped how well it would look on the door, which, at the time of writing, it still embellishes, and took it to London without revealing to my father that I had done so, for though he had several years previously handed Renishaw over to me, he yet liked to be consulted, and I knew from experience that the words which came most easily to his lips were 'No, certainly not!' or, with a note of warning in his voice, 'Oh, I *shouldn't* do that if I were you!'

All those dreary long winter weeks, therefore, I was obliged to conceal the knocker, my father having sought refuge in London for reasons which I will shortly disclose. . . . In the days of which I write, Scarborough, ancient and historic borough, and modern pleasure resort, yet retained a

[76]

marked character of its own. . . . Many incidents of past years there I could relate: and, though varied, they would be equally grotesque. Of them all, the Adventure of the Phantom Special Commissioner of Inland Revenue is perhaps the most exceptional—as unexpected as the episode in London to which, by causing my father to spend the winter there, it led up. In those days we still had a house in Scarborough—Wood End—always referred to by a writer in the local Press as 'Sir George and Lady Ida's marine residence'; a description which ever summoned to mind the image of some submerged and finny grot at sea bottom with huge fish darting in and out in strictest privacy: the words certainly served to make the place sound cool and remote. However, Wood End was not so isolated or lonely as the description suggests. Several taller houses overlooked its rectangular block, built of dark, golden stone, set in a large garden and within range of all the sea's voices, its roarings, its tremendous thunder and lion-voice threats, its occasional purring and light-hearted delusive promises.

It was some time during the late summer that my father first noticed one of the Special Commissioners of Inland Revenue, so he asserted and continued to maintain, skulking on the roof of the nearest house, observing him through binoculars. My father declared him to be a dignified-looking individual, wearing striped trousers, a morning coat, and a tall hat—no very suitable garb, I reflected, for someone literally 'on the tiles' who must wish to escape attention. Apparently the stranger stood there for hours, patiently watching Wood End. At the beginning my father was furiously angry, and would stare back through the spy-glass which he always carried about with him when at Renishaw or Wood End, so as to be able to 'obtain the distant view'—in other words, in case he should see a chance of knocking down some building, and beginning to erect another in its place. . . . I was never able myself to discern the mysterious stranger, and my own feeling was that he must be either my father's Narcissus-like *doppelgänger*, a projection from and of his own personality such as Edgar Allan Poe was concerned with in his story of *William Wilson*, or else that victim of *delirium tremens* who had lived ten years before—and apparently was still living—in the house in question. From time to time the prey of the most oppressive alcoholic nightmares, he was probably—if it were he—scanning our garden for stray pink elephant or undulant boa-constrictor; but my suggestions to that effect were contemptuously rejected. No, my father had guessed the identity of the prowler immediately, and once and for all. He did not believe in ghosts, but with his whole being he believed in the existence of his Special Commissioner. Nothing could shake him. When I said to him: 'How can you be so sure that he is one of the Special Commissioners of Inland Revenue?', he resorted to the use of one of his favourite and most irrefutable replies:

'*We happen to know.*'

The phantom continued to haunt him, so he decided to go away. He would not visit Renishaw as my guest, for the insolent intruder might follow him there, hide in one of the stables or outhouses, and steal out unobserved, to watch and follow and pry, and, in fact, like the hosts of Midian, to 'prowl and prowl around'. Instead, he took the lease for the autumn and winter of a furnished apartment on the sixth floor of a block of flats in Knightsbridge: at least there he would not be over-looked, and would be free from the daily persecution—as he had grown to regard it—that he had suffered at Scarborough.

So it came about that my door remained for several long months without its customary knocker. . . . From his new and temporary eyrie my father could pursue his many interests: he could be seen—if the Commissioner in question had followed him—wearing frock-coat and silk hat, the well-known air-cushion like a lifebuoy on his arm, leaving the building every morning for the Reading Room of the British Museum, where he was at last in the final round of a long hand-to-hand tussle with the Grosvenor pedigree. He was, however, no longer attended to the door by Henry Moat, now superseded by my former soldier servant, the nimble Robins. . . . Though the conduct of his life followed its customary course in London, the experiences of the last few weeks had left him in a more than usually suspicious frame of mind. When, therefore, he received a letter from a stranger, asking him to visit his house, my father's reactions were mixed (the Commissioner again?). The correspondent claimed to be an ex-naval captain, lived somewhere at the top of Hampstead Heath, and had written to say that he had lately purchased at a sale a small portrait which had formerly hung at Renishaw, and depicted a Sitwell ancestress as a child. He never sold—he proceeded to write—anything he had bought, but on this occasion would like to make an exception and offer the picture to my father. He would be at home on Tuesday afternoon, and could show the painting.

This letter at once excited my father's predominant interest —in family history—but also roused his latent fear that, since his life was of such great importance to the country, someone might attempt to kidnap him for ransom, or even to kill him. (He used, I cannot imagine by what means, to acquire certain slang phrases, and I recall him saying, in this connection, 'I fear that one of these gangs may bump me off!') There had been that odd incident, he recalled for my benefit, of the sample of cocoa that had reached him through the post, addressed in handwriting unknown to him (he had caused it to be put on the fire at once, but even then it had burnt with a curiously coloured flame, and had made a spluttering noise). But at whatever cost to himself, he intended to inspect the portrait (which would it prove to be, Katherine Sacheverell who had married George Sitwell, or Francis Sitwell's wife, or Mary Reresby? much depended on that); there was no point, however, in incurring needless risk, so he would take with him Robins, who could carry a harquebus—what did they call it now?—of course, a revolver! Robins no doubt would require considerable coaching beforehand in how to act and how to handle the weapon, but my father would give him a few hints, so he could not go far wrong.

The instructions which Robins received were that he was to sit beside the driver, to draw a revolver ostentatiously from its holster directly he arrived outside the house, and, when my father alighted, was to remain holding it in an obvious and menacing manner, at the same time lolling to show he felt no fear himself, till my father should give a signal. (My father said he would know by the atmosphere of the house after he had been in it for five or ten minutes what course of action to follow. If all were well he would make certain faces and gestures, which he had previously taught Robins to interpret, from a window or possibly from the garden: if he failed to appear within a quarter of an hour Robins was to fight his way in at the point—or, rather, at the barrel—of his revolver—for if the owner were really an ex-naval officer he might be a good hand with a cutlass.)

The day came, the taxicab was hired. The driver, however, at first objected to Robins sitting beside him, protesting that it was contrary to the law that governed the life of taxicabs, but as soon as he saw my father in tall hat and topcoat, with a collar

The Dining-Room, Renishaw

Staircase at Renishaw

of Irish beaver, a fur which he claimed to be extinct (and it looked to me as if the allegation were justified), the driver's objections were overcome, and they started on their singular quest.· They arrived, and the house seemed an ordinary, rather pretty Hampstead dwelling. My father rang the bell and the door was opened almost immediately by a neatly dressed parlourmaid. Robins, therefore, watched the house and garden with anxious attention and was relieved, after some eight and a half minutes had passed, to see my father's face grimacing at him from a shrubbery just the other side of some oak palings, and to read its message and that of the accompanying gestures: '*All Clear*'. . . . What the ex-naval officer—who proved to be of a well-known type, bluff, hearty, adventurous, and intelligent —can have made of the highly unconventional behaviour of his visitor, who in every other respect seemed so dignified and courteous, we shall never know. The taxi-driver, for his part, from whom some reaction might have been expected, did not seem in the least astonished: he commented, as my father got out: 'Nice gentleman, that, quite of the old school,' but certainly my father, with his beard, as he had signalled across the fence from among the speckled laurels, laburnums, and privets of a suburban garden, must have looked rather strange, unusual today as a satyr in a glade. The adventure had, it is true, a happy ending—no one was killed; my father left the house with the picture under his arm, the ex-naval officer had acquired the twenty-five pounds he had asked for it, and in time I was able to restore the door-knocker to its accustomed place. Nevertheless, the expedition had left a tender spot in my father's memory, for when one day, some years later, I began to question him about it, he gave me a severe look, and said:

'Don't ask silly questions, dear boy.'

10

LA GALLINA

WHEN the Campanile of St Mark's had but lately col-
lapsed, the Saint on his pinnacle landing from the air
in so gentle a manner, as if knocking at the great doors of the
cathedral in order to crave sanctuary, and by this unique
gesture of abdication had given back to the golden church
and to the Piazza their ancient and proper proportion, my
father went to Venice to meet Signor Bracciaforte, so that with
the aid of this expert he might try to find and buy for Renishaw
a pair of garden statues and a fountain. That they should be fine
and beautiful works of art was all the more important because
he relied on architectural rather than horticultural features for
his effects. Flowers, in fact, were only admitted to the garden
if innocuous and indeed insipid enough not to attract attention
to themselves. In short, he hated strong colours, and in this
connection a friend recalled to me one more instance of it. . . .
Ernest de Taye, for very many years head gardener at
Renishaw, but at the time of which I write new to the job,

asked one morning to see my father. He obtained permission, entered my father's study, and said to him in his soft foreign voice—he was a Belgian from Ghent:

'Sir George, I am sorry to inform you that the large very brightly coloured rhododendron near the fern-leaf beech was blown down in last night's gale'—only to receive the to him startling reply:

'All I wish is that it had been blown right out of the garden!'

It will be appreciated, therefore, to what a degree my father had to depend on the more permanent and organic features of a garden. The best examples of statuary of the kind he sought were to be found scattered over the former Venetian territories on the mainland. Accordingly, my father and Signor Bracciaforte set off at eight or eight-fifteen of a morning either to worry and beat down the dealers in Venice itself or to ransack throughout the day one of the neighbouring little cities.

Here I must turn aside to establish the character of Signor Bracciaforte. I have written of him elsewhere, that he was the Pécuchet to my father's Bouvard. My father always referred to him not as a dealer of perspicacity and principle, but as 'our little artist friend', and it was true that before becoming a dealer he had been a painter. Indeed, to that very day he continued to see life in terms of Murger's *Vie de Bohème* and still wore a beard as a declaration of his faith, though it was a rather thin and token beard. Nevertheless, all that he lacked in order to complete the costume of the part was a floppy brown velvet beret. Born out of wedlock, Bracciaforte was the warm-hearted offspring of a peasant woman and an Italian Count, who had seen her working in the fields. He had married an English-woman who had a fortune of her own, but he continually looked to left and right. He was kind and gay by nature, and a creditable human being, though one not lacking in absurdities and contradictions. He loved nature, and liked especially birds. His English was a language fluent but consisting of words which were unidentifiable, and he would deplore for many minutes at a time—and choosing my sister as audience—the character of the cuckoo as a mother, always beginning: 'Miss Edit, have you tor' what it min . . . ?' (Miss Edith, have you thought what it means . . . ?)

I saw him last in 1949, at the age of ninety-three, when he suddenly materialized with a suitcase and a niece, who deposited it and him at Montegufoni. Unexpected things had happened to him during the war years. His pictures, painted sixty years before, had suddenly become the favourites and paragons of the advanced Italian painters of the day. Articles had appeared in the papers demanding the facts of his life and death. Nobody knew, of course, that he was, or could be, at such a great age, still living; so his fame was posthumous in his lifetime. His house (his wife was by then dead) had been commandeered during the war, and well though he knew the city, he was unable to find anywhere to live in his adopted Florence, so he returned to his native Romagna and had chosen to make his home there in a remote valley, because it looked so pastoral and untouched by war. Indeed, there seemed no reason why it should ever be affected: but quite soon after he had settled in his new home, the Allies started to bomb the valley so regularly and to such an extent that it became known to the world as the Death Valley. He then moved to a hotel, and from hotel to hotel, till the end of the war. Some time during the years he had taken under his wing—if one can use the expression in this connection—a hen that he had found in the yard of a deserted and bombed farmhouse. She quickly became devoted to him and was widely known as La Gallina. She lived between his shirt and coat, buttoned in for security, and was the cause of most of his moves from hotel to hotel in the small cities of the region: for the other guests sitting in the public rooms of the establishment would object to the sudden contented sound of clucking and the emergence of a bright eye and the scruffy feathered neck above the lapel of Signor Bracciaforte's coat. The lounge, as the residents called it, was no place for fowls: she should never have been taken away from the farm. But he refused to abandon her and together they moved from place to place, from one hotel to another. Eventually, however, La Gallina died from old age, but tears still came into Signor Bracciaforte's eyes when he spoke of her. . . .

Signor Bracciaforte, I was explaining, was accompanying my father in his search for garden ornaments, as so often before on previous similar occasions, and leading the way, would turn to my father and say as he always did: 'Mebbee, we fine old t'ing.'

II

THE FOUNTAIN

Y FATHER was apt to drive too hard a bargain. . . . One morning in Treviso, whither he, with Signor Braccia-forte in attendance, had gone for the day from Venice, in the back garden of a dealer who lived on the ground floor of an old palace, and with whom they had transacted business on more than one occasion in the past—so that the *antiquario* must have grasped what technique would be used and what treatment to expect—my father at last discovered a fountain of the very size and shape he required. It was made of marble that when it had first been cut had been pure white, but now had assumed with the passing of time a tone of dark honey, and had been invested, further, with a perfect patina by centuries of exposure to salt air and to the lion-maned glare of the Venetian lagoons. It was plainly intended for him—indeed, the sole hindrance to its immediate purchase was the high price demanded by the dealer; too high even when my father had in his own mind deducted one third of the sum first asked, which constituted the

customary overcharge made by the vendor in order to allow
ample room for bargaining. Such was the common practice in
those days. Obviously the dealer enjoyed exercise in this
important art: he liked to bargain (in the manner, no doubt,
that a trout might enjoy being tickled). This my father
remembered from earlier visits to him.

In order to obtain the best results, my father, with Bracciaforte and Henry Moat in waiting, decided to move out to
Treviso for two weeks, during which period—fortunately the
hotel was situated near the apartment of the dealer—my
father could descend on him at any moment he chose of the
day or night. (The dealer, he averred, did not mind. It gave an
antiquario the feeling that he was doing his selfless duty—like
doctors whom 'we happen to know' nothing pleases more
than to be called up from their beds during the darkest and
most slumberous hours to attend an unknown patient with
little wrong with him. . . . But by this time the simile had
grown rather muddled and he abandoned it). . . . Treviso was a
pleasant place in which to make a stay and the hotel was a
singularly fine building, not very imaginative, he owned, but
built as if to battle against eternity single-handed; in fact it was
of a mysterious size and solidity, since few people would want
to stay there for long with Venice so near to entice them. There
did not seem to be even the usual solitary tourist looking as if
he had been pressed between the pages of a Baedeker. No, the
hotel was plainly empty and he and Signor Bracciaforte had
the undivided attention of the proprietor and staff.

The *antiquario* was a dapper little man with a charming
smile, albeit, after the first few mornings, afternoons, and
evenings of bargaining with my father that smile began to
crack, while by the last few days it had plainly gone rancid.
Nevertheless, he still retained at times an air of smiling to

himself at some joke which only himself could perceive.

My father conducted the proceedings with considerable skill: sudden bouts of bullying alternating with stretches of long but gentle persistence. By the ninth day the price had been brought to a reasonable level and by the thirteenth it became obvious that my father would get his way and that the next morning the *antiquario* was bound to accept the final offer, so that in the afternoon my father would be able to return to Venice floating in triumph from the station through the apotheositic splendours of a Venetian sunset to Danieli's Hotel.

Consequently, on the morning of the fourteenth day, and accompanied of course by Signor Bracciaforte, he arrived at the dealer's in a very genial humour, at an hour unusually early even for him, and ready to clinch his bargain. He rang the bell happily: but nobody answered. No doubt he had not pulled it hard enough. He rang again, more heavily: this time they both heard it ring. . . . Still no one came. Just as he was going to ring a third time, he happened to look down, and saw an envelope projecting from under the door. He picked it up. It was addressed to *Monsieur Sitwell*. He tore it open and read. . . . It began with many professions of esteem, and went on to say how much the dealer had enjoyed the sessions of bargaining at pleasantly unconventional hours, but now that he had sold this fountain at the same low price at which he had offered it to my father the previous afternoon, he felt the need of change and fresh air, and had decided on impulse to go to the country for a few days' shooting. . . . The purchaser of the fountain, as my father would undoubtedly know, was his compatriot, the Duke of Meldrum. . . . The Duke of Meldrum was reputed to be the richest man in England, with an income to spend—for this was before the introduction of surtax—of a thousand pounds a day. . . . My father was flabbergasted. He had not

[88]

even been aware that the Duke was in the vicinity, far less that he was staying, as it transpired, at the same hotel; whereas the Duke had known that my father was there and bidding—one cannot say briskly, but seriously—and had arranged for the *antiquario* to telephone every evening to his courier, giving the score, as it were, of both parties at the close of play. Nor, even had my father known of the Duke being so near, would he have connected him with works of art: no, race-horses, polo, hunting, and yachts were his domain and speciality. My father was enraged. The more he thought about it, the more angry he became, as he dwelt in his mind on the hours he had wasted in unwitting preparations of a vicarious super-bargain for his invisible rival; in short, for having done all the work and got nothing for it.

If, during the years that immediately followed, a tourist were to obtain permission to visit Meldrum Abbey, after being taken to see the gold trophies won by the race-horses, which were displayed in a specially constructed chamber, a kind of strong-room cellar, and to marvel at the private post-office, police station, and dental surgery, he would then be sure to be conducted through the garden to admire the fountain, looking very out of keeping with grey skies in a damp yew-enclosed setting. By its side stood a wooden notice, painted green, with the following words inscribed on it in white letters:

This fountain, a gem of the Italian Renaissance, sculptured by the hand of Bartolomeo di Treviso, was discovered abroad by Henry Victor Fitzroy Fawcett, eleventh Duke of Meldrum, and erected by him in its present suitable position.

Further, to this very hour, when parties of tourists are shown round by the present Duke, a grandson, this cicerone will point out the fountain to his flocks and read aloud to them the legend.

[89]

12

IDEAS FROM THE BUREAU

ONE morning not long ago I was sitting in the dentist's chair when, just as he was walking away from it to make sure what was happening in the next room from which sounded a loud groaning, and leaving me with my mouth full of looking-glasses, drills, steel crochet-hooks, and other instruments of his profession, he remarked: 'I will say one thing for you: you're a good listener.' At the time I was not amused, but thinking it over I began to believe that there might be a little truth in it, and that it was as the result of many years of silent observation and suffering that I had become something of an expert on parents and how to manage them. Indeed, at one time in the twenties I had considered opening an office where it would be possible to obtain professional advice on payment of a fee. It was to be called *The Sons and Daughters Advice Bureau* and would have existed in order to advise children how to treat their parents, whether to try temporarily to pacify or further to inflame them, always with a view to subsequent relaxation. For this purpose, new techniques had to be devised.

Means of increasing nervous tension—in fact the waging of a private cold war—are not difficult to invent. . . . It was during the twenties, after my father had been vouchsafed the vision of the Phantom Tax-inspector and when, as a result, he was in a rather nervous condition, that I considered using on him one of the three techniques that I had devised for the harrying of Percy Wyndham Lewis, a person also of deeply suspicious nature. The first process is called *The Masked Musicians*, the second I named *The Unexpected Gift*, and the third *The Quick-change Artiste*.

At Renishaw one year I had spent a long, wet summer morning looking round a lumber-room—limbo-room would have been a more precise description of this place where the William Morris paper hung from the walls like the tattered regimental banners of a defeated foreign foe in a cathedral, and a piled-up clutter of unwanted objects led an existence in a half-world of dust: an old piano, a stuffed bird of dull but unknown species—a sort of seagull I suppose—a Venetian vase of blue-green glass over six foot in height and resembling in shape a trumpet only with a crinkled edge, a few assegais and a shield made from some kind of Zulu esparto grass, a carved, carpenter's-gothic armchair, a harp, a plumed hat in a case, belonging to an extinct uniform which had got itself elsewhere, a great many cut-glass scent-bottles with silver tops now black, bits of broken cups and saucers, a hare made of blue china with an eyeglass and high white collar, and a box of photographs all faded to the colour of khaki. Among these one caught my eye and filled me with curiosity. It showed two men sitting side by side, both dressed in the same way and looking exactly alike. They were wearing black felt hats drawn down over their eyes and enveloping black cloaks, very mysterious; but what captivated me was that they were both the very image of Wyndham Lewis. My mother was the only person who might be able to identify them. I went to find her. She looked at them and said:

'Of course, they are the Masked Musicians.'

This was tantalizing because she could tell me no more. The photograph must have been very nearly forty years old. . . . I acted at once and ordered five hundred picture postcards to be reproduced from it, and when they arrived I sent a large number of them to Wyndham Lewis's particular friends and particular enemies: but the first card of all I posted was addressed to Wyndham Lewis himself at his studio with written on it anonymously the intimidating message: 'So there *are* two of you!' . . .

Puzzled and alarmed, he went round to see various friends and found them with the same photograph, placed in a conspicuous position on the mantelpiece, but everyone was equally unable to explain the meaning.

I will now tell the reader how the idea of the second method came to me as the happy result of a fortunate concatenation of circumstances. . . . One morning I came downstairs and said to my secretary, who was always most co-operative: 'I feel just in the mood to send Wyndham Lewis an unsolicited gift. . . . I wonder what we could find for him today.'

She replied: 'I've the very thing for him in an envelope in my bag. It's a tooth, extracted by the dentist yesterday. . . . Here it is!' and she triumphantly produced on the palm of her hand an opalescent molar.

I at once accepted the kind offer: first I wrapped the precious object in cotton wool and next placed it in a cardboard box, which had contained a watch, was of a pale shade of lilac, and bore on the lid in gold lettering the famous name of Cartier. I then added a card that I found lying on my desk, and which bore engraved on it the legend: *With Sir Gerald du Maurier's Compliments*. (It must have reached me, I think, accompanying an appeal for some charity connected with the stage, and affords another instance of the folly of throwing anything away—you can never tell when the most improbable article may come in useful.) The whole surprise packet, after it had been wound in layer after layer of rustling tissue paper, was then encased in sober brown paper, on which was pasted securely a label bearing Wyndham Lewis's name and address in typescript. Finally, when all this had been accomplished, it was posted to him from the G.P.O. . . . The essence of the Unsolicited Gift is the artful combination of unrelated objects. I tried to think of some equally exciting present for my father, but no inspiration came. . . . Perhaps the third technique I had invented, known as *The Quick-change Artiste*, could be more easily applied to parents.

There were turns—now I fear defunct—still lingering in the superb music-hall programmes of those days, announced as being performed by Professor So-and-So, 'the World-famous Quick-change Artiste'. Dapper and clean-shaven, a man would walk on to the stage, empty except for one piece of furniture, a cross between a desk and a table, and bow to the audience; when the applause had died down, he would explain that his first impersonation would be of Gounod. He would then turn his back on the auditorium and go to the table, as we will call it, where his fingers would move quickly among a collection of wigs, false noses, and looking-glasses; having transformed himself, he would whisk round to the audience, at the same time striking a supposedly characteristic attitude, such as, in this instance, holding a conductor's baton as if about to launch on the world a new masterpiece. This portrayal would be greeted with rapturous applause, though in spite of the reception the artiste had won, he had not, I apprehend, the slightest conception, any more than I had myself, of what the composer had looked like in real life. When the clapping had died down, the performer would announce his next impersonation, which was nearly sure to be of the Abbé Liszt, an item that appeared in such turns, as did that of Gounod, to be almost obligatory. . . . Indeed, the imitations given by quick-change artistes were almost always the same, and it was difficult to grasp what principle of selection governed their choice, except that a lot of hair on head and face made the impersonation easier. The repertory generally included, in addition to Gounod and the Abbé, Charles Dickens and some of the following: Zola, Mr Gladstone, Lord Tennyson, Bismarck, and, to finish up with, W. G. Grace, wearing a round cricket cap and carrying a bat. (This last was a certain winner.) It will have been noticed that those who were impersonated all belonged roughly to the same period, then the recent past, and were seldom earlier than the Emperor Napoleon the Third or later than President Kruger (Oom Paul, always such a great target for fish-heads when they were in supply). Most of these figures, in short, belonged to the limbo of those who had died some thirty years before, and though in life they may have looked immensely distinguished, the mimicry of them seemed now to bring with it a whiff of Madame Tussaud's Chamber of Horrors, and to declare their relationship to the wax effigies of Doctor Neil Cream or of Charley Peace—who, we may recollect, was himself a quick-change artiste, adept at totally changing his appearance, even the lines of his face, in the shortest possible time.

It will be appreciated that my father would have been

astonished if his eyes, wandering from the Phantom Tax-inspector on the roof of the next-door house down to the drive, had suddenly beheld there the apparition of Gounod, and hurrying into the house to fetch Robins or Henry to look at the startling new arrival, had returned in the space of two minutes only to find in his place Mr Gladstone or the Abbé Liszt. The prospect of his reactions would be fascinating—so alluring, indeed, that it was difficult to banish the idea: but there proved to be too many practical difficulties to its fruition. Quick-change artistes had already become very rare and those who still existed were old, and age has little liking for adventure, as we are frequently informed, so that the idea of hanging about all day under the damp shelter of umbrageous trees, and then meeting with an uncertain reception at the end of it, did not appeal to them. Moreover, if they agreed to perform for a day, they must be paid, they insisted, for a full week's engagement. . . . We had therefore to remain content with the Phantom Tax-inspector.

13

LOOKING AHEAD

ONE morning in the hot summer of 1921 I was walking with my father in the park at Renishaw, where great patches of shadow lay under the old trees and at the edges of the plantations. He was wearing a very neat, pale grey suit and a grey wide-awake hat. As we were approaching a fence with a wooden gate, he suddenly took a little run and vaulted lightly over it. I was astonished, for he was over sixty years of age, complained always that the slightest exertion tired him out, and, additional cause for wonder, I had never seen him do this before. He must have noticed my surprise, for he said to me: 'I try to keep up my vaulting, to amuse my friends.' My father, though he never saw any member of the spectral band, continued often to allude to it.

My father always liked to pose to himself as a fine sportsman, and the exploit I have just related helped to foster this illusion. Certainly I can never recollect his hunting or riding for pleasure—albeit I remember my mother telling me that he

Author's bedroom with Staffordshire Figures

Author standing by the Gothick Temple, Renishaw

had as a young man won a point-to-point; a victory the status
of which she somewhat disparaged by alleging that his horse
had run away with him. Nevertheless it brought him in some
votes at the subsequent Election, though of course it may have
cost him others. My mother also recalled how my grandmother
Sitwell, who disapproved of any form of racing because of the
opportunity it afforded for gambling, had remained in her
room in prayer, not for the victory of her son, but for his
safety, and how when eventually she rose from her knees,
and went downstairs and heard the result, she felt that such an
answer to her supplications had been almost overwhelmingly
too swift, direct, and triumphant: so she climbed upstairs again,
and spent the rest of the day imploring the Deity to turn
a disapproving eye on any further racing exploits of my
father's.

My father also objected strongly to gambling—and with
every reason—because his family had twice been ruined by
addiction to it—objected to it, that is to say, except on the
Stock Exchange, where it was promoted and given a new
name, being transformed into investment, that pillar of Church
and State, and at the worst being dignified by the word
speculation. Notwithstanding his principles, he liked to stay in
the metropolis of the gambling world, Monte Carlo. He never
entered the Rooms (a paternal deprivation which, indeed, I
welcomed, since it meant that I could frequent them with the
certainty of not meeting him), nor could he enjoy walking
through the acres of garden, of which he deplored the lay-out
('Such a pity not to have consulted *me*') as much as the floral
extravagance of the subtropical blossoms that flourished therein
in certain parts, plants such as the hibiscus with its red trumpet.
The tidiness of the ordinary Riviera flowers offended him
equally, beds of carnations, for instance, covered with sacking

every night during the winter months for protection against possible cold air. In short, he could take no pleasure in any of the flowers set in emeraldine grass with not a blade awry. So neat was everything that it seemed that the only explanation could be that every blade and blossom must have its own attendant. No, what he enjoyed, what drew him here, was the sense of lavishness which made the visitor realize that more money was spent on him than it cost him (so long as he did not go into the Rooms), that his stay was subsidized indirectly by the losses at the tables incurred by gamblers of many nations, and all these amenities just described, together with many others, were provided for him gratis through the errors and cupidity of people more foolish than himself. Moreover, all empty pockets were in his view deserved, for he would not allow the existence of good or bad fortune. In support, he would quote a favourite dictum: 'There is no such thing as good or bad luck, only good or bad management.' There were, of course, other drawbacks besides those enumerated which also prevented complete contentment. Thus in spite of his liking for the principality, he took exception to the architectural style of the Casino and its immediate neighbours, and I recall his remarking to me at tea one afternoon in the Café de Paris:

'Have you noticed that the buildings here have a most objectionable gaiety about them?'

It was during the visit to my father at Monte Carlo that he issued the wildest and most terrifying of all his warnings to me. Readers of those books of mine in which my father occurs may remember that he was wont to give strange cautions to those round him. As he grew older these seemed to become more unexpected and frequent. We had been talking the previous evening of my projected first visit to the United States early in

the New Year. In the morning he sent for me to his room. As
I entered, he said: 'Good morning, Osbert, come in and shut
the door. . . . There are two things of which I should warn you
before you start for America.'

My heart sank at the familiar opening, usually the preliminary to trouble.

'What are they, Father?'

'Never play with a dead cat, and above all never make
friends with a monkey.'

Even I, accustomed though I was to receiving from him
cautions at once morbid and startling, was on this occasion
somewhat disconcerted, because the warnings thus addressed
to me seemed to fit in with no proclivities of my nature of
which I was conscious. Good heavens, what could he mean?
Indeed, I was so much taken aback that I rather foolishly
asked: 'Why?', and received a yet more bewildering Delphic
reply delivered in his most withering style:

'Because if you do you'll get diphtheria!'

The explanation proved to be that my father had read in
one of the papers of an outbreak in New York of this illness,
which a small boy had developed; and the child had been seen
playing in Central Park, throwing the body of a dead cat up
in the air and catching it over and over again. The second
warning derived also from a newspaper, in the columns of
which he had read how some children had been observed,
pressed against the bars of a cage in the Zoo, talking for a long
time to a great ape, and that in view of the fact that the animal
had developed diphtheria the next day, it was surmised in
medical circles that the children, who fell ill a week or two
later, had contracted the disease from their anthropoid chum.
(My father was fond of animals, and I have often seen him go
up to the cage of a monkey, and talk to the sad-eyed but

[99]

insouciant inmate. . . . His special interest in the simian tribes was no doubt a tribute to the part they played in the evolutionary theories of his great hero Charles Darwin.) That, however, which rendered my father's warnings disturbing as well as entertaining was that you could not just dismiss them, because you never knew what might not come next, and because often under their *prima facie* absurdity would lurk, hidden by piles of rubbish though it might be, an unexpected truth. Equally, his mind, with its conflicting streaks of conventional and unconventional, on occasions enabled him to arrive at startling but perhaps correct conclusions—as, for example, when we entered into argument about a contemporary trial for murder; in the course of our dispute I opined that the man found guilty was plainly a lunatic and should, therefore, not be executed: my father agreed, rather surprisingly, that the man was mad, but added: 'and one of his delusions may be that he can always commit a murder with absolute impunity'.

My father had a great belief in 'Looking Ahead', which had become with him a special process and one which was concerned with material affairs and not, as might have been presumed from its name, with some spiritual state in the future. No, 'Looking Ahead' was included in good management and was avoided whenever possible by my mother. The concentration necessary to its formulation sometimes gave 'Looking Ahead' an impression of insensibility which was not altogether deserved. It had to be impersonal as a proposition in geometry, and who has ever complained that Euclid was heartless? . . . My mother related to me one of the most singular instances of it. The scene had taken place in March 1916, while I was in the trenches. My father had one morning rushed like a whirlwind into the room, and said at great speed: 'I have just been looking ahead. We may hear at any moment that Osbert's been killed, and the other dear boy will probably go too; in which case you will certainly pass away, and what I want to know is, would the money in your settlement be available for the sons of my second marriage?'

14

UNFORGOTTEN FEASTS

P ROVERBS are often supposed to embalm and preserve an
ancient truth: nevertheless, to the precise contrary, they
may on occasion present in its stead a stunning falsity. Thus,
enough is *not* as good as a feast and never will be. An adequacy
may be honest and healthy but lacks the glamour of a feast.
The idea of the banquets given by the City Companies
fascinated me as a small boy and conferred upon my father a
special prestige in my eyes, because he would from time to
time go up to London in order to attend a gala of this kind,
and return the next day bringing with him an elaborate box of
chocolates or some piece of glass or china which had been
given to him as a memento. Ordinarily, however, banquets
and feasts bore no part in my father's life, though he took an
interest in the decorative and esthetic side of them and would
sometimes talk with apparent airy approval of the singular
entertainments offered in Rome by that Syrian esthete, the
teen-age Emperor Heliogabalus, some two thousand years

before. No! A nourishing and unexciting sufficiency was as a rule the culinary standard my father supported. He liked food to be tasteless and to be served tepid: though he had a good appetite and ate very quickly—a habit which he was fond of attributing to the rapidity of the working of his brain. His favourite dish was blancmange, that quaking white confection that masquerades under a bogus foreign title but is quite unknown in the whole gastronomic repertory of the French. So fond was he of it, and so often did it figure in the menu, that Henry would warn us beforehand: 'He's having his old rock of ages again for luncheon.' It will be understood that for a good cook to have to send up that concoction would be derogatory; and how often have I not heard my mother declare that he could ruin the best chef in the world, if left alone with him for two days to order and superintend the meals. The poor cook would hereafter abide in a fog of frustrated virtuosity. Yet though my father in no whit resembled or aspired to resemble either Lucullus as gourmet or Trimalchio as host, nevertheless at least two of the dinner-parties he gave in his later years at Montegufoni attained a certain more than local celebrity.

While the first dinner-party described pertained to the ancient and international world of slap-stick, it is really with the second and in essence fantastic and mysterious occasion that I am chiefly concerned. It was essentially of a socialitic nature. The guests were comparatively few and chosen on no very evident principle. For that reason it is necessary to consider and describe two of the persons present, but although they occur in the second part of this chapter, I present them here so as not to allow the description of the persons to interfere with the detailing of the two parties placed together for comparison.

First, Mrs George Keppel: a most unusual person who

naturally dominated, but never domineered over, the people in her company. To such a degree was this the case that I may add that when in 1940 at the end of the phoney war I stayed at Monte Carlo on my way back from Italy about ten days before the occupation of Paris by the Germans and just before Italy joined in the war, I saw in the dining-room of the Hôtel de Paris several of those who frequented the same circles as she did; when they in turn beckoned to me, the question they asked was identical. It was not, as I had rather expected: 'Is Italy coming into the war?' but instead: 'Is Alice Keppel still in Florence?' . . . She was not a beautiful woman, but had a handsome and very individual appearance. In addition, she was, to use a colloquialism of her time, 'great fun'. Jewels suited her and there was about her a certain natural magnificence which was always reflected in her surroundings. Thus her villa in Florence had the same splendour about it that her house in Grosvenor Street had formerly shown. . . . She added an ambience of amusement, good nature, and keen appreciation both of the surface and of what was occurring underneath it to any occasion at which she was present. As she talked in her clear and level voice, her bold and humorous grey-green eyes raked the scene and took in all that was happening. To give an example of her particular quality, I recall an incident that took place a year or two earlier at Renishaw when she was staying with us. A man whom we had never seen before was wished on us for luncheon one day. He was placed next to my sister, and took it into his head to enquire of her: 'Do you remember this house being built, Miss Sitwell?' Mrs Keppel overheard this, and said to him quickly: 'My dear man, be careful! Not even the nicest girl in the world likes to be asked if she is four hundred years old.'

Then, my aunt Londesborough: she was by now an old

lady. Without being fat, she gave the impression of being over life-size, and when she walked into a room, with a slight limp that was the result of a fall out hunting, she certainly looked an imposing figure, an Amazonian wreck, a substantial ruin of the Edwardian Age of which—in every sense of the word—she had been a prop. . . . My father did not share my views of her personal appearance, and when I one day asked him how my aunt had looked as a girl, he had replied: 'Just as she does now —always very flashy-looking'! But then he was prejudiced. He had never forgiven her for having bought at a local Conservative Bazaar a stone garden seat, somewhat fancifully classified as Italian, but whatever its origin may have been, of a quite unusual ugliness and an excruciating discomfort, and then, having declared in public that she had purchased it as a present for her brother-in-law, for having sent him in a bill of fourteen pounds for it—after which there was yet more talk than customarily of its being 'easy to be generous with other people's money'. Even now, after the passage of many years, the gift had been neither forgiven nor forgotten. Of course it may be that the bill was an error due to her absent-mindedness. She was, as will be seen, very vague. . . .

Here I produce in evidence a scrap of conversation I heard at dinner one night during this same visit to Montegufoni; a fragment typical of both participants.

'George,' my aunt said, 'on my way home I'd like to stay at Monte Carlo—if only I knew where it was.'

My father, always delighted at the thought of perhaps being able to stop anyone from doing something pleasurable, at any rate in prospect, and as if he could detect some terrible danger lurking and looming, at once replied:

'Oh, I shouldn't do anything as rash as that if I were you.'

I recalled, as I looked at her, how a cousin of mine had told me that at the Coronation of King Edward the Seventh, instructions having been specially issued by the Earl Marshal that peeresses were not to wear flowers, a distracted court official had rushed up to my cousin and wailed: 'What *am* I to do? Lady Londesborough has entered the Abbey wearing a large bouquet of pink malmaisons on her chest!' 'What are you to do?' my cousin replied. 'Go back to the Abbey and thank God that she isn't wearing them in her hair!' . . .

In her talk my aunt combined a singular eighteenth-century frankness with a degree of nineteenth-century squeamishness as well. To illustrate this trait, Henry Moat alleged that when, during this visit to Montegufoni, he went upstairs, he would often meet my aunt passing by in a dressing-gown, and each time it had occurred, feeling that some explanation was due from her, he asserted that she would invariably remark:

'I am just on my way to wash my feet.'

THE NIGHT OF THE PARTY

I

The International Festival of Modern Music, under the chairmanship of our old friend Edward Dent, was holding its annual festival at Siena in September 1929. This was for him a fortunate choice because Dent was never happier than when in Italy, and—which constituted an astonishing achievement for an Englishman—or, as for that, for an Italian—he could speak perfectly the dialect of every district and former sovereign state. For the festival the ancient city was crammed for ten days with visitors of a different kind from the ordinary tourist:

with those who brought to music a modern ear. . . . There was a house-party for the occasion at Montegufoni, because among works to be presented was *Façade*, and the author, the composer, and the reciter—my sister, William Walton, and Constant Lambert—were all three staying with us, and were eager to observe the impact of this entertainment upon the two worlds that would form its audience: the cosmopolitan, including advanced composers from nearly every civilized country, superimposed upon the lively Italian main body of it. In addition to the concert, a very full programme of festivities included a special performance of the *Palio*, that great Sienese spectacle, which had been arranged in honour of the visitors. (I recall that just before the *Palio* was due to start, William and Constant, plainly after a very good luncheon, walked with dignity, though with a slight but telling lurch, across the Piazza del Campo, the centre of which had now been cleared for the imminent horse-race, and that their stately intrepidity won them a resounding cheer from the great crowds pressed but jostling behind the barriers.) Though every day was crammed, there was a free evening at the end of the last concert, and accordingly we determined to try to induce my father to invite the delegates to dinner. We cherished little hope of success, but to our surprise he proved on this occasion to be malleable, and even eager to fall in with our plan.

Invitations were sent out and accepted; and on the last day of the festival, dinner was laid for seventy-two persons in the Great Dining-Room. The room had certainly not been used for a century and a half for this, its appointed purpose, and my father's choice of it on this occasion no doubt explained why he had allowed himself to be so easily persuaded; because he had lately restored it, made a kitchen underneath, and had installed as well a service lift to communicate with it. Now he wanted to see the room in action. It is nearly sixty feet long, and has a high coved ceiling, in the centre of which is shown, in a framing of decorative white stucco, an attractive piece of colour, a painted apotheosis, not so much of Cardinal Acciai-uoli, as of his hat, which is being conveyed up to heaven in a swirl of fleecy clouds and angels. On the north side five windows look toward Mont' Albano—in a village at the foot of which Leonardo da Vinci was born—and to the south, on to the Great Court. Between the windows are seventeenth-century plaster pedestal-brackets culminating in bat-like faces which in their deliberate distortion rival gothic gargoyles. My father as he hurried past them was wont to murmur: '*Brutto Seicento!*', but they must have nobly fulfilled their evident purpose: to support baroque dynastic busts which had long vanished, for all the pomp and pride of their full-bottomed wigs and Habsburg features.

Dinner was to be at quarter to seven, and the first guests, headed by Edward Dent, arrived at four-thirty, in order to help in welcoming the delegates unknown to us: the main body was to make the journey in two specially chartered charabancs, due to appear at six. Unfortunately, someone— and I can guess who it was, an indefatigable, indeed relentless, sightseer—had advised the organizers to pay a visit first to San Gimignano, and then to Volterra, so that the parties could see these ancient cities. It would take no time, he had said, as they were practically on the way. . . . But that afternoon they seemed a long distance out of it. The drivers of the charabancs continually lost their bearings, and wandered hither and thither for hours over Tuscany in the gloaming. Meanwhile my father stood in the Court of the Dukes of Athens, watch in hand, and would not be comforted. The waiters, hired for the occasion from Doney's in Florence, tall, melancholy, distinguished-looking individuals, immaculately tailored, spent the spare hours in musing or in throwing the stones with which we provided them down the Well of Polidora in the Great Court and, as its full depth was revealed to them by the sound and sight of the falling pebbles, they would exclaim in tones of astonished pleasure: '*Mamma Mia! Mamma Mia!*': but darkness soon crept over the world and we had to substitute burning straw for pebbles.

Electric light had not yet been installed, and although candles and lamps were provided in great quantities, the enormous blackness within the Castle seemed to swallow and suffocate such light as there was. Gloom brooded and doubts began to develop as to whether our expected guests would ever make their appearance. The principals were at a loss to explain the breakdown of the programme, and my father was full of reproaches, spoken and unspoken, and worked himself up into almost a fever of fussing. In fact he began to 'create'. What could have occurred? Motor-coaches were always dangerous. Perhaps they had fallen over a precipice—a dreadful thing to happen—or one of the drivers might have had a stroke at the wheel, or perhaps he had run amok—driving, he had always understood, could impose a great strain on a man—or, worse still, had the two charabancs through some mischance telescoped each other?—or—but here another side of the matter struck him: if there were no explanation of the sort he had outlined, it was grossly inconsiderate of the delegates. It was now long past the hour for dinner. . . . The sole consolation in our present quandary was that Henry Moat had entered my father's service once again, and though he was by now physically very heavy, lightness had returned to the air, and it was amusing to see how quickly he and my father took up their accustomed roles opposite each other. On this occasion my father called to him.

'Henry, it is now eight-thirty: if they don't arrive in ten minutes' time, I intend to sit down to dinner—if necessary by myself.'

'Well, Sir George, you couldn't ask for more cheerful company, could you?'

My father was just going to reply to this double-edged compliment when at that very moment an excited clamour composed of the shouts, shrieks, and lamentations of a furious mob could be heard approaching; it was the first contingent of guests. Distracted by the nightmare journey to which they had been subjected, always, it seemed to them, brought up with a sudden creaking of overstrained brakes on the very edge of an abyss, lost on mountain roads and in forests of total blackness—difficult enough to find your way about in even by daylight—now maddened by hunger and thirst and other natural needs of the human body, in their search for comfort the herd broke loose and charged about in the vast interior darkness of the Castle. The members of our house-party tried to help them, but they would not be guided; as they dashed down passages, they engaged in personal combat with inanimate objects, hitting here the corner of a cupboard, receiving there a black eye from a toppling *torciere*, were tripped by a lurking footstool, had a K.O. administered to them by an invisible table, or were victims of some infamous attack by a carved saint, who had apparently become an adept at all-in wrestling. Suddenly the vociferation, bawling, and trampling were redoubled; the second charabanc had at last made its appearance. Mob fought mob. Pandemonium reigned. The scene, as occasionally a lamp or candle revealed this conflict of shadows, was memorable, and in spite of the international composition of the mob, it was plain that only an English artist, Rowlandson, could have faithfully recorded the riot.

Eventually, however, the guests were rounded up and the mob began to break down into individuals again, as they were conducted to the places reserved for them in the Great Dining-Room, where we found friends and acquaintances—among them Edwin Evans and Spike Hughes—already in their chairs. We sat down exactly three hours late, but miraculously the food was not spoilt. . . . The waiters had recovered their official mien, and Henry Moat could be seen growing more portly and more dignified with every passing moment. Upstairs and downstairs wine flowed like—I was going to write 'like water', but in Tuscany water only flows in fountains—no, flowed like *wine*. When dinner was over, and the ladies retired, several of the male guests—especially those from Balkan countries—instead of standing up, fell down.

No one was tempted to stop and sightsee on the way home, for even this simple return journey to Siena in the dark would take two hours. At the Castle silence once more clothed the walls, though the sense of mystery was a little dispelled by the commonsense croaking of mud-happy frogs.

THE NIGHT OF THE PARTY[1]

II

The dinner-party to which we must now direct our attention took place in 1930; in early May, when the wistaria is in flower uncontaminated as yet by rain and distils its perfume far and

---

[1] I am grateful to Mrs Sacheverell Sitwell and to Mr David Horner for the help they have given me. . . . There were present, as well, Lady Londesborough and Lord Berners, who were both staying in the house, Mrs George Keppel who brought over from her villa at Bellosguardo her two daughters Violet and Sonia and her brother-in-law Lord Albemarle with his son Lord Bury and his daughter, and Sir John Aird.

wide, when the banksia roses cascade over the high walls of the terraces and in the evening love-hungry female fire-flies signal their presence to the more reticent males, and points of light wax and wane and flicker through the warm and fragrant darkness. . . . My sister-in-law Georgia and my brother and David Horner and myself had been on a tour in Greece. We stopped in Rome on our way to Montegufoni, where we had been commanded to stay without fail during the last days of April, but when we reached our hotel we found letters waiting for us from my father. He asked Georgia to go there three days earlier for some mysterious reason which he did not divulge, and requested the rest of the party to delay their arrival for a few days. Berners, who was going with us, suggested that we should spend three or four nights at Assisi. (I shall always remember the first dinner there. . . . The dining-room was full of mute esthetes and pallid ascetics whispering over their meal and half a bottle of white wine—when suddenly shock-treatment was administered by Sir John Squire, who— we did not know he was in Assisi; neither, I think, did he— burst through the door and shouted at us: 'Have you any whisky in your pub? Mine has completely run out.' As a result guests at the other tables fell silent and then began to talk in ordinary tones.) It was during this visit to Assisi that I heard of the death, following a sudden operation for appendicitis, of Mrs Powell, my dear housekeeper in London, which greatly saddened me and made me feel unusually impatient with what was about to take place.

Later Georgia described to me her reception. . . . On arrival, the motor—the Ark, which the readers of *Laughter in the Next Room* may remember—had met her at the station. Even the conniving manner of the driver seemed to suggest a share in some mystification. . . . My mother was in one of her rages, due to the fact that she could tell that some arcane matter was in the air and that my father was evidently planning something big but was determined not to let her into the secret. On the other hand, directly Georgia set foot in the precincts of the Castle my father, adopting a most confidential mien, dragged her off to talk in a distant room, thereby increasing my mother's anger. Our aunt Londesborough, the only other guest who had appeared as yet, vainly and ineptly tried to keep the peace between my parents, but the effort remained unsuccessful. To Georgia, though my father gave the impression that he was going to tell her of his schemes, he refused to reveal at present what he was planning, but his aim was plain: to work her up to a state of excitement rivalling his own. . . . Next morning he sent for her again, and again gave her non-cohering pieces of information. But at last he made clear what he wanted from her: her help in making the whole of the plans as dramatic as possible. For the remaining days before the party he would dash into the gallery beckoning wildly to Georgia; thus continuing further to inflame my mother's mood. On Tuesday my sister-in-law had been obliged to start for Florence with my father at eight o'clock in the morning in order to complete arrangements for the all-important Thursday evening. When they returned, he immediately kidnapped her again, still without revealing the entire plans. Her diary for the day contains the entry 'sinister, eccentric, delirious'; no doubt an accurate summing up of the atmosphere.

The next day Georgia was to dine at the Keppels' villa, but in the morning came the not infrequent announcement that the Ark had broken down. The prospect seemed hopeless, as there was no means of letting her hostess know. However, Mrs Keppel discovered somehow or other and rescued her. . . . When she reached the villa she found a large party, members of which besieged her with questions about what was to happen the following evening. They were all aware that some mystery brooded. Her position was more especially difficult because my father had at last revealed to her the full plans, first having sworn her to an embarrassing secrecy; which, the next day, was to make her relations with my mother still more unenviable.

My mother, dressed in black, spent the day in her favourite armchair by an open french window, and with numberless copies of English newspapers drifting round her feet, as if deposited there by a receding tide. Occasionally she would lunge ineffectually with a fly-whisk at some large velvety insect that steered itself in on a puff of golden fragrance from the garden, or would remark to someone passing through the gallery: 'All one can do is to live from day to day.'

I remember that in the afternoon my father passed rapidly by her in the Cardinal's Garden, and she called out: 'George, you're looking just like Bobby Arthington'—a cousin of his for whom she entertained no admiration, so that the alleged resemblance was certainly not intended as a compliment. My father, however, treated it as such, fluttered his hand at her and with a radiant air called back: 'So glad!'

However, in any case, my mother took a dejected view of the party. Her own contribution to the evening had been to order two dozen bottles of champagne, but my father, who had only found out about them when the cases were at the door, refused to accept delivery, explaining to my mother that the red wine of the Castle would be much more appreciated by the guests. My mother said:

'But, George, champagne makes everyone feel so cheerful.'

'But I'm not sure that I *want* them to feel *cheerful*. It isn't the mood I'm aiming at.'

This reply must have related to the special character of the party which was to take place—as no doubt did the fact that the dinner was laid in the Grand Sala, a large very high room across the Great Court opposite that room in which the dinner already described had taken place.

On arrival at Montegufoni it was plain that some mystery was hatching, but nobody seemed to know what or why. Henry refused to enlighten us—if, indeed, he were in the secret. . . . A volcanic air permeated everything and everyone seemed in bad humour. From the symptoms I could not diagnose the illness, though I ought from previous experience to have been able to deduce what sort of business was brewing; it was presumably one of those dim, demi-practical jokes to which my father was partial; as for example when he brought out on the 1st January 1901 a prophetic issue of the *Scarborough Post* (a local paper which for many years belonged to him), dated 1st January 2001—one of those jokes the fun of which resided more in the months of preparation they required beforehand than in the whimper and splutter of the resulting finale.

Georgia could not, or rather would not, enlighten us.

. . . . .

The Sala commanded the sharp declivities of the garden; the walls, slanting back at the angle only to be found in walls built in Rome and Tuscany, and seeming to bring a remote echo of temple terraces in Cambodia, were hidden now under the clustered knots and buds of the climbing roses, and revealed the wide expanse of country beyond the cypress groves and spring woods and the fields redolent of flowering bean. On the west was a door which disclosed, when open, a vista of painted rooms. . . . A meal in the Grand Sala was in itself an innovation, and therefore probably the choice of it must be connected with the nature of the mystery, but I held no clue.

My father sat at the head of a long table, looking imperturbably good-humoured, by no means a true or at any rate an abiding aspect of his character. He also had somewhat the air of a conjurer about to produce a rabbit from his hat. Occasionally he would look round in a rapt manner, which I took to signify that he was thinking of early times when the Duke of Athens used to come here attended by five hundred Greeklings to visit his brother.

Dinner had started and continued in an ordinary enough way until the last course was handed round, when Angelo the *contadino* came in and whispered something to my father, who got up, saying: 'Somebody wants to speak to me', and hurried away, returning in about five minutes. He then said to Mrs Keppel, who was sitting on his right: 'The workmen have found a ghost: will you come and inspect it with me?' . . . When they came back he went up to someone else, and said the same thing, repeating the formula to each guest in turn. . . . The guests came back looking startled and bewildered. My aunt Londesborough looked frightened. Sachie was worried and distraught. 'It's simply Bouvard and Pécuchet,' he complained, 'and makes us all look such fools.' I remember one old gentleman saying to me over and over again: 'But what does it *mean*? I can't make head or tail of it!'

I could not enlighten him, since I had not yet been conducted, but at last my turn came. I did not want to go, for I am not by nature very inquisitive: moreover I thought it just possible that a ghost *had* been found. Nevertheless, since the visit was clearly obligatory, I went. My father led me through the painted apartments, to the end of the Galleria, the principal drawing-room, then he opened a door, which could not be seen unless you knew of it, and took me down a few break-neck stairs and through a crack-skull door into another room of the very existence of which we had been unaware: in the far wall a large jagged hole had been knocked, and through it could be seen a further secret chamber. In the foreground stood a table at which sat a middle-aged man with a sallow face, dressed in the scarlet robes of a Cardinal. On the table lay a vellum-coloured holy book of some sort, and a human skull. The Cardinal was repeating over and over again with a strong cockney accent: *'Perchè non mi lasciano in pace?'* I soon recognized him as an Englishman, an habitual of the Castle.

The room was lofty for its size, and behind the figure stood, fixed to the wall, a series of gothic cupboards, in cypress wood, with elaborately carved borders to the larger panels and with a fretwork cornice. The table, a rare example of its kind, belonged to the earliest days of Italian furniture.

By the time we had returned to the dinner table we found an atmosphere of bewilderment amounting almost to stupe-faction brooding over the guests. (This was, I think, the mood at which my father was aiming; he may not have wished his guests to feel cheerful, but he *did* want them to feel astonished, even flabbergasted.) The same old gentleman as before was still loud in his demand for help in understanding what was taking place. 'What is the old fellow supposed to *be?*' he repeated. *'Someone must know.'* But nobody could or would enlighten him. Looking back, I suppose the correct answer would have been: 'One of the two Cardinals produced by the Acciaiuoli family.' . . . But though the reply would have sounded so indefinite, even then the dates would not tally. . . . I should have told him that my father had designed the whole occasion as an attempt, as so often before, 'to amuse my friends', that phantom company to whose existence he so often and loyally referred. I ought to have added that 'amuse my friends' was a common phrase with my father, and that the fun in this instance resided in the fact that, except for himself and Georgia, no one present, my mother included, had been aware of the existence of the room disclosed this evening, that it must have taken months to prepare, workmen labouring at it day after day, always from the other side of the wall, and that they had only broken through it during the time occupied by the first few courses at dinner. I ought, too, to have explained to him that the bookshelves, so-called, had been copied in detail from a cupboard in a picture by Carpaccio—and in this connection I should have indicated to him what I have, I hope, elsewhere made clear to my readers, that in this characteristic we reach an instance of one of my father's special mental attitudes. At first anyone acquainted with him would have presumed, because of his general esthetic outlook, that he was interested in early Italian painting because of its beauty: but this would have been a false deduction; no, he only took notice of any particular painting if it contained some object, spoon or fork for example, or, as in this instance, a cupboard, that would be suitable for him to reproduce at Montegufoni (at the restoration of which he had now been at work for at least twenty years without apparently coming any nearer the end of it); otherwise he would give a picture only a cursory glance, and hurry on, saying: 'It has nothing in it for me!' as if pictures had been painted with only that sole prophetic aim in view, and if they failed in this respect were a complete waste of time and effort. When, on the other hand, he succeeded in finding some detail that might be suitable, he would stand in front of the picture for an unconscionable time, gazing at it intently, and would then scribble some notes with a stub of a pencil on the back of an old envelope which he carried about with him in his pocket for that purpose, and perhaps he would also add a little rough drawing—but now we must return to the party.

Everybody appeared to be embarrassed, but I was told that my aunt Londesborough had kept her head and had attempted an explanation to her escort, remarking: 'It must be a sort of tomb, I think. I can't hear what he's saying. He must be a Cardinal . . . or one of those what-d'you-callums . . . you know, dear boy.'

In any case, however, though she had made the best of it, this cannot have been her idea of a party. Skulls and hermits were not in her line: no, for her the word *party* summoned up the memory of great entertainments given at St Dunstan's for King Edward and Queen Alexandra, the gardens illuminated, the rooms crammed with malmaisons and roses, and quails and champagne, and, behind her, her Indian page in pink clothes with a pink turban.

Soon the questionings of his guests were drowned by the clamour and clatter of the brass band of *La Società Filarmònica di Montegufoni* which started to play outside in the court. Their programme began with a village version of 'God Save the King', with many idiosyncratic variations: these lasted for half an hour, during which time we had all to stand to attention in the court facing the bandsmen. As the piece at last began to show signs of abating, my aunt, who stood beside me, said in my ear:

'Osbert, you were in the Brigade of Guards. Stand in front of Alice Keppel immediately! Otherwise she'll take the salute.' I looked round, and there, sure enough, was Mrs Keppel preparing to charge through the vanguard.

After the National Anthem had finished we danced in the court to the strains of lively, outmoded waltzes, grown rustic by the passage of time. It was a hot night and my aunt Londesborough and her partner had found seats in a window. The conversation went somewhat as follows:

'I've bought a new house called Mill Hill Lodge,' she observed.

'Where is it?'

'I'm not quite sure *where*, but it's on Barnes Common, wherever that is. There are two roads to London; which make it very convenient in a fog.'

I then came up to ask my aunt to dance. We glided off rather stiffly. She returned out of breath, but elated by the waltz. 'I know what,' she exclaimed, 'I'll give a ball at Mill Hill Lodge when I get back! Electric lights—coloured ones—in the garden in the trees, and *you* will choose the band, but we must have plenty of valses, dear boy. But of course there are those couples on Barnes Common . . . they lie there, you know.'

Time passed, and our guests departed into the darkness, which, on the point of 'What is it all about?', matched this incident; but the darkness was thronged with dancing dots of light, supplied by the fire-flies, and fragrant with the scent of honeysuckle. Most of the guests were still in a daze, but, to this day, if they meet, the survivors still discuss the party and the memory of it forms a link between them.

The following morning an edict was issued that the newly discovered room would be known in future as the Gothic Library. For a time it served a purpose; whenever anything particularly absurd happened it was possible to go there quietly and laugh it out—such an incident had occurred the following evening when my aunt Londesborough decided to read aloud the current *Fragrant Minute* by Wilhelmina Stitch from the latest copy of the *Daily Sketch*. . . . It also at moments served the purpose of supplying a solemn background for family announcements, as the reader will see in another chapter 'Making a Bolt for It'. . . . During the war the Castle was occupied in turn by the troops of many nations. The Fortuny curtains of the Gothic Library were subsequently used by the German soldiers to clean their boots. The smooth, vellum-coloured walls still palely retain on them, drawn in chalk, the regimental emblems of victorious South African and New Zealand regiments.

15

BY RAIL AND BOAT

Travelling by rail with my father and mother always presented its own tortures as well as its own pleasures. What vistas of journeys with one or other or both my memory treasures and re-creates; journeys from Scarborough to London, for instance, in an extinct kind of railway carriage called a saloon, rather resembling, only of course much smaller than, a private Pullman car. It had wide windows and on the ceiling a gas jet blossomed like an evening primrose under its thick bell-glass. It also contained a table on which to place the luncheon baskets, made of polished and creaking brown wicker, which we would invariably buy at York station. There we would stop just long enough to take them on board and to be formally greeted by one of Henry Moat's elder brothers who was for many years stationmaster and, when on duty, always wore a top hat and frock-coat as became his dignity. Then we would be shunted to join the London train. The luncheon, when taken out of the baskets with a great rustling

and crackling of grease-proof paper—and after we had survived
the recurrent disappointment caused by unwrapping layer after
layer from one large packet to find it consisted only of a
particle of salt—always in the end revealed cold chicken,
cooked long ago, or, it may be, smoked by the engines that
snorted their funnels off in York station. These chickens posed
as well an educational puzzle: were they claiming to have been
educated at Eton or at Harrow, because, though they had
plainly been the right age to enter—or, as for that, to leave—
either school, they wore the colours of both, being striped
laterally with light blue and dark blue? It was difficult to tell. . . .
(My father had his own views about railway food, as upon
many other matters, thinking it excellent, and I recall his
saying to me when he was going by train to Renishaw: 'I shall
lunch at Chesterfield station. You can't beat it.')

As I was saying, travelling with my father and mother
presented its own special difficulties, beginning with the train
you caught. My mother always kept her travelling clock half
an hour slow, my father his watch ten minutes fast; my father
liked to be two hours early for any journey—indeed, my
mother told me that on one occasion she decided to be there
first, and arrived at the station two and a quarter hours too
soon, only to find him already waiting on the platform. Then,
in addition, he liked to break the journey unnecessarily at unexpected places, whereas she liked to go straight through to the
end and object of her journey. She liked to read and rustle as
many newspapers as she could, and, particularly, nearly to miss
the train by buying them at the last minute ('Where is your
mother? The train is just going.'); or sometimes she would send
her maid, who always returned with the wrong papers. My
father liked to rest on his round, lifebuoy air-cushion and read
about the palaces erected by the Emperor Frederick II, or

technical papers such as the *Lancet*, whence he derived his medical theories, subtly changed when passed through his temperament, or one of the architectural magazines and the *Saturday Review* (of the board of which he had once been chairman, when Frank Harris had been editor) or the latest volume on *Leaden Jewellery in the Middle Ages*. My mother would look at the *Tatler* or the *Field*, but liked best to talk on the journey, my father to be silent, except occasionally to administer a snub where it was not needed. In consequence, of later years, they often occupied seats in separate railway carriages and had to be rounded up at their destination by my mother's maid or by Henry or Robins.

Once, when travelling from Scarborough to Renishaw, I remember that our governess decided to take us for a stroll in the station and contrived to become lost as utterly as if we had been in the Green Hell of the Amazon Valley. We got back to the train too late, just as it was snorting out of the station. She then found out that she had not any money on her and was obliged to borrow five pounds from the stationmaster: though why she should want five pounds for that short distance could not be imagined. . . . My own time was spent—as by most children in a train—in screaming and looking out of window, so that I can see that parents also had much to complain about.

One occasion, the most startling that occurred, comes back to me with particular clarity. It took place while the whole family were travelling together. The train was standing in Dijon station when a ticket inspector entered my father's sleeping-car and discovered that our tickets had been issued the wrong way round—from Venice to Paris instead of from Paris to Venice. He threatened to turn us off the train. My father was furious with the inspector—more indignant, I think, than with the people who had issued the tickets—and I recall his announcing with a very English accent:

'*J'ai été plusieurs fois membre du parlement anglais et vous ne pouvez pas jouer avec moi comme ça!*'

Eventually, however, we were allowed to continue our journey. . . .

My father and mother, as I have said, rarely sat together of later years but when they did there was no knowing what might not happen. During the Channel crossing she needed fresh air and would sit in a chair on deck, while he would usually lie down and stretch at full length on a sofa in the stuffiest of the public rooms downstairs. On a hot September day, for example, we were on the way to Paris and Florence, and were going to spend the first night at Boulogne (where, incidentally, when we reached our hotel we discovered that our luggage had been registered through to Paris). My mother and father had decided to recline side by side in deck-chairs placed just near enough to the main gangway to cause passengers when they boarded the Channel steamer to stumble over their feet and drop the bags they were holding.

It was one of those sporadically extra-fine days which sometimes descend on the Channel after weeks of rainstorms and roaring and moaning gales. There were the customary broadcast appeals to Mr Spiridion Gentleflower and Mr MacKickle to report *immediately* to the purser's office—where, one felt, they would hear no good of themselves. . . . On the other side of my mother sat a middle-aged couple. They told her all their history, that their name was Leonard and that they were on their way to visit the grave of their only son, who had died of wounds in the first effort to make the world safe for democracy. My mother felt an instant pity for them; especially when she learned that Mr Leonard had a bad heart, and had shown signs of an attack the previous evening. His wife said she only hoped he would be able to complete their tragic expedition. They were to be met at Boulogne and motor straight to the cemetery—about an hour's run. My mother thought that Mr Leonard looked very ill. Emotional and generous by nature, she longed to help. . . . Suddenly she remembered that her doctor had given her a medicine for the heart, which had proved wonderful in her case. She explained this to Mrs Leonard, and they resolved to give the invalid a dose of it at once. My mother sent me to find her maid, and when I had traced her, despatched her to open a dressing-bag and fetch the medicine bottle and a measured glass. The right amount was poured out and administered to the surprisingly acquiescent invalid. . . . The effect had been instantaneous: he became purple in the face, and seemed to swell all over. A doctor had to be found, and the poor man had to be carried below. The explanation was, of course, that his heart normally beat too fast, my mother's too slow. . . . As a result, my mother was terribly worried and angry with the world in general. . . . When we arrived, however, we had the satisfaction of hearing that Mr Leonard was better, and of seeing him drive off. . . .

My father, who had sat there and said nothing to stop what was happening, now spoke:

'Typical of your mother! . . . You'd think that the poor man had suffered enough without being given a heart attack!'

16

A WINK FROM THE GREAT BEYOND

MY FATHER took what can only be described as a mystical view of double-entry book-keeping, as if some unexpected and particular virtue resided in it like a djinn in a bottle. The world was divided for him into two classes, the one consisting of those who were at home in this esoteric language of mathematics and the other of those who were not. It constituted a test in his mind. A man's character would be finally summarized and dismissed with the words: 'He doesn't understand Double Entry.'

My father had an only sister, Florence, two years older than himself, and it was a great grief to him that she preferred religious mysticism to material calculation. I could never persuade her to tell me much about her beliefs. This was, no doubt, my fault for not knowing how to lead up to the subject, but it was difficult to do so without committing oneself, and English reticence also debarred it. I recall an approach on this theme made to me by a former soldier servant of mine who was apt on occasion to drink too much. One evening when I went up to my bedroom I found him sitting on the arm of a chair. As I came in he did not stand up but gradually revolved on to the floor, saying with unnaturally precise diction as he did so: 'Excuse me, sir, but do you believe in a Great Beyond?', and then fell peacefully asleep where he lay. No, that means of getting close to the subject was forbidden, so I had to be content with other ways. Since my aunt's death I have read and edited her diaries[1] and greatly enjoyed them. The journal opens at Renishaw in the 1870s, when she was very young, with the ingenuous entry: 'George and I have been revelling all the morning in dirty books.' This, of course, is straightforward fun, though not meant as such, and intended to be taken with absolute literalness, but there are further fascinating entries such as that made after dining at Lambeth Palace with her great-uncle Archbishop Tait: 'A musical little Mr Maxwell made a horrid joke about the millennium.' What can it have been, I wonder? I long to know, for it would seem to be a difficult event about which to make jokes, whether horrid or not—no laughing matter, in short. Her journal is evidence that, however absurd on occasion—curates move through its pages with, shining on them, the fierce light that today beats on film stars only—she had a natural gift for writing. She was also a past master in the art of tantalizing a reader. For instance, an entry in her journal runs: 'Better news of Claude, only a bullet through his helmet.' . . . Where was his head, I wonder? Alas, as the years went by, she became more and more lost in her private maze of religious theory. Moreover, things so seldom took the direction she thought—or hoped—they would take.

In illustration of this: when she was living with my

[1] *Two Generations*, Part II.

Landscape, Montegufoni

The Tower and Baroque Façade. Montegufoni

grandmother at Gosden in Surrey it was her habit to teach a
Sunday School class which consisted of gypsy children, among
them two gypsy boys. In the first volume of my autobiography[1] I published the following passage from my aunt's journal:
'. . . then to our tiny school for the Gypsies which Mother has
had arranged in the little wood.' (This sentence inevitably
recalls the patter of a music-hall song, usually rendered by a
hefty-looking female impersonator:

> My mother said,
> I never should
> Play with the gypsies
> In the wood.)

However, to return to the entry in my aunt's journal:

They [the gypsy children] take such an earnest interest in the
simple lessons on the New Testament at the end and now several
of them can say a few words of prayer themselves after the lesson.
Coralina, aged about fifteen, is, it seems, beginning a true Christian
life. Their name is Symes, and they live in a van two miles away.

These words caught the eye of Miss Dora Yates, editor of the
Gypsy Lore Society's Journal, who wrote to me and asked if I
had any objections to her making enquiries concerning their
subsequent development and careers. I was naturally delighted
for her to do this. . . . What happened to the truly Christian
Coralina I do not know, but Miss Yates was able to trace the
histories of the two boys, and found that in early adult life one
of them had been tried for murder and the other had often
been in the courts for petty theft and robbery. The whole

---

[1] *Left Hand, Right Hand!* page 236.

episode is typical of the sort of thing that happened to my aunt and to her religious enterprises.

In her appearance, as in her conduct, my aunt was plainly not of this world. There was about her an atmosphere of submission to the will of God, and her chief joy was to be found in holy books. She had a gentle, early Christian expression on her face, and lovely hair, reminiscent of Mélisande in *Pelléas et Mélisande*. Her old maid used to say: 'Miss Florence's hair is beautiful and golden, and so long that she can jump on it,' which would somehow seem to be a far-fetched and even painful form of exercise for her. Looking back and since reading her journal, I find my aunt a much more interesting character than I thought. Her extraordinary humility and innocence had something wonderful about them, and I recall at my grandmother's the daily family prayers—that now extinct festival—and how her meek voice would sound reading great rolling passages about lions and eagles. She might well in another age have been a saint; except that she was very Low Church and a halo would not have appealed to her nor would she have approved, I think, of saints but only of their saintliness. The great drawback to her everyday existence was her credulity. She believed any story—such as that of the Angels of Mons—which came her way. . . . She never married but at one time she very nearly made a sensational match, becoming engaged to a man who was subsequently tried for murder, which he was alleged to have committed in order to obtain insurance money. He had run a small establishment in Scotland for cramming backward boys, and one youth, on whose life a large insurance policy had been suddenly taken out a short time before the fracas, suffered on the same day a number of attempts to kill him. Of the several methods that had been tried during the space of a few hours, the first was the simple device of pulling out a piece of wood from the bottom of a boat (the young man could not swim) and another of shooting him with a revolver. One of these kindly experiments was at last successful. The case was tried in Scotland and the judgment Not Proven was brought in. But the jury must have been the only persons who felt, or at any rate expressed, any doubt about his guilt. Had my aunt married him, with her vagueness and lack of interest in everyday affairs, he would have found his perfect prey.

I suppose my father was fond of her. At any rate my grandmother's death in 1911 afforded him the opportunity of providing for the use of his sister and her companion two houses—although she only wanted one. It also gave him the chance to enlarge them and to decorate the rooms and make gardens, although my aunt so seldom noticed her surroundings in this world. Of these dwellings one was a Tudor timber house of some architectural interest. It had been bought as an investment in the middle of the eighteenth century by a member of my family, but none of us had ever lived there. In the course of time it had become first a public house—the Flower-de-Luce—and then a farm, and was situated about a hundred miles from Renishaw at Long Itchington in Warwickshire, a village where lived a few of the farming community only. The other suggested residence was just outside the gates of Renishaw. My father laid out an elaborate garden for it, and the place soon became known as 'Ginger's Folly'.

A few days after my aunt's death, her companion saw—or said that she had seen—the ghost of the deceased. The phantom had also appeared to the cook—so it was alleged. The spectre was walking in the gallery of her house in Long Itchington. My father, who usually refused to take ghosts seriously, had chosen to believe this story and said to me:

'Your aunt and I often discussed the possibility of there being a future life. She had probably come back—what is that slang phrase I have heard you use, Osbert?—to tip me . . . ?'

'To tip you the wink from the Great Beyond,' I interrupted.

'Exactly,' my father replied. 'She had probably come to tell me that there is a future existence.'

'Or that there isn't,' I suggested encouragingly.

'No,' he said, 'there would be no point in it. It would mean all that long journey for nothing.'

'In any case,' I protested, 'I'm sure she never winked at anyone in this life and I can't see her doing so in another.'

17

UNUSUAL HOLIDAYS

M Y FATHER had a talent for providing unusual holidays: though a great part of the fun to be derived from them consisted in the elaborate preparations that had to be made beforehand.

It must have been in May or June of the early twenties that my father, who had returned to England after a stay of some months in Italy, wrote to my brother and myself, asking us to meet him at Renishaw. He wished us, he explained, to accompany him on a tour of the tombs of his Sacheverell ancestors in Derbyshire and Nottinghamshire; that is to say in the churches of Morley, Barton, and Ratcliffe-on-Soar. He had long planned such a pilgrimage in the company of his two sons—a ceremony comparable to the initiation rites that mark the beginning of adult life in savage tribes—but then the first German war had come and had cut across the traditional texture of life and prevented him from carrying out all his schemes. Now that he could at last put this project into execution, a strange wind blew from Russia, a new and ice-cold wind, so that the journey seemed remarkable and demoded instead of customary, because roots were mocked at and ancestors were at a discount.

The arrangements he made for this journey were truly tremendous, even though no incident worthy of them occurred during the four long days in which they culminated. . . . When we arrived (yes, it must have been in the month of May, for I recall the expanse of bluebells flowering in every glade and coppice) we found that he was in process of mobilizing the machinery and assembling the backcloths for the unconscious comedy—a comedy big enough to reach over chasms of tragedy—that he could always be relied upon to provide; he had hired a rusty, bumpy motor-car, large and antiquated, he had brought his air-cushion to support him during what he chose to consider the long and tiring expedition before him, while the agile and forthright Robins, who had passed into his service from mine, was darting crab-like through the house executing, so far as was possible in an imperfect world, my father's instructions. . . . My father had resolved to spend the first night thirty miles away at Derby (one could only be astonished that he had not proposed an extra night at Chester-field, some seven miles from Renishaw). Robins had to pack an array of medicine bottles, the labels on which had all been interchanged, for my father believed that it was the aim of every hotel servant to swallow 'a dessertspoonful, as pre-scribed', from any bottle that might seem appropriate to the complaint from which they were suffering. If any of them attempted this trick with him now they would get something they had not bargained for—but then my father was frequently his own victim and suffered similarly: for though he maintained that he could identify the contents of each bottle by the look of it, his memory had been known to play him false. . . . There were also to be packed quantities of sunset-coloured Thermogene wool against lumbago, whole sets of the very elaborate system of clothing which he had gradually evolved for himself, mounds of books, most of them in the dingy livery of the London Library, a mosquito-net from the misty shelter of which he could emerge to quell possible trouble from the insect world, many notebooks, the special pens which I have described elsewhere, and last but not least several luncheon-baskets containing cold hard-boiled eggs and roast chickens, iron rations in case we found the towns without provisions. In fact, the preparations more resembled those that would be made to withstand a siege than those intended for a peaceable expedition.

We started in the early afternoon, and from time to time my father would command the driver to stop, in order that he could 'rest his back'. This he did by rocking and rolling backward and forward on the seat, so that his companions felt themselves to be crossing the Channel on a rough day. On our way, about three miles before we reached Derby, we passed a signpost with a pointer saying: 'Morley—$\frac{1}{2}$ mile', but to go there today would, he alleged, be too tiring. So we rattled on to Derby, where we arrived in time for dinner and, in order to be ready for an early start the next morning, went soon to bed.... But first my father's bed had to be arranged as he liked it by Robins, and several boxes unpacked. (Looking at them, he remarked to me: 'Next time we do this sort of thing I must really bring enough luggage to make myself comfortable.') Then the curtains had to be tightly drawn, but proved intractable owing to some technical and no doubt permanent difficulty with the curtain rings. A hotel porter had to be summoned. He had just come on duty and was very tipsy, so that the act which he put on with a ladder took an immense time to effect and was as full of danger to himself as to others. Indeed, it was sufficiently farcical to rank in the Bloomsbury pejorative phrase of the time as being 'rather music-hall'.

The three days that followed were a series of triumphant anticlimaxes. It rained all the time. . . . At one place we visited the house had just been pulled down and there only remained a square red-brick pigeon-cote, like a truncated tower, which still bore the arms of the Sacheverells—a building, no doubt, with an economic purpose: for my father told me as we drove up how in the Middle Ages the Lord of the Manor could with absolute impunity train his birds to raid the fields of independent farmers no less than those of the villeins, so that the pigeons grew plump for his table in the monotonous and remorseless winters of Plantagenet and Tudor times. . . . Then, again, when we reached what should have been the culmination of our pilgrimage, the church of Ratcliffe-on-Soar, we found the floor of the sacred edifice under water, to the height of half a foot. It was impossible to examine the series of tombs closely without wading, but from the door they looked, it must be admitted, impressive and beautiful. Four or five great rectangular masses, fashioned of Nottinghamshire alabaster and Derbyshire marble, bearing on them the recumbent effigies of knights and their ladies, seemed to float on a flat mirror of water. . . . My father refused to be depressed, and merely called to Robins, who was in attendance outside:

'Robins, another time remember to put in my gumboots!'

At last those four days ended, but they certainly ranked as an unusual holiday. Still more out of the ordinary, however, was a vacation my father had later, with my aid, planned for himself—though in the end it had to be abandoned, owing, as will be seen, to a leakage of information. But first of all let me

[136]

recount the singular incident that was responsible for reviving the memory of it.

One year during the thirties I sold our house at Scarborough —Wood End—to the municipality. During the 1939–45 war it suffered damage of various kinds, from the hands of a destructive indigenous generation no less than from enemy bombs. The plain structure in golden stone had stood there for several years with windows void of glass and ceilings fallen: especially the enormous conservatory in the middle of the house looked derelict, an airy ruin of twisted iron frames. To build it up once more must have seemed a difficult and expensive proposition, and consequently some time passed before the Corporation determined to redecorate the house and to bring it back as much as possible to its former style and condition, planning to devote part of the space to a Sitwell Museum and part of it to giving shelter to a collection of stuffed animals—a bequest to the town by the same Colonel Harrison who first brought the pygmies to England from Equatorial Africa.

Five or six years after the end of the war my sister and I drove over to Scarborough to inspect the house, the restoration of which was nearing completion. . . . It was late in August, and we arrived in sunshine, particularly hot and luminous, but scarcely had our feet touched the pavement in front of our hotel before the wettest imaginable blanket of sea-reek enveloped us and prevented us from even seeing across the road to the Town Hall where the Mayor gave us luncheon. After the meal was over we were conducted directly to the Sitwell Museum. The fog had cleared, but as soon as we entered our former home, a brick, inoffensive enough to look at, shot out of the wall at me, hitting the back of my neck and bouncing off it on to the shoulder of the Borough Librarian. There were only one or two workmen about at the time and they faced the phenomenon with true British phlegm, but my companions were visibly astonished and shaken. No explanation of this incident was ever forthcoming: but subsequently, when I allowed my mind to run on it, I wondered which, if it were really a manifestation, of many provocative incidents had been responsible for such sharp retaliation from the spirit world. . . . After this manner, then, the memory of an episode that had taken place at Renishaw returned to me.

It had happened during one of the peerless summers of the early twenties, when the sun seemed always to shine, and the scent of box and tobacco plant lay heavy on the air which carried the melancholy of a long vanished prosperity. . . . Parents and children were having luncheon together. It was an ordinary enough everyday British scene—except in one respect: that the younger members of the family—my brother, my sister, and myself—were wearing beards, designed by my sister, and made out of the hideous, lightly tasselled fringe of an orange-coloured rug; they fastened over the ears with two loops of tape, and had small bells attached to them, which, with the movement of the jaws when eating, gave out a melodious alpine tinkle. These artificial and extraneous adjuncts we had adopted as an outward sign of compliance and out of respect for my father's wishes; because one day, not long before, he had remarked, in a self-congratulatory tone while stroking his red beard: 'It's a pity that you three children haven't got a little of this sort of thing.' We could never, notwithstanding, be certain—since he was as curiously unobservant in some matters as observant in others—whether he had noticed the new fashion we had launched on the world that day. Howbeit, during the course of the meal he had suddenly informed us that there were to be no guests this year, though he knew we were expecting

[138]

several friends the next day, that it was too late to put them off. My mother, always surrounded by people, but never by so many as she would have liked, looked at him severely with her mournful brown eyes and said, as she had said many times before:

'George, you want me to lead a hermit's life.'

The announcement he had made must have been a disciplinary measure, for we had begun to understand that he liked to entertain at Renishaw—other people's friends, of course, for he had none of his own.

We no longer paid attention to his home-made and favourite maxim: 'Such a mistake to have friends: they waste one's time', because on the evening of the same day he might give vent to an opposite opinion, as when at Montegufoni, pointing to the fragments of a terracotta pot bearing the Acciaiuoli arms on it, he remarked: 'I really must have copies made of that pot, it need not be expensive. I could have them made at Impruneta, or better still Montelupo—it's nearer here, and I could constantly run over there, and give them my advice. As to the cost, I could take six dozen myself for the lemon trees on the middle terrace, and get several friends to join with me and order an equal number. It always works out cheaper if you order a great many. That's the advantage of having friends!'

As always a stickler for facts, I cautiously enquired:

'Which friends are you thinking of?'

I received, snapped back at me, the daunting reply:

'Don't ask unnecessary questions. They'd *all* be only too pleased to be given the chance.'

In short, as he grew older, he became more sociable. When there were guests in the house or when my mother was giving a luncheon-party in London, he no longer had luncheon by himself at twelve noon because he found the company tedious; and now, on one occasion, when I complained that one of the guests had told me the same anecdote three times running, he declared:

'I like it: he keeps the ball rolling.'

My father was due, just after seven the next evening, to catch a train to London, there to spend the rest of the week, and one singular consequence of the edict he had thus abruptly promulgated was that from the morning of the following day until he left, the Wilderness—a wood that closed in the garden to the east—became full of figures hidden there as soon as they arrived; friends who had been invited to stay but now found themselves, in order to avoid discovery, obliged to inhabit this bosky thebaid. We had arranged for food to be brought to them at midday, and immediately after my father had departed these involuntary hermits, who remained singularly amiable considering the way in which we had been obliged to treat them, were liberated and dragged in triumph from their leafy refuge to dine with us. We felt compelled, nevertheless, to ask them to leave before my father returned.

During the unfolding of the summer he had become the most wretched victim of his own austere decree. Without guests to amuse him he was in reality immensely bored, though he continually denied this, because boredom (no one had even known the word in the Middle Ages) ranked in his mind as one of the greatest of sins. Although he would not rescind his edict, he felt that something had to be done to combat his ennui, so one morning he sent for me and announced that he felt he needed rest and recreation and to get away for a little (from what, he did not specify); in brief, he must have a holiday, but if possible in some rather remote place, but where there would be plenty of other residents to whom he could talk and who could talk with him in return. He would prefer a house with a fine garden which offered as well a distant view and his bedroom must look over flower-beds. It should be situated in a park with a lake in it—which was to him as running water, h. and c., to those of a more modern and practical outlook. Now as it happened I had only that very morning read in one of the daily papers an advertisement of what was obviously a privately run home for the demented, and was described as 'set in peaceful surroundings with a park and a lake'. Accordingly I told my father about this establishment but did not disclose to him its true nature.

'It sounds just what I need,' he said.

'Well, all I can tell you is that most people, once they've got there, never leave. . . . They like it so much that they've even invented a pet-name for it—"the Bin".'

This appeared to satisfy him, though he added: 'I should like my fellow guests to have hobbies which they could discuss with me, and to be people, too, of some importance.'

'I believe that one of them claims to be a steam-roller, which I suppose in a way *could* be important,' I replied in imaginative frenzy before I could stop myself, 'and another resident maintains that he is the Emperor of China.'

Fortunately, my father never listened very carefully to what was said to him and caught nothing before the last part of the sentence. Indeed, he seemed gratified, and remarked in answer that revolutions usually did a great deal of harm. My brother and my sister also spoke to him of the place with enthusiasm. Indeed, we succeeded in painting for him so attractive a picture of this peaceful retreat that he told his secretary to write immediately for *pension* terms. When the answer came, he said to me: 'Though expensive, it is not exorbitant,' and at once instructed his secretary to engage a room on his behalf for the whole of the month of September. Unfortunately, in their reply, the asylum authorities added to the letter a postscript:

'Ought a strait-waistcoat to be sent for Sir George to wear during the journey, which will be made by van? Three strong and practised male nurses will, of course, be in attendance, and prepared to quell any disturbance on the way.'

This, though it abruptly terminated our design, was by no means the last we were to hear of it. I was packed off to our house at Scarborough, which my father was at that time using as a kind of private Siberia. . . . I was sorry to leave Renishaw in its full August glory, the trees showing as yet no trace of the yellow fingers of the sun, the scent of lilies and stocks lying long on the heavy air, though an occasional gust of wind stirred the tree-tops of the avenue, and left the butterflies clinging precariously to their flowers. Nevertheless, I reflected as I walked to the station, the project had been worth while for its own sake, and my father had nearly enjoyed a long and for once really unusual holiday.

18

CREATING

M Y FATHER, as by this time the reader will have concluded, worked himself up easily into an exaggerative
state of mind with few or no facts to support this condition.
His imagination was wont to catch fire suddenly, but he was
more likely to repine and deplore than to rejoice. When at last
an auditor would enquire: 'From what are you deducing these
catastrophic events that you foresee?' he would take refuge
once again in that favourite apothegm, delivered with an
Olympian air: 'We happen to know'. Thus, albeit he was not to
be numbered among all those thousands who glimpsed
bearded Cossacks with the snow still on their boots from
crossing the fringe of the Arctic Circle—yet had he seen them,
he would certainly have concluded that they were German
troops dressed up as Russians and ordered here specially to nab
him (I have elsewhere related how he thought the German
Fleet was sent after him to Scarborough when that town was
bombarded): nor could he be counted among those later

mystics who, so many of them, beheld the Angels of Mons: nevertheless, he too had his visions, but of a depressing order and equally divorced from fact.

One morning in the autumn of the second year of the 1914–18 war, when he was deeply engaged in farming and I was just off to the Battle of Loos—which, incidentally, gave me the idea for my first alliterative entry in *Who's Who*, where, under *Recreations*, I entered: 'Fighting in Flanders and Farming with Father'—he rushed into the estate office, flourishing in one hand a paper of some sort. It was the end of September, the guests were leaving, everything was closing down for the winter, and the family was just off to Scarborough. He was agitated and called to Maynard Hollingworth, the agent:

'I have just received notice that troops are to be billeted in the house. The servants will all leave, and there will be no one to look after anything. It means the ruin of the estate, for they will probably take it over.'

Here Maynard Hollingworth interrupted, saying:

'Can I see the Billeting Order, Sir George?'

My father continued to wave the paper about without troubling to answer Hollingworth. This refusal to let anyone see a paper clutched in his hand was a well-known symptom of his working-up; thus, when he stood there, the document could be seen to resemble that sole shilling that is buried under the foundation stone of some great structure. (These huge edifices that my father built for himself were plainly a form of creation, albeit somewhat gloomy, and it demonstrates what a useful thing slang is, for the slang use of the word 'creating' expresses perfectly the mental processes. 'Sir George is creating this morning something terrible!')

Maynard Hollingworth reiterated: 'Isn't that a cheque in

Montegufoni from under an Olive Branch

Stone Lion, Montegufon

your hand, Sir George? If you'd let me look at it I might be able to help.'

My father made no attempt to reply or to give it him but went on adumbrating his dream of destruction.

'There is no knowing what may not happen,' he continued. 'The books in the library will all be burnt, and no doubt my Family History, which has taken many years of work, will disappear. The stables will be pulled to pieces, all the trees in the park will be cut down for firewood. . . .'

Later in the day Hollingworth contrived to obtain a glance at the paper. He found it to be a cheque in payment for the billeting of horses in the stables which had ended a month before he received the document. . . .

My father was later deeply distressed by the Government's granting permission to Lord Cowdray's firm, S. Pearson & Son Ltd., to bore for oil on the Sitwell estate just outside the park near Foxton Wood. Accordingly, he permitted himself to be persuaded by the general manager of the neighbouring coal mine that oil could be reached much more easily and quickly in Eckington Woods, also on Sitwell property. The reader will not be surprised to learn that after reading a single pamphlet on oil my father had become a self-decreed expert on it. ('Such a pity not to consult *me* before they started work.') In a few days he sent a telegram to Lloyd George, who was by then Prime Minister: 'Have I your permission to bore for oil? Can reach it months before Cowdray.' He received no reply.

On the other hand, nobody ever struck oil there, though Lord Cowdray's experts drilled through the coal measures, and through Mountain Limestone and Millstone Grit, only at the end to be faced with brine. . . . Creating, in its other and opposite form, now began. When he heard that brine had been found my father remarked that they would soon have to abandon the site and perhaps he would be able to build a health resort, similar to Harrogate or Droitwich, and inaugurate brine baths as a cure for arthritis. 'The men who built Bath as a cure town made a fortune,' so he told me when I next saw him. 'The doctors, I know, will be enthusiastic about it, and I could go to Lutyens for the plan of the town—luckily, he has had plenty of practice with New Delhi—nothing too ambitious, just a group of stone nymphs and another group illustrating the Seven Ages of Man, but in an opposite order from that in which they generally appear, so as not to depress the patients unduly. First of all there would have to be hotels and shops. These could easily be built within a few months after the war ends. The doctors would all be housed in a separate quarter. (They would enjoy being together.) Then there would have to be an arcade for patients to walk in on rainy days, and the nature of the ground gives ample opportunity for me to make a fine garden for them. Nothing rheumatic patients enjoy so much as being able to sit in a garden. It needn't be big—about twelve acres. . . . Then there is the question of the swimming-bath itself. It should be two or three hundred yards long with an arcade and made of scagliola. And the Opening Ceremony—what would you advise for that?'

'I think you should dive in to open the pool,' I suggested.

'Yes, that would amuse my friends, but I'm afraid my diving days are over'—and they certainly were. None of us had ever known him to swim.

19

A RAP OVER THE KNUCKLES

Readers of my autobiography may recall that upon one occasion, when I was occupying the next bedroom to my father's at Renishaw, I woke up in the small hours to hear his voice declaring in a very sinister manner: 'They May Think I Shall—But I Shan't!' This pronouncement was followed by a prolonged chuckle. Now whether these words were spoken in his sleep or when awake I shall never know, but certainly they describe and define very precisely an attitude he often struck in his conscious hours. Indeed, 'They May Think I Shall—But I Shan't' ranked with him as a game, and one which, I believe, he was proud to have invented. First, you led your opponent on by niggling and worrying him over what course of action to pursue in a particular quandary and then, just as, after a fever of fussing, you had induced him to think that you had settled on a specific line of action, you switched off that plan and on to another, which would then have to be argued all over again from the beginning.

My mind reverts especially to one instance of his using this very personal technique. It occurred sometime during the few enchanted years just before the First World War, when summer appeared as if it would last for ever and each hour showed its own special glow and lustre: when Clio, the Muse of History, had apparently settled down to a placid middle age, and the only events she produced would turn out to be menus of pleasure. Such disputes as existed were the result of particular political problems such as Home Rule for Ireland, Lloyd George's Budget—always afterwards referred to as *The* Budget, as though no other had ever been brought in—and that child of The Budget, the Veto Bill; a bill intended to curb still further the powers of the House of Lords. This, apparently, could only be effected by Mr Asquith, the Prime Minister, advising the King to create at once a large number of Liberal Peers—a large enough number to pass the measure—but they, alas, always showed a most retrogressive tendency to adopt the Conservative creed, however much they had denounced it previously, the moment they entered the august precincts.

Many people were much concerned about these matters, my father among them. He had at last recovered from a long illness and was full of energy again. As usual he constituted himself, as it were, a self-elected one-man government. Continually he wrestled in his mind with this problem; what, in particular, could be done to defeat the machinations of the Liberal politicians? although himself had recently, and publicly, adopted the Liberal faith! At last his ingenious mind found a way out. Accordingly, he wrote to the Conservative chief, Mr Balfour, and in spite of personally holding the poorest opinion of him, whom he regarded as little more than a half-baked philosopher, an amateur esthete unduly fond of music, with none of the qualities of a leader, and as a man who had founded his position on the support of numerous influential relations and of a particular set in the social world—my father, in short, wrote to Mr Balfour to tell him that he had thought out a plan by which Mr Asquith's threatened action could be averted, and wondered whether the statesman would care to know about it. After a day or two an answer arrived stating that Mr Balfour would indeed be very interested, and asking my father if he would write to him and communicate it. My father then just wrote back, no, he would not; a prime instance of 'They May Think I Shall—But I Shan't!'. . . . Probably Mr Balfour in his vagueness hardly registered the rap inflicted, for truly he was very absent-minded. (Did he not during a luncheon given at Claridge's by a transatlantic hostess, pass to me under the table a note which ran: 'Can you tell me the name of our hostess and where she is sitting?'; a classic instance. . . .)

Another of my father's favourite phrases was: 'He needs a rap over the knuckles', such as the one administered below. He had a habit of discussing the high political questions of the day with his secretary and asking for his opinion on them. One day his secretary said to him at last: 'How can I advise you about such matters, Sir George, when you know far more about them than I do?' and my father replied: 'It isn't *your* advice I want. I need to hear somebody else's view, it doesn't matter whose, so that by a process of contrast and comparison I can more clearly formulate my own opinion.'

If my father's principal motto was 'They May Think I Shall—But I Shan't!', my mother's, obversely, and though she would never declare it in words, was 'They May Think I Shan't—But I Shall!' . . . There comes to my mind a particular instance of what I am trying to indicate. . . . One cold winter my father decided to move from the country into an hotel in Florence: it would be warmer and he could economize: my mother would not be able to entertain so lavishly nor to give such large parties as at Montegufoni. After a week or so at the hotel my father suffered one of his recurrent attacks of imaginary illness and resolved to move again; this time into the Nursing Home of the Blue Nuns for a month.

When he mentioned this decision to my mother he was rather surprised to find her in such a co-operative mood, for usually she would insinuate that his illnesses were hypothetical: but on this occasion she told him that she thought he was quite right to take his indisposition seriously, and so, after having given a valedictory exhortation to the strictest economy in his absence, he was wafted off in the Ark the same evening for a month's rest on the sunny heights of Fiesole. . . . There Henry would bring him up the English papers every afternoon—but one day they were late. In consequence, one of the nurses, feeling sorry for my father, confined as he was to the reading matter he had brought with him—*A Flutter Through Manorial Dovecotes in the Sixteenth Century, Over the Border, an Account of Flodden Field, Wool-Gathering in Nottinghamshire in the Dark Ages, Rotherham before the Norman Conquest, Medieval Fools, a Study of Court Jesters during the Wars of the Roses*, and *The Stone Age on the Yorkshire Moors*—took pity on him and brought him a weekly paper, printed in French and published in Florence in the cause of tourism. It was devoted in the main to most favourable accounts of local social events and to fascinating lists of the guests staying in the various hotels—a paper which he had not seen before and probably would never have set eyes on at all if Henry had not failed him on this single occasion. My father opened it at random, and the first paragraph that caught his eye was headed: 'Lady Ida Sitwell gives a fête at the *Hôtel Ali Baba et Macheath*.' The account of it said that Lady Ida Sitwell had offered a dinner to forty people in honour of the visit of her sister Lady Mildred Cooke. (It did not say, however, how shy Lady Mildred was, nor how much she must have hated it.) Then came the menu of the dinner, the names and order of the wines and liqueurs, and an account of the table, decorated with pink roses that had been specially flown from the Riviera. It was fortunate that my father was already in a nursing home, for certainly this information would have sent him to one, in order to recover from the shock of the announcement of my mother's determined stand for economy during his absence. . . . The feast occupied his mind for weeks. In the list of *convives*, as the paper called them, occurred the names of all the best-known *pique-assiette* in Florence, and I remember his telling me that when the bill came in and he queried the amounts charged for liqueurs, he was informed that some of the guests had ordered full bottles of brandy and Cointreau and other imported liqueurs to take home with them. . . . Henry Moat was the person who suffered most: for not having told my father about it. He ought to have known, my father said. It was disgraceful of him.

'But I heard nothing about it, Sir George.'

'Well then, you ought to have found out.'

'But how could I, Sir George?'

'Don't argue, it stimulates the brain cells and prevents me from sleeping.'

20

POPULARITY

IT WAS in May 1923, when tenants who would not
be moved were still many of them living in the Castle,
that my father asked me to go for a walk with him in the
Great Court. The summer heat, which in certain years
begins in Tuscany as early as the second week in May,
was not yet in full glow and the shafts of sunlight, instead
of piercing like spears, lay light as feathers on the dark
stone of the pavement. Even from this distance, too, the
bees could be heard swarming in the dark-leaved golden
blossoms of the ivy which completely covered the stone
medieval tower at the garden's end. As we strode up and down,
my father talked, I remember, of the translation of books, and
remarked to me what a pity it was that if the English Bishops
of King James I's reign had felt obliged to translate a volume of
some kind, they could not have found for their purpose a more
interesting book than the Bible. I did not attempt to enter into

argument with him as I did not think that it would lead very far. Occasionally, as he talked, the shutter of an upper window would silently shift a little, and a face would be seen framed in it, glowering and glaring down at us. My father seemed pleased, taking it to be a token of interest and popularity: indeed, he observed to me that it was nice to feel that you could always make yourself liked if you wanted to. But facts have an awkward way of asserting themselves and when, shortly afterwards, an old woman was arrested by the police, she was found to be carrying on her a list of people whom she meant to kill when the Revolution came: my father's name was at the head of the list. Yet even if his assumption had been rather too sanguine, there were fragments of truth in it. He could make himself generally and lightly popular with great numbers but had no gift for intimacy. Thus he would be popular at a large meeting rather than in talking to an individual as a person. In this respect I think the house-to-house canvassing that was formerly conducted in between general elections by the candidates of both parties must have been a great strain on him, for he had difficulty in remembering people (as I have written elsewhere, he would frequently pass his own children in the street without recognizing them) and, if he remembered them, in associating them with their names. Thus, on one occasion he went into a small house under the Castle Hill at Scarborough and asked a woman who was ironing shirts to obtain for him her husband's vote. She looked at him and said: 'But I am *Mrs Jones*, Sir George.'

This information conveyed nothing to my father. He did not identify her as the wife of his personal servant who had been his scout at Christ Church and had remained with him to serve him ever since. (He was butler when Henry Moat first came to us as footman, a day which Henry always lamented as being the last on which free beer was provided in the servants' hall. He used to say: 'I joined up too late.')

A more obvious instance of the falsity of my father's happy conviction comes back to me when I think of my first visit to Chiswick House. It proved a memorable occasion and took place in the early twenties when the building was still in use as a private mental home. It was necessary beforehand to obtain permission to go over it from the Commissioners of Lunacy, who kindly granted my request. Accordingly, my brother Sacheverell and I went there about four o'clock one hot afternoon in July. The house, built for the great patron Lord Burlington by Colin Campbell, then existed, of course, on a larger scale than it does today, when the two later eighteenth-century wings have been blown up or pulled down to show the purity of design of the original Palladian villa. . . . We were to have tea with the resident doctor, but on arrival we were not certain by which of the doors to enter. However, we opened one of them and there, coming down the staircase, was a good-looking grey-haired man already wearing a dinner jacket—it seemed an odd hour to be clad in this manner. We enquired from him where the doctor lived and he replied by whistling, but—and this was the most extraordinary part of it—the words were absolutely distinct, yet enunciated by—not through—the whistling. He was, in short, whistling and not speaking. It was obviously a natural and original gift, though he must have cultivated it, too, to the highest degree and surely must have been the only person who could communicate in this way. In addition, had he so desired, it would have placed him among the most highly paid stars of the music-hall stage. This virtuoso, then, informed us that we were on the right track. . . . When we reached the doctor upstairs, we found a most splendid and impressive tea ready for us, sandwiches very thinly cut and bearing flags on them, cut out of paper, on which were written such descriptions as PÂTÉ DE FOIE GRAS and CAVIARE. My brother commented on this smart labelling to our host, who asked:

'Did you happen, when you came in, to notice the whistling man who was wearing a dinner jacket?'

We said: 'Yes.'

'Well,' he explained, 'he arranged the tea. He always does it for me. A most curious history. His father was one of the Marshals of France during the reign of Napoleon III and a great favourite at court. His son inherited a fine fortune, but dissipated it on prima donnas. I had known him for a long time, but some ten years ago we received a letter from him telling us that he felt he was going off his head, and asking whether we would take him in here to be under my care, in return for which he would act as a servant—but every now and then he asks permission to go out for the evening and the next day we read in the *Morning Post* that he was at some social gathering to which I should never be invited.'

It was, as I was saying, a peculiarly sultry day and after tea the doctor led us through the suites of rooms which, richly decorated, with gilded cornices and painted ceilings, formed a strange setting for the wretched lunatics, all over-excited by the heat. Many of them shook as if with fever, and their faces were yellow from the glow of the gilding as much as from illness. You could hear cries and roars and screams on every side. When we had completed our tour we went out on to the platform at the top of the staircase leading down to the garden. The vista was a perfect instance of the esthetic beauties caused by neglect. It was not a flower garden, but a large pleasance, though owing to the skilful planning it looked immensely larger than it really was. An idyllic rusticity prevailed, aided by the greensward, stone vases, pools of bracken and groves of

[155]

old trees. We wandered about there for a while and talked. Then, as we turned to climb up to the portico, we saw approaching a tall, lank man with an air of some distinction, who carried over his shoulder a bag of golf clubs.

'Oh, I am so glad,' the doctor remarked to me, 'that this particular patient has come out. He must be on his way to the golf course. I'd like you to meet him. Don't feel the slightest alarm: he has never been violent and is a very charming person.'

The doctor beckoned to him to join us and he was formally introduced to me.

'This is Mr Osbert Sitwell,' the doctor announced.

'Are you Sir George's son?' the lunatic at once demanded.

I admitted it, and before you could say Jack Robinson—or whatever other proverbial name you use to describe the swiftest passage of time—his demeanour changed and, rather hastily selecting a golf club, he shouted: 'Then I should like to kill you.'

By some means or other the doctor persuaded him to disarm and go away without any of us incurring injury. But it was a breath-taking moment. Having successfully spirited the patient away, the doctor hurried back to us, saying:

'Oh, I am so sorry! What a dreadful thing to happen! He has never been known to behave like that before.'

In that same instant I recalled my father striding along in the Great Court at Montegufoni, and the faces peering down at him, and I wondered by what precise act of his I had so nearly, if vicariously, shared his popularity. I never found out.

21

NEAPOLITAN STREET SCENE

IN THE autumns of the years immediately following the
First World War my brother Sacheverell and I would
sometimes join my father and mother at Naples, where we
would stay at Bertolini's, a hotel like a ship that floated on a
hill half-way between the heights of Vomero and the city
below. The hotel possessed a good deal of character. You entered it at a level considerably lower than the body of the
hotel itself, through an opening in the rock face, a little resembling the so-called Tomb of Virgil at Posillipo, except that
after you had walked to some depth inside, you found a lift
which soon whirled you up to the hotel public rooms, situated here above the bedrooms, and to terraces that recalled the
decks of a ship. At all hours, terraces and windows offered an
unparalleled view of grandiose but dilapidated palaces, and of
the domes of churches striped in herringbone patterns of
yellow and green tiles, and set among palms and orange trees.
At times when the wind was in the right direction the noises

of the city, so unlike those of any other in the world, would mount to one sound, a characteristically vital and yet sinister diapason. . . . Moreover, each month offered its own features: thus one day in mid-December, during one of the visits to Naples, I walked to the Piazza Oberdan and saw there two men disguised as clowns of a sort striding on stilts which brought them to the same height as the tip of the marble Guglia, and then entering the church found two shepherds playing on bagpipe and wooden trumpet, serenading the Virgin in her *presepio*.

My father enjoyed staying at this hotel, albeit he considered it rather expensive; he did not, however, like the bread provided. Therefore it was one of Robins's duties to go every afternoon to Caflisch's, a café and bakery in the Piazza dei Martiri below, to purchase rolls for breakfast the next day, but when he asked at intervals for money on account in order to pay for them, I always noticed a drop in paternal enthusiasm.

A particular instance of this, when my father, Sacheverell, and I had walked down to the town, comes back to me. . . . It was a golden October afternoon and the whole town glowed with its own vital forces as well as with the heat and noise of what seemed a summer day. As we neared the Piazza dei Martiri the tide and force of sound was amazing; this hymn to life was composed of the music of barrel-organs, of hoarse voices shouting and singing, as well as of the conventional cries of the men who presided over the stalls in the piazza; stalls decorated with tufts of pampas-grass, where they sold peeled Indian figs, piled in pyramids, ready to be eaten, showing the colours of a blood orange, water-melons, the scarlet flesh of which was exposed, peppered with large black pips, and drinks made from fresh oranges and pomegranate juice. Further, there were the sad oriental groans and moans of the beggars, still in those days to be encountered in great numbers haunting popular corners and parading their infirmities. . . . Into this scene my father fitted well, in spite of his fair skin, prominent nose and red beard; indeed, I remember thinking he a little resembled Captain Fracasse or another one of the figures of the Italian Comedy. . . . At the end of the Via Roma we met Robins looking very worried. He touched his hat, came up to us, and said to my father:

'I was hoping to catch you, Sir George. I'm on my way to get your rolls for tomorrow, but I haven't a penny to pay for them. Could you let me have a few *lire* on account or I don't know what I shall do?'

My father did not answer directly to him, but observed to me in a voice calculated to be very distinctly overheard:

'Disgusting, I call it, stopping one in the street and asking for money like a beggar!' He then walked on, angrily humming to himself—but the rolls were there the next morning.

LORD HENRY

LORD HENRY was my mother's first cousin, though he seemed to belong to a much earlier generation, and, indeed, must have been much older than she, for when he had sat in the House of Commons he had been one of that handful of young aristocrats chosen by Disraeli to be trained and ready to hold high office in the future. Besides, *he* had really belonged to the days mentioned before in these pages, when in the drawing-room after dinner men would sing ballads; and the music of one of the worst and most popular of them—'O Dry Those Tears'—as well as of several others less celebrated, had been composed by Lord Henry. . . . He never, in fact, attained the position in politics predicted for him, because a personal scandal of a non-explosive order—if a scandal can ever be non-explosive—had wafted him to Italy when he was twenty-eight, and he had never returned to England. However light and almost private the scandal may have been, it had, of course, proved sufficient to blast the life of everyone connected with it, although my mother and the members of her family would hear no word in his dispraise.

Eventually he had settled down in Florence, where he built himself a house—or, more accurately, an elaborate and, taken all in all, rather hideous little palace in one of the styles associated with King Ludwig II of Bavaria (so that perhaps he saw himself as being his own Wagner—but with what a difference —to his own 'Mad King'). Everything that could be gilded —and much that could not—had been gilded. Nevertheless, the house was fascinating, for it was full of personality, and it was clear that a great deal of thinking had gone into its planning and into the contrivance of every detail. In so far as the house possessed a theme it was that of family pride. The coat-of-arms, much in evidence, was that of the Plantagenet Kings and still displayed, as well as the Lions of England, the Lilies of France; a claim discarded for his successors by King George III. Otherwise the house was a pure experiment.

In the Tuscan spring you entered from a whirl of dust and dry fallen blossoms of wistaria and lilac blown by the hot wind into spirals, to find yourself in a gilded oasis of tall potted palm trees and carved pillars. There were among the clusters of rather small rooms that composed each floor some designed to look larger than they were by the aid of various structural stratagems and decorative tricks: others offered their own inherent interest. One room, for example, had an inner ceiling resembling a canopy supported by gilded pillars and was enclosed by transparent walls of plate glass. (When one day I asked my cousin why he had built it in this way, he had replied that he had always wanted to know what it would be like to sit in a room without walls.) Another room had yellow walls that, when the electric light was turned on, changed their colour to a tone of rosy copper. The house was crammed with precious and decorative objects, but contained few pictures; of these the finest was a panel by Bernard van Orly.

The occupant and owner of this house was very tall, six foot four, and to his last days never stooped but held himself absolutely erect. To look at, he resembled a very well bred pelican and he also presented a certain likeness to Don Quixote, which was emphasized as life drew progressively further away from him. As he grew older he seldom went out, but feeling at last that he should have more fresh air, he had caused a motor-bicycle and side-car to be built to his specifications. He had carefully planned the whole matter: the machine must be controlled by one of his menservants, and himself was to sit in the side-car, but—and in this consisted its originality—the side-car was built at right angles, instead of being parallel, to the motor-bicycle. He had arranged for it to be made after this fashion in order, he explained, not to attract attention. Alas, it did not have that effect, but produced quite an opposite result. The start was quiet enough. He had intended to ride up to the heights of Fiesole, but somehow or other he never reached them. Dressed as usual in a dark, well-cut suit and large-brimmed hat, he wore invariably, indoors and out, a pair of carpet slippers on which were emblazoned his initials in gold thread. He was not, in any case, of the sort of build or appearance that would be associated with a side-car: but this side-car, in which he sat with his long legs stretched out in front of him, proved irresistible as a popular spectacle. Word had somehow gone round and the streets were lined with an appreciative, indeed rocking, crowd. After a short hour he was forced to abandon the machine and he never used it again.

As he grew older Lord Henry felt himself to be out of

sympathy with the age that was clearly shaping itself, and the affair of the motor-cycle confirmed him in his prejudices. Towards the end of his life this was manifested by his never going out at all and by his moving up a storey a year, until, finally, he could rise in this world no further above ground level. You would find him ready to receive you in a large, ornate bathroom at the top of the house dressed in a cowled white bath-robe and wearing on his head a biretta of purple silk propped up and kept in place by a small lump on his forehead. Here he would be ready at six o'clock to give his visitors a cup of black coffee—never tea, for tea he forbade to be brought into his house, since, he would explain, tea-drinking was 'responsible for all the terrible scandal talked in English drawing-rooms'.

In these later years how Lord Henry spent his days I cannot imagine. He cannot even have sat in the garden, which was a dark tangle of laurel leaves and very umbrageous plants, so overgrown that there was no room to move, though it looked cool and refreshing when seen through the windows. There did not seem to be many books in the house. He would, however, write every day and receive in return a diurnal letter from an old lady. This correspondence went back to the days when he left England: but what they can have found to write to each other about is beyond comprehension, for each hour that passed was increasingly empty of events. To his visitors, Lord Henry liked, after the manner of all old people, to dwell on times past. He would talk about Disraeli, or mimic him—an imitation which those who remembered the dead statesman would say was very true to life—or he would describe how himself would walk away from the House of Commons very late and suddenly feel a small arm hooked in his. It would be Lord Beaconsfield on his way home after speaking in the

House of Lords. Lord Beaconsfield would invite Lord Henry to supper and, when they arrived, they would find Lady Beaconsfield, bejewelled and in full evening dress, waiting as always for her husband. Lord Beaconsfield at first seemed too utterly exhausted to open his mouth, but directly his lips had touched a glass of champagne he would revive suddenly and become again the brilliant person he was. . . . Lord Henry also liked to tell us about d'Annunzio, who was a friend of his.

Lord Henry's ivory tower was very different from that my father had through the years constructed for himself; though both were alike in the failure of their original purpose —to find total refuge from the present day and the future. . . . My father, rather unexpectedly, liked Lord Henry, who, he said, had the best manners of anyone he knew, though being in essence an art and cultivated to the highest degree, they were perhaps a little over-elaborate and formal—but my father's regard for him did not prevent Lord Henry from giving, or my father from receiving, one or two jumbo-sized snubs; a process to which my father was not used, being accustomed to deliver them himself.

The first time I saw my cousin was during the Easter holidays from Eton which I spent in Florence in the year 1908. He had invited us to dinner. We arrived punctually in spite of the delaying tactics of my mother. My father rang the bell. Immediately, an oblong piece of metal slid away from an aperture in the door and a dark eye was visible looking through it. Apparently the inspection was favourable, for the bolts shot back, and the door was thrown open by two servants dressed seemingly as wrestlers in jerseys with alternate blue and red lateral stripes. We entered and were conducted by a footman in livery to the Glass Room in which our host was waiting for us. After we had greeted him he led us to the Blue Dining-

Room, reserved for guests of royal blood, or at least with a drop of it in their veins. At the side of each guest was a gold case full of Turkish cigarettes. (I was greatly flattered by this compliment to my years.) I now think, looking back, that these cigarette-cases must have been made by Fabergé, but at that time I did not know the name. The dinner was excellent and everything, including the ice, but excluding the young turkey which was the main dish, bore his coat-of-arms on it. When dinner was finished and we were drinking our coffee, my father turned to Lord Henry and asked:

'Why do you have that silver-gilt statue of King Arthur in the middle of the table?'

'Because I am descended from him,' Lord Henry replied syllogistically and with an air of finality.

My father had to accept this, though he was a well-known debunker of pedigrees—including his own—for he held that genealogical truth was of more interest than any invented descent. But what could he say against this bland assumption? He could neither retort: 'You're a liar', nor even: 'I think you are mistaken.'

23

MUSIC

I NEVER knew my father to go to a concert in spite of his liking for 'a little music after dinner'. He regarded it as the least important of the arts. It was not practical and you could not touch it. Even painting, he used to maintain, was a more useful art because you could often gather from the pictures, for instance from those of the Florentine and Sienese Primitives, the most interesting facts about contemporary life in the thirteenth and fourteenth centuries, how the people dressed and what they ate and with what implements. The facts that he gathered were submitted to a well-known process. He would not divulge them, but would probably 'keep them up his sleeve' for the future. (The reader may perhaps recall that on one occasion my father said to me: 'Between ourselves, I have the whole history of the two-pronged fork up my sleeve,' and on another: 'Between ourselves, I have two miles of lead-piping up my sleeve.') Further, music gave the patron —to whom rather than to the composer or the executant,

the chief glory in his opinion was due—little opportunity
to show off. He had, he would protest, many *useful* things
to do. He could, for example, go round to the College
of Arms and worry the Chester Herald about the Barons of
Pulford, or he could look up in the British Museum fascinating
details about life in Rotherham under Cromwell, full of helpful
hints about economy. (The household bills were a revelation.)
There also always remained the Black Death to study if other
subjects failed. Whereas music was of no practical use whatso-
ever. Therein he was wrong, as I will show.

For example, in 1923 my sister, my brother, and myself
were staying in Munich. By chance this visit coincided with
that of our intermittent friend Siegfried Sassoon. I had
apparently in some manner unknown to me succeeded in
annoying him so that, as happened not infrequently, we were
for the moment not on speaking terms. Hearing that he was to
dine one night at a fashionable restaurant to which we were
also going and which had a band, I persuaded the conductor
to watch me and at a prearranged signal to strike up the March
from *William Tell*, knowing that the strains would go to
Siegfried's feet, as it were, and compel him to march in time to
them through the whole length of the restaurant to his table
in a distant corner.... The moment I saw Siegfried enter I gave
the signal to the conductor and we watched the victim advance
in a procession of one to his table exactly as planned. After that
it was difficult for him to be so very dignified and in consequence the temperature of the whole dispute was lowered....

Few restaurants, I suppose, now supply their own music,
but there is always the radio or a juke-box to take its place. In
the hotel—a monastery until the suppression of the monastic
orders—in which between the wars I used to spend the winter
months in the company of various friends, there was a band

which played by fits and starts—mostly, one would have presumed, by fits. The winter patronage of this long white building, which fitted into the cliffs high up on its wall of rock, was in the main exercised, not as at one time by a steady resident population, but by parties of passengers from boats bound on pleasure cruises. They were not much used to travelling. (I recall a member of one of them opening a conversation with me by saying: 'There seem to be a lot of Roman Catholic churches in Italy.') The party would arrive from Naples by charabanc. Directly it had left that city for the Salernitan Gulf—to travel at horrifying speed—especially, it seemed, round corners—along the coast road between, on one side high limestone cliffs where jonquils grew in every crevice and cranny, and on the other side a precipitous fall with the sea coloured like a peacock's tail lapping, or occasionally roaring, at its base—the manager would be informed by telephone that a party was on its way. He would then in turn send messages down to the members of the band, telling them to cast away their cobblers' lasts, to abandon the cutting out of shirts and the clipping of hair and climb up the long steep flights of steps to make music for the pleasure crusaders.

The music supplied—'Santa Lucia' ad lib. and the odiously sportive and lubricious 'Funiculì, Funiculà'—was abominable. The band consisted of five men in all. The barber played a mandolin, while the cobbler blew into a pitcher, thereby provoking a deep and dull reverberation. In front of these men, a little girl wearing a pink dress was stationed who would sing very nasally, making peculiarly rigid and conventional gestures, first with one hand and then with the other, expressing nothing. Such an entertainment might have afforded the entrancing rustic fun of Pyramus and Thisbe in *A Midsummer Night's Dream*, or of the music of the *Società Filarmònica di*

Montegufoni; a group composed of peasants and shepherds playing in a superbly pastoral setting: but it did not. By those who were to be borne away on a ship the same night, it may have been thought to be characteristic or to rank as a piece of debased local colour, but to those making a long stay in the hotel it became insupportable and nauseating. Something had to be done about it.

With the more than willing support of the friends who were of our party, I arranged a plan. At luncheon one day, when a charabanc company was present, we waited until the band began to play a near-'Santa Lucia'—'Santa Lucia' itself was too well known for our purpose—and then abruptly rose to our feet and remained standing in the tense manner associated with national anthems. The guests, though puzzled concerning what country it could be that had adopted this tune, were anxious not to hurt any national feelings and hastily rose until the whole company was on its feet. The band was flabbergasted. Its members had played the tune hundreds of times without anything of this sort ever happening. What new nation had come to birth in the last few days, they asked themselves? The little girl in front was so startled that she forgot to make her gestures, and the members of the band were taken aback to the degree that one or two of them even played the right note. They had, they must have felt, inadvertently trodden on a national anthem.

Thus it can be seen that music has its uses.

24

MAGIC

A s a child the toys I most enjoyed playing with—and in
this I think I was typical of every child—all had about
them an aura of the inexplicable. Thus I was specially fascinated
at the Guy Fawkes season by the magnesium tapes which when
burnt turned into the likeness of a coiled serpent, the dried
pieces of paper from Japan that resembled dirty matchsticks
but swelled into highly coloured flowers when immersed in
water, and even a simple magnet shaped like a horseshoe with
which to pick up steel filings, or any puzzle that made use of
that alchemist's liquid metal, quicksilver, never to be made
fast. But if I liked to be astonished, my father, I believe, liked
to astonish; even his own small children; and when I was four
or five he used to make magic for me by causing a penny to
disappear from his hand, and by shaping with his fingers and
with the aid of a light the shadows of rabbits and cats and goats
upon the wall. I was immensely impressed by these achievements and my mind was very much occupied by them. I can

recall easily today the tall, authoritative man that he then was. Sometimes he would come to visit me on his way down to the drawing-room before dinner, when he would be wearing full evening dress. This must have been at our Scarborough house: but at Renishaw he was able to produce a piece of magic which for me outshone all the others. . . . I would be playing in the garden when I would hear him suddenly call my name from a distance: then, looking up, would see him waving at me from between the battlements on the roof. How did he rise to that altitude, by some process which many years later I learnt to refer to as levitation? How did he get there? I wondered, rather in the style of the well-known question attributed to King George III, who, when faced with an apple-dumpling, is supposed to have asked repeatedly on one occasion: 'How did the apple get *inside* the dumpling?' It never entered my head that he could do anything so prosaic as just climb a staircase. I did not find this out until a year or two later, but when I did discover it, his prestige suffered immensely in my eyes: because, from being a sorcerer, he had sunk to being a mere conjurer, and sleight of hand was shown to have masqueraded as magic.

Nevertheless I took a great fancy to the roof myself, and the door, on the third storey, of the wooden staircase that led to it was conveniently opposite a nursery. By the side of the staircase stood a large dappled rocking-horse, which had been drawn a century before by Octavius Oakley, showing my grandfather holding, and two of his sisters riding it, the elder girl dressed in the manner of some Cruikshank drawing with knickers showing beneath her short skirts. I was not, of course, aware of this at the time, but I knew that I was forbidden to ride the rocking-horse myself, on the score that a great-uncle of mine had fallen off it and had been killed: whether this was true or an improvisation by my nurse, I never found out; but if it was an invention it was outstandingly successful in frightening me, and nothing would have induced me to climb on its back. Conversely, it seemed impossible to keep me off the roof for long. By stretching, I could just reach the handle of the first door leading to the little wooden staircase and with more difficulty the handle of the door at the top, within one of the three gothic spires, leading to the roof itself. The keys had been lost, so there was no difficulty about locking or unlocking.

I made the expedition twice before I was caught. I was supposed to be resting after luncheon, but in the manner of all children my one idea after a meal was to rush round the room at tremendous speed and never to stop running, jumping, and singing for hours. So my nurse, on the first two occasions to which I refer, had been puzzled to find it much easier than usual to persuade me to lie down, and when she saw my hands at the end of my rest she could not think how they had got so black. Though she had been in the next room, she had heard nothing, so quiet and careful had I been. As I have said elsewhere, her favourite motto was: 'Even a slave has an hour for his dinner', and she might have added 'and another hour for digestion', for that was the amount of time she liked. . . . But the fiasco of my third visit to the roof was entirely my own fault: if I had not acted foolishly, I should again have reached home safely. It was a particularly fine day, however, calm and full of sunlight, and the roof was fascinating; the best place possible from which to seize the beauty of the whole lay-out, the counterpoint of light and shadow, of water and dark yew hedge, and from which to look down on the golden mounds of the tree-tops. The roof also afforded an easy way to compute the age of the original house and the various additions to it; for the part with stone tiles belonged to the time of King Charles I, and the grey-blue slates to different periods in the eighteenth century, while the chimney-stacks also afforded their clues. Of course, I did not realize this at the time, but the beauty of it, of the light and colour, excited me and seems to have warped my judgment. By standing on the flat part of the roof and stretching on tiptoe, I could just get my head over the gap between two battlements. Everything looked beautiful. Suddenly I saw my father walking across the lawn alone. Overcome by the feeling of my own cleverness in reaching here unaided and by my pleasure at seeing him, because he was usually indoors at this hour, I determined to give him a pleasant surprise, and shouted as loud as I could: 'Father! Father!'[1] I saw him turn round immediately, look up, and then begin running towards the house. What I think chiefly frightened him was the thought of the wooden planks which led from one ridge to another. It would be easy for a child to trip and fall over, and the valleys between the ridges were often very deep. I was happily playing in the sunshine when the hasty tread of feet on the creaking stairs announced his arrival, accompanied by my nurse, who on this occasion wore the woebegone expression of a saint in a picture by some Flemish artist such as Roger van der Weyden, and a flustered nurserymaid. I was carried downstairs kicking, and put to bed. My mother, however, did her best for me as soon as she found out what had happened, pointing out to my father how lovely the day had been and how playing in the rare sunshine of our climate could do me nothing but good. . . . I did not quite understand what I had done, but whatever it might have been, I regretted it because my nurse and Jenny were in disgrace,

---

[1] To some of my readers it may seem strange that I called father 'father', but the more intimate 'daddy' belongs to a later generation, as the use of 'papa' and 'mamma' belonged to a generation earlier.

though my nurse never blamed me for it. She was, however, usually in disgrace with my father, because she had been nurserymaid to my mother, and any faults my mother had developed in his eyes were attributed to her regime.

There was staying in the house at this moment one whom my father considered more culpable still, my nurse's exalted guest, Mrs Ayton, who had been nurse to my mother and her sisters. Indeed, in a sense my father was right, for if Mrs Ayton had not been there and had not been immersed in conversation about nameless scandals (nameless because it was her belief that if you omitted to refer to the persons of whom you were talking by their full names, but only in some way indicated them, then it did not count as scandal at all), my nurse would have heard me moving about. . . . Mrs Ayton may have been the villain of this piece, but she enjoyed the widest esteem in the world of the Housekeepers' Rooms of the country houses she went to: and she settled herself annually for a full month on my mother and each of her three sisters. She had now retired and lived for the rest of the year with her three children —two daughters and a bachelor son—in a small house at Balham. She was an old woman with grey hair, worn out-of-doors under an old-fashioned bonnet decorated with sequins, and she found her chief pleasure in talking. Upon her upper lip grew the ghost of a grey moustache, always moist from tea-drinking, which made being kissed by her a horrid experience; but for her faults she would atone by bringing with her always a special kind of chocolate cake of which she alone knew the secret recipe. She seemed to me very ancient at that time, but she lived another twenty years to be ninety-one and to be bombed out of her house in one of the comparatively rare air raids in 1917. Indeed, preparations against air raids became the chief interest of her life in later days, when she could not visit my mother and her sisters since country houses, if not all shut up, were not in a state to receive anyone. Directly an air raid announced itself, she would get up, dress, and sit near the kitchen fire surrounded by her children, talking about the event—ample scope for her conversation—and waiting for the end, and on one occasion the end had nearly arrived. All that my father said when he heard of her misfortune was:

'So like her!'

25

THE ROCKING-HORSE

I T MUST have been in the autumn of 1935 that I was dining
with my father. He seemed in a jaunty mood that evening,
and asked me—which was unusual—what sort of day I had
spent.

'A singular day in two respects,' I replied, and began to
tell him what they had been.

In the morning I had been listening to the speeches of the
orators at Marble Arch. I had watched the solitary figures
coalesce into crowds and then the crowds gradually disperse
again. As I had turned away from the particular clump I had
joined, it was with the accustomed feelings of disappointment
and dissatisfaction. The words of the speaker, floating on the
air, followed me.

'Only co-operation can save the world,' he was saying.

The slogan might be true, I had reflected, but as a programme it seemed somewhat vague.

'Co-operation can be a disaster,' my father objected.

he Grotto, Montegufoni. The Goddess Latona

The Grotto, Montegufoni. Peasant throwing a ston

'In what way?' I enquired.

'Look at our coalition governments. Always when this country is in danger there is an outcry to have a coalition. The idea is, I suppose, that it's safer to place your life in the hands of two fools rather than of one.'

I resumed and told my father how I had been thinking about co-operation when I reached the Serpentine. Then I had turned along by the water's edge. The day and the place were beautiful, elegiac with fallen leaves, wraith-like mists, and the scent of bonfires, the flames of which flickered like gonfalons on a light breeze. I had reflected how melancholy the people looked who passed, whether lingering by themselves or even in companies—but suddenly there had been an abrupt change to another tempo. Faces broke into smiles, feet into runs rather than walks, movement in general became lively and bustling. The centre of this cheerful commotion was the bridge, just as the sun which had come out was the centre of such heat as there was. The feeling was one of liveliness and expectation. I had wondered whether the crowd had gathered here to watch a film star go by; but then I noticed that all the faces were turned outwards towards the water. The cheerfulness was now such that complete strangers talked to one another. What could it be, I asked myself, that had caused this stir? A man pulled me by the sleeve and said:

'Have you seen the suicide, they've just found the corpse? He's there, under the blanket.' . . . So that was it.

Looking down at the lake, I saw an oozing mass under a sodden brown army blanket on the asphalt path. The water spread out, trickling over the hard surface. . . . It's difficult to know what governs such matters or what will make people talk, but a shock of some sort is patently required.

The second unusual incident had taken place in the

afternoon in the toy department of one of the big London stores.

I was choosing a kind of game and in reaching up to a shelf to get something which the assistant thought I wanted, upset a pile of light flat white cardboard boxes on to a stranger's head. I knew they weren't heavy enough to have hurt him, but still it must have been annoying. I had noticed him when I came in, a rather distinguished-looking man examining a rocking-horse. . . . I apologized profusely, and then added:

'That's a fine rocking-horse you've got your eye on!'

'Yes,' he said, 'I'm buying it as a birthday present for a small son. I'm determined that he shall have the toys of which the children of our generation were deprived.' . . .

The shower of cardboard boxes seemed to have melted the ice.

He spoke English with a slightly foreign intonation, no accent, but the rhythm of his speech wasn't English. He talked in rather a formal way.

'What good English you speak.'

'Do you think so? I'm afraid I talk like a book, for all my English was first learnt by reading. Are you the writer?' he went on.

I admitted it.

'Well, I'm the pianist Boris Michaelis,' he said. 'I don't know whether you've heard me play, but your books have given me great pleasure. When you've finished your purchases, perhaps you'd come and have a cup of coffee with me downstairs and I'll tell you more about the rocking-horse.'

I looked at my watch and finding it was only four o'clock accepted the invitation. When coffee was brought he said to me:

'I'll tell you something about myself, a subject about which I usually speak little, but as an author you'll understand. I was born and brought up in Cernauti, or Czernowitz, as it is now, in Rumania. This town was formerly a centre from which quite a disproportionate number of creators poured through to Europe and America. My father combined the rather contradictory professions of music teacher and impresario, but he was a poor man. I worshipped him. He had designed my career directly I was born. His aim was to produce me as a virtuoso pianist and from the very first I was trained to be, and in fact was, a child prodigy. I gave my first concert in Czernowitz under my father's auspices at the age of five. It had all been extremely well organized and the hall was crowded with genuine musical enthusiasts, as well as with kind ladies who doted on children. At the end of the concert there was tremendous applause, and it rose to a climax when a huge rocking-horse, brilliantly dappled, was carried on to the stage by two men and presented to me. Children up to the age of seven have little self-consciousness and, as a child would at that age, I clambered on to the horse the moment it was put down, and began to rock. That was certainly the greatest moment of my childhood. I had longed for a rocking-horse as far back as I could remember. The applause doubled and increased to the volume of thunder. It was a triumph, though I say so myself, and earned great praise in the local Press, which compared me as a virtuoso—for such I was—with Mozart at the harpsichord at a similar age. As for me, the rocking-horse claimed all my attention. I didn't respond much to the applause, but felt I could go on rocking all night. I was soon rushed home, however, given a bowl of soup, and sent to bed. I wanted to have the rocking-horse stabled in my bedroom so that I could rock to my heart's content the moment I woke, but my father wouldn't allow it to be put anywhere except near the front door. I wondered why, as I fell into a sleep of exhaustion.

'Though I was woken early by a van arriving and driving away again almost immediately, my first thought was of the rocking-horse. I went out into the passage, to discover that my toy had vanished. . . . When later I discovered what had happened—that it was all a deception, that my father had hired the horse for the evening, and that I should never see it again —I lost all my great love for him, and from then until today the very sight of a rocking-horse has made me feel sick—or it did until I chose that one upstairs for my boy.'

My father gave all the well-known symptoms of being displeased, fidgeting and flickering his eyes sideways. I often made the mistake of expecting an ordinary response from him.

'Of course, his father was quite right,' he said, 'in sending away the rocking-horse. He couldn't afford it, and was determined not to encourage the boy in extravagant habits. It would have been much more sensible if he had been able to save up and later obtain for his son a commission in a good English cavalry regiment.'

'But he wasn't English,' I objected.

'Well, no doubt the boy could easily have got naturalized,' my father remarked. 'He could always have consulted me. I'm afraid I've no patience with him.'

26

MAKING A BOLT FOR IT

M Y MOTHER died in a nursing home in London on the 12th of July 1937, and in August my father left England for Switzerland, and thence, after a month's visit, returned to Montegufoni. For the long stay he proposed to make there he had provided himself with some companions—acquaintances, it must be admitted, more than buddies—and others we had found for him, in order that he should not be lonely—or, to be precise, not more lonely than the complete suit of armour he had grown for himself in the past half-century rendered inevitable. In it he was now ever encased impenetrably, the vizor down, so that he revealed his face only a little less seldom than his hand. In addition, I had told him that I would join him in Italy whenever he wished, but I became aware in talking to him that he was not really eager for me to do so, because he liked to be in a position of absolute command, with nobody to gainsay him, and since I, too, was accustomed to having my own way, this encroached on his prerogative. However, during the course of a few weeks he came to cherish a certain sense of grievance, most carefully nurtured by various of his acquaintances, at his children not being round him, and towards the end of November, some two months after his return to Italy, telegrams were suddenly shot at me from all sides with such vigour and poignance that they inevitably recalled the multitude of arrows that pierced the writhing body of St Sebastian. This barbed shower revealed behind the shafts a formidable power of organization. They sped from people young and old, men and women, worldly and unworldly, Italian and English, prelates and laymen, but all united to tell me that my father was very ill and that it had now become my duty, however disagreeable, to be at his side. I at once took the train for Florence.

On arrival at the Castle I found arranged for my benefit a tableau, a death-bed scene like one of those that occur in the paintings of the Italian Primitive masters. My father lay in a four-poster—baroque in style, I must confess, rather than gothic —receiving fruit, fresh eggs, game, and sympathy—but not flowers. These last he rejected outright because they were prone to give him hay-fever. . . . As I entered the room, the figures relaxed and the tableau broke up. My father proceeded to dismiss the guests with a little ceremonial flutter of the hand, and went on to tell me at once of his serious illness, although there were no outward signs of it in his physical appearance. I therefore asked him to be allowed to talk to his doctor, Giglioli. He gave me permission, and accordingly I bumped into Florence in the Ark, described at some length elsewhere, to interview this sympathetic and most intelligent Italian doctor. When I asked him if my father was very ill, he replied:

'The disease which Sir George assumes he has developed is

a matter of X-ray plates and not of faith alone. He is an old man of seventy-seven years of age, and of course if he gets a cold it may always turn to pneumonia: but probably he will outlive me and be with us for another twenty years.' (My father did in fact survive his doctor by some five.)

On my return from the city I found the invalid still in bed, and looking intensely depressed. As I opened the door of his room, he enquired in a drooping voice:

'How long does the doctor give me?'

'About twenty years,' I replied.

At this he suddenly jumped out of bed with an agility that would have done credit to a man half his age, and said: 'I must dress now.' That night he came down to dinner.

The long journey and change of climate had afflicted me with a bad attack of lumbago, and the next morning I had breakfast in bed, and was therefore rather late in making my appearance. First, from a small room above the Cardinal's Garden, protected from the wind, and full of late November sunlight, of roses and stocks and of drowsy butterflies in the last florid stage before their hibernation, I had observed my father holding court in a deck-chair—or rather in the kind of long wicker chair that he liked because he could put his feet up and thus rest the heart, and one of which was always reserved for him in any garden that he owned. He reclined on these hard open-work planes of wicker at the top of a flight of steps commanding the view: the valley of vines, and nearer, climbing the Castle Hill in steep terraces, the long tank-like stone beds full of blue plumbago, leading up in turn to the surrounding box parterre, in which were growing the flowers he had chosen for it in pale, pastel colours. . . . Round him were grouped the courtiers. . . . There was a man with more false teeth in one mouth than I had ever previously seen gathered

[183]

together, and rather ill-balanced they were, too, so that his conversation was an act of perpetual conjuring. There was Signor Bracciaforte, smiling as always, full of childish benevolence, easily moved to tears or laughter. There was a young girl, a student of history, her figure slightly foreshortened by fate and a-clink with the old paste jewellery with which my father delighted to hang it. Her eyes, I noticed, seemed to be perpetually full of tears and she had a sweet smile of sympathy showing from a head hung rather on one side. There was another girl, a cousin of ours, and then there was my friend Francis Bamford, who had kindly offered to accompany my father to Italy and to look after him. (To him my father had in the past months uttered some of his more sudden, startling, and Delphic warnings and aphorisms, such as 'Never be Kind to a Dowager', and 'One can see in my grandchildren how Nature is trying to reproduce *Me*!')

When I got downstairs—with some difficulty—and appeared in the garden under that cloud of awkwardness that always overshadows the latecomer, I said: 'Good morning, Father.' He greeted me in return and then gave a significant, rather ominous glance at those round him from under eyelids that seemed to work sideways rather than up and down; a signal which the court knew from experience was calculated to convey dismissal. Watching in silence till his guests were out of earshot, he remarked to me in a voice of unusual dignity and importance:

'Osbert, I wish to speak to you alone.'

I replied rather carelessly:

'Then I'll get a chair and sit by you. How delicious it is out here, Father! This is the first sun I've seen for months.'

To my surprise, for he usually liked to warm himself in the winter sunshine, he answered:

'No, I would prefer to speak to you in the Gothic Library.'

He proceeded to lead the way to the small, cold, high room, which I have described earlier in the second part of 'Unforgotten Feasts', on the north side of the house. On the faking of it he had for some years been engaged, spending on the process a very considerable sum of money. It was, of course, a library without books—I say of course, for it could always be noticed that, though he loved books and lived surrounded by them, none the less in any room which he called a library no single volume was ever to be found. At Scarborough, similarly, his library had been bookless, though each of his several sitting-rooms even had books piled up all over the floor. But this library was, its very appearance proclaimed, a State Apartment, to be used solely for giving audiences and making special pronouncements. No book had ever been brought into it or was ever likely to be, and people, it was plain, seldom entered it. Indeed, it proved difficult to do so. First you had to find your way down some break-neck steps set at odd angles at the bottom of a spiral staircase, and then to get yourself through a doorway forbiddingly narrow, like a coffin. When finally you reached the room, it had a recess lined with cypress-wood cupboards. Too shallow to hold books, they were crowned with a flat, gothic fretting as cornice, and their panels were edged with a margin of leaves, rabbits, and human figures cut in very flat relief, expertly carved. The detail of the presses, lightly touched with colour, and of the vaulted ceiling, dis-proportionately high, had, if I am not mistaken, been derived from one of the nine canvases by Carpaccio, depicting the life of St Ursula, to be seen in San Giorgio degli Schiavoni in Venice. The cupboards had below them, attached to their base, seats that resembled medieval instruments of torture; although, as if in mockery, they were thinly padded in places with flat cushions, soft stone pancakes, covered in blue and silver velvet. Herein and hereon we sat, the two of us facing each other, for the cupboards took up three sides of a square. We bore our discomfort manfully, pretending not to notice it. I can see my father now, as he sat there, very upright, with the sun through the barred window catching the gold glint of his red but greying beard. He was wearing a grey suit and one hand rested on a cushion. In his manner could be perceived, by one familiar with his ways, both a certain air of tension and a wish to surprise. Thus I was prepared for something portentous—and sure enough it came.

He gave a slight bow and said:

'I thought I ought to inform you, Osbert, that Mrs FitzDudley Gudgeon wishes to marry me.'

This unusual announcement winded me. I had seen Mrs FitzDudley Gudgeon. She was a widow with no background but a past, and a past of peculiarly unpleasant character, who had for half a century and more trailed behind her a long train of unsavoury financial transactions merging into love affairs, and vice versa. . . . She had contrived to cultivate my father's society for some years. Once at a concert at the Queen's Hall she had come cringing up to me in the interval, and had said: 'I know your father'—to which I had replied: 'Yes. Better than I do, I believe.' But most clearly I remember the first occasion on which I had seen her. It was at a party, and I recall it vividly because a friend of mine, much older than myself, who had been standing by my side, had turned to me as she entered the room, and had said:

'Here comes the wickedest woman in Europe.'

This had naturally focussed my attention on the neatly dressed, discreet-looking, grey-haired woman who entered. What he said might be true: but here was, I found out, an unaudacious, flat, mousy, money-grubbing kind of wickedness without any endowment of wit or wits, and lacking in the fun that sometimes attends and makes lively the company of sinners. It demanded a guaranteed sound return, and constituted a real four-per-cent-preference-share brand of evil.

Naturally, I had noticed my father's unusual choice of words. So now I asked him:

'Do *you* wish to marry *her*?'

He replied: 'I am not certain, but she has written to me to say that she would like to come here for a long stay.'

'Well,' I enquired, 'what will you do if she insists on marrying you, and you don't want to?'

'Make a bolt for it, I suppose, as I had to once before. . . .'

Recollecting previous conversations with my father, I seized immediately the implications of this gallant reply: because, when I was younger and he had been fond of warning me of the dangers of everyday life, he had often related to me how, when just down from Christ Church, he had arrived to stay in a famous country-house for a ball. The two daughters of his hostess would be great heiresses; but unfortunately, though he liked them, and they, so he claimed, entertained feelings deeper than friendship for him, yet my father disapproved of both the young ladies: for he considered that they were over fond of pleasure, and feared, moreover, that they might like to spend money too freely. Another motive influenced him even more profoundly. As I have related before, he held very strict views on eugenics, and their noses too nearly resembled his own in shape (so he had told me), and this, if he had married either of them, might have tended to accentuate the aquiline profiles of his offspring, and so have deprived his children of the classical mould of feature for which he hoped, and which indeed he was determined, to secure for them. . . . It was difficult to follow precisely what happened. Howbeit, so far as I could make out, on his entering the hall a footman as usual had taken the heavy leather portmanteau with which a man then always travelled—when, to his surprise, he had discovered that the heiress who was his particular friend was waiting for him there as well. Her presence at once convinced him that the young lady expected him immediately to propose to her; indeed, beyond the hall lay a vista of rooms, and at the end of it the conservatory door could be seen open in invitation. He had felt it imperative, if his children were to avoid nasal catastrophe, to act at once. Therefore, hastily snatching back his luggage from the footman's arms, he had pelted back down the drive and through the park without offering to anyone a word of explanation or apology, either at the time or subsequently. . . . This—though I may have gathered some of the details incorrectly—I could have no doubt was one occasion on which he had been obliged to 'make a bolt for it'. . . . But that was nearly sixty years ago, and at the moment I was concerned with stopping the threatened alliance. To take first the most obvious of present difficulties, plainly he would not be able to run so fast at his present age, while Mrs FitzDudley Gudgeon was quite capable of running after and catching him! The best way, I concluded, of preventing the marriage was to find for him a rival attraction to Mrs FitzDudley Gudgeon, because obviously he felt a need for feminine sympathy and for presenting himself in a new light and as a centre of interest. What could be done? Fortunately my mind lighted on Mrs Rippon: a woman of character and humour and formerly a celebrated beauty; a pirate, but kind and audacious, and of quite a different sort. . . . He liked her, and her husband was rumoured to be dying. Accordingly I improvised.

[188]

'Well, I must admit I always saw a different future for you,' I remarked.

He said: 'What do you mean?'

I replied: 'After Colonel Rippon's death, I thought Ethel Rippon would marry you.'

At this he looked very pleased with himself, and I realized that I had defeated Mrs FitzDudley Gudgeon's scheme once and for all.

.   .   .   .   .

There is little more to add, except that after my father's death, when I returned to Montegufoni at the end of the war, I found among his papers all the correspondence that had passed between him and Mrs FitzDudley Gudgeon—for he kept and filed copies of letters he wrote, as well as preserving those he received. Just as the letters quoted in the Bardell *v.* Pickwick Trial were said by Serjeant Buzfuz to have been written in code, so that an order for 'Chops and Tomata sauce. Yours, Pickwick', conveyed the declaration 'I love you', so these unusual *billets-doux* were couched in the current technical terms of the English and European, but especially of the American and Canadian, Stock Exchanges. It was easily to be deduced: the tenderness of Mrs FitzDudley Gudgeon's requests for information about Abitibi shares and the prospects of Brazilian Traction spelt ardent and everlasting devotion for my father and the respect she cherished for his wisdom—still more for his wealth: while his affectionate response to these demonstrations took the form of such phrases as, 'I hear Beralts may pay a bonus' or 'I advise you to stick to Chinese Customs 1882.' Moreover, alas, I am bound to conclude that the counsel he gave her in his final communication, to avoid further 'flutters' and to invest all her 'loose money' in Consols, constituted both a reproof and a call to order, equivalent in that language of love which they had evolved for themselves to the words: 'Let us part on terms of friendship; I wish to be let alone, and have no intention of marrying you.' After that, there came no more letters.

27

THALIA

MY FATHER had made a bolt for it—or, rather, his mother had made it for him—once before, a year or two earlier than that just described. . . . The opening scene of this bolt is set at Renishaw, but it was a very different place from that of today: since my father had not yet had time to begin the numerous improvements which, in spite of many plans started and never concluded, he effected there during the following half-century: the yew hedges had not been planted yet, nor had he built the terraces of the formal garden with which he was to re-establish and increase the beauty of the immediate surroundings: nor was the magic mirror of the lake below yet in place to double the prospect of trees and sky; these were all to be begun some ten years later. I do not remember the landscape garden which he destroyed: and it is difficult for me to construct it in my mind. A fine green lawn, over which flower-beds were dispersed for no particular reason, swept down in front of the house from the Avenue to the Wilderness.

The house, my father told me, seemed unanchored to the ground it stood upon, though the lie of the land must always have been magnificent. I once asked my great-aunt Blanche—whom readers of my autobiography may remember—what the garden was like before the changes, and she said: 'Renishaw had always an enchantment about it.' . . .

Everything indeed seemed golden, everything was at its brightest and best in those particular days at the end of May and beginning of June in the early eighties of the last century. My father had just come of age after a minority of nineteen years. So capable a woman had my grandmother proved herself to be that she had contrived to pull the estate together, and by the end of this period to pay off the heavy debts contracted many years before my grandfather had succeeded, and which had for long been such an encumbrance. The old ship was afloat again. Everything looked golden. My grandmother still presided over the house for her son, and at Church of England services rich and poor alike joined in the singing of hymns with such words as:

> The rich man in his castle,
> The poor man at his gate,
> He made them high or lowly,
> And ordered their estate.

Everything seemed golden, and even my grandmother, though apt to take a dark, dramatic view, did not discern through the golden mists of the eighties and nineties the ruin that was in the next generation to descend both on the houses of this kind and on the way of life to which they gave shelter. . . . For several hours a day my grandmother would rest on a sofa, her face, with its melancholy smile, a mask of Christian resignation. This year she, together with my aunt Florence, had presided over a succession of parties—lasting much longer than the Friday to Monday visits of today. Florence, her only daughter, had never, I apprehend, been of much help to her in mundane affairs, her head full, as it was, of the approaching millennium to the utter exclusion of all else. Charitable and ineffably religious, my grandmother had been obliged for the time being to become worldly—but at least she could still enjoy putting away all secular books on a Saturday night in preparation for the intensive all-in religious wrestling to occupy the next day. Every party over which she had presided had been based on a sound foundation of religion and family relationships, and had culminated in the visit of Archibald Campbell Tait, Archbishop of Canterbury, guardian and great-uncle to my father, and who thus belonged to both worlds.

His visit, however, was over, but the house was again full of guests. It is not necessary to name and describe them all here, but they must be kept in mind as a background to the action. The relations present, in addition to my aunt Blanche, included a cousin of my father's, Hildebrand Sitwell, who proudly filled the position of black sheep to the family—in those days every county family possessed its own black sheep—and to whom my aunt Blanche was in consequence much attached. Black sheep could always count on her sympathy and affection: and there was nothing in which she so much delighted as helping a lame black sheep over a stile, though the effort would sometimes require all her strength, tenacity, and love of fighting. On this occasion, moreover, Hildebrand had come here to introduce his new betrothed, named curiously Thalia, and to show once more that he had turned over a new leaf—for though still young, twenty-six—he had become an almost professional turner-over of new leaves.

Thalia, to whom he was now engaged, was dazzlingly pretty and everyone liked her immediately for her appealing looks and charm. On this visit the couple had already spent ten days here, and were expected to stay another week. But fate decreed otherwise.

Thalia seemed to like everyone and, in short, liked my father so much that she made a declaration of her feelings to him. It is always, I believe, difficult for a girl to isolate a man from his surroundings which, in her mind, have become part of him, or to separate from him his achievements and possessions. Thus it is unfair to deduce that a girl has married a man because, let us say, he is Prime Minister. To her the man and his office are one, so that the quality of enchantment mentioned by my aunt Blanche as always belonging to Renishaw had been in part responsible for Thalia's switch-over, as well as the fact that here was a distinguished-looking young man in a preordained, Meredithian mist of golden fortune and destiny.

My grandmother's version of what occurred dates from many years later, but had by no means shed the romantic lustre with which her turn of mind had invested it, and by her manner of speaking which those relations who did not like her —and there were not many—would have characterized as 'affectation'. Be that as it may, she had, so she said, suddenly felt—owing to what was known then as 'a mother's intuition', but would now be called 'E.S.P.'[1]—that my father needed her help, though she could not tell in what connection. So she went straight to his room, entered it, and found him with his head in his hands 'in an attitude of, oh, but despair!' She gently asked: 'George, what is the matter?'

He replied: 'Mother, Thalia has proposed to me.'

[1] Extra-Sensory Perception.

[194]

'But, George,' my grandmother pointed out, 'Thalia is already engaged to Hildebrand.'

'Yes, but this morning she broke off her engagement with him and told him that she had fallen in love with me.'

My grandmother soon had the situation in hand. She had chosen from the background a friend and contemporary of my father's—subsequently to develop into that quaking, cultured Silver Bore who, as I relate in *Laughter in the Next Room*, was to cost me in the future a galleryful of Modiglianis—and had swiftly arranged for him to set out at once for a walking tour with her son. It was to occupy ten days. (This was, nevertheless, essentially a bolt for it, though rather longer and slower, and covering less distance, than was to be expected.) Meanwhile, Hildebrand had declared his intention of shooting someone, either himself, Thalia, or my father—or, better still, all three together—and, carrying with him an unloaded revolver, which had, however, no bullets with which to fill the cylinder, had proceeded to lock himself into the box-room, where he brooded for several hours. What the other guests thought, I do not know, but my aunt Blanche, of course, championed Hildebrand and gave expression to the opinion that 'George has behaved disgracefully', a pronouncement which, when repeated to him, was one of the main reasons for my father's subsequent life-long feud with her. It was my aunt who eventually persuaded Hildebrand to join the outside world once more for dinner, though when he had come out most of the party wished he were in again. This she accomplished by saying brusquely: 'Come out of there, Tom!' (she would never call him Hildebrand) 'and don't be such a damned donkey!' ...
Later he settled in China, and was no longer able almost professionally to darken doors in London. (The injunction:

'Leave my house, sir, and never dare to darken my doors again' was still in current use in the eighties, left over from and popularized by mid-Victorian melodrama. Indeed, sons and lovers would have felt deprived of something if they were spared this admonition. The next step would be the threat of a horsewhip.)

My grandmother had spoken quietly to Thalia and persuaded her to return home in two days' time. During this interval my grandmother and Thalia were much together and took their meals upstairs in the boudoir. This propinquity through many trying hours was responsible for a mutual friendship, improbable though it may have seemed at this juncture, especially in the present circumstances for which Thalia was plainly responsible. Thalia now officially broke off her engagement to Hildebrand and even promised my grandmother to lay off my father, in fact not to see him again.

The last chapter of the story took place some twenty-five years later, one spring in the Boltons; the Boltons, that late Victorian haven, nebulous island of houses and gardens and dogs, of church spires showing dimly through the fog, that floating island, so solid when you are in it, so difficult to find when you are looking for it—perhaps because it survives in its own separate pocket of time, different from that of today. . . . Be that as it may, my grandmother had bought a house there in the last years of her life, and one day when my sister was staying with her, my grandmother told her the postscript to the story, with its unusual choral culmination.

After two years had passed Thalia married an English officer in an Indian cavalry regiment. From India for many years she kept up a regular correspondence with my grandmother. . . . Her life, I think, had not been very interesting. Indeed, the most unusual feature of it was the number of children born of this marriage. Eventually, the entire family had come home to England for a brief visit.

My grandmother asked them to tea. . . . I can imagine the scene, the drawing-room full of the sunlight of a May evening in London, in which the silver cabinet glittered and the gilded rococo chairs—now in the next room to that in which I am writing—glowed. It must have seemed to her when Thalia entered the drawing-room, as if she were leading a procession, a well drilled procession dwindling in height, which gave a false perspective to it, making it look even longer than it was. When the children were all drawn up in single file to be introduced, my grandmother related how Thalia had re-marked:

' "Mother"—for she always called me Mother—"would these were George's": and the Dear Nineteen joined in, chanting: "Yes, Mother." '

28

THE NEW JERUSALEM

O F A fine evening in August during the twenties, after a solitary and early tea, my father—wearing a light-weight grey suit, and brown brogue shoes rather too delicate for country mud and for the wet tufts of rank grass near the water—liked to walk down to the lake and round it, in order to see how the plantations he had made were prospering, and to examine the distant views revealed by the fellings that had taken place. As a younger man, he would have been found at this hour paddling along in a canoe, with Monarch, a black spaniel, following behind in the water at a discreet distance, though one from which he could still splash his master if he wished, or even try to board the boat and succeed in swamping it. But Monarch was long dead and my father now preferred to walk round the lake. Sometimes he would ask me to join him. We would descend the flight of steps in the middle of the garden and then go through the iron gate at the top of the hill. At this season, the yellowing grass was close-cropped and the only flowers in the park would be drifts of harebells with their translucent blue cups swinging on invisible stalks, clumps of toadflax in their two tones of yellow and jungle tangles of convolvulus engaged in gradually strangling the green bushes on which they climbed: but in spite of this nefarious procedure they produced large white trumpet flowers having an air of unusual innocence and beauty. Partly running down the hill, for it was so steep that it impelled us to run, we reached the lake through a thicket of wild raspberries. Here at the water's edge was an entirely different set of flowers, fragrant clumps of lilac-coloured wild mint, the clustered spires of magenta loosestrife, and, just inside the banks, groups of meadowsweet and bulrushes. On the water itself, in the middle of the lake, two kinds of yellow lilies floated, one a large round-petalled nenuphar with a red centre resembling the inside of a pome-granate, the other a small yellow flower, insignificant except for the abundance of its blossoms, but the leaves of both formed big golden circles floating on the darkness of the water. . . . A difference was visible, too, in the insect world: here the dragonflies darted and skimmed: it was too late in the year for the great quantities of azure dragonflies which were to be seen in July, though a few might survive, but it was those of a larger species which now attracted attention as they sped on dark gauze wings in dry crackling flight. Their bodies were brown and varnished or marked with green, blue, and yellow like a grass-snake's belly, their eyes protuberant and endowed with more facets than man has ever contrived to cut in the largest and finest diamond. Occasionally a kingfisher would flash by and, more rarely, a heron would be seen fishing in the marshy part of the lake opposite Half-Moon Plantation, having flown apparently some forty miles for an evening's sport, since the heronry nearest to us was at Kedleston.

My father walked very fast and, as was his wont, would stop suddenly—abruptly enough, indeed, to make anyone walking behind him collide with him—and raise binoculars up to his eyes in order to obtain the distant views. Sometimes we would cross the path of a trespasser, a miner off work for a day or two and engaged in gathering a bunch of wild flowers to make into a posy to compete at a local horticultural show, where there would be competitions in flower arrangements: and very pretty the bouquets would be, with flower heads of each sort, pressed together in concentric, concolorous circles; very pretty and unexpectedly fastidious, with their contrasts of texture, of the lacy interweaving cow-parsley and meadowsweet contrasting with more robust flowers, and reminiscent of the bouquets clasped in the hot hands of bridesmaids, dressed in early-Victorian style, at fashionable weddings. It seemed odd that miners, after their heavy work, should indulge in such fragile and elegant fantasies, but in those days people made their own amusements and were happier for it. . . . My father would not notice the interloper, his mind being occupied with other matters, and distant enough to bring out sometimes a real surprise. Thus one evening, suddenly interrupting himself in the middle of explaining how unselfish of him it had been to make all the improvements he had effected here—lakes and plantations and a drive through the wood—for the benefit of generations unborn, he looked up at the hill and, forgetting what he had said, just pronounced:

'This wicked taxation will most probably drive you out of England, in which case you must emigrate to Canada or America and build a copy of the house there: but though I shan't, I fear, still be here to help you and the architect with my advice, I can give you a few tips now. The new Renishaw must be an exact replica of the present house and garden, except in one respect: the stones needn't be numbered and moved one by one across the Atlantic, nor need it even be built of the same stone: but you must find a position for it with a natural resemblance to the original site.'

I was floored and stunned by the outlining of these new measures of economy.

'How am I to pay for it?' I asked.

'You must keep expenses down in every other direction. It needn't cost so much: it would be unnecessary, for instance, to make the lake at first. You could wait for that until you had settled in the house, then you could keep an eye on the work yourself.'

'But what I want to know,' I reiterated, 'is how I am to pay for the purchase of the site and for building a house?'

'As for that, there are always the Building Societies. I understand they exist, as their name implies, for the purpose of encouraging building. They'd be only too pleased to help, I imagine. It'd be a real chance for them. Now you'll see, my dear boy, why it is so important to be economical in small things. The pocket-money you have enjoyed might have come in very useful, for a shilling a week soon mounts up at compound interest.'

'It's too late to do anything about that now, I'm afraid,' I said rather unsympathetically. 'The question is, who is going to find the money for everything?'

'I have already told you—the Building Societies. You may have to draw on the resources of more than one of them, of two or three perhaps, but of course they'd jump at it. It's the sort of opportunity they don't often get.'

'The building operations you suggest are not of the kind that the directors would support,' I objected.

[201]

'Then they've no right to call themselves *Building Societies*,' he replied crossly. 'It's a piece of imposture. I never heard of such a thing. But of course you're wrong. They'd jump at it. Meanwhile I can continue, as long as I am still with you, to advise you about details which will save you money. . . . For example, when you've made the lake, you needn't plant English wild flowers round the water at once. You can take your time over it. You'll find all the arrangements very enjoyable. Then, in making the lake, you can leave out the island. That'll mean a big saving, and it's not really necessary, anyhow not at present. You'll have, of course, to make a copy of the Lake Pavilion. But you can't do that until I've built the original, so you see why it's so important for me to get on with it. It ought to be started immediately. All the plans are ready. One other point: it would pay you probably to sell the furniture and pictures in the house and to have exact copies made to furnish the new Renishaw. This is an age of copying and we ought to learn to make use of it. No one out there would know the difference, and it would mean a great saving.' . . . At this moment, those elegant cannibals, the jays, burst out from their dark castles in the trees, gave a screech and a mocking cackle of laughter, and my father, suddenly recalled to himself, said:

'I suppose it's time to start back now.'

INDEX

The Economics of Corporation Finance

Sergei P. Dobrovolsky

Professor of Economics
Rensselaer Polytechnic Institute

The Economics of
Corporation Finance

McGraw-Hill Book Company

New York St. Louis San Francisco Düsseldorf Johannesburg
Kuala Lumpur   London   Mexico   Montreal   New Delhi
Panama   Rio de Janeiro   Singapore   Sydney   Toronto

THE ECONOMICS OF CORPORATION FINANCE

Library of Congress Catalog Card Number 70-150458
07–017205–6
1234567890MAMM7987654321

This book was set in Times, and was printed on permanent paper and bound by The Maple Press Company. The drawings were done by John Cordes, J. & R. Technical Services, Inc. The editors were Jack R. Crutchfield and Sonia Sheldon. Annette Wentz supervised production.

Contents

Preface

The purpose of this book is to provide a theoretical framework for analyzing business financial policies and problems. It is intended to be used as a text —or one of the texts—in an advanced course in business finance offered to undergraduate or graduate students who have already taken an introductory course in this field and are, therefore, familiar with the basic terms, definitions, and distinguishing characteristics of the major types of financial transactions.

Since most of the problems discussed are of a quantitative nature, a good deal of algebra and some calculus are involved. However, the student is not expected to have taken more than a first course in calculus and a first course in statistics. Numerical examples are presented to illustrate complex algebraic equations, so that even the students with a relatively weak mathematical background should be able to grasp the essence of the propositions discussed. The emphasis is generally on the theoretical principles applicable to the problems involved rather than on the mathematical techniques available for their solution.

The book has grown out of teaching advanced courses in business finance for a good many years, first at Wayne State University and later at Rensselaer Polytechnic Institute. It has consistently been my experience that a large proportion of students enrolled in these courses have been handicapped in their analytical efforts by an insufficient knowledge of economic theory. I have, therefore, found it useful and, in fact, essential to spend some time reviewing those parts of economic theory (both micro and macro) which are most relevant to the analytical problems encountered in the field of business finance. This explains the inclusion in the present volume of Chapter 2, which contains a review of the marginal productivity theory as it applies to capital as a factor of production, and of Chapter 12, which contains a review of the theory of interest and of the interest-investment-income relationships in the national economy. These reviews are relatively compact and limited in scope, but the topics selected for discussion are treated so as to acquaint the student with a fairly advanced level of economic analysis.

More specifically, the plan of the book is as follows. Part I is concerned with microfinance: the financial problems and policies of an individual firm, particularly a corporate enterprise with marketable securities. Chapter 1 contains a brief outline of the basic accounting and economic concepts required for a meaningful financial analysis. Chapter 2, as already mentioned above, contains an economic analysis of capital as a factor of production. Chapter 3 examines alternative profit maximization criteria and the optimal amounts and time periods of investment. Chapters 4, 5, and 6 are devoted to stock valuation problems. The discussion in these chapters is based on the assumption that the firm's objective is to maximize the present value of the expected dividend stream. It is assumed at first that only internal financing (profit retention) is available to the firm; next, external equity financing is introduced and its effects are examined; and finally, the effects of debt financing and financial leverage are analyzed.

In Chapter 7, the concepts of the cost of funds obtained from various sources and of the average cost of the firm's total capital are analyzed. Chapter 8 is concerned with depreciation as a source of funds. Whereas in the earlier chapters only the net component of internal financing (i.e., the retained profit) is taken into account, the depreciation component is now examined in some detail. Finally, in Chapter 9, some alternative valuation and investment criteria are discussed. The problem of total profit versus dividend maximization is considered and the hypothesis of sales rather than profit maximization is discussed.

Part II is concerned with macrofinance: the capital market, the flow of capital funds, and the factors determining the aggregate volume of investment in the economic system. The basic financial flows and the major types of financial intermediaries are discussed in Chapter 10. The flow-of-

funds accounting system is described in Chapter 11. Following this description of the capital markets and financial flows, an analysis of the factors
determining the price of loanable funds—i.e., the interest rate—is presented
in Chapter 12. Both nonmonetary and monetary theories of the interest rate
are examined and a simple static macroeconomic model is outlined in that
chapter. A more complex dynamic model is presented in the Appendix.

Chapters 13, 14, and 15 are concerned with a more detailed analysis
of some of the factors and relationships which could not be adequately
treated in the simple models presented in Chapter 12. In Chapter 13, corporate internal financing is introduced as a separate variable in a macro-
economic model, and certain theoretical implications of a switch from
external to internal financing (and vice versa) are explored. Chapter 14
contains a discussion—on both theoretical and empirical levels—of the factors determining the aggregate volume of business investment in our
economy. Chapter 15 gives recognition to the fact that in the real world
there is a variety of interest rates rather than a single rate for all financial
transactions at a given time. The problem of the term structure of interest
rates is examined in some detail. Finally, Chapter 16 may be considered as
a historical appendix. It examines the long-term trends in financing capital
formation in the United States over the period comprising roughly the last
quarter of the nineteenth and the first half of the twentieth century.

Since the book is relatively short, most instructors will probably want
to supplement it with additional reading assignments. On the other hand,
some instructors may wish to omit a chapter or two, which I believe could
be done without making the rest of the text unintelligible.

It is a pleasure to acknowledge my indebtedness to all those who have
helped so generously in the preparation of this volume. Professor Charles
A. D'Ambrosio of the University of Washington has reviewed the entire
manuscript and made numerous valuable suggestions. Substantial portions
of the manuscript have also been reviewed by Professor William J. Baumol
of Princeton University and Professor Eugene F. Brigham of the University
of Wisconsin, whose comments have been most helpful. My colleagues in
the Department of Economics at Rensselaer, especially Professors Stanley
B. Brzyski, Romesh K. Diwan, Earl S. Paul, and Alexej Wynnyczuk, have
been very cooperative in reading some of the chapters and discussing various
points with me. Dean Ronald A. Mueller offered continual encouragement over the entire period of my involvement with this project.

I am also indebted to all graduate students who have taken my courses
and helpfully participated in the discussions—in and out of the classroom—
of the various problems concerned. Special thanks are due to Leonard
Bronitsky, my regular student assistant, who has carefully read the entire
manuscript, checked most of the algebra, and helped weed out a number of
numerical and other errors. Mrs. Beverly Barlow tirelessly and efficiently

typed and retyped chapter after chapter of the successive versions of the manuscript. And last, but not least, my wife, Tamara, deserves credit not only for her general encouragement of my work, but also for the many hours spent in proofreading the typescript.

Sergei P. Dobrovolsky

The Economics of Corporation Finance

part one

Financial Problems of the Firm

1
Introduction

Broadly defined, the area of business finance comprises all operations of business firms directed toward the procurement of capital funds and their investment in the various types of assets. Capital funds are obtained from a variety of sources and may be classified in different ways. To begin with, two major categories must be distinguished: the internal and the external financing.

Internal funds are obtained by retention of a portion of the firm's own revenue stream. There are two major components of internal financing: (a) capital consumption allowances, which essentially represent funds retained for the purpose of durable asset replacement, and (b) undistributed net profits, which, in principle, represent funds available for asset expansion. The sum of components (a) and (b) will be referred to as "gross internal financing," whereas component (b) alone will be referred to as "net internal financing."[1]

---

[1] This corresponds to the terms "gross investment" and "net investment," as used in the national income accounting. As is well known, in actual practice it is sometimes difficult to draw the line precisely between replacement and expansion of assets. The problems involved in this connection are discussed in Chap. 8.

External financing represents a transfer of capital funds to the firm in question from other business units or individuals in the form of loans or additional ownership (equity) capital. When such a transfer takes place, the unit releasing the funds acquires a claim (or a financial asset), while the unit receiving the funds incurs a liability. To put it differently, the same transaction represents a use of funds from the standpoint of the releasing unit and a source of funds from the standpoint of the receiving unit.

When all economic units in a national economy are considered as a whole, all domestic claims and liabilities cancel out and the economy's total assets are equal to its stock of physical goods plus the net balance of claims and liabilities vis-à-vis foreign countries. From the standpoint of an individual firm, however, claims on other economic units within the national economy usually represent a significant component of its total operating assets. In fact, in the case of financial institutions, total assets consist almost entirely of such claims.

THE ACCOUNTING FRAMEWORK

A firm's financial policy is reflected in its basic accounting statements: the balance sheet, the income account, and the statement of sources and uses of funds.

The balance sheet is a "stock" statement. It presents the data on the firm's assets, liabilities, and net worth as of a given moment of time, usually at the end of the firm's accounting year. In a simplified form the balance sheet of a manufacturing corporation may be drawn up as follows:

Balance Sheet of XYZ Corporation
December 31, 1969
(in thousands of dollars)

Cash	100	Accounts payable	220
Marketable securities	200	Accrued taxes	180
Accounts receivable	300	Total current liabilities	400
Inventories	400	Long-term debt	600
Total current assets	1,000	Capital stock	400
Plant and equipment (gross)	2,000	Capital (paid-in) surplus	200
Less: Depreciation reserve	800	Earned surplus	600
Plant and equipment (net)	1,200		
Total assets	2,200	Total liabilities and net worth	2,200

The statement indicates that on December 31, 1969 the firm's net worth—the sum of Capital Stock, Paid-in Surplus, and Earned Surplus—was $1,200,000; its total debt—the sum of short-term liabilities and long-term debt—was $1,000,000; and its total invested capital was $2,200,000. The sum of Capital Stock and Paid-in Surplus represents total paid-in equity. In the absence of accounting revaluations and transfers, it is equal to the actual amount of funds received by the firm from its stockholders. Earned Surplus represents the accumulated amount of net internal financing. If stock dividends have never been declared, it will show total accumulation of profits retained since the company's inception. But if stock dividends have been declared, this must have involved transfers from the Earned Surplus to the Capital Stock account. When such transfers take place, the subsequent balance sheets will no longer give an accurate indication of how much of the firm's equity has been paid in and how much has resulted from profit retention.

The asset side of the balance sheet indicates that on December 31, 1969, the company's physical assets—Inventories, Plant, and Equipment— amounted to $1,600,000, while its financial assets—Cash, Marketable Securities, and Receivables—totaled $600,000.

The balance sheet figures on both sides represent book values, which may differ widely from current market values, especially under inflationary (or deflationary) conditions when the general price level shows significant and persistent changes. Investors in corporate stocks usually focus attention on the market price of a firm's stock and pay relatively little attention to the book value of the firm's equity. When business assets are sold by one firm to another, the buyer is also interested primarily in the market value of the property acquired. However, the balance sheet figures tell a significant story of their own, inasmuch as they indicate the amounts of funds actually invested by the firm in its various assets.[2] They are, therefore, of importance to the financial analyst and the economist engaged in financial research.

In contrast to the balance sheet, the income statement is a "flow" statement. It indicates the amount of revenues received and of expenditures incurred *during* a stated period of time, typically one year. In a simplified form, a corporate income statement may be presented as follows:

**Income Statement of XYZ Corporation
for the Year 1970
(in thousands of dollars)**

Total revenue (sales)	3,000
Cost of sales (includes depreciation allowance of 200)	2,570
	430
Interest on debt	30
	400
Corporate income tax*	200
	200
Dividends	120
Retained profit	80

* It is assumed that the corporate income tax for 1970 is accrued during that year but paid in 1971.

[2] The picture may, however, be seriously distorted if major asset revaluations have been made.

The statement indicates that the company's net profit after tax for the year 1970 was $200,000, of which $120,000 was distributed as dividends and $80,000 was retained. The latter amount represents the company's net internal financing in 1970. The statement also indicates that the depreciation allowance in that year was $200,000. The company's gross internal financing was, therefore, equal to $80,000 + $200,000 = $280,000.

Both the internal and the external financing obtained by the company during the year must be reflected in its end-of-the-year balance sheet. Let the company's balance sheet at the end of 1970 be as follows:

Balance Sheet of XYZ Corporation
December 31, 1970
(in thousands of dollars)

Cash	100	Accounts payable	270
Marketable securities	200	Accrued taxes	200
Accounts receivable	350	Total current liabilities	470
Inventories	500	Long-term debt	700
Total current assets	1,150	Capital stock	400
Plant and equipment (gross)	2,200	Capital surplus	200
Depreciation reserve	900	Earned surplus	680
Plant and equipment (net)	1,300		
Total assets	2,450	Total liabilities and net worth	2,450

Comparing the end-of-the-year figures with those at the beginning of the year, we see that Earned Surplus increased by $80,000, which corresponds to the amount of profit retained, as shown in the income statement. Notice, however, that Depreciation Reserve shows an increase of only $100,000, although the depreciation allowance for the year is equal to $200,000. This difference is due to the fact that some items have been fully depreciated during the year, and therefore, removed from both Plant and Equipment and Depreciation Reserve accounts. If we assume that $300,000 worth of new equipment was purchased during the year, while $100,000 worth of old equipment was written off, then the following entries must be recorded in the accounts concerned.

Plant and Equipment				*Depreciation Reserve*			
Balance,		Written off		Written off		Balance,	
1/1/70	2,000	during 1970	100	during 1970	100	1/1/70	800
Purchased		Balance,		Balance,		Allowance	
during 1970	300	12/31/70	2,200	12/31/70	900	for 1970	200
	2,300		2,300		1,000		1,000

The net amount of Plant and Equipment at the end of 1970 is equal to $2,200,000 − $900,000 = $1,300,000, and the net increase over the year is $100,000. We may say, then, that of the $300,000 spent on new equipment, $200,000 represents replacement investment and $100,000 net investment.

By comparing the two balance sheets we may also determine changes in the other accounts, both on the asset and on the liability side. Combining all the information provided by the balance sheets, the income statement, the Plant and Equipment account, and the Depreciation Reserve account, we may draw up a statement of sources and uses of funds for the year 1970.

Statement of Sources and Uses of Funds of XYZ Corporation for the Year 1970

Uses		*Sources*	
Accounts receivable	50	External:	
Inventory	100	Accounts payable	50
Plant and equipment	300	Accrued taxes	20
		Long-term debt	100
			170
		Internal:	
		Depreciation allowance	200
		Retained profit	80
			280
Total	450	Total	450

The statement shows that the company absorbed during the year $170,000 of external funds and $280,000 of internal funds. These funds were used to purchase new equipment, expand the inventory, and extend more credit to the company's customers.

The above is, of course, only a thumbnail sketch of corporate financial accounting. The accounting nomenclature and procedures have been greatly simplified. Yet, it should convey the gist of the concepts and relationships involved.

THE ECONOMIC FRAMEWORK

In economic theory the business firm's operations have traditionally been analyzed in terms of revenue and cost functions. It has been assumed that the objective of the firm is the maximization of profit, i.e., of the difference between total revenue and total cost.

The firm's total revenue is equal to its physical output times the unit price at which the output is sold. Under conditions of pure competition, the market price cannot be influenced by an individual firm, and its total revenue is a linear function of its output. When competition is imperfect, the price declines as the firm's output increases and the revenue function assumes a nonlinear shape.

The firm's total cost is equal to the sum of the quantities of the various inputs (or factors of production), each multiplied by its price. Again, if pure competition prevails in the factor markets, the factor prices cannot be influenced by the firm's actions. Under conditions of imperfect competition, however, the factor prices rise as the quantities employed by the firm increase.

In the short run, the firm's invested capital is assumed to remain constant. In order to maximize profit, the firm must then determine, first, the least-cost combination of variable inputs for each of the different outputs that can be produced and, secondly, the particular output that will result in the greatest amount of profit. In a competitive equilibrium position, each variable factor will be employed up to the point at which its marginal cost is equal to the marginal revenue attributable to it.

In the long run, on the other hand, the invested capital may be changed. The firm will maximize profit by making additional capital investments up to the point at which their marginal cost is equal to the marginal revenue attributable to them. But the revenues resulting from an investment outlay made at a particular time can be realized only in a later period, and usually not in one lump sum but as a series of receipts distributed over time. It follows that, in comparing receipts with expenditures, not only the amounts involved but also their timing must be taken into account. Moreover, since the realization of future revenues may not, as a rule, be taken as certain, the risks associated with expected streams of receipts must also be given consideration.

In order to take account of the timing and risk factors, it becomes necessary to compare not the expected revenue and expenditure streams as such, but their present (capitalized) values. For each stream, an appropriate capitalization factor must be applied, reflecting the degree of risk involved. The advantages of the present value concept are such that some economists now prefer to define the objective of the firm in terms of wealth maximization rather than profit maximization. According to this view, to produce the greatest amount of benefits for its owners, the firm must seek to maximize its net worth—not the book value, of course, but the market value of its equity, which is determined by capitalizing the expected net profit stream. This approach brings into sharper focus the close relation between economic theory and financial analysis.

Realization of the firm's objectives requires a close coordination between its financial plans and policies and its production, pricing, and marketing policies. Our concern in Part I of this book is with the major financial problems relating to the optimal size and structure of the firm's capital, the cost of capital and the rate of return, capital expansion opportunities with internal and external funds, the choice between debt and equity financing, and the effect of financial leverage. These problems will be examined in the following chapters in considerable detail, within the framework of basic economic theory. We shall begin by reviewing the essential characteristics of capital as a factor of production.

SELECTED REFERENCES

Lerner, Eugene M., and Willard T. Carleton: *A Theory of Financial Analysis*, Harcourt, Brace and World, Inc., New York, 1966, chaps. 1 and 2.
Solomon, Ezra: *The Theory of Financial Management*, Columbia University Press, New York, 1963, chaps. I and II.
Vickers, Douglas: *The Theory of the Firm*, McGraw-Hill Book Company, New York, 1968, chap. 1.
Weston, Fred J., and Eugene F. Brigham: *Managerial Finance*, Holt, Rinehart and Winston, New York, 1966, chap. 1.

2
Capital as a Factor
of Production

In the traditional economic theory, the things which are necessary for production to be carried on, or factors of production, have been grouped into three major classes: labor, land, and capital.[1] Land and capital both represent stocks of physical goods; but while land includes all non-reproducible natural resources, "capital" is defined as the sum of all goods that have been produced in the economy and are used for further production rather than immediate consumption.

Of course, this threefold classification is oversimplified. Neither labor nor land nor capital consists of simple homogeneous units. In modern production theory, output is considered to be the function of a multitude of productive factors or inputs. Algebraically, this may be expressed as

$$Q = f(a_1, a_2, \ldots, a_n)$$

---

[1] Sometimes, management has been treated as a separate factor of production, making four factors in all. However, it may also be considered as a special high-level kind of labor.

where Q is the output and $a_1, a_2, \ldots, a_n$ are the quantities used of the factors $A_1, A_2, \ldots, A_n$, respectively. Some of these inputs represent different kinds of labor; others, different kinds of natural resources; still others, different kinds of reproducible capital goods.

In analyzing capital inputs on the individual firm level, account must be taken of both physical and financial assets. The economic calculus used for the determination of optimum input amounts is basically the same for both types of assets. In totaling the stock of capital employed by the entire national economy, on the other hand, the financial assets representing domestic claims are offset by the domestic obligations. National capital therefore consists of physical assets plus the net balance (positive or negative) of foreign claims.

MARGINAL COST AND MARGINAL REVENUE CONCEPTS

It is a familiar proposition in economic theory that a firm trying to maximize its profits should employ each factor up to the point at which its marginal cost (total cost increment resulting from hiring the last unit of the factor in question) is equal to its marginal revenue product (total revenue increment due to the production and sale of a larger output as a result of hiring that last factor unit). Of course, in virtually every realistic situation there is a significant interval that separates the time when the costs are incurred from the time when the revenues are realized. A certain adjustment is, therefore, required in order to make the costs and the revenues strictly comparable to each other. To begin with, however, we shall briefly consider a simplified situation in which the production period is assumed to be so short that the time factor may be ignored.

The marginal physical product of each productive factor is represented in mathematical terms by the first partial derivative of output with respect to the input in question:

$$\frac{\partial Q}{\partial a_1}, \frac{\partial Q}{\partial a_2}, \ldots, \frac{\partial Q}{\partial a_n}$$

If the firm operates under conditions of pure competition in the factor market, the price it pays for the factors will remain the same irrespective of the quantities employed. Therefore, the marginal cost of each factor will be equal to its price per unit, w_i:

Marginal cost of $a_1 = w_1$
. . . .
Marginal cost of $a_n = w_n$

Furthermore, if the conditions of pure competition prevail also in the market for the firm's product, the product price p will also remain constant irrespective of the firm's output. The marginal revenue product of each factor will then be equal to its marginal physical product times the product price:

$$\text{Marginal revenue product of } a_1 = \frac{\partial Q}{\partial a_1} p$$

. . . .

$$\text{Marginal revenue product of } a_n = \frac{\partial Q}{\partial a_n} p$$

The firm's total profit P is equal to its total revenue R less total cost C:

$$P = R - C = Qp - (a_1 w_1 + a_2 w_2 + \cdots + a_n w_n)$$

or

$$P = pf(a_1, a_2, \ldots, a_n) - a_1 w_1 - a_2 w_2 - \cdots - a_n w_n$$

Total profit is maximized when

$$\frac{\partial P}{\partial a_1} = p \frac{\partial Q}{\partial a_1} - w_1 = 0 \qquad \text{or} \qquad w_1 = p \frac{\partial Q}{\partial a_1}$$

. . . .

$$\frac{\partial P}{\partial a_n} = p \frac{\partial Q}{\partial a_n} - w_n = 0 \qquad \text{or} \qquad w_n = \frac{\partial Q}{\partial a_n}$$

It should be mentioned that economists define "profit" as the excess of total revenue over the cost of *all* factors employed, including equity capital and managerial services. Under purely competitive conditions, the maximum *economic* profit, realizable with an optimum combination of factors, is zero. Any other—less than optimum—combination of factors would result in a negative economic profit.[2]

---

[2] In a competitive equilibrium the output of a firm employing the optimum quantities of inputs may be written (according to Euler's theorem) as follows:

$$Q = \frac{\partial Q}{\partial a_1} a_1 + \cdots + \frac{\partial Q}{\partial a_n} a_n$$

Multiplying both sides by p we obtain

$$Qp = \frac{\partial Q}{\partial a_1} pa_1 + \cdots + \frac{\partial Q}{\partial a_n} pa_n$$

But when profit is maximized, we have $(\partial Q/\partial a_1)p = w_1$, etc., and it follows that

$$Qp = w_1 a_1 + \cdots + w_n a_n \qquad \text{or} \qquad R = C$$

If the factor prices and the product price vary depending on the quantities employed and sold by the firm (which means that the firm is operating under conditions of imperfect competition), then the marginal cost of each factor exceeds the price paid per unit of this factor, and the marginal revenue product falls short of the marginal physical product times the product price. The marginal cost of input a_i is now equal to

$$\frac{\partial C}{\partial a_i} = \frac{\partial w_i}{\partial a_i}a_i + w_i$$

and the marginal revenue product of input a_i is now equal to:

$$\frac{\partial R}{\partial a_i} = \frac{\partial(Qp)}{\partial a_i} = \frac{\partial Q}{\partial a_i}p + \frac{\partial p}{\partial Q}\frac{\partial Q}{\partial a_i}Q = \frac{\partial Q}{\partial a_i}\left(p + \frac{\partial P}{\partial Q}Q\right)$$

where $\partial P/\partial Q < 0$.

When the firm's profit is maximized, the following equations must hold:

$$w_1 + \frac{\partial w_1}{\partial a_1}a_1 = \frac{\partial Q}{\partial a_1}\left(p + \frac{\partial P}{\partial Q}Q\right)$$

$$\cdots \cdots \cdots \cdots \cdots \cdots$$

$$w_n + \frac{\partial w_n}{\partial a_n}a_n = \frac{\partial Q}{\partial a_n}\left(p + \frac{\partial p}{\partial Q}Q\right)$$

THE ROLE OF THE TIME FACTOR IN PRODUCTION: A SIMPLE CASE

Let us now consider more realistic situations in which the time factor plays a significant role. To take the simplest possible case, let us assume that output is a function of only one factor (labor, L), but that it takes a significant period of time for this factor to produce a finished product. We shall also assume that the wages are paid at the beginning of the production period, while the product is finished and sold at the beginning of the next period, and that the wage rate w and product price p remain constant over time. We may then write the production function as:

$$Q_{t+1} = f(L_t)$$

Total revenue realized at the beginning of period $t + 1$ is

$$R_{t+1} = Q_{t+1}p$$

and the marginal revenue product of labor is

$$\frac{dR_{t+1}}{dL_t} = \frac{dp}{dL_t}Q_{t+1} + \frac{dQ_{t+1}}{dL_t}p$$

If we assume that the price of the product p is independent of the number of units sold (pure competition in the product market), then the first term on the right-hand side of the last equation is equal to zero, and the marginal revenue product is

$$\frac{dQ_{t+1}}{dL_t}p$$

Total cost incurred at the beginning of period t is

$$C_t = wL_t$$

In order to compare the cost incurred at the beginning of period t with the revenue realized at the beginning of period $t + 1$, one must take into account the interest on the capital funds invested for one period. If the funds had not been used to pay the wages of the workers concerned, they could have been invested outside of the firm at a certain rate of interest. The maximum rate available to the firm, without incurring greater risks than those involved in its own operations, represents the opportunity cost which must be added to the wages paid at the beginning of period t in order to arrive at the firm's total cost of producing the output Q_{t+1}. Total cost incurred over the entire production period t may then be written as

$$C_{t+1} = wL_t(1 + i)$$

where i is the highest interest rate available to the firm on outside investments.[3]

---

[3] In this and the following formulas, the interest rate is expressed not in percentage points but as a fraction: e.g., the rate of 5 percent would be stated as .05. The reader may be reminded that the basic compound interest formula for annual compounding is

$$y = x(1 + r)^t$$

where x is the initial amount invested, r is the annual interest rate, and t is the number of years for which x is invested.

If interest is compounded n times a year, the formula becomes

$$y = x\left(1 + \frac{r}{n}\right)^{nt}$$

and if n is infinitely large, as it is in the case of continuous compounding, we obtain

$$y = xe^{rt} \qquad e = 2.71828 \ldots$$

The present value of an amount to be received or paid in the future is derived by discounting this amount over the period concerned at an appropriate interest rate. In the case of

The marginal cost of labor is

$$\frac{dC_{t+1}}{dL_t} = \frac{d[wL_t(1+i)]}{dL_t} = \frac{dw}{dL_t}L_t(1+i) + w(1+i)$$

Again, if the wage rate w is independent of the number of labor units employed by the firm (pure competition in the labor market), then the first term on the right-hand side is equal to zero, and the marginal cost of labor is equal to $w(1+i)$. The firm will maximize its profit by employing labor up to the point at which the marginal cost of labor, including the interest, is equal to its marginal revenue product:

$$w(1+i) = \frac{dQ_{t+1}}{dL_t}p$$

Alternatively, one may say that the firm's profit is maximized when the wage rate is equal to the marginal revenue product of labor discounted for one period at the market rate of interest or, in other words, when it is equal to the present value (at the beginning of period t) of the marginal revenue product

$$w = \frac{dQ_{t+1}}{dL_t}p(1+i)^{-1}$$

Consider now a slightly more complex situation, in which the output sold at the beginning of period $t + 1$ is a function of both labor and capital goods used during period t. With respect to labor, we assume again that it was hired and paid at the beginning of period t. As for the capital goods, we shall begin by assuming that (1) they were produced by only one factor (labor), which was hired and paid at the beginning of period $t - 1$, and (2) they can last only one period, so that the goods acquired by the firm at the beginning of period t are completely used up by the end of that period. We may then write the production function as follows:

$$Q_{t+1} = f(L_t, K_t)$$

---

annual discounting, we may write

$$v = z(1 + r)^{-t}$$

while in the case of continuous discounting we have

$$v = ze^{-rt}$$

where z is the amount to be discounted and v is its present value.

where K_t denotes the capital goods used during period t. Since these goods were produced by labor employed in period $t - 1$, L_{t-1}, we may also write

$$K_t = F(L_{t-1})$$

As in the previous case, total revenue realized at the beginning of period $t + 1$ is equal to

$$R_{t+1} = Q_{t+1}p$$

Under conditions of pure competition the marginal revenue product of the labor employed in period t is equal to

$$\frac{\partial R_{t+1}}{\partial L_t} = \frac{\partial Q_{t+1}}{\partial L_t} p$$

and the marginal revenue product of the capital goods used during period t is

$$\frac{\partial R_{t+1}}{\partial K_t} = \frac{\partial Q_{t+1}}{\partial K_t} p$$

Total cost of producing the output Q_{t+1} consists of the wages paid to the labor employed in period t plus the wages paid to the labor employed in period $t - 1$ (to produce the capital goods) plus the interest on the capital funds invested in both periods. The funds invested at the beginning of period $t - 1$ amount to wL_{t-1}, and interest must be computed on this amount for two periods. The funds invested at the beginning of period t amount to wL_t, and interest must be computed on this amount for one period. Total cost incurred over the two periods in question is

$$C_{t+1} = wL_t(1 + i) + wL_{t-1}(1 + i)^2$$

The marginal cost of L_t and L_{t-1} is

$$\frac{\partial C_{t+1}}{\partial L_t} = w(1 + i)$$

and

$$\frac{\partial C_{t+1}}{\partial L_{t-1}} = w(1 + i)^2$$

In order to maximize its profit, the firm must employ each factor to the point at which its marginal cost equals its marginal revenue product. For the labor employed in period t we have

$$w(1 + i) = \frac{\partial Q_{t+1}}{\partial L_t}p \qquad \text{or} \qquad w = \frac{\partial Q_{t+1}}{\partial L_t}p(1 + i)^{-1}$$

For the capital goods (i.e., for the labor employed in period $t - 1$) we have

$$w(1 + i)^2 = \left(\frac{\partial Q_{t+1}}{\partial K_t}\right)\left(\frac{\partial K_t}{\partial L_{t-1}}\right)p = \frac{\partial Q_{t+1}}{\partial L_{t-1}}p$$

or

$$w = \frac{\partial Q_{t+1}}{\partial L_{t-1}}p(1 + i)^{-2}$$

Since $(1 + i)^2$ is greater than $1 + i$, the marginal cost and the marginal revenue product of L_{t-1} are greater than the marginal cost and the marginal revenue product of L_t. And since p remains the same in both expressions, it is clear that the difference must be due entirely to greater physical productivity of L_{t-1}, as compared with L_t. If this were not so, it would obviously be more profitable for the owners of capital funds to invest them for one period by paying the wages of L_t than to make an investment for two periods by paying the wages of L_{t-1}. In order for both these investments to earn the same rate of return, the ratio of the marginal revenue product of L_t to the marginal revenue product of L_{t-1} must be equal to $(1 + i)/(1 + i)^2 = 1/(1 + i)$.

The importance of the time element in production processes was analyzed most elaborately by the economists of the Austrian school. One of the leading representatives of this school, E. von Böhm-Bawerk, distinguished between the more time-consuming, "roundabout" methods of production and the less time-consuming direct methods, and argued that the former are more productive than the latter. Few would deny the validity of this proposition in a general way. There is no uniform agreement, however, as to von Böhm-Bawerk's more specific and stronger proposition that every increase in the length of the productive process necessarily increases total output, although at a diminishing rate.[4]

LONGER PRODUCTION PERIODS

Suppose now that production of capital goods takes longer than just one period, $t - 1$, while their useful lifetime is still limited to one period, t. If

[4] For a summary of von Böhm-Bawerk's theory, see M. Blaug: *Economic Theory in Retrospect*, Richard D. Irwin, Inc., Homewood, Ill., 1968, chap. 12.

we assume that production of K_t extends over two previous periods, but only one factor—labor—is involved, we may write

$$Q_{t+1} = f(L_t, K_t)$$

and

$$K_t = F(L_{t-1}, L_{t-2})$$

Total cost of Q_{t+1} is then equal to

$$C_{t+1} = wL_t(1 + i) + wL_{t-1}(1 + i)^2 + wL_{t-2}(1 + i)^3$$

The marginal cost of labor is, as before, equal to

$$\frac{\partial C_{t+1}}{\partial L_t} = w(1 + i)$$

But the marginal cost of capital is now

$$\frac{\partial C_{t+1}}{\partial K_t} = \frac{\partial C_{t+1}}{\partial [F(L_{t-1}, L_{t-2})]}$$

If we assume, for simplicity's sake, that the two labor inputs in the two periods must always be applied in the same proportion, so that $L_{t-2} = \alpha L_{t-1}$, we may write

$$C_{t+1} = wL_t(1 + i) + wL_{t-1}[(1 + i)^2 + \alpha(1 + i)^3]$$

and we may then express the marginal cost of capital in terms of L_{t-1} alone:

$$\frac{\partial C_{t+1}}{\partial L_{t-1}} = w[(1 + i)^2 + \alpha(1 + i)^3]$$

The optimal amount of capital to be employed is again at the point at which

$$\frac{\partial C_{t+1}}{\partial L_{t-1}} = \frac{\partial R_{t+1}}{\partial L_{t-1}}$$

But our assumption that capital goods were produced in periods $t - 1$ and $t - 2$ by labor alone is, of course, unrealistic. In the real world capital goods cannot be produced by workers using their bare hands.

Their production always involves the use of both labor and previously manufactured tools. Suppose that the currently used capital equipment K_t was manufactured in the preceding period $t - 1$ by employing labor L_{t-1} and previously manufactured equipment K_{t-1}^*; that K_{t-1}^* in its turn was produced in period $t - 2$ by labor L_{t-2} and previously manufactured equipment K_{t-2}^*; and so on. We then have an infinite series of labor inputs: $L_{t-1}, L_{t-2}, L_{t-3}, \ldots, L_{t-n}$, where $n \to \infty$. This does not, however, mean that the total amount of labor involved in producing K_t is infinitely large. The series concerned consists of successively diminishing values ($L_{t-1} > L_{t-2} > L_{t-3} > \cdots$) and the sum of its terms approaches a finite limit.

To put it differently, we may say that while the absolute period of production may be infinite, the *average* period (i.e., the weighted average of all the intervals betwen the input of labor and the final output) has a finite value.[5]

The cost of K_t must, of course, also be finite—no firm could afford to use equipment whose cost was infinitely high. It is equal to

$$C_{K_t} = wL_{t-1}(1 + i) + wL_{t-2}(1 + i)^2 + \cdots$$

when computed at the beginning of period t. The marginal cost of K_t is equal to

$$\frac{\partial C_{K_t}}{\partial K_t} = \frac{\partial[wL_{t-1}(1 + i) + wL_{t-2}(1 + i)^2 \cdots]}{\partial[F(L_{t-1}, L_{t-2}, \ldots)]}$$

The optimum amount of K_t is, as before, at the point where

$$\frac{\partial C_{K_t}}{\partial K_t} = \frac{\partial V_t}{\partial K_t}$$

where V is the present value of total revenue, computed at time t.

PRODUCTION WITH DURABLE CAPITAL GOODS

Let us now consider a case in which the durability of the capital goods is longer than one period. For simplicity's sake, however, we shall assume once more that capital equipment can be produced during one period and

---

[5] Attempts to provide a precise definition and a generally acceptable formula for measuring the average period of production have met with considerable difficulties. This has led some authors to deny the usefulness of this concept. However, others have defended its use, at least for some types of production processes. For a brief discussion of conflicting views, followed by notes for further reading, see M. Blaug, *ibid.*, pp. 510–530 and 569–570.

by one factor only—labor. The initial cost of this equipment is, therefore, equal to the wages paid to the workers who produced it in period $t - 1$. The output sold at the beginning of period $t + 1$ is, as before, a function of labor and capital equipment used during period t:

$$Q_{t+1} = f(L_t, K_t) = F(L_t, L_{t-1})$$

But in this case, the capital goods K are not completely used up during period t but will continue to be used in the following periods. Assume that the equipment's lifetime is three periods. We may then write

$$Q_{t+2} = F(L_{t+1}, L_{t-1})$$
$$Q_{t+3} = F(L_{t+2}, L_{t-1})$$

At the end of period $t + 3$, however, the old equipment will have to be replaced by new equipment, and the output sold at the beginning of period $t + 4$ will be a function of the labor and the capital goods purchased at the beginning of period $t + 3$:

$$Q_{t+4} = f(L_{t+3}, K_{t+3}) = F(L_{t+3}, L_{t+2})$$

The marginal revenue product and the marginal cost of labor employed in each of the three periods t, $t + 1$, and $t + 2$ may be written as follows:

$$\frac{\partial R_{t+1}}{\partial L_t} = \frac{\partial Q_{t+1}}{\partial L_t} p \quad \text{and} \quad \frac{\partial C_{t+1}}{\partial L_t} = w(1 + i)$$

$$\frac{\partial R_{t+2}}{\partial L_{t+1}} = \frac{\partial Q_{t+2}}{\partial L_{t+1}} p \quad \text{and} \quad \frac{\partial C_{t+2}}{\partial L_{t+1}} = w(1 + i)$$

$$\frac{\partial R_{t+3}}{\partial L_{t+2}} = \frac{\partial Q_{t+3}}{\partial L_{t+2}} p \quad \text{and} \quad \frac{\partial C_{t+3}}{\partial L_{t+2}} = w(1 + i)$$

In each period, the optimal employment of labor will be achieved by equating the marginal revenue product of labor with its marginal cost.

Unfortunately, considerable difficulty is encountered in trying to apply a similar procedure to the determination of the optimal employment of durable capital goods. An increase in capital equipment at the beginning of period t may be expected to result in increased revenues in all three periods: $t, t + 1$, and $t + 2$. The marginal revenue product of the capital equipment in each of the three periods may be written as follows:

$$\frac{\partial R_{t+1}}{\partial K_t} = \frac{\partial Q_{t+1}}{\partial K_t} p$$

$$\frac{\partial R_{t+2}}{\partial K_t} = \frac{\partial Q_{t+2}}{\partial K_t} p$$

$$\frac{\partial R_{t+3}}{\partial K_t} = \frac{\partial Q_{t+3}}{\partial K_t} p$$

On the other hand, the entire cost of the new equipment installed at the beginning of period t is, by our assumption, incurred at that time. We cannot, therefore, compute the marginal cost of this equipment for each of the three periods separately, unless an appropriate method is used to allocate cost over time. Accountants and economists have been struggling with this problem for a long time, but no fully satisfactory and universally accepted method of such allocation has as yet been found.

In theoretical economics, another approach to the problem has been found more convenient and appropriate. The entire initial cost of durable capital equipment is compared with the entire stream of revenues attributable to this equipment, net of the cost of the other factors employed by the firm. (In the language of economic theory, these net revenues represent *quasi rents* earned by the durable capital equipment.) Of course, in order to be comparable to the original cost, the revenues realized in later periods must be discounted at an appropriate rate; in other words, their *present value* must be computed.

The optimum amount of capital is found at the point at which the cost of the marginal unit of equipment is equal to the present value of the sum of revenue increments attributable to the unit during its entire lifetime. In our example the present value of the sum of the marginal revenue products of capital equipment, computed at the beginning of period t, is equal to

$$\frac{\partial V_t}{\partial K_t} = \frac{\partial Q_{t+1}}{\partial K_t} p(1+i)^{-1} + \frac{\partial Q_{t+2}}{\partial K_t} p(1+i)^{-2} + \frac{\partial Q_{t+3}}{\partial K_t} p(1+i)^{-3}$$

where V_t is the present value of the entire revenue stream, computed at the beginning of period t—when capital equipment K_t is first put into operation.

Since the marginal cost of the capital equipment is, under our assumptions, equal to $w(1 + i)$ at the beginning of period t, the optimal amount of capital equipment is at the point at which

$$\frac{\partial V_t}{\partial K_t} = w(1 + i)$$

CONTINUOUS INPUTS AND OUTPUTS

In all the preceding sections it was assumed that factors were hired and paid for at stated discrete intervals and that outputs became available and were sold also at stated intervals (point-input–point-output process). We shall conclude by examining briefly the case in which both costs and revenues are continual flows during certain periods of time.

Let us make the following assumptions:

1. Labor is the only input, and it is used and paid for continually during the period $t - k$ to $t + m$. The rate of labor input need not be constant, but the rate of pay, w, remains constant over the entire period.

2. Outputs become available and are sold continually during the period t to $t + n$.

We wish to compute and compare the present values, at time t, of all the costs and all the revenues involved. The present value of all the costs is equal to the sum of the costs incurred during the period $t - k$ to t, compounded to the present, plus the sum of the costs incurred during the period t to $t + m$, discounted to the present. This may be written as

$$C_t = \int_{t-k}^{t} L(t)we^{rt}\, dt + \int_{t}^{t+m} L(t)we^{-rt}\, dt$$

where r is the "instantaneous" rate of interest, which assumes continuous compounding.

The present value of the sum of all the revenues realized during the period t to $t + n$ is equal to

$$V_t = \int_{t}^{t+n} R(t)e^{-rt}\, dt$$

Now, if the rate of input during the entire period $t - k$ to $t + m$ is increased by a small margin, the present value of all the costs incurred will also rise and the increment will be equal to

$$dC_t = d\left[\int_{t-k}^{t} L(t)we^{rt}\, dt + \int_{t}^{t+m} L(t)we^{-rt}\, dt\right]$$

$$= \int_{t-k}^{t} dL(t)we^{rt}\, dt + \int_{t}^{t+m} dL(t)we^{-rt}\, dt$$

Furthermore, the rate of output during the entire period t to $t + n$ will also rise, and the present value of all the revenues will show an increment equal to

$$dV_t = d \int_t^{t+n} R(t)e^{-rt} \, dt = \int_t^{t+n} dR(t)e^{-rt} \, dt$$

The firm's total profit will be maximized when the point is reached at which the present values of all the cost increments and of all the revenue increments are equal to each other: $dC_t = dV_t$.

SUMMARY

In production theory, output is considered to be a function of a large number of productive factors or inputs, some of which represent different kinds of labor, others represent different kinds of non-reproducible natural resources, and still others represent different kinds of reproducible capital goods.

In order to maximize profit, the firm must employ each factor up to the point at which its marginal cost equals its marginal revenue product. But since expenditures and revenues do not, as a rule, occur simultaneously, an adjustment must be made for the intervals that separate them. This can be made by computing the present (discounted) values of the amounts involved.

The time factor is especially important in connection with capital inputs. Capital goods are goods which have been produced in a previous time period and are being used for further production in the current period. If they are of a durable type, they will also be used in one or more subsequent periods. Therefore, in order to make a comparison between their cost and the revenues attributable to them, at a particular point in time, e.g., at the beginning of the current accounting period, one must take the initial expenditure plus the interest accrued up to this point and compare this total amount with the present value of the entire revenue stream which is expected to result from this investment. To maximize profit, the firm must increase the input of capital goods of each specific type up to the point at which the marginal cost increment (with interest) is equal to the discounted sum of all expected revenue increments.

In a going concern, inputs are made and outputs are realized continuously, and this involves continuous expenditure and revenue streams. The firm will maximize profit by increasing the rate of inputs per unit of time up to the point at which the present values of the entire streams of cost increments and revenue increments are equal to each other.

SELECTED REFERENCES

Henderson, James M., and R. E. Quandt: *Microeconomic Theory: A Mathematical Approach*, McGraw-Hill Book Company, New York, 1958, chap. 3.
Hirshleifer, J.: *Investment, Interest, and Capital*, Prentice-Hall, Inc., Englewood Cliffs, N.J., 1970, chap. 2.
Lutz, Friedrich, and Vera Lutz: *The Theory of Investment of the Firm*, Princeton University Press, Princeton, N.J., 1951, chap. 1.
Wicksell, Knut: *Lectures on Political Economy*, Routledge and Kegan Paul Ltd., London, 1961, vol. 1, part 2.

3
Profitability Measures and Profit Maximization Criteria

In the preceding chapter we considered the significance of the time element in production and emphasized the importance, from the standpoint of profit calculations, of comparing the cost of the marginal unit of each factor with the present (discounted) value of the future revenue increments attributable to the marginal unit concerned. We shall now take a closer look at the concept of profit and consider some alternative methods of measuring profitability of capital outlays.

THE AMOUNT OF PROFIT AND THE RATE OF RETURN

When investment in new durable equipment is considered, the following financial variables must be taken into account: the initial or "fixed" cost of the equipment, the operating or "variable" costs that will be incurred continually over the entire lifetime of the equipment, and the revenues attributable to the equipment over its entire lifetime. The initial cost is known exactly, while the operating costs and the revenues expected in the future can only be estimated with a varying degree of accuracy. We shall assume for the present that the estimates can be made quite accurately and that the degree of uncertainty is, therefore, negligible. The problems arising when there is a significant element of uncertainty, which must be taken into consideration, will be considered later.

In each unit period of time during its lifetime the equipment will yield a certain net revenue equal to the total revenue resulting from its use less the operating cost incurred during the unit period in question.[1] In the language of economic theory this net revenue represents a quasi rent earned by the equipment. Algebraically, we may write:

$$Q_t = R_t - E_t = p_t q_t - E_t$$

where Q_t is the quasi rent on the equipment in period t; R_t is total revenue, which is equal to price per unit of product, p_t, times the quantity sold, q_t; and E_t is the operating cost, which must be expected to vary with the volume of production.

The firm's total profit from the investment in question, P, is equal to the difference between the sum of the present values of all the quasi rents over the entire lifetime of the equipment, V, and the initial cost of the equipment, C. Mathematically:

$$P = V - C$$

$$V = \sum_{1}^{n} Q_t(1 + i)^{-t}$$

If Q is assumed to be a continuous variable, the present value V is equal to

$$V = \int_{1}^{n} Q_t e^{-it} \, dt \tag{3-1}$$

In the above expressions i represents the market rate of interest. If we assume that the firm operates in a simplified situation, in which it can borrow additional capital funds at a given constant rate of interest, and in which it can also lend its own funds at the same rate, then there is no question that this single market rate of interest must be used in computing the present value of every additional investment expenditure. In the actual world, there are, of course, not one but a variety of interest rates, applicable to different types of funds, but we shall ignore this complication for the present.

[1] The operating cost must be taken here exclusive of depreciation and interest charges.

In order to maximize its total profit, the firm must expand investment of capital funds in new equipment up to the point at which the present value of all the quasi rents attributable to the marginal unit of equipment equals its initial cost. At that point the marginal increment of profit will be equal to zero, and any further increase in capital investment will make the profit increment negative, thus reducing the total profit of the firm.

Mathematically, the condition for profit maximization may be written as

$$\frac{dP}{dC} = \frac{dV}{dC} - \frac{dC}{dC} = 0$$

or

$$\frac{dV}{dC} = \frac{dC}{dC} = 1 \tag{3-2}$$

The question now arises whether the maximization of the dollar amount of profit (P) also means the maximization of the rate of return on invested capital. In order to examine the relationships involved, we must introduce the concepts of the average and the marginal internal rate of return. To take a simple example, assume that a given amount C is invested for n years and that total revenue R is realized in one lump sum at the end of n years. The average internal rate of return on C is then equal to r_a in the compound interest formula

$$C(1 + r_a)^n = R$$

We may say that r_a represents the rate at which C must grow during the period of n years in order to become equal to R at the end of this period.

Alternatively, we may write:

$$C = R(1 + r_a)^{-n}$$

We may also say, then, that r_a represents the discount rate which equates the revenue R, realized at the end of n years, with the initial investment C, made at the beginning of the first year. Now, if C is increased by ΔC and this results in revenue increment equal to ΔR, the marginal internal rate of return is then equal to r_m in the equation

$$\Delta C = \Delta R(1 + r_m)^{-n}$$

When revenue is received as a series of quasi rents, distributed over the entire investment period, we may write

$$C = \frac{Q_1}{1 + r_a} + \frac{Q_2}{(1 + r_a)^2} + \cdots + \frac{Q_n}{(1 + r_a)^n} = \sum_1^n Q_t(1 + r_a)^{-n}$$

or

$$C = \int_1^n Q_t e^{-r_a t}\, dt \tag{3-3}$$

Here again, the average internal rate of return on C is equal to r_a.

The marginal internal rate of return is represented by r_m in the following expressions:

$$\Delta C = \sum_1^n \Delta Q_t(1 + r_m)^{-t}$$

or

$$dC = \int_1^n dQ_t e^{-r_m t}\, dt \tag{3-4}$$

The reader will observe that these expressions are similar to the one given above for the present value of a series of quasi rents (Equation 3-1) except for the substitution of r_a (or r_m) for i. It should be clear that if a firm's total profit is positive ($V > C$), then the average internal rate of return must exceed the interest rate ($r_a > i$). Similarly, if the marginal unit of the firm's investment yields a positive profit increment, then the marginal rate of return must exceed the interest rate ($r_m > i$). It does not follow, however, that the firm will maximize its total profit by maximizing either the average or the marginal rate of return on its invested capital. It will be shown in the next section that total profit is maximized by extending investment to the point at which $r_m = i$, and that neither r_m nor r_a is, as a rule, at its maximum at that point.

OPTIMAL INVESTMENT IN A GIVEN TIME PERIOD

Assume that capital investment C is made at the beginning of time period t and that revenue R is received in one lump sum at the end of this period. The investment period cannot be changed and the revenue is a function of the original investment C alone. We may then write:

$$R = f(C)$$
$$V = f(C)e^{-it}$$
$$P = V - C = f(C)e^{-it} - C$$

Profit is maximized when $dP/dC = 0$. Therefore, we have

$$\frac{dV}{dC} - \frac{dC}{dC} = f'(C)e^{-it} - \frac{dC}{dC} = 0$$

or

$$\frac{dV}{dC} = f'(C)e^{-it} = \frac{dR}{dC}e^{-it} = 1 \tag{3-5}$$

It will be recalled that i in the above expressions represents the market interest rate. The marginal rate of return in this case is represented by r_m in the expression

$$\frac{dC}{dC} = \frac{dR}{dC}e^{-r_m t} = 1 \tag{3-6}$$

Thus, when profit is maximized, we have

$$\frac{dR}{dC}e^{-it} = \frac{dR}{dC}e^{-r_m t} \tag{3-7}$$

from which it follows that $r_m = i$ at that point.[2] These relationships are illustrated diagrammatically in Figure 3-1, in which the initial cost of investment, C, is measured on the horizontal axis, while the undiscounted revenue R and the present value of this revenue, V, are measured on the vertical axis. The interest rate i and the period of investment are assumed constant for all values of C. If the interest rate were zero, V would be equal to R and maximum profit $(R - C)$ would be realized by making investment equal to Oa, since at that point the slope of the OR curve, dR/dC, is equal to the slope of the OC curve, $dC/dC = 1$. The marginal rate of return at that

---

[2] For a more detailed discussion see Friedrich and Vera Lutz, *The Theory of Investment of the Firm*, Princeton University Press, Princeton, N.J., 1951, chap. 2.

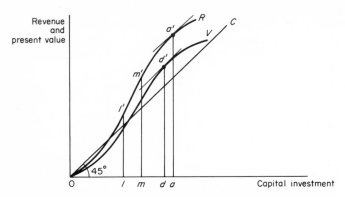

Figure 3-1   Determination of the most profitable volume of investment.

point is equal to zero, as is, by assumption, the interest rate:

$$\frac{dC}{dC} = 1 = \frac{dR}{dC}e^{-r_m t} = \frac{dR}{dC} \qquad \text{if } r_m = 0$$

The average rate of return, which is r_a in the expression $Ce^{r_a t} = R$, is greater than zero at the point of maximum profit since $R > C$. But, as shown below, it does not have its highest value when investment is equal to Oa.

At a positive rate of interest, on the other hand, V must be smaller than R. With the interest rate and the investment period being constant, the ratio of V to R also remains constant, irrespective of the value of C (i.e., V is equal to R multiplied by a constant factor e^{-it}). Profit must now be defined as $V - C$, and the point of maximum profit is reached when $dV/dC = dC/dC = 1$. Since the slope of V is less steep than the slope of R, the point of maximum profit is now reached with a smaller value of C than that found in the case of zero interest rate. In the diagram the maximum profit is now obtained when the capital investment is equal to Od.

The slope of the R curve, dR/dC, is now greater than 1 at the point of maximum profit. When discounted at the rate r_m, however, dR/dC becomes equal to $dC/dC = 1$. On the other hand, when discounted at the rate i, dR/dC becomes equal to dV/dC. But since $dV/dC = dC/dC$ when profit is maximized, it follows that $r_m = i$ at that point.

The amount of investment, C, which results in the greatest total amount of profit, $V - C$, does not coincide with the amount which yields either the highest average rate of return, r_a, or the highest marginal rate of return, r_m. The highest marginal rate of return is at the point at which the slope of the OR curve is greatest. This is the inflection point l' on the diagram. The amount

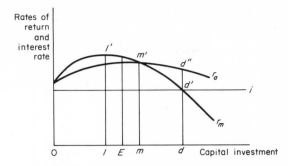

Figure 3-2 The relation between the average and the marginal rates of return and the interest rate.

of investment corresponding to this point is Ol. The highest average rate of return is at the point m', at which the marginal and the average rates are equal to each other. The amount of investment corresponding to this point is Om.

The relationship between the average and the marginal rates of return and the rate of interest may be seen more clearly by inspecting Figure 3-2.

The highest marginal rate of return, ll', is obtained by making investment equal to Ol, while the greatest average rate of return, mm', is obtained by extending investment to Om. But the maximum total profit is realized when investment is equal to Od, at which point the marginal rate of return, dd', is equal to the interest rate di. As the figure indicates, the average rate of return at the point of maximum profit is lower than it is when investment is limited to Om or, in fact, to any amount between Om and Od.

Table 3-1   The relation between cost, revenue, profit, and the rates of return

C	R_1	R_2	$R_1 + R_2$	V	P	r_a	r_m
100	60.00	60.00	120.00	104.13	4.13	.137	
110	67.00	67.00	134.00	116.28	6.28	.142	.251
120	75.00	75.00	150.00	130.17	10.17	.163	.380
130	85.00	85.00	170.00	147.52	17.52	.199	.618*
140	94.00	94.00	188.00	163.14	23.14	.221	.500
150	103.00	103.00	206.00	178.76	28.76	.240	.500
160	111.00	111.00	222.00	192.65	32.65	.249	.380
170	118.00	118.00	236.00	204.79	34.79	.250*	.251
180	124.00	124.00	248.00	215.10	35.10	.243	.131
190	129.75	129.75	258.50	225.19	35.19*	.233	.099
200	135.00	135.00	270.00	234.30	34.30	.226	.019
210	140.00	140.00	280.00	242.97	32.97	.215	.000

* Maximum value.

A simple numerical example, presented in Table 3-1, should help to clarify the relationships involved. It is assumed that the amount of initial investment, C, may vary from \$100 to \$210 by \$10 increments. The amount selected is invested at the beginning of year 1. Total revenue in each case is the sum of two amounts: R_1, which is received at the end of year 1, and R_2, which is received at the end of year 2. The present value of total revenue is derived as follows:

$$V = \frac{R_1}{1 + i} + \frac{R_2}{(1 + i)^2}$$

where i is the market interest rate, assumed to be equal to .1.

The average rate of return is equal to r_a in the expression

$$C = \frac{R_1}{1 + r_a} + \frac{R_2}{(1 + r_a)^2}$$

and the marginal rate of return is equal to r_m in the expression

$$\Delta C = \frac{\Delta R_1}{1 + r_m} + \frac{\Delta R_2}{(1 + r_m)^2}$$

It may be seen that r_m is maximized when $C = 130$ and that r_a is maximized when $C = 170$. But total profit, $P = V - C$, is maximized when $C = 190$, at which level r_m is very close to i (since investment is raised by finite increments, the exact equality of r_m and i cannot be attained).

The fact that the average rate of return is not at its highest point when total profit is maximized may seem surprising at first glance. But it must be borne in mind that we are discussing here the rate of return on the firm's total investment capital, which consists partly of the owners' equity and partly of borrowed funds. Assume, for example, that the owners' equity is equal to OE. Clearly, the owners will increase the average rate of return on their own funds and on the total capital by borrowing the amount Em. Furthermore, they will continue to increase the average rate of return on their own funds by additional borrowing—up to the point d—even though the average rate of return on total capital will begin to decline after point m has been reached. If they continue to borrow beyond the point d, however, the average rate of return on their own funds will begin to decline also.

Suppose, however, that the owners' equity is equal to Od. Would it not then be preferable, from the owners' standpoint, to limit investment to Om and maximize the average rate of return? The answer is no, because in that case the owners would realize the higher rate of return only on the portion of their capital equal to *Om*, while the other part of their capital, *md*, could be loaned out at only the market interest rate. The combined rate of return on the entire equity would be lower in this case than it would be if the entire amount were invested in the business, yielding an average return equal to *dd"*.

The mathematical proof that the average rate of return on the owners' equity is maximized at the same point at which total profit is maximized is as follows: Let E be the amount of equity and C the total amount of invested capital. Borrowed funds are then equal to $C - E$. The average rate of return on E is then equal to k in the expression

$$Ee^{kt} = R - (C - E)e^{it}$$

Since both E and t are constants, maximization of k coincides with maximization of Ee^{kt}. If we differentiate with respect to C and put the result equal to zero, we obtain

$$\frac{dR}{dC} - e^{it} = 0$$

or

$$\frac{dR}{dC}e^{-it} = 1$$

Thus, k is maximized at the same point at which $V - C$ is maximized, as shown above.

If the interest rate at which the firm can borrow funds is not constant but varies with the amount borrowed, the maximum profit position is obtained at the point of equality between the marginal internal rate of return and the marginal borrowing rate of interest. This is illustrated in Figure 3-3.

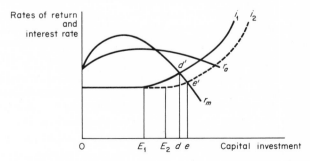

Figure 3-3 The effect of a rising interest rate on the maximum profit position.

It is interesting to note that in this case the total amount of invested capital will not be independent of the amount of equity funds, as was established above in the case of constant interest rate, but will increase as the amount of equity becomes greater. Thus, if the firm's equity were equal to OE_1, it would maximize profits by borrowing the amount $E_1 d$ and paying the rate dd' on the last increment of debt. But if equity were equal to OE_2, maximum profit would be obtained by borrowing the amount $E_2 e$. The marginal interest rate would now be ee', which is equal to the marginal rate of return when total capital is equal to Oe. (See footnote 3.)

THE OPTIMAL INVESTMENT PERIOD

In the preceding section we assumed that the investment period t remained constant while the amount of invested capital C could be varied by the firm. We shall now reverse the procedure and assume that C remains constant while the investment period may be shortened or lengthened as desired by the firm. As discussed in an earlier section, there is reason to believe that, in general, total revenue can be increased by lengthening the investment period (i.e., by adopting a more roundabout method of production), even though the initial capital investment remains unchanged.

Here again, it can be shown that total profit, defined as $V - C$, is maximized at the point at which the marginal rate of return is equal to the market interest rate. The marginal rate of return, however, must be defined in this case as the rate at which total revenue will increase when the investment period is lengthened by one (small) unit of time.

Since we now consider revenue as a function of time, we may write

$$R = f(t)$$

The present value of this revenue is equal to

$$V = f(t)e^{-it}$$

---

[3] If the firm has to pay a different (higher) interest rate for each successive unit of borrowed funds, then the marginal interest rate is equal to the rate charged for the last unit borrowed. If, however, the situation is such that the firm has to pay a different (higher) rate on the *entire* amount of debt each time it borrows an additional unit of funds, then the marginal rate of interest must be defined as the increase in the total interest charge, resulting from borrowing an additional unit of funds, divided by that unit. Mathematically:

$$\frac{dI}{dD} = \frac{d(iD)}{dD} = \frac{di}{dD}D + i$$

It is clear that the marginal interest rate, thus defined, is higher than the new (increased) interest rate charged by the lender.

where i is, as before, the market interest rate. Since C remains constant in this case, maximization of $P = V - C$ coincides with maximization of V. The condition for maximizing V is:

$$\frac{dV}{dt} = 0 = \frac{dR}{dt}e^{-it} - Re^{-it}i$$

Consequently, profit is maximized when

$$\frac{dR/dt}{R} = i$$

It can be shown that the expression on the left-hand side of the above equation is equal to the marginal rate of return with respect to time. The average rate of return is represented by r_a in the equation

$$C = Re^{-r_a t}$$

By differentiating with respect to t, we obtain

$$\frac{dC}{dt} = \frac{dR}{dt}e^{-r_a t} - Re^{-r_a t}\left(\frac{dr_a}{dt}t + r_a\right)$$

The expression in parentheses represents the marginal rate of return, r_m. (See footnote 4.) Since $dC/dt = 0$, it follows that

$$\frac{dr_a}{dt}t + r_a = \frac{dR/dt}{R} = r_m$$

Thus, profit is maximized at the point at which $r_m = i$.

The relationships involved are illustrated graphically in Figure 3-4. In this diagram, time is measured on the horizontal axis while the initial investment and revenue are measured on the vertical axis. For convenience in drawing, a logarithmic scale is used vertically, so that curves of uniform growth become straight lines.

Let the initial investment be equal to OC. The revenue, R, increases with time—at first at an increasing rate and later at a decreasing rate. The lines DV_1, EV_2, FV_3, etc., represent a system of growth curves accumulating from various present values OD, OE, OF, etc. Growth in each case

---

[4] This conforms to the general relationship between the average and the marginal values of the dependent variable. Let $y = f(x)$. Then the average value of y is y/x and the marginal value of y is dy/dx, which is equal to $y/x + [d(y/x)/dx]x$.

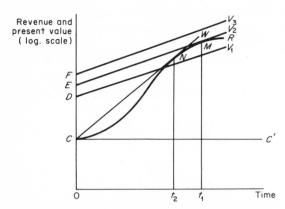

Figure 3-4 Determination of the most profitable investment period.

proceeds at the market rate of interest, which is assumed to remain constant. Only one of these growth lines is tangent to the revenue curve CR: it is the line EV_2, which touches the curve CR at the point M. It is clear that at this point the marginal rate of return is equal to the interest rate and that the distance CE represents the maximum profit $(V - C)$ that can be realized with the given revenue function and interest rate. The investment period which yields the maximum profit is Ot_1. The diagram also shows that the investment period Ot_1, which maximizes profit $(V - C)$, does not coincide with the period which maximizes the average internal rate of return on the invested capital. The highest average rate of return is indicated by the slope of the steepest line drawn from C, which touches the revenue curve CR. This is the line CW, which is tangent to the CR curve at point N. The investment period corresponding to that point is Ot_2, which is shorter than Ot_1.

In order to decide which of the two investment periods $(Ot_1$ or $Ot_2)$ is preferable in the long run, the firm must consider the possibilities for reinvestment of its capital funds at the end of each period. If the profit opportunities existing at the beginning of the initial investment period are not expected to recur at the beginning of the next period, and if the firm does not expect to be able to earn in the next period a return higher than the market rate of interest, then it will find the longer investment period Ot_1 preferable to the shorter period Ot_2. Our diagram indicates that if the revenue t_2N, realized at the end of the period Ot_2, is reinvested at the market rate of interest for the period t_2t_1, its accumulated value will be smaller than t_1M at the end of the period Ot_1. In contrast, if the present profit opportunities are expected to continue in the future, so that the firm can reinvest its funds at the same

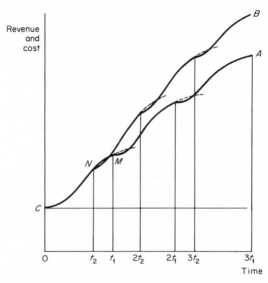

Figure 3-5 Selection of an optimal series of investment periods.

rate of return as that earned in the initial investment period, then the shorter period Ot_2 will be found preferable to the longer period Ot_1. This proposition is illustrated in Figure 3-5.

In this graph, as in the preceding one, the amount OC represents the initial capital investment of the firm; at the end of the first investment period this amount will accumulate to t_2N if the period is equal to Ot_2, or to t_1M if the period is equal to Ot_1. The line CA indicates the rate at which the initial investment will grow if the investment period is made equal to Ot_1 (the marginal internal rate of return is equated to the interest rate) and the entire revenue is reinvested repeatedly. The line CB indicates the rate of growth when the investment period is made equal to Ot_2 (maximizing the average internal rate of return) and the entire revenue is reinvested repeatedly. It is clear that the initial capital will grow at a faster rate with the shorter investment period Ot_2.

SIMULTANEOUS VARIABILITY OF CAPITAL AND INVESTMENT PERIOD

In the above discussion we considered two types of situations. In one of them, the length of the investment period was held constant and the revenue was assumed to be a function of the invested capital alone. In the other, the invested capital was held constant and the revenue was assumed to be a function of the investment period alone. In actual practice, of course, neither one of these factors remains constant.

It can be shown that when time and capital are variable, the firm will maximize profit at the point at which the marginal internal rate of return with respect to time, as well as the marginal internal rate of return with respect to capital, is equal to the marginal market interest rate. The mathematical proof of this statement is rather complex and will not be given here.[5] The relationship between the variables involved may, however, be illustrated by a three-dimensional diagram (Figure 3-6).

In this diagram the interest rate and the internal rate of return are measured on the vertical axis. Capital investment is measured on the horizontal axis OC and the investment period is measured on the horizontal axis OT. Let us assume that the firm begins operations with equity capital equal to OC_1. If the capital is held constant, it will maximize profit by making the investment period equal to $Ot_1 = C_1 a$, since at that point the marginal rate of return with respect to time, represented by the curve r_{t_1}, equals the interest rate, which is assumed to remain constant at $OB = ab$.† The diagram indicates, however, that the firm could increase its profit if it expanded the invested capital beyond the point C_1, even without any change in the investment period. (It can be seen that with the capital held at $OC_1 = t_1 a$ the marginal rate of return with respect to capital—represented by the curve r_{c_1}—exceeds the interest rate at point a.) Thus, the firm will

[5] See F. and V. Lutz, *op. cit.*, p. 37.
† We assume here that the firm's planning horizon does not extend beyond a single investment period.

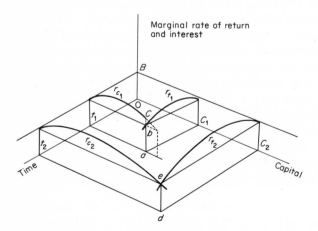

Figure 3-6 Selection of optimal capital and optimal investment period.

find it advantageous to supplement its equity capital by borrowing. But as total invested capital (equity plus debt) increases, the firm may find it advantageous to lengthen the investment period. The expansion may then proceed along both the C and the T axes until an equilibrium position is reached with the capital being equal to OC_2 and the investment period to Ot_2. As the diagram indicates, at that point, d, the marginal internal rate with respect to time and the marginal internal rate with respect to capital are *both* equal to the interest rate.

It is clear that at this point the firm cannot increase profit by either increasing C (while holding t constant) or increasing t (while holding C constant). But would it not be possible to increase profit further by employing more capital and lengthening the investment period simultaneously? This would depend, of course, on the nature of the production function, but it does not seem realistic to assume that such a simultaneous expansion can proceed without limit. It is true that up to a certain point an increase in capital will probably allow the firm to employ more roundabout methods of production. But there are technological constraints limiting the degree of roundaboutness that can be profitably utilized even when additional capital resources are available at a constant rate of interest. In a realistic situation, however, additional borrowing is bound to result eventually in a rise in the interest rate, which will place an additional constraint on the firm's scale of operations.

THE RISK FACTOR IN CAPITAL INVESTMENT

In the preceding sections it was assumed that future costs and revenues could be estimated with a high degree of accuracy; in other words, invest-ment projects were considered to be virtually riskless. But in reality, expected future values may not be taken as certain, and the risk factor involved must be carefully considered in the evaluation of investment projects.[6] In connection with this factor, one must distinguish between the degree of risk inherent in the expectation, on the one hand, and the degree of aversion to risk on the part of the investor, on the other.

Once again, let us begin by considering a simplified situation which involves an initial expenditure C and a revenue R expected to be received in one lump sum at the end of n years. But instead of a single-valued expecta-tion of R we now assume that there is a range of possible values of R, and that each value within this range has a certain probability associated with it.

---

[6] In the economic literature, a distinction is usually drawn between risk and uncertainty. Risk is involved in situations in which the probabilities of occurrence of particular events are known; uncertainty characterizes situations in which these probabilities are not known. We shall be concerned in this section with the former class of situations.

In other words, we now have a probability distribution of expected revenues :

Values	Probabilities	
R_1	p_1	
$\vdots$	$\vdots$	
R_n	p_n	$\Sigma p_n = 1$

By taking the weighted average of all the R's, we can compute the expected value of R :

$$\bar{R} = \sum_{i=1}^{n} R_i p_i$$

The dispersion of R's may be measured by the variance :

$$\sigma^2 = \sum_{i=1}^{n} (R_i - \bar{R})^2 p_i$$

or by the standard deviation, which is the square root of the above expression.

It should be clear that the values of both $\bar{R}$ and σ^2 must have an effect on the present value of the project. As will be recalled, the basic present value formula for riskless projects was given above as

$$V = R(1 + i)^{-t}$$

where R is the single-valued revenue expectation and i is the market interest rate for riskless investments (which is sometimes referred to in economic theory as the "pure" interest rate). We now have to make the following adjustments. First, we must substitute the expected value of revenue, $\bar{R}$, for the single-valued R. Secondly, we must show the effect of the variance, which can be done by adjusting either the value of i or the value of $\bar{R}$. The first of these alternatives is known as the "risk-adjusted discount rate" approach and the second one as the "certainty-equivalent" approach.

If we wish to adjust the discount rate, we may proceed as follows. Assume that the required rate for any given project, r_r, is equal to the basic (risk-free) interest rate i_0 plus a premium for risk which increases with the variance of R. A simple linear function may then be written as follows:

$$r_r = i_0 + \alpha \operatorname{Var}(R)$$

where α is the risk-aversion coefficient and $\alpha \operatorname{Var}(R)$ is the risk premium component of the required discount rate. The present value of the project is then equal to

$$V = \bar{R}(1 + r_r)^{-t}$$

If the expected revenues are distributed over several years and we have a probability distribution of revenues for each year, the present value of the project may then be written as

$$V = \sum_{t=1}^{n} \bar{R}_t(1 + r_r)^{-t}$$

Thus, if two investment projects, A and B, are considered which have the same expected values of R but different dispersions of R's, the variance being greater in the case of A, then the required discount rate must be higher for Project A, and its present value must be lower than the present value of Project B.

The certainty-equivalent approach is based on the proposition that an uncertain future revenue, expected to be received at a given date, may generally be considered equivalent (in terms of the investor's total satisfaction) to a smaller amount expected with certainty at the same date. Consequently, if we know the ratio between the uncertain and the certain amounts in question, we may substitute the latter for the former and then determine the present value by using the risk-free interest rate. Algebraically, we may write:

$$V = \frac{\beta\bar{R}}{(1 + i)^{-t}}$$

where $\beta\bar{R}$ is the certainty equivalent of $\bar{R}$. The coefficient β must be less than 1 and must vary inversely with the degree of risk involved (as measured by the variance of R or any other means).

The certainty-equivalent method may also be stated in a different way, by introducing the concept of utility of the value outcome of an investment project. If investment is riskless, total utility, U, may be regarded as a function of the present value of the expected revenue, V, the latter being derived by using the "pure" interest rate. But it is not a linear function: as V increases, U will increase at a declining rate, in conformity with the principle of diminishing marginal utility of money (or wealth). We may write

$$U = f(V)$$

where $dU/dV > 0$ but $d^2U/dV^2 < 0$.

If instead of a single-valued revenue expectation we have a probability distribution of expected revenues, then the expected utility of the project, $E(U)$, may be derived by multiplying the utility associated with each possible present value V_i by the probability of its occurrence, $p_i(V_i)$:

$$E(U) = \sum_1^n U(V_i)p_i(V_i)$$

Here again, all present values must be computed by discounting expected revenues at the risk-free interest rate.

SUMMARY

The present value of an expected revenue (or a series of revenues spread over a period of time) is derived by discounting it by an appropriate interest rate. If the revenue is regarded as certain, the risk-free or "pure" interest rate should be applied. If the revenue is not certain, a premium for risk taking should be incorporated into the discount factor used. "Profit" is defined as the difference between the present value of the expected net revenues and the initial capital expenditure.

The internal rate of return on invested capital is the discount rate which equates the expected revenues with the initial capital expenditure. If the internal rate exceeds the interest rate, a positive amount of profit, as defined above, will be realized.

If the investment period is held constant and the revenue is considered to be a function of the initial capital expenditure, profit is maximized at the point at which the internal rate of return on the marginal unit of capital is equal to the interest rate. This is not, as a rule, the point at which the average internal rate of return on total invested capital is at its maximum. However, when the opportunity of borrowing (or lending) in the market exists, the extension of investment to the point of equality between the marginal internal rate of return and the interest rate will result in maximizing the average internal rate of return on the investor's own funds.

When the amount of investment is held constant, but the investment period can be varied, profit is maximized at the point at which the internal rate of return realized in the marginal unit of time is equal to the interest rate. If a single investment period is considered, the point of maximum profit will not, as a rule, coincide with the point of the highest average internal rate of return on the invested capital. In the long run, however, one must consider the opportunities for reinvestment of capital funds at the end of the time period selected. Under certain conditions, long-term profits may be maximized by selecting investment periods so as to maximize the average rate of return in each of them.

When both the amount of capital investment and the investment period are variable, profit is maximized at the point at which the marginal internal rate of return with respect to time, as well as the marginal internal rate of return with respect to capital, is equal to the interest rate.

When investment involves an element of risk, one must distinguish between the degree of risk inherent in the expectation, on the one hand, and the degree of aversion to risk on the part of the investor, on the other. If instead of a single-valued revenue expectation, we have a probability distribution of expected revenues, the variance of such a distribution may be taken as a measure of the risk involved, and the required premium for risk taking may be considered as a function of this variance. In order to find the present value of a risky investment, we must, first, compute the expected value of revenue and, secondly, discount this value by using the rate equal to the sum of the risk-free interest rate plus the required risk premium. An alternative method consists of reducing the uncertain expected revenue value to its certainty-equivalent value and then discounting the latter by using the risk-free interest rate.

SELECTED REFERENCES

Bailey, Martin J.: "Formal Criteria for Investment Decisions," *Journal of Political Economy*, vol. 67, October, 1959, pp. 476–488.

Beranek, William: *Analysis for Financial Decisions*, Richard D. Irwin, Inc., Homewood, Ill., 1963, chaps. 5 and 6.

Bierman, Harold, Jr., and Seymour Smidt: *The Capital Budgeting Decision*, 2d ed., The Macmillan Company, New York, 1966, chaps. 2, 3, and 4.

Farrar, Donald: *The Investment Decision under Uncertainty*, Prentice-Hall, Inc., Englewood Cliffs, N.J., 1962.

Gordon, Myron J.: *The Investment, Financing, and Valuation of the Corporation*, Richard D. Irwin, Inc., Homewood, Ill., 1962, chaps. 2 and 3.

Hirshleifer, Jack: "Efficient Allocation of Capital in an Uncertain World," *American Economic Review*, vol. 54, May, 1964, pp. 77–85.

———: "On the Theory of Optimal Investment Decision," *Journal of Political Economy*, vol. 66, August, 1958, pp. 329–352.

Lutz, Friedrich, and Vera Lutz: *The Theory of Investment of the Firm*, Princeton University Press, Princeton, N.J., 1951, chap. 2.

Renshaw, E.: "A Note on the Arithmetic of Capital-budgeting Decisions," *Journal of Business*, July, 1957.

Solomon, Ezra: "The Arithmetic of Capital-budgeting Decisions," *Journal of Business*, vol. 29, April, 1956, pp. 124–129.

Weston, J. Fred, and Eugene F. Brigham: *Managerial Finance*, 2d ed., Holt, Rinehart and Winston, New York, 1966, chap. 7.

Present Value and Internal-rate Criteria for Selecting Projects

In the preceding sections we have established that, in order to maximize profit, the firm must expand capital investment up to the point at which the marginal internal rate of return on capital is equal to the interest rate at which additional funds can be borrowed in the capital market. "Profit" has been defined as the difference between the present value of the sum of the expected net revenues (quasi rents) and the initial capital expenditure: $P = V - C$. As has been shown, total profit is maximized when marginal profit, i.e., the profit made on the marginal unit of investment, is zero. In other words, the present value of the marginal revenue is equal to the marginal capital expenditure: $\Delta V = \Delta C$ or $\Delta V - \Delta C = \Delta P = 0$.

Let us now consider a somewhat different kind of problem. Suppose that for some institutional reasons, a firm is unable to expand capital up to the point of maximum total profit. It has a fixed sum of money to invest in a given period and is, therefore, unable to accept all projects promising a positive profit increment. It seems clear that under such conditions the firm should select the projects which promise the greatest addition to its total profit. Suppose that two alternative projects are considered which involve equal initial capital outlays C. Then, if the present value of the revenues expected from Project I, V_1, is greater than the present value of the revenues expected from Project II, V_2, Project I should be selected. However, the present values V_1 and V_2 depend on the interest rate used for their computation. Generally speaking, as the discount rate increases, both V_1 and V_2 will become smaller; but the degree in which V_1 and V_2 will be reduced need not be the same. And it may be shown that for some types of projects the difference in the relative change in the present values is so large that while $V_1 > V_2$ within a certain range of interest rates, the reverse is true outside of that particular range of interest rates. In other words, while Project I seems to be preferable to Project II if the interest rate remains within a given range, Project II begins to look more attractive than Project I if the interest rate moves into a different range.

On the other hand, the average internal rate of return, which has been defined above as r_a in the equation

$$C = \frac{R_1}{1 + r_a} + \frac{R_2}{(1 + r_a)^2} + \cdots + \frac{R_n}{(1 + r_a)^n}$$

is clearly independent of the market rate of interest. If the internal rate is higher for Project I than for Project II, this seems to indicate that Project I is preferable to Project II irrespective of the level of the market interest rate. Thus, there appears to be a conflict between the present value and the internal rate of return criteria. It will be shown, however, that the conflict may be resolved once it is determined how the future revenues $R_1, R_2, \ldots, R_n$ will be disposed of: whether they will be reinvested and, if so, at what rate of return.

A couple of specific examples may be helpful at this point. Consider first the following pair of alternative projects:

	C	R_1	R_2
Project I	100	80	80
Project II	100	60	60

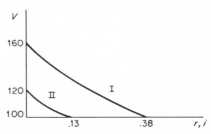

Figure 3-7 Present values of Projects I and II.

By using the above formula we find that the internal rate of return for Project I is .38 or 38 percent and for Project II .13 or 13 percent.[7] By using this criterion, then, Project I is preferable to Project II.

The present values of the revenue streams expected from these two projects are represented by V_1 and V_2 in the following equations:

$$V_1 = \frac{80}{1 + i} + \frac{80}{(1 + i)^2}$$

$$V_2 = \frac{60}{1 + i} + \frac{60}{(1 + i)^2}$$

Both V_1 and V_2 are functions of i, which is the market rate of interest. These functions are presented graphically in Figure 3-7. If the interest rate is zero, the present worth of each project is equal to the undiscounted sum of the expected revenues. V_1 is then equal to 160 and V_2 to 120. If the interest rate is 13 percent, V_2 is reduced to 100, which is the same as the project's cost. At this rate, which is equal to the internal rate of return of Project II, it becomes marginal, yielding zero profit. Project I, on the other hand, still yields considerable profit when the interest rate equals 13 percent. At this rate, $V_1 = 133.45$ and $P_1 = 33.45$. Project I becomes marginal when the interest rate reaches 38 percent, which is equal to this project's internal rate of return.

It will be observed that in Figure 3-7 the V_1 curve remains above the V_2 curve at any rate of interest. Thus, in this case, the net present value and the internal-rate criteria give identical results: Project I is preferable to Project II irrespective of the level of the interest rate. In general, it may be stated that projects with equal life spans, whose revenues, period by period, differ by a proportionality factor, will have nonintersecting V curves. The ranking of such projects will not depend on the interest rate.

Consider now the following pair of projects:

	C	R_1	R_2
Project A	100	112	0
Project B	100	55	60.50

[7] Since the projects extend over a two-year period, the computation of the internal rate involves in each case solving a quadratic equation which has two roots. Thus, for Project I the roots are .38 and -1.58, but the negative value has no meaning in terms of the rate of return and may be disregarded. It should be noted that for other types of projects two (or more) positive rates of return may be obtained. Situations of this kind are discussed in the following section.

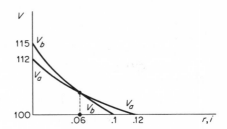

Figure 3-8 Present values of Projects A and B.

Again, by using the formula given above, we find that the average internal rate of return is .12 or 12 percent for Project A and .1 or 10 percent for Project B.

The present values of the expected revenues are given for both projects in Table 3-2. The V_a and V_b functions are also presented graphically in Figure 3-8. It may be seen that the present worth of Project A exceeds the present worth of Project B when the interest rate is above 6 percent, but the reverse is true when the interest rate is reduced below the 6 percent level. Thus, in this case, the internal rate and the present value criteria give the same results in the higher interest range, but conflicting results in the lower range. However, this apparent discrepancy disappears when the assumptions concerning reinvestment opportunities are stated explicitly. Actually, when the two projects are ranked on the basis of their internal rates of return, an

Table 3-2 Present values and internal rates of return for projects A and B, assuming reinvestment of the first year's revenues at market interest rates

Interest rate	Revenue at the end of		Present value	Average internal rate of return
	Year 1	Year 2		
Project A				
12%	112	112 × 1.12 = 125.44	100	.12
10%	112	112 × 1.1 = 123.20	101.82	.102
8%	112	112 × 1.08 = 120.96	103.70	.098
6%	112	112 × 1.06 = 118.72	105.73	.089
3%	112	112 × 1.03 = 115.36	108.73	.074
0%	112	112 × 1.00 = 112.00	112.00	.058
Project B				
10%	55	(55 × 1.1) + 60.50 = 121.00	100	.10
8%	55	(55 × 1.08) + 60.50 = 119.90	102.79	.095
6%	55	(55 × 1.06) + 60.50 = 118.00	105.73	.089
3%	55	(55 × 1.03) + 60.50 = 117.15	110.42	.080
0%	55	(55 × 1.00) + 60.50 = 115.50	115.50	.073

implicit assumption is made that in each case the revenue realized in year 1 can be reinvested in year 2 at the same rate: 12 percent for Project A and 10 percent for Project B.

Suppose, however, that the revenue of year 1 can be reinvested in year 2 only at the market rate of interest, which is the same irrespective of which project is accepted by the firm. The equation, which must be solved to determine the average internal rate of return over the two-year period, then assumes the following form:

$$C = \frac{R_1(1 + i)}{(1 + r)^2} + \frac{R_2}{(1 + r)^2}$$

If the market interest rate (i) is 3 percent, the internal rate of return over the two-year period is found to be 7.4 percent for Project A and 8 percent for Project B. The present worth of Project A with the interest rate at 3 percent is 108.73 while the present worth of Project B is 110.42. Thus, both criteria indicate that Project B is preferable to Project A under the conditions assumed.

In general, as Table 3-2 indicates, both the present values and the average internal rates of return computed in accordance with the above formula are higher for Project A than for Project B when the rate of interest is over 6 percent. The reverse is true when the rate of interest is below 6 percent.

MULTIPLE RATES OF RETURN

The types of project considered above involved an initial capital outlay followed by a stream of positive revenues in subsequent periods of time. The present value of the future revenues for such projects is inversely related to the discount rate used. This is illustrated in Figure 3-9a.

The initial capital outlay is equal to OC. If the interest rate is zero, then the present value is equal to the undiscounted sum of the net revenues attributable to the project, which is represented by OB. If the interest rate is equal to Oi_1, then the present value (V) is equal to OD and net profit (P) is equal to CD. When the interest rate is increased to Oi_2, the present value is reduced to OC, and net profit drops to zero.

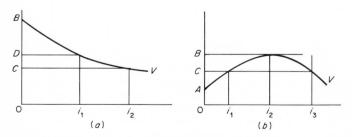

Figure 3-9   Present values of different types of projects.

A different situation is encountered, however, when projects are considered which involve a stream of revenues consisting of negative as well as positive items (in other words, projects which involve a net loss in some periods and a net profit in other periods).

In the case of such projects, the relationship between the present value and the interest rate is more complex; it is inverse over a certain range of interest rates but becomes direct over a different range of rates. This is shown diagrammatically in Figure 3-9b. The undiscounted sum of revenues is represented by the distance OA. Net profit at this point is a negative quantity AC. As the interest rate increases from zero to Oi_1, and then to Oi_2, the present value also increases. At the rate Oi_1, the present value is equal to the initial cost, OC, and net profit is zero. At the rate Oi_2, the present value is equal to OB and net profit is represented by BC. In contrast, when the interest rate increases beyond the Oi_2 level, the present value begins to decline. When the rate reaches the level Oi_3, the present value is once more equal to the cost and net profit is once again zero.

We know that when $V = C$, the interest rate is equal to the average internal rate of return. It follows, therefore, that the project in question has not one but two internal rates of return, both of which are positive (Oi_1 and Oi_3). With any interest rate within this range, we have $V > C$ and $P > 0$ (positive net profit). With any interest rate outside this range, we have $V < C$ and $P < 0$ (net deficit).

A specific example should help to clarify the relationships.[8] Consider an investment project which involves replacement of a pump installed in an oil well with a larger pump that can get a fixed amount of oil out of the ground at a faster rate. Assume that by operating the existing pump the investor's expected revenue is $10,000 in period t_1 and $10,000 in period t_2. Assume further that by installing the larger pump at an initial net cost of $1,600 he can expect $20,000 in period t_1 but nothing in period t_2. The alternative cash flows may be presented in tabular form as follows:

Time period	Alternative A (investment in a larger pump)	Alternative B (no additional investment)	Incremental cash flow due to investment in a larger pump
t_0	−1,600	0	−1,600
t_1	20,000	10,000	10,000
t_2	0	10,000	−10,000

[8] The example given below was originally presented by E. Solomon in "The Arithmetic of Capital-budgeting Decisions," *Journal of Business*, April, 1956, and was further discussed and elaborated upon in E. Renshaw's "A Note on the Arithmetic of Capital-budgeting Decisions," *Journal of Business*, July, 1957. Both articles were reprinted in *The Management of Corporate Capital*, edited by E. Solomon, The Free Press of Glencoe, Ill., New York, 1959.

As the last column of the table shows, an investment of $1,600 in a larger pump results in a redistribution of revenues over time ($+10,000$ in period t_1 and $-10,000$ in period t_2), without a change in the total amount of realizable revenue. The internal rate of return for this project is found by solving for r the following equation:

$$1,600 = \frac{10,000}{1 + r} - \frac{10,000}{(1 + r)^2}$$

This quadratic equation has two roots, both of which are positive: $r_1 = .25$ and $r_2 = 4.00$. Thus, we find that the project has two internal rates of return: 25 percent and 400 percent.

The present value of the incremental revenues is equal to the cost, making net profit equal to zero at both of the above rates. At any interest rate between 25 percent and 400 percent the present value exceeds the cost and there is a positive net profit. For example, at the rate of 50 percent, we have $V = 2,223$ and $P = 2,223 - 1,600 = 623$. At any interest rate lower than 25 percent or higher than 400 percent, the present value is below the cost and there is a net loss. For example, at the rate of 20 percent, $V = 1,389$ and $P = -211$. In this case, the advantage resulting from the acceleration of the revenue stream is not large enough to outweigh the additional expenditure involved. At the rate of 600 percent, $V = 1,224$ and $P = -376$. In this case the advantage of the accelerated revenue stream is, of course, much greater; but the opportunity cost of the additional funds required is so high that, on balance, the project must be rejected.

4
Stock Valuation: Dividend Capitalization Model

Theoretically, a firm's net profit—after fixed charges and taxes—represents net return on its equity capital. But in the corporate enterprise, dividends paid to the stockholders are not, as a rule, equal to the profit earned in any given accounting period. Historical records show that during prosperity periods most companies have been retaining a substantial proportion of net profit for reinvestment in the business. In contrast, during major depression periods many companies have paid dividends in excess of the sharply reduced current net earnings. In the long run, however, the stream of cash dividends received by the stockholders has in most cases remained considerably smaller than the stream of net profits earned by the company.

Since the policy of net profit retention increases the company's equity capital, it also tends to raise its earning power. If the number of shares remains unchanged, this policy should produce an expanding stream of net profits per share, accompanied by an expanding stream of dividends per share (although the rate of dividend expansion need not, of course, be the same as the rate of profit expansion). An investor in such shares who intends to hold them for a considerable but finite period of time may then expect a series of expanding dividend receipts during his investment period plus a realized capital gain, reflecting the company's increased earning power, at the end of this period—when he sells the shares.

In view of these rather complex relationships, it is not surprising to find conflicting opinions among the writers on corporation finance as to the relative importance of the dividend, retained profit, and total net profit factors in the determination of the market values of corporate stocks. In this chapter we shall consider a valuation model which assumes that stock values are determined by the expected dividend streams alone. It is important to realize at the outset that this model does not ignore retained profit altogether, but rather assumes that retentions influence stock values indirectly—through their effect on future dividends. In a later chapter we shall compare this model with some other valuation models.

THE PRESENT VALUE OF A GROWING DIVIDEND STREAM

The stock-valuation model presented in this chapter is based on the following assumptions:

1. Corporate capital consists of equity funds alone.
2. No external financing is available and, consequently, capital expansion is possible through profit retention only.
3. No corporate income tax is imposed.
4. Once decided upon, the retention ratio (the proportion of profit that is retained) remains constant at all times.
5. The value of a company's stock is determined by the expected stream of dividend payments.

To begin with, let us consider a simplified situation in which the firm's capital K and the average internal rate of return, r, are assumed to remain constant over time. This implies that the amount of profit, $P = rk$, also remains constant and that the entire profit is distributed each year as dividends $(D = P)$. For, if any part of profit were retained and reinvested, the firm's capital would obviously no longer remain constant. Under these conditions, the market value of the company's stock is equal to the present value V_0 of an infinite series of constant dividend payments:

$$V_0 = \frac{rK_0}{1 + k} + \frac{rK_0}{(1 + k)^2} + \cdots = \frac{rK_0}{k} = \frac{P}{k} = \frac{D}{k} \qquad (4\text{-}1)$$

Under competitive conditions, the discount factor k must be equal to the rate of return generally available in the market to investors in stock of this particular risk class.[1] It may be observed that if $r = k$, then $V_0 = K_0$: the present market value of the company's stock is equal to the initial amount of its paid-in capital.[2] On the other hand, if r rises above k (or if k drops below r), then V_0 will exceed K_0 and the initial stockholders will be able to realize a capital gain equal to $V_0 - K_0$ by selling their stock at its present market value. One should note, however, that if the value of r (or k) changes only once and then remains constant at its new level, the capital gain can also be realized only once. The new stockholders, who have purchased the stock at a higher price, will not be able to realize any further capital gain unless there is a new change in either r or k.

The static situation described above is not, of course, a typical one in our growing economy. Most firms in our economy pursue expansionary policies and most investors in common stocks look forward to an increasing, rather than constant, dividend rate per share. To come closer to reality, let us now assume that the firm decides to expand its capital each year by retaining and reinvesting a certain proportion of its annual net profit. The ratio of retained profit to total net profit, b, will be subsequently referred to as the *retention ratio* and the ratio of dividends to net profit, which must be equal to $1 - b$, as the *payout ratio*.

Since the firm's net profit in the initial year is equal to rK_0, its retained profit must be equal to brK_0 and its capital in the following year will be equal to $K_0 + brK_0$. The rate of capital growth, g, is then equal to

$$g = \frac{K_1 - K_0}{K_0} = \frac{brK_0}{K_0} = br \tag{4-2}$$

The firm's dividends for the initial year are equal to $(1 - b)rK_0$, and its dividends the next year are equal to $(1 - b)r(K_0 + brK_0)$. It can be easily seen that the rate of dividend growth must then be exactly the same as the rate of capital growth, g:

$$g = \frac{D_1 - D_0}{D_0} = \frac{(1 - b)r(K + brK_0) - (1 - b)rK_0}{(1 - b)rK_0} = rb \tag{4-3}$$

As long as r and b remain constant, the rate of growth in the firm's capital, net profit, dividends, and retained profit will also remain unchanged in all the future years. Algebraically we may write:

$$\frac{K_t - K_{t-1}}{K_{t-1}} = \frac{P_t - P_{t-1}}{P_{t-1}} = \frac{D_t - D_{t-1}}{D_{t-1}} = \frac{RP_t - RP_{t-1}}{RP_{t-1}} = br = g \tag{4-4}$$

---

[1] The value of k for a given firm may change if the firm begins to expand operations. See the section entitled "The Relation between k and b."

[2] It should be clear that V_0 in Equation 4-1 represents the aggregate market value of the company's outstanding common stock. The market price of a single share may be obtained by dividing this aggregate amount by the number of shares outstanding: V_0/N.

Under these assumptions, the market value of the company's stock will be equal to an infinite stream of dividend payments expanding at the annual rate g:

$$V_0 = \frac{D_0}{1 + k} + \frac{D_0(1 + g)}{(1 + k)^2} + \frac{D_0(1 + g)^2}{(1 + k)^3} + \cdots = \frac{D_0}{k - g} \tag{4-5}$$

Or, by substituting rb for g and $(1 - b)rK_0$ for D_0, we may write:

$$V_0 = \frac{(1 - b)rK_0}{k - br} \tag{4-6}$$

The following questions must be considered: (1) Do changes in the retention ratio b have a significant effect on the stock value V_0; (2) if they do, what particular value of b will result in the maximum possible value of V_0.

If the retention ratio is zero, the firm's dividends are equal to its net profit and remain constant over time. When the retention ratio is raised above zero, the initial amount of dividend declines, but the future amounts will expand in each successive period. After a certain period of time, the expanding dividends will reach, and then exceed, the constant dividend level maintained when $b = 0$. The greater the value of b, the lower is the initial amount of dividend but the higher will be the rate of growth. This is illustrated in Figure 4-1.

The straight line P_1D_1 represents both dividends and net profit on the assumption that $b = 0$. The curve D_2D_2 is drawn on the assumption that

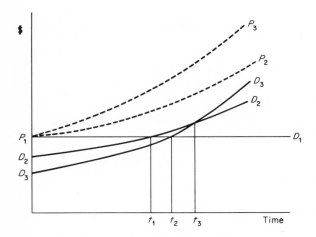

Figure 4-1 Dividend and profit streams resulting from different retention ratios.

$b = .25$. The initial dividend OD_2 is now equal to only 75 percent of the initial net profit, OP_1, but both dividends and profit expand continually at the same rate. (Profit expansion is indicated by the curve P_1P_2.) It will be noticed that the curve D_2D_2 remains below the straight line P_1D_1 during the period Ot_1, crosses that line at point t_1, and is above that line in all subsequent periods.

The figure also includes the curve D_3D_3 drawn on the assumption that $b = .5$. The initial dividend in this case, OD_3, is equal to only one-half of the initial profit OP_1, but the rate of growth now is faster. It will be seen that the curve D_3D_3 crosses the straight line P_1D_1 at point t_2 and crosses the curve D_2D_2 at point t_3.

Evidently, any further increase in the retention ratio would reduce the initial dividend even more but would also result in a further increase in the rate of dividend growth. What we wish to find out is whether the present values of the various possible dividend streams differ significantly from one another and, if so, which particular value is the maximum one. In dealing with this question, we find that different answers are obtained depending on whether the relation between the internal rate of return, r, and the discount rate k is such that $r > k$, $r = k$, or $r < k$.

First, it can be easily shown that the retention ratio, b, has no effect on the stock value, V_0, when $r = k$. This becomes evident by substituting k for r (or r for k) in Equation 4-6. We may then write:

$$V_0 = \frac{(1 - b)kK_0}{k - bk} = K_0 \tag{4-7}$$

Thus, when $r = k$, the present value of the stock is equal to the firm's paid-in capital, irrespective of the value of b. The economic interpretation of this finding is simple. As already mentioned above, under competitive conditions, k must be equal to the rate of return generally available to investors in comparable stocks. This means that any funds distributed as dividends may be invested in the market at the rate equal to the firm's internal rate of return. Consequently, the stockholders can neither lose nor gain by any change in the company's retention policy, and the market value of their stock must remain the same.[3]

Next, let us consider the case in which the internal rate of return is smaller than the discount rate. Equation 4-6 indicates that, if the retention ratio b is zero, the stock value V_0 is equal to rK/k. Since in this case $r/k < 1$, it follows that V_0 is smaller than the firm's paid-in capital, K_0.

---

[3] In this discussion we assume that there are no transaction costs in connection with purchasing stocks in the market and that there is no tax differential between the retained and the distributed parts of net profit. These factors will be examined later.

Moreover, it can be shown that as the value of b increases, the value of the stock is continually reduced. By differentiating V_0 with respect to b we obtain

$$\frac{\partial V_0}{\partial b} = \frac{rK_0}{(k - rb)^2}(r - k) \tag{4-8}$$

Since the first term of the right-hand side of the above equation is always positive for a profitable firm, it follows that $\partial V/\partial b$ must be positive if $r > k$, zero if $r = k$, and negative if $r < k$, over the entire range of possible values of b (from 0 to 1). To give a numerical example, assume that $K_0 = 100$, $r = .08$, and $k = .1$. If $b = 0$, we have

$$V_0 = \frac{.08 \times 100}{.1} = 80$$

By a similar computation we find that $V_0 = 78$ when $b = .1$; $V_0 = 66.67$ when $b = .5$; $V_0 = 28$ when $b = .9$; and $V_0 = 0$ when $b = 1$.

The results obtained should not be surprising. If the internal rate of return is smaller than k, which is equal to the rate available in the market, profit retention clearly becomes undesirable from the stockholder's standpoint. Each additional dollar retained reduces the amount of funds that the stockholders could invest at a higher rate elsewhere and thus further depresses the value of the company's stock. Under such conditions, the company should adopt a policy of contraction and disinvestment, which would allow the owners to transfer not only the net profit but also the paid-in capital (or part of it) to some other, more remunerative enterprise.

Finally, let us consider the most important and interesting case, in which the internal rate of return is greater than the discount rate ($r > k$).

Equation 4-8 indicates that if $r > k$, $\partial V/\partial b$ must be positive over the entire range of possible numerical values of b. Thus, it appears that in this case the firm will maximize its stock value by raising b to its upper limit of unity. However, a closer look at Equation 4-6 reveals that the denominator $k - br$ becomes zero, thus making V_0 infinitely large, when $b = k/r$. Since in the present case $r > k$, it follows that this point is reached when $b < 1$. If the retention ratio is raised to a level greater than k/r, then the present value of the firm's stock becomes negative.[4]

[4] Mathematically, $\partial V/\partial b$ continues to increase even when V_0 becomes negative. As b continues to increase, after it has reached the value equal to k/r, the absolute value of the denominator of Equation 4-6 also increases and the absolute value of V_0 decreases. But a negative quantity with a smaller absolute value is larger than a negative quantity with a greater absolute value (e.g., $-50 > -100$). However, since in the real world negative stock values are not feasible, the mathematical relationships between them are of no practical importance.

A numerical example should be helpful at this point. Assume that $K_0 = 66.67$, $r = .15$, and $k = .1$. By inserting these numbers in Equation 4-6, the following stock values are obtained for different retention ratios:

V	b
100	0
200	.5
400	.6
∞	.667
-600	.7
-100	.8

Under these assumptions, then, the value of the firm's stock increases from 100 to infinity as the retention ratio increases from zero to .667. (It will be observed that at the latter point $b = k/r = .1/.15 = .667$.) If the retention ratio is raised beyond .667, negative stock values are obtained. (But since the absolute values of V_0 decline, it follows that $\partial V/\partial b$ remains positive.)

The results obtained in this case are obviously unrealistic. No actual company, no matter how profitable, has ever been able to make the value of its stock approach infinity by manipulating its retention ratio—or, for that matter, by any other means. We must conclude, therefore, that the assumptions made at the beginning of this chapter failed to take account of some important factors restraining the rise in stock values in actual practice. Let us take another look at Equation 4-6 and examine more closely the variables involved.

It is clear that K_0, which represents the amount of the company's paid-in capital at the beginning of the period concerned, is a constant. But are we justified in assuming—as we did above—that the values of r and k also remain constant, irrespective of changes in the retention ratio b? We shall consider this question in the next two sections.

THE RELATION BETWEEN r AND b

The relation between the internal rate of return, r, and the retention ratio, b, is rather complex. A change in the retention ratio has a direct effect on the amount of internal funds and, therefore, on the total amount of invested capital. But as the amount of invested capital changes, this may or may not have a significant effect on the internal rate of return. Furthermore, if there is a significant effect, it may be either positive or negative, depending on whether the firm operates within the region of increasing or of diminishing returns.

In analyzing the relation between the input of productive factors and the resulting output of goods, economic theory distinguishes between the following two cases:

1. We may assume that the quantity of one factor (e.g., labor) is variable, while the quantities of the other factors remain constant. In this case, if the initial quantity of the variable factor is small in relation to the quantities of the fixed factors, employment of additional units of this factor will expand output at an increasing rate. In other words, the marginal product of the factor in question will be rising. The possibility of realizing increasing returns is not, however, unlimited. As the quantity of the variable factor is further increased, a turning point will eventually be reached, after which the employment of additional units of the variable factor can expand output only at a decreasing rate. The well-known "law of diminishing returns" will come into play.[5]

2. Let us now assume that the quantities of all productive factors can be varied simultaneously and proportionately. At first galance, it would seem that if all inputs are increased at the same rate, the output must also rise at an equal rate. But actually this need not be so, if there are important economies or diseconomies of scale. If the initial scale of production is too small, relative to the optimum scale for the industry in question, a proportionate increase in all inputs will yield a more than proportionate increase in output. But the reverse will be true if expansion continues after the optimum scale has already been reached.

In discussing changes in the return to scale, however, one must distinguish between an increase in the size of an individual plant on the one hand and an increase in the size of a firm, which may own several plants, on the other. If the plants owned by a firm are already of the optimum size, the firm may still continue to expand by acquiring additional plants of the same optimum size, in which case the physical productivity will remain undiminished. But even if the physical productivity remains the same, the firm may still experience a reduction in r because of price fluctuations. If the firm operates under conditions of imperfect competition, an expansion of its operations may involve a rise in the input prices it has to pay or a decline in the product prices it receives, or both.

---

[5] It must be pointed out that in economic theory the tendency of diminishing (or increasing) returns is usually discussed in terms of the marginal rate of return, whereas the r in the above formulas represents the average internal rate of return on invested capital. However, as has been shown in Chap. 3, when the marginal return is rising, the average return is also rising, although at a lower rate. When the marginal return begins to decline, the average return continues to rise for a while, but then begins to decline, too. Here again, the rate of decline is lower for the average return than for the marginal return. Thus, when the amount of invested capital changes, the two rates will, for the most part, move in the same direction.

Of the above two cases the second one is clearly more relevant to our discussion here than the first one. If the amount of invested capital increases, there is no reason why the firm should keep the quantities of the other factors constant. Most probably, it will expand all inputs so as to maintain their optimal combination and, therefore, the greatest possible efficiency of operations. Consequently, if r begins to decline, this is most likely to be due to the diminishing returns to scale.

Turning to the relation between the retention ratio b and the invested capital K, it is clear that an increase in b in any particular year will result in a greater capital increment in that year, which may have either a positive or a negative effect on r depending on whether the firm is initially below or above the optimum scale of operations. But, as will be recalled, in this chapter it has been assumed that the value of b, once set, will remain constant at all times. A firm which continually retains part of its net profit will obviously experience a continual capital expansion as long as it earns a positive net profit. Does this mean that it will inevitably reach at some point in the future the stage of diminishing returns to scale, even though initially it may be of less than an optimum size?

Clearly, if the economy as a whole remains stationary, a continual expansion by an individual firm must indeed, sooner or later, result in diseconomies of scale owing to either the physical or the financial factors mentioned above. But it need not be so in the case of a growing economy. First, if the economy is expanding, new technological developments may increase the optimum physical size of an individual plant. Secondly, even in the absence of technological changes, in a growing economy both the factor and the product markets will expand continually, so that an individual firm may continually increase the volume of its operations without experiencing unfavorable price changes in either of these markets.

As was already stated above, the capital of a firm which uses only internal financing will expand at the rate equal to br. We now find that if b is set so that, with a given initial value of r, br is equal to the rate of expansion of the firm's markets, then this value of r may be expected to remain constant in the future. But if b is raised above this level, we may expect r to decline in the future, because of the diseconomies of scale. Moreover, if b drops below this level, r may be expected also to decline in the future, for, in this case, the firm will be losing ground to its competitors in terms of its market share, ability to modernize its equipment, etc.

As a first approximation, we may represent the relation between r and b by the following quadratic equation:

$$r = \alpha_1 + \alpha_2 b - \alpha_3 b^2$$

Assuming that $\alpha_1 = .2$, $\alpha_2 = .3$, and $\alpha_3 = .2$, we may write

$$r = .2 + .3b - .2b^2$$

We then obtain the following values of r for selected values of b:

b	r
0	.2
.1	.228
.25	.2625
.50	.3
.75	.3125
.8	.3120
1.0	.3

As can be seen, the value of r increases from .2 to .3125 as b is raised from zero to .75. After that the value of r decreases to .3 (when $b = 1$).

In mathematical terms, the maximum value of r is reached when $\partial r / \partial b = 0$. With the numerical values assumed above, we obtain:

$$\frac{\partial r}{\partial b} = .3 - .2 \times 2.0 \times b = 0$$

$$b = .75$$

Since the second derivative is negative ($\partial^2 r / \partial b^2 = -4$), we know that this value of r is a maximum and not a minimum value.

If the firm sets its retention ratio at .75, its expansion rate, which is equal to br, will be $.75 \times .312 = .234$. If this rate corresponds to the market expansion rate, the firm may continue to retain 75 percent of its net profit year after year without any adverse effect on its average rate of return.[6]

THE RELATION BETWEEN b AND V_0 WHEN r IS A FUNCTION OF b

Under the assumptions made above, the stockholders are interested in maximizing the present value of the expected dividend stream rather than

[6] It should be noticed that the quadratic equation used implies that the value of r will remain constant over time with any value of b. Strictly speaking, if b is set so that br does not correspond to the market expansion rate, r should be expected to decline continually as the difference between the size of the firm and the size of its market widens. Therefore, instead of one value of r we should have a series of values, such that $r_1 > r_2 > r_3 > \cdots$, for every given value of b. Consequently, if we use the above equation, we must assume that r represents an average of continually changing annual values of r, except for the one specific value of b which makes br equal to the market expansion rate, in which case we have $r_1 = r_2 = r_3 = \cdots$.

the average rate of return on the firm's capital. We must, therefore, consider the relation between the retention ratio b and the present value of the stock V_0, when r is a function of b. As will be recalled, V_0 is equal to

$$V_0 = \frac{(1 - b)P_0}{k - rb}$$

where $P_0 = r_0 K_0$. (See Equation 4-6.)

As was pointed out above, if r is greater than k and is expected to remain constant irrespective of changes in b, the denominator of the above equation becomes zero and V_0 becomes infinitely large when b reaches the value equal to k/r. But if r declines as b increases, rb may remain smaller than k, and V_0 may remain finite over the entire range of feasible values of b (from zero to 1).

The value of V_0 is maximized when $\partial V/\partial b = 0$. If $r = f(b)$, $\partial V/\partial b$ is equal to

$$\frac{\partial V_0}{\partial b} = \frac{P_0}{(k - rb)^2}\left[r - k + b(1 - b)\frac{\partial r}{\partial b}\right] \tag{4-9}$$

Since $P_0/(k - rb)^2$ is always positive for a profitable firm, it is clear that the sign of $\partial V/\partial b$ depends on whether the expression $r - k + b(1 - b) \times (\partial r/\partial b)$ is positive or negative. If $r > k$ when $b = 0$, $\partial V/\partial b$ must be positive at that point, which means that V_0 can be increased by a small rise in b above the zero level. A continual rise in b, however, may either increase or decrease $\partial V/\partial b$ depending on whether $\partial r/\partial b$ is positive or negative.

If the firm has entered the stage of diminishing returns, $\partial r/\partial b$ is negative and $\partial V/\partial b$ may be reduced to zero—at which point V_0 is maximized before b reaches its upper limit of 1.

The following numerical examples may help to clarify the relationships involved:

1. Let us assume at first, for simplicity's sake, that r is a decreasing linear function of b, as follows:

$$r = .25 - .2b$$

This simple function makes the computations much easier, but its implications must be clearly understood. According to this equation the internal rate of return is highest when $b = 0$. Any degree of profit retention and, consequently, any degree of capital expansion will result in a lower value of r. This implies that the firm has already reached the stage of diminishing returns and, furthermore, that there is no prospect of market expansion that could shift the point at which this stage begins in the future.

Let us also assume that the firm's initial capital K_0 is 100, its profit in the initial year, P_0, is 25, and the discount rate k is .1. Then, if the firm decides not to make any profit retentions at all ($b = 0$), the present value of its stock will be equal to

$$V_0 = \frac{(1 - 0)25}{.1 - 0} = 250$$

This is not, however, the maximum value of V_0. To maximize V_0 we must have $\partial V/\partial b = 0$, and, as pointed out above, this condition is satisfied when

$$r - k + b(1 - b)\frac{\partial r}{\partial b} = 0$$

By substituting the numerical values assumed above, we obtain the following quadratic equation:

$$.2b^2 - .4b + .15 = 0$$

Solving for b, we obtain two roots: $b = .5$ and $b = 1.5$, but the latter value is outside the range of admissible retention ratios and may be disregarded. We may conclude, therefore, that the firm will maximize the present value of its stock by retaining each year one-half of its net profit.

In order to compute the maximum present value of the firm's stock, we first find the value of r corresponding to $b = .5$. This is found to be $.25 - .2(.5) = .15$. We then find that the maximum V_0 is

$$V_{max} = \frac{(1 - b)P_0}{k - rb} = \frac{(1 - .5)25}{.1 - (.15)(.5)} = 500$$

The reader may easily verify that an increase in the retention ratio above the level of .5 will result in a decrease in the value of V_0. For example, when $b = .6$, V_0 is found to be 454.55. A decrease in b below the level of .5 will also result in a lower value of V_0. For example, when $b = .4$, V_0 is found to be 468.75.†

† It should be noted that, in all cases, the initial profit, P_0, is equal to 25. This is so because of our assumption that profit retained in the initial year is invested in operating assets at the beginning of the following year. Therefore, a change in b can begin to influence the firm's operations and profit only in the following year.

2. Let us now assume that the relation between r and b can be expressed by the following quadratic equation:

$$r = .2 + .1b - .2b^2$$

In this case, the value of r increases from .2 to .2125 as the value of b is raised from zero to .25. Further increases in b will, however, have a decreasing effect on r.†

If we assume that $K_0 = 100$, $P_0 = 20$, and $k = .15$, then the present value of the firm's stock is equal to

$$V_0 = \frac{(1 - b)20}{.15 - (.2 + .1b - .2b^2)b}$$

Again, to maximize V_0 we must set $\partial V_0/\partial b = 0$, and this condition is satisfied when

$$r - k + b(1 - b)\frac{\partial r}{\partial b} = 0$$

By substituting the numerical values assumed above we obtain the following cubic equation:

$$.4b^3 - .7b^2 + .2b + .05 = 0$$

which has two real roots: 1.46 and .62. Since the retention ratio cannot be larger than 1, the relevant value of b must be .62 and the maximum value of V_0 is then found to be 219.0. Other values of V_0, corresponding to several selected values of b, are given hereunder.

Value of b	Value of r	Value of V_0
0	.2	133.33
.25	.2125 max.	154.50
.5	.2	200.00
.62	.185	219.00 max.
.8	.152	143.00
1.0	.1	0

Thus, if the firm distributed its entire net profit as dividends ($b = 0$), the present value of its stock would be $133.33. If it continually retained

† From the above equation it follows that $\partial r/\partial b = .1 - .4b$. By setting $\partial r/\partial b = 0$, we find that r is maximized when $b = .25$.

one-quarter of its net profit, it would maximize the average internal rate of return (as shown above), but not the present value of its stock. An increase in the retention ratio above 25 percent would result in a decline in r but a further rise in V_0. After the retention ratio has reached the value of .62, however, a further increase in it will result in a decline in both r and V_0.

THE RELATION BETWEEN k AND b

We shall now consider the question whether the market capitalization rate k applicable to a particular firm may be affected by a change in its retention ratio b. As will be recalled, we are assuming for the present that there is no external financing and that, therefore, the rate of the firm's capital expansion g is equal to rb. If r remains constant, an increase in b will clearly result in a proportionate rise in g. If r is a decreasing function of b, an increase in b should still be expected in most cases to raise g, although less than proportionately. Is there reason to expect that the degree of risk assumed by the firm's stockholders is increased when its capital expansion is accelerated through greater profit retentions?

Several factors must be considered in this connection. In many cases a faster expansion of capital and output involves greater efforts to develop new production methods, introduce new products, or enter new markets, all of which tend to increase the degree of risk assumed by the firm's stockholders. An increase in b in such cases would lead to an increase in the expected rate of growth of the firm's capital, profit, and dividends, but would also result in an increase in the degree of risk that this higher growth rate may not actually be realized. To put it in statistical terms, we may say that as the expected growth rate increases, the variance in the growth rate (which is equal to the sum of squared deviations from the mean) will also increase. And we may then write k as the sum of the risk-free interest rate i and a risk premium related to the growth rate g:

$$k = i + \alpha \operatorname{Var}(g)$$

It should be pointed out, however, that even if a higher growth rate did not involve an increase in variance, some investors would probably still feel justified in applying a higher discount factor to a dividend stream resulting from the adoption of a higher retention ratio. Some people, especially in the more advanced age groups, may be influenced by the feeling of uncertainty as to whether their remaining life span will permit them to realize the benefits of a policy that aims to reduce the amount of dividends in the near future in order to accelerate capital expansion and thereby increase the amounts to be paid in the more distant future.

Another relevant factor may emerge during periods of general uncertainty and concern about the prevailing price trends in the economy.

If an inflationary price trend is expected, most investors will feel justified in discounting more heavily the dividend streams consisting of lower amounts in the near future (when the purchasing power of the dollar is expected to be relatively high) and of higher amounts in the more remote future (when the purchasing power of the dollar is expected to decline considerably).

In general, we may conclude that, other things being equal, an increase in a company's retention ratio b may be expected to induce many—though not necessarily all—stockholders to apply a higher discount factor, k.† Consequently, our valuation formula will be more realistic if we treat k, as well as r, as a function of b.

Let us assume that k is an increasing function of b, as follows:[7]

$$k = \alpha + \beta b^2$$

Substituting this expression for k in the valuation formula (Equation 4-6), we obtain

$$V_0 = \frac{(1 - b)P_0}{\alpha + \beta b^2 - rb}$$

† Actually, when the degree of risk increases with time, a different k should be applied to each term of the dividend stream:

$$V = \frac{D_0(1 + g)}{1 + k_1} + \frac{D_0(1 + g)^2}{1 + k_2} + \cdots$$

When a single value of k is used in all the terms, it must be interpreted as an average of all k_i's $(k_1, k_2, k_3, \ldots)$ in the series. Some further problems arise in connection with the process of averaging, but they need not concern us at this point. (See Myron J. Gordon, *The Investment, Financing, and Valuation of the Corporation*, Richard D. Irwin, Inc., Homewood, Ill., 1962, p. 65.)

[7] We are using a quadratic equation because a linear function does not yield realistic results. If we set $k = \alpha + \beta b$, we have

$$V = \frac{(1 - b)P_0}{\alpha + \beta b - rb}$$

and

$$\frac{\partial V}{\partial b} b = \frac{P_0}{(\alpha + \beta b - rb)^2} (r - \alpha - \beta)$$

The first term of the last expression must always be positive. Therefore, $\partial V/\partial b$ will be positive, zero, or negative depending on the sign of the second term: $r - \alpha - \beta$. If $r > \alpha + \beta$, then $\partial V/\partial b$ is positive, which means that V increases continually as b is raised. When $b = \alpha/(r - \beta)$, the value of V becomes infinite. If $r = \alpha + \beta$, then $\partial V/\partial b = 0$ and V remains constant irrespective of the value of b. The firm's retention policy then becomes a matter of indifference. Finally, if $r < \alpha + \beta$, then $\partial V/\partial b$ is negative and V declines as b increases. Under these conditions, the firm should not retain any part of its profit at all.

If we assume for the moment that r remains constant (this assumption will be dropped later), differentiation of V_0 with respect to b gives us

$$\frac{\partial V}{\partial b} = \frac{(\alpha + \beta b^2 - rb)(-P_0) - (P_0 - bP_0)(2\beta b - r)}{(\alpha + \beta b^2 - rb)^2}$$

$$= \frac{P_0}{(\alpha + \beta b^2 - rb)^2}(\beta b^2 - 2\beta b + r - \alpha) \tag{4-10}$$

To maximize V_0 we must set $\partial V/\partial b = 0$. This condition is satisfied when $\beta b^2 - 2\beta b + r - \alpha = 0$.

By solving this quadratic equation, we can obtain the value of b which maximizes V_0, and by substituting this value of b in the valuation equation we can compute the maximum value of V_0.

To take a numerical example, assume that

$$k = .03 + .1b^2$$

and that $r = .1$ and $K_0 = 100$, which makes $P_0 = 10$.

By solving the equation

$$.1b^2 - .2b + .1 - .03 = 0$$

we find that the value of b that maximizes V_0 is equal to .45. The maximum value of V is then equal to

$$V_{max} = \frac{(1 - .45)10}{.03 + .1(.45)^2 - (.1)(.45)} = \$1,048$$

Other values of V, corresponding to several selected values of b, are given hereunder:

$b = 0$ $V = 333$

$b = .1$ $V = 429$

$b = .25$ $V = 667$

$b = .45$ $V = 1,048$ max.

$b = .6$ $V = 667$

$b = .9$ $V = 48$

It remains to consider the case in which the values of both k and r are affected by changes in the value of b. Let us assume that k is an increasing and r a decreasing function of b, as follows:

$$k = \alpha_1 + \alpha_2 b^2$$
$$r = \beta_1 + \beta_2 b - \beta_3 b^2$$

The valuation formula then assumes the following form

$$V_0 = \frac{(1 - b)P_0}{\alpha_1 + \alpha_2 b^2 - (\beta_1 + \beta_2 b - \beta_3 b^2)b}$$

and the first derivative of V with respect to b is equal to

$$\frac{\partial V}{\partial b} = \frac{P_0}{[\alpha_1 + \alpha_2 b^2 - (\beta_1 + \beta_2 b - \beta_3 b^2)b]^2}$$
$$\times [2\beta_3 b^3 + (\alpha_2 - \beta_2 - 3\beta_3)b^2 + (2\beta_2 - 2\alpha_2)b + \beta_1 - \alpha_1]$$

$$(4\text{-}11)$$

Once again, the value of b corresponding to the maximum value of V may be found by setting $\partial V/\partial b = 0$.

To give a numerical illustration, let us use the same equation for k as we did above

$$k = .03 + .1b^2$$

but assume that r, instead of being a constant, is the following function of b:

$$r = .1 + .1b - .3b^2$$

By substituting these values in the valuation formula and by setting $\partial V/\partial b = 0$, we find that the value of b which maximizes V can be obtained by solving the following cubic equation:

$$.6b^3 - .9b^2 + .07 = 0$$

The relevant root of this equation is found to be .3, and V_{max} is now equal to \$864. Other selected values of V are given hereunder:

$b = 0$ $V = 333$

$b = .1$ $V = 443$

$b = .3$ $V = 864$ max.

$b = .4$ $V = 652$

$b = .9$ $V = 6$

It will be noted that, with $b = 0$, the value of V is the same (\$333) both when $r = .1$ and when $r = .1 + .1b - .3b^2$. When b is relatively small (e.g., $b = .1$), V is larger in the latter case, because the firm is operating in the area of increasing returns. But as b becomes larger, the tendency of diminishing returns sets in and begins to exercise a depressing effect on V. The maximum value of V obtainable when r is a function of b is considerably below the value obtainable with a constant r.

SUMMARY

The problem discussed in this chapter concerns the relation between the firm's dividend policy and the present value of its stock. It is assumed that (1) the present value of stock is determined by the expected dividend stream, (2) profit retention is the only source of new financing, and (3) the retention ratio, once set, remains constant at all times. If a higher retention ratio is selected, lower dividends will be paid in the immediate future, but the rate of capital expansion will be increased and, consequently, greater dividends may be expected in the more distant future. The problem then is to determine which of the various possible dividend streams has the maximum present value.

If the internal rate of return, r, and the rate at which the dividend stream is capitalized, k, are held constant, the following results are obtained: when $r = k$, the present value remains the same, irrespective of changes in the retention ratio b; when $r < k$, the present value is maximized by reducing b to zero; finally, when $r > k$, the present value increases with b and becomes infinitely large when $b = k/r$. Since these results are obviously unrealistic, we must conclude that in reality either r, or k, or both do not remain unaffected by changes in the value of b.

The internal rate of return may be influenced by the retention ratio because of the latter's effect on the capital expansion rate. In a static market situation, a firm which attempts to increase its capital continually will sooner or later reach the stage of diminishing returns. But in an expanding market situation, a firm may be able to increase capital continually without experiencing diminishing returns, provided its rate of growth is in keeping with the growing capacity of the market. If this condition is not satisfied, however, a rise in the retention ratio and the resulting rise in the rate of capital expansion will probably lead to a decline in the internal rate of return.

The capitalization rate may also be affected by the firm's rate of expansion, and consequently, by its retention ratio. An increase in the rate of growth may involve introducing new products, or entering new markets, or both, and these developments may enhance the risks associated with the firm's operations. Consequently, the investors may feel justified in using a higher capitalization rate to derive the present value of the expected dividend stream.

If we assume that the internal rate of return is a decreasing function and the capitalization rate is an increasing function of the retention ratio, we obtain a more realistic range of the present values of the expected dividend streams. We find that the present value V increases as the retention ratio b is raised above its lower limit of zero; that V reaches its maximum when b is at a certain point; and that V begins to decline as b gets closer to its upper limit of 1. Under these conditions, the best interests of the stockholders clearly would not be served by pushing dividend payments upward without regard to the capital expansion needs; nor would they be served by pushing retentions upward without regard to the amount left for distribution.

SELECTED REFERENCES

See Chapter 5.

5

Stock Valuation: The Effect of External Equity Financing

In the preceding chapter we ruled out any inflow of external funds. Therefore, the rate of capital growth was determined solely by the retention ratio b and the average rate of return r. We shall now drop this restriction and consider situations in which the firm has a choice of using either internal or external funds, or a combination of both.[1] In this chapter, we shall assume, however, that external financing is available only in the form of additional stock sales. In other words, the firm's capital will still consist entirely of equity funds, irrespective of the method of financing used. The problems arising in connection with debt financing will be considered in Chapter 6.

EQUIVALENCE OF EXTERNAL AND INTERNAL FINANCING UNDER SIMPLIFIED CONDITIONS

Let us assume at first that the firm has already decided on the rate of capital expansion and is now considering whether it should use the internal or

[1] This means that we are removing item 2 from the list of assumptions made at the beginning of Chap. 4. All the other assumptions (1, 3, 4, and 5) are, however, still retained for the present.

the external source of new financing. As before, let K_0 be the firm's initial capital and r be the average rate of return (which is assumed to remain constant over time). If the firm wishes to expand at the rate g and decides to use the internal source, it must set the retention ratio b so as to make $rb = g$. The firm's profit in the initial year is rK_0; the amount retained and reinvested is $brK_0 = I_0$; and the amount of dividends paid is $(1 - b)rK_0 = rK_0 - I_0$. The series of dividends paid in the initial and subsequent years may then be written as follows:

$$D_0 = rK_0 - I_0$$
$$D_1 = rK_0 + rI_0 - I_1$$
$$D_2 = rK_0 + rI_0 + rI_1 - I_2$$
$$\cdots\cdots\cdots\cdots\cdots\cdots\cdots$$

In accordance with assumption 5 made at the beginning of Chapter 4, the value of the firm's stock is equal to the present value of the expected dividend stream. By summing up the terms on the right-hand side of the above equations and by applying the discount factor k, we obtain

$$\frac{rK_0}{1 + k} + \frac{rK_0}{(1 + k)^2} + \cdots = \frac{rK_0}{k}$$

$$\frac{-I_0}{1 + k} + \frac{rI_0}{(1 + k)^2} + \frac{rI_0}{(1 + k)^3} + \cdots = \frac{-I_0}{1 + k} + \frac{rI_0}{(1 + k)k} = \frac{(r - k)I_0}{(1 + k)k}$$

$$\frac{-I_1}{(1 + k)^2} + \frac{rI_1}{(1 + k)^3} + \frac{rI_1}{(1 + k)^4} + \cdots = \frac{-I_1}{(1 + k)^2} + \frac{rI_1}{(1 + k)^2 k}$$

$$= \frac{(r - k)I_1}{(1 + k)^2 k}$$

$$\cdots\cdots\cdots\cdots\cdots\cdots\cdots\cdots\cdots\cdots\cdots\cdots$$

It follows that the present value of the firm's stock, V_0, is equal to[2]

$$V_0 = \frac{rK_0}{k} + \frac{(r - k)I_0}{(1 + k)k} + \frac{(r - k)I_1}{(1 + k)^2 k} + \cdots \tag{5-1}$$

[2] This expression is, of course, equivalent to the one used in the preceding chapter, namely:

$$V_0 = \frac{(1 - b)rK_0}{k - rb}$$

It must be realized in this connection that $I_1 = I_0(1 + rb)$, $I_2 = I_0(1 + rb)^2$, etc. After making these substitutions, the reader can easily verify the equivalence of these two equations for V_0.

Suppose now that the firm wishes to expand at the same rate, g, but decides to use external instead of internal funds. In this case, the entire amount of profit, rK_t, will be distributed as dividends each year. New investment I_t will again be equal to rbK_t, but will now be financed each year by selling additional shares of stock instead of by profit retention. The firm's total dividends in the initial and subsequent years will then be

$$D_0 = rK_0$$

$$D_1 = rK_0 + rI_0$$

$$D_2 = rK_0 + rI_0 + rI_1$$

. . . .

Again, by summing up the terms on the right-hand side and applying the discount factor k, we obtain

$$\frac{rK_0}{k} + \frac{rI_0}{(1 + k)k} + \frac{rI_1}{(1 + k)^2 k} + \cdots \tag{5-2}$$

However, the present value of the shares held by the initial stockholders (in year 0) is determined not by the firm's total expected dividends but by the dividends expected to be paid on the initially held shares in all the future years. We must, therefore, deduct from the above expression the present value of all dividends to be paid to the new stockholders who will invest in the new shares to be issued at the beginning of year 1, year 2, etc.

If k is the prevailing market rate of return on comparable securities, the new stockholders at the end of year 0 would not be willing to invest the amount I_0 unless they expected a dividend stream equivalent to kI_0 per year in perpetuity. If the expected dividends were lower, the market value of the shares issued at the end of year 0 would drop below I_0; and if the expected dividends were higher, the market value of these shares would rise above I_0. The same is true of the stockholders investing in the firm's new shares in the subsequent years: they will have to be paid dividends equivalent to a perpetual stream of $kI_1, kI_2, kI_3, \ldots$ per annum, respectively. The dividends on the first issue of new shares, sold at the end of year 0, will begin to be paid at the end of year 1. Consequently, their present value is equal to $kI_0/k = I_0$ when computed at the end of year 0, and $I_0/(1 + k)$ when computed at the beginning of that year. The present value of the dividends paid on the subsequent new issues, all computed at the beginning of year 0, is equal to $I_1/(1 + k)^2$, $I_2/(1 + k)^3$, etc.

By deducting these amounts from Equation 5-2 we obtain the present value of all the future dividends to be paid on the initial shares held in year 0:

$$V'_0 = \frac{rK_0}{k} + \frac{(r - k)I_0}{(1 + k)k} + \frac{(r - k)I_1}{(1 + k)^2 k} + \cdots \qquad (5\text{-}3)$$

Since the right-hand side of Equation 5-3 is identical with the right-hand side of Equation 5-1, we conclude that the present value of the stock held in year 0 is the same ($V_0 = V'_0$) irrespective of whether the expansion (at a given rate g) is to be financed from the internal or the external source.

This conclusion may at first seem surprising. One can readily understand that the method of financing should have no effect on the present value of the old stockholder's stock when the internal rate of return r, is equal to the market rate of return, k. In such a case, the stockholder's additional revenues, resulting from reinvestment of a given amount of profit in the same firm, are clearly equivalent to the revenues obtainable by investment of the same amount of funds in other comparable securities. The values of V_0 and V'_0 would, in this case, both be reduced to $rK_0/k = K_0$. But when $r > k$, it may seem, at first glance, that the policy of profit reinvestment should be preferable from the stockholder's standpoint to the policy of total profit distribution accompanied by external financing. We have shown, however, that when total profit is distributed and external funds are obtained, the old stockholders still obtain a revenue increment resulting from the fact that $r > k$. The interpretation of this result may be made easier by observing the expansion process more closely, year by year.

In year 0, the firm's profit is rK_0. In the case of internal financing, I_0 is retained and reinvested, while $rK_0 - I_0$ is distributed as dividends at the end of the year. The amount retained I_0 represents, from the stockholder's standpoint, the cost of the new investment made at the end of the year 0. The discounted value of this cost at the beginning of year 0 is equal to $I_0/(1 + k)$. The revenues from this investment will consist of a perpetual stream of rI_0 per annum, beginning at the end of year 1. The present value of this perpetual stream at the beginning of year 0 is equal to $rI_0/(1 + k)k$ and the stockholder's net gain from the investment made in year 0 is equal to

$$\frac{rI_0}{(1 + k)k} - \frac{I_0}{1 + k} = \frac{(r - k)I_0}{(1 + k)k}$$

In the external-financing case, no part of the firm's profit is retained and the old stockholders incur no cost in connection with the new investment. The new funds, amounting to I_0, are provided at the end of year 0 by new stockholders who will be receiving a perpetual dividend stream equivalent to kI_0 per annum beginning at the end of year 1. The present value of this dividend stream at the beginning of year 0 is equal to $kI_0/(1 + k)k$. But the revenues which the firm will derive from the new investment are equal to rI_0 per annum beginning at the end of year 1, and the present value of this perpetual revenue stream at the beginning of year 0 is $rI_0/(1 + k)k$. Consequently, the net gain of the old stockholders, resulting from the new external investment in year 0, amounts to

$$\frac{rI_0}{(1 + k)k} - \frac{kI_0}{(1 + k)k} = \frac{(r - k)I_0}{(1 + k)k}$$

which is exactly the same as the net gain realized in the internal-financing case. The same relationship between the internal and the external financing will hold true in each of the subsequent years of the expansion process.

Once again, a simplified numerical example should be helpful. Assume that:

$$K_0 = \$1,000$$
$$r = .16$$
$$k = .1$$
$$b = .5$$

It follows, therefore, that the firm's profit in year 0 is $160; the desired rate of growth is $rb = .16 \times .5 = .08$; and the new investment in year 0 is $I_0 = 80$. To simplify computations, let us also assume in this example that, instead of planning continuous expansion, the firm plans to expand its capital by $80 only once, in year 0. In all the subsequent years new investment will be zero $(I_1 = I_2 = I_3 = \cdots = 0)$ and the firm's capital will remain at the level reached at the end of year 0 ($1,080). Under these conditions, the present value of the firm's stock at the beginning of the year 0 must be equal to

$$V_0 = \frac{.16 \times 1,000}{.1} + \frac{(.16 - .1)80}{1.1 \times .1} = 1,643.63$$

irrespective of whether the internal or the external method of financing is used in year 0. If the firm decided to use the internal method, retention of $80 at the end of year 0 would represent a cost to the stockholders, and the present value of this cost at the beginning of year 0 would be $80/1.1 = 72.73$.

On the other hand, reinvestment of $80 in the business would give rise to an additional revenue (and dividend) stream equal to $.16 \times 80$ per annum, beginning with year 1. The present value of this revenue stream at the beginning of year 0 would be $(.16 \times 80)/(1.1 \times .1) = 116.36$. The present value of the net gain to the stockholders resulting from this reinvestment would be equal to $116.36 - 72.73 = 43.63$.

If the firm decided to use the external method of financing, the old stockholders would incur no cost. The new stockholders, investing $80 at the end of year 0, would receive dividends amounting to $8 per annum, beginning at the end of year 1. The present value of this stream at the beginning of year 0 is equal to $8/.11 = 72.73$. But the firm's total profit and dividends will increase from $160 to $172.80 beginning at the end of year 1 (and will remain at that level thereafter because there will be no further new investment). At the beginning of year 0 the present value of this profit increment is equal to $12.80/.11 = 116.36$. The difference between 116.36 and 72.73 represents the present value of the old stockholder's net gain, which is exactly the same here (43.63) as in the internal-financing case.

It must be emphasized, however, that Equations 5-1 and 5-3 were derived on the basis of certain specific assumptions which are not entirely realistic. We have disregarded such factors as the cost of new stock flotations and the cost arising from the tax differential between the retained and the distributed part of corporate profit. We have also disregarded the diversification factor, which may significantly affect the value of k in Equations 5–1 and 5-3. It has been assumed above that the discount factor k is equal to the prevailing market rate of return for all securities belonging to the same risk class as the stock of the firm in question, and it has been further assumed that the same value of k may be used regardless of the method of financing chosen by the firm. However, if the investors are strongly motivated to diversify their portfolios, they may prefer to have the firm's profits distributed so that the funds may be invested in other firms (even if they are in the same risk class) rather than have the profits continually retained and reinvested in the same firm. Under these circumstances, the investors will be inclined to use a higher value of k if they expect the firm to use internal financing, and a lower value of k if they expect it to use external financing. Other things being equal, this will tend to reduce the value of V_0 in Equation 5-1 relative to the value of V_0' in Equation 5-3.

Finally it must be borne in mind that the availability of internal financing is limited by the firm's profitability. If the desired rate of expansion, g, does not exceed rb when $b = 1$, then the firm has, in theory, a choice between the internal and the external methods of financing. But if $g > rb$, even when $b = 1$, an inflow of external funds clearly becomes unavoidable. Of course, even in this case the firm has a choice of either using internal financing to the maximum extent possible and supplementing it with the required amount of external funds, or distributing the entire net profit and using external financing exclusively. However, the alternatives are obviously different here from what they are when $g \leq rb$.

THE EFFECT OF THE TAX FACTOR

We shall now drop the assumption that corporate profits are not subject to taxation and consider the effect of the tax factor on the value of corporate stock under the internal and the external methods of financing. In the United States corporate profits are taxed on both the corporate and the personal tax levels. The entire amount of net profit—irrespective of how much is paid out as dividends and how much is retained—is subject to the corporate income tax. In addition, dividends—but not retained profits— must be included in the stockholder's personal taxable income.[3] Profit retention may influence the stockholder's personal tax liability only indirectly, because of its effect on the value of the firm's shares. If shares, purchased at a certain price, are later sold at a higher price, the realized capital gain is subject to the personal income tax at a special (lower) rate. The problem of "double taxation" of corporate profits is complex and cannot be considered here in all its ramifications. Our present task is confined to an examination of the effect of both the corporate and the personal income tax factors on the conclusions reached above with respect to corporate stock valuation.[4]

First, it can be easily shown that the imposition of a corporate income tax does not, in itself, change our earlier conclusion that the value of a firm's stock remains the same irrespective of whether its expansion is financed by profit retention or via new stock issues. This is demonstrated in Parts A and B of Table 5-1. This table is set up on the assumption that the stockholders are given a choice of (a) having a certain amount, I, retained and reinvested in the same firms or (b) having the entire profit distributed and then investing the same amount, I, outside of the firm. In the latter case, the firm maintains the same rate of expansion by securing funds from external sources. It is also assumed that the same market rate of return, k, applies to the outside investments made by the firm's stockholders and to the investments made by the buyers of the firm's new shares.

In Part A of the table, the tax factor is entirely absent. It may be seen that the financial position of the initial stockholders is not affected by the method of financing used by their firm. In Part B, a corporate income tax is introduced at a flat rate t_c. As a result, profits and dividends are reduced in the same proportion, irrespective of whether the firm uses internal or

[3] A small dividend exclusion ($100 for a single person, $200 for husband and wife) is, however, allowed by the tax law.

[4] In connection with the "double taxation" argument, it should be mentioned that there is no general agreement among economists as to the incidence of the corporate income tax. To the extent that the tax is shifted to consumers (through higher prices), the stockholders escape the alleged extra tax burden. But since an individual company cannot affect the incidence of the tax by changing its own dividend policy, such a change is bound to have an effect on the stockholder's personal tax liability.

Table 5-1—Part A: No taxes Comparison of the stockholder's income under internal and external methods of financing

(a) Internal Financing

Year	Profit	Retained profit	Dividends
0	$P_0 = rK_0$	I_0	$D_0 = rK_0 - I_0$
1	$P_1 = rK_0 + rI_0$	I_1	$D_1 = rK_0 + rI_0 - I_1$
2	$P_2 = rK_0 + rI_0 + rI_1$	I_2	$D_2 = rK_0 + rI_0 + rI_1 - I_2$
....			

(b) External Financing

Year	Profit = dividends (1)	External funds (2)	Dividends on new shares (3)	Dividends on initial shares (4)	Outside investment by initial stockholders (5)	Dividends on outside investment (6)	Total dividends of initial stockholders less outside investment (Col. 4 + Col. 6 – Col. 5)
0	$P_0 = D_0 = rK_0$	I_0	kI_0	rK_0	I_0	kI_0	$rK_0 - I_0$
1	$P_1 = D_1 = rK_0 + rI_0$	I_1	kI_1	$rK_0 + rI_0 - kI_0$	I_1	$kI_0 + kI_1$	$rK_0 + rI_0 - I_1$
2	$P_2 = D_2 = rK_0 + rI_0 + rI_1$	I_2		$rK_0 + rI_0 + rI_1 - kI_0 - kI_1$	I_2		$rK_0 + rI_0 + rI_1 - I_2$
....							

Table 5-1—Part B Corporate income tax only

(a) Internal Financing

Year	Profit	Retained profit	Dividends
0	$P_0 = (1 - t_c)rK_0$	I_0	$D_0 = (1 - t_c)rK_0 - I_0$
1	$P_1 = (1 - t_c)(rK_0 + rI_0)$	I_1	$D_1 = (1 - t_c)(rK_0 + rI_0) - I_1$
2	$P_2 = (1 - t_c)(rK_0 + rI_0 + rI_1)$	I_2	$D_2 = (1 - t_c)(rK_0 + rI_0 + rI_1) - I_2$
.....	.....	.....	.....

(b) External Financing

Year	Profit = dividends (1)	External funds (2)	Dividends on new shares (3)	Dividends on initial shares (4)	Outside investment by initial stockholders (5)	Dividends on outside investment (6)	Total dividends of initial stockholders less outside investment (Col. 4 + Col. 6 − Col. 5)
0	$P_0 = D_0 = (1 - t_c)rK_0$	I_0		$(1 - t_c)rK_0$	I_0		$(1 - t_c)rK_0 - I_0$
1	$P_1 = D_1 = (1 - t_c)(rK_0 + rI_0)$	I_1	kI_0	$(1 - t_c)(rK_0 + rI_0) - kI_0$	I_1	kI_0	$(1 - t_c)(rK_0 + rI_0) - I_1$
2	$P_2 = D_2 = (1 - t_c)(rK_0 + rI_0 + rI_1)$	I_2	kI_1	$(1 - t_c)(rK_0 + rI_0 + rI_1) - kI_0 - kI_1$	I_2	$kI_0 + kI_1$	$(1 - t_c)(rK_0 + rI_0 + rI_1) - I_2$
.....	.....	.....	.....	.....	.....	.....	.....

Table 5-1—Part C Corporate and personal income taxes

(a) Internal Financing

Year	Profit	Retained profit	Dividends less personal income tax
0	$P_0 = rK_0$	I_0	$D_0 = (rK_0 - I_0)(1 - t_p)$
1	$P_1 = rK_0 + rI_0$	I_1	$D_1 = (rK_0 + rI_0 - I_1)(1 - t_p)$
2	$P_2 = rK_0 + rI_0 + rI_1$	I_2	$D_2 = (rK_0 + rI_0 + rI_1 - I_2)(1 - t_p)$
...			

(b) External Financing

Year	Profit = dividends (1)	External funds (2)	Dividends on new shares (3)	Dividends on initial shares less personal income tax (4)	Outside investment by initial stockholders (5)	Dividends on outside investment less personal income tax (6)	Total dividends of initial stockholders less outside investment (Col. 4 + Col. 6 − Col. 5)
0	$P_0 = D_0 = rK_0$	I_0	kI_0	$rK_0(1 - t_p)$	I_0	$kI_0(1 - t_p)$	$rK_0(1 - t_p) - I_0$
1	$P_1 = D_1 = rK_0 + rI_0$	I_1	kI_1	$(rK_0 + rI_0 - kI_0)(1 - t_p)$	I_1	$(kI_0 + kI_1)(1 - t_p)$	$(rK_0 + rI_0)(1 - t_p) - I_1$
2	$P_2 = D_2 = rK_0 + rI_0 + rI_1$	I_2		$(rK_0 + rI_0 + rI_1 - kI_0 - kI_1)(1 - t_p)$	I_2		$(rK_0 + rI_0 + rI_1)(1 - t_p) - I_2$
...							

external financing. Thus, here again the stockholder's financial position is not affected by the method of financing.

Finally, in Part C of Table 5-1, a personal income tax is assumed to be imposed on the dividend income at a flat rate t_p. In this part of the table it is also assumed that r represents the average internal rate of return *after* corporate income tax. Consequently, $P_0 = rK_0$ is the amount of profit after corporate tax in year 0. In the case of internal financing, in the initial year the amount of dividends before personal income tax is equal to $D_0 = rK_0 - I_0$ and the amount of dividends after personal income tax is equal to $(1 - t_p)(rK_0 - I_0)$. In the case of external financing, the amounts of dividends before and after the personal income tax are rK_0 and $(1 - t_p)rK_0$, respectively. It can be readily seen that, if the stockholders in the external-financing case invest outside of the firm an amount equal to the firm's retained profit in the internal-financing case, I_0, their remaining cash on hand will be smaller than the cash dividends received in the latter case by an amount equal to t_pI_0. In other words, t_pI_0 represents the tax saving that can be made in year 0 by reinvesting the amount I_0 in the same firm rather than taking it out in the form of cash dividends.

As the table indicates, in each of the subsequent years the amount of tax savings is equal to $t_pI_1, t_pI_2, t_pI_3, \ldots$, respectively. The present value of all future tax savings is equal to:

$$t_p\left[\frac{I_0}{1 + k} + \frac{I_1}{(1 + k)^2} + \cdots\right] = \sum_{t=0}^{\infty} \frac{t_pI_t}{(1 + k)^{t+1}} \tag{5-4}$$

Consequently, if the present value of the stock of an externally financed firm is equal to $_eV_0$, the present value of the stock of an internally financed firm must, under the conditions assumed, be equal to

$$_iV_0 = {_eV_0} + \sum_{t=0}^{\infty} \frac{t_pI_t}{(1 + k)^{t+1}} \tag{5-5}$$

THE PROBLEM OF CAPITAL GAINS

In the preceding sections it was assumed that the present value of a firm's stock is determined by the expected future stream of dividends extending over an infinitely long period of time. But in real life, the investor's time horizon is not infinitely long. In fact, in many cases it is rather short: shares are purchased with a view to a resale at a higher price in a relatively brief period of time. Under such conditions, it would seem that the main factor determining the present value should be the expected future price rather than the expected dividend yield.

If an investor buys stock with the intention of holding it for n years and then selling it at the market price, his expected stream of receipts is

$$D_0 + D_1 + \cdots + D_n + N_n$$

where D_t denotes annual dividend and N_n is the market value of the stock at the end of year n.

The present value of this stream is equal to

$$V_0 = \sum_{t=0}^{t=n} \frac{D_t}{(1 + k)^{t+1}} + \frac{N_n}{(1 + k)^{n+1}} \tag{5-6}$$

But the price of the stock in year n is determined by the dividend stream beginning at the end of that year. Thus we may write

$$N_n = \frac{D_{n+1}}{1 + k} + \frac{D_{n+2}}{(1 + k)^2} + \cdots = \sum_{t=n+1}^{\infty} \frac{D_t}{(1 + k)^{t-n}}$$

The present value (in year 0) of this stream is equal to

$$\frac{N_n}{(1 + k)^{n+1}} = \frac{D_{n+1}}{(1 + k)^{n+2}} + \frac{D_{n+2}}{(1 + k)^{n+3}} + \cdots = \sum_{t=n+1}^{\infty} \frac{D_t}{(1 + k)^{t+1}}$$

By substituting we obtain

$$V_0 = \sum_{t=0}^{\infty} \frac{D_t}{(1 + k)^{t+1}} \tag{5-7}$$

It follows that the present value of a finite stream of dividends plus the present value of a future price of the stock is mathematically equal to the present value of an infinite stream of dividends. In other words, the length of the present stockholder's investment horizon has no effect on the present value of the stock. This is true both when the firm is expanding by means of profit retention and when it is expanding by means of new stock flotations.

Let us now consider the effect of the tax factor when investors purchase stock and then resell it within a finite period of time. The imposition of a corporate income tax at a given rate, which remains constant over time, will reduce the firm's profit P_t in the same proportion year after year. If b remains constant, dividends will also be reduced in the same proportion each year. Equations 5-1 and 5-2 will, therefore, remain valid if D_t is made equal to $(1 - t_c)(1 - b)P_t$.

The imposition of a personal income tax on the distributed part of profit above will result in a series of annual tax savings in the case of internal financing, as has already been shown above. Suppose that an investor buys stock with the intention of holding it for n years and then selling it at its market value. In the case of internal financing, he will pay less tax each year, and the present value of the tax savings over the period of n years will be

$$TS_0 = \sum_{t=0}^{n} \frac{t_p \alpha I_t}{(1 + k)^{t+1}}$$

where αI_t is the investor's share of the firm's total retained profit. Furthermore, the tax savings expected in the subsequent period, beginning with year $n + 1$, should be incorporated in the price at which the stock will be sold. The present value of these tax savings, at the beginning of year 0, is

$$TS_0' = \sum_{t=n}^{\infty} \frac{t_p I_t \alpha}{(1 + k)^{t+1}}$$

Consequently, the present value of the stock of an internally financed firm should exceed that of an externally financed firm by an amount equal to

$$TS_0 + TS_0' = \sum_{0}^{\infty} \frac{t_p \alpha I_t}{(1 + k)^{t+1}} \tag{5-8}$$

This, of course, is the same result as that obtained above on the assumption that the initial owner holds the stock indefinitely. As can be seen, Equation 5-8 differs from Equation 5-4 only in that it includes the fraction α in its numerator. It must be borne in mind in this connection that Equation 5-4 shows the tax savings accruing to all stockholders combined. If we wanted to compute the tax savings accruing to a stockholder holding indefinitely a certain fraction of the firm's stock, we would have to include α in the numerator of Equation 5-4 too.

Finally, suppose that a tax on realized capital gains is imposed at a flat rate t_{cg}. The amount of the tax, which will have to be paid when the stock is sold at the end of the nth year, will be equal to

$$t_{cg}(N_n - N_0)$$

where N_0 and N_n are the market values of the investor's shares at the beginning and the end of this holding period, respectively. Now, since the value of his shares should increase at a faster rate in the internal-financing case than in the external-financing one, the amount of taxable capital gain should be correspondingly higher in the former case. The net amount of tax savings resulting from internal financing will then be equal to the personal income tax saved because of lower dividends less the additional tax paid because of the greater capital gain.

If the firm's rate of return is average for its class, internal financing should tend, other things being equal, to raise the value of its stock by the amount of profit retained each year. The investor's total capital gain, over the period of n years, would then be equal to $\sum_0^n \alpha I_t$, and the present value of his net tax saving over this period would be

$$t_p \sum_{t=0}^n \frac{\alpha I_t}{(1 + k)^{t+1}} - t_{cg} \sum_0^n \frac{\alpha I_t}{(1 + k)^{t+1}} = (t_p - t_{cg}) \sum_0^n \frac{\alpha I_t}{(1 + k)^{t+1}}$$

Clearly, in this case, net saving would be positive only as long as t_p exceeded t_{cg}.

TRANSACTION COSTS

An additional factor, tending to disturb the equivalence of internal and external financing, is found in the costs involved in purchasing and selling securities in the capital market. These transaction costs include (a) underwriters' fees and other expenses incurred by the corporations issuing new shares and (b) brokers' commissions and transfer taxes paid by the investors buying and selling outstanding shares.

To isolate the effect of this factor, let us once more consider a situation in which income taxes—both corporate and personal—are absent. But we shall now assume that the investors buying or selling shares in the market must pay a broker's commission at a constant rate c, and that the corporations selling new issues must pay an underwriter's fee at a constant rate f. If a firm retains an amount I out of its net profit, there are no transaction costs and the entire amount can be invested in profit-earning assets. But if an equivalent sum is paid out as dividends and is used by the stockholders for purchasing other securities, the net value of the shares acquired (after the broker's commission) will be only $(1 - c)I$. Moreover, if the firm resorts to external financing and raises an amount I by selling new shares through investment bankers, the net amount (after the banker's fee) that can be invested in profit-earning assets will be only $(1 - f)I$.

In the case of internal financing, the stockholder's dividend stream is still the same as that shown in Table 5-1, Part A, Section (a), viz.,

Year 0 $D_0 = rK_0 - I_0$

Year 1 $D_1 = rK_0 + rI_0 - I_1$

Year 2 $D_2 = rK_0 + rI_0 + rI_1 - I_2$

· ·

In the case of external financing, however, we now have a different situation from that presented in Section (b) of the Table 5-1. The initial stockholder's total income, less the amount of outside investment, is now equal to

Year 0 $rK_0 - I_0$

Year 1 $rK_0 + k(1 - c)I_0 + r(1 - f)I_0 - kI_0 - I_1$

Year 2 $rK_0 + k(1 - c)I_0 + k(1 - c)I_1 + r(1 - f)I_0 + r(1 - f)I_1$
$$- kI_0 - kI_1$$

. . . .

The annual difference between these two income streams are found to be

Year 0   0

Year 1 $(rf + kc)I_0$

Year 2 $(rf + kc)I_0 + (rf + kc)I_1$

. . . .

and the present value of this series of differences, capitalized at the rate k, is equal to

$$\frac{(rf + ck)I_0}{k} + \frac{(rf + kc)I_1}{(1 + k)k} + \frac{(rf + kc)I_2}{(1 + k)^2 k} + \cdots = TR_0$$

Thus, if the present value of the stockholder's income stream in the case of internal financing is equal to $_iV_0$, the present value of his income stream in the case of external financing, $_eV_0$, must be equal to

$$_eV_0 = {}_iV_0 - TR_0$$

In the absence of transaction costs (and income taxes), it should be possible for investors to convert securities into cash, or vice versa, without any diminution in their total net worth. Under such conditions, therefore, the stockholders would not be penalized if the payout ratio adopted by the firm did not exactly meet their cash requirements for consumption and—if they wish to diversify their portfolios—for investment in other securities.

But if we assume that there are transaction costs amounting to, say, 5 percent of the value of the securities sold, the sale of $100 worth of securities would bring in only $95 in cash. Clearly, under these conditions, the stockholders would prefer that the firm not retain profit in excess of the amount which they themselves would wish to add to its capital, considering all of their other financial needs.

The effect of the transaction cost is illustrated diagrammatically in Figure 5-1, in which retained profit is measured along the vertical axis and dividends are measured along the horizontal axis. The maximum possible amount that could be retained is equal to OB, which is the total amount of profit. The maximum possible amount of dividends is equal to OC, which is, of course, equal to OB. The line BC is the locus of all possible combinations of profit retention and dividends. The slope of this line is equal to -1, since an increase in dividends by a given amount always means a decrease of retained profit by exactly the same amount.

Lines I_1, I_2, and I_3 are the stockholder's indifference curves for different combinations of retained profit and dividends. Their preferred combination is at point F, where the line BC is tangent to the highest indifference curve, $I_1 I_1$. At this point, retained profit is equal to $FD = OE$ and dividends are equal to $EF = OD$. But suppose that instead of point F the firm selects point G on the line BC, which means that it retains an amount equal to $GK = OH$ and pays dividends amounting to $HG = OK$. It can be seen that point G lies on a lower indifference curve, $I_3 I_3$. However, in the absence of transaction costs, the stockholders can make an adjustment and reach point F on the curve $I_1 I_1$ by selling a package of shares, whose total value is equal to HE, and adding the cash received ($HE = KD$) to the dividends paid by the firm (OK).

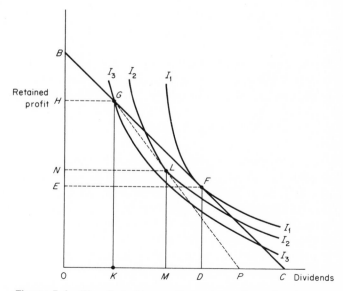

Figure 5-1   The effect of transaction costs on the preferred payout ratio.

On the other hand, when transaction costs are present, it becomes impossible to convert shares into cash on a dollar-for-dollar basis. The conversion rate is now indicated by the slope of the broken line GP. If the firm selects point G, the stockholders can adjust their position only by moving along this broken line, and the best combination would be reached at point L, which lies on the indifference curve I_2I_2. The stockholder's cash increments (the dividends plus the cash realized by selling shares) are now equal to OM, and the increase in the value of their remaining shares is equal to ON.

It should also be pointed out that if the firm decided to adopt a higher payout ratio than that preferred by the stockholders. i.e., if it selected a point on the BC line to the right of the point F, the stockholders would not be able to convert cash into additional securities on a dollar-for-dollar basis, as long as they had to incur transaction costs.

Let us now consider the combined effect of the personal income tax and the transaction cost factors. Dividends, as we know, are subject to the regular personal income tax rate, while realized capital gains (long-term) are subject to a lower tax rate. Therefore, a high payout ratio may, on balance, be advantageous to the stockholders if the tax saving resulting from the lower dividend payments exceeds the transaction cost involved in obtaining additional cash by selling some of the shares owned.

The combined effect of these factors is illustrated in Figure 5-2. In the absence of taxes and transaction costs, the stockholder's preferred

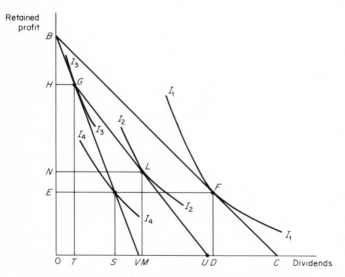

Figure 5-2 The combined effect of taxes and transaction costs on the preferred payout ratio.

position is again at point F, with the retained profit being equal to OE and dividends to OD. However, when dividends are subject to a personal income tax, a one-dollar reduction in the retained profit adds less than one dollar to the stockholder's disposable income. The rate of substitution between retained profit and dividends is indicated in this case not by the line BC, but by the steeper line BV. If the firm retained an amount OE, the dividend income after tax would be equal to OS instead of OD, and the stockholders would be on a lower indifference curve, I_4I_4.

As the diagram shows the stockholders would in this case be in a better position if the firm retained a higher amount OH. Although dividends after taxes would then amount only to OT, this combination would place the stockholders on a higher indifference curve I_3I_3 (cutting through point G). But the stockholders could further improve their position by moving along the line GU. This line is drawn on the assumption that a sale of the firm's shares involves payment of the broker's commission and of the capital gains tax, but that this combined cost is less than the regular income tax imposed on the dividend income. As can be seen, a sale of shares with a total value equal to HN will yield a net amount of cash TM. This combination, which is denoted by point L, will place the stockholders on the indifference curve I_2I_2, which is higher than I_3I_3.

In conclusion, it should also be pointed out that for simplicity's sake we assumed in the above discussion that all stockholders of a given company have the same payout preferences. Actually, in a publicly owned corporation, there are bound to be substantial differences between individual stockholders in this respect because of the wide range of income and wealth classes to which they belong. Therefore, it would be virtually impossible for such a firm to find a single payout ratio that would eliminate the conversion of shares into cash (or vice versa) and the payment of transaction costs by any of its owners. Even if the management, in setting the dividend policy, was motivated primarily by the desire to meet the stockholders' payout preferences—which is not generally the case—the most it could hope for would be to find a ratio most closely approximating the preferences of the largest possible sector of its owners.

SUMMARY

In this chapter we have introduced external financing, but only in the form of additional equity funds obtained by issuing new shares of stock.

In a simplified situation, in which there are no taxes and no transaction costs, the financial position of a firm's stockholders should not be affected by switching from internal to external financing, or vice versa, as long as the same rate of capital expansion is maintained. This can be easily seen in the case in which the firm's internal rate of return is equal to the market rate of return available on securities of other firms in the same risk class: the stockholder's income increment will clearly be the same whether the firm's profit is retained or paid out and invested elsewhere.

As has been shown, however, this is also true in the case in which the internal rate exceeds the available market rate: if profit is distributed, the stockholders can invest the funds outside the firm only at the lower market rate; but the firm will pay the same lower rate on the new external funds received, as a result of which the amount of profit accruing to the old stockholders will increase and this profit increment will offset the loss sustained because of the lower rate available on outside investments.

The equivalence of internal and external financing is disturbed, however, when the income tax factor is taken into account. Since in our tax system dividends are subject to the personal income tax (except for minor exclusions), whereas retained profits are not (as long as the stock is not sold), retentions tend to lower the stockholder's personal income tax liability.

An investor who intends to hold his shares indefinitely may look forward to an indefinite postponement of the tax on the retained part of profit. Consequently, the present value of his shares should be higher if the firm intends to use internal financing. On the other hand, an investor who intends to sell his shares within a finite period of time must take into consideration the capital gains tax to be paid when the sale is made. Since profit retention should tend to increase the value of his shares at the time of their sale, the amount of capital gain should be higher in the internal-financing case. The resulting increase in the capital gains tax would then tend to diminish the positive effect of profit retention on the present value of the shares.

Transaction costs represent another factor tending to disturb the equivalence of internal and external financing. These costs include underwriting costs and other expenses involved in the selling of new issues by corporations as well as brokers' commissions and transfer taxes paid when existing securities change hands.

When profits are retained and reinvested in the same firm, transaction costs are avoided. However, if an investor expects to convert these retained funds into cash at a later time by selling some of his shares in the market, transaction costs will be involved and must be taken into account along with the expected amount of the capital gains tax.

SELECTED REFERENCES

Bodenhorn, Diran: "A Cash Flow Concept of Profit," *Journal of Finance*, vol. 19, March, 1964, pp. 16–31.
————: "On the Problem of Capital Budgeting," *Journal of Finance*, vol. 14, December, 1959, pp. 473–492.
Brittain, J. A.: *Corporate Dividend Policy*, The Brookings Institution, Washington, D.C., 1966.

Friend, Irwin, and Marshall Puckett: "Dividends and Stock Prices," *American Economic Review*, vol. 54, September, 1964, reprinted in *Foundations for Financial Management*, ed. James Van Horne, Richard D. Irwin, Inc., Homewood, Ill., 1966, pp. 535–561.

Gordon, Myron J.: *The Investment, Financing and Valuation of the Corporation*, Richard D. Irwin, Inc., Homewood, Ill., 1962, chap. 5.

Harkavy, Oscar: "The Relation between Retained Earnings and Common Stock Prices for Large Listed Corporations," *Journal of Finance*, vol. 8, September, 1953, pp. 283–297.

Lerner, Eugene M., and Willard T. Carleton: *A Theory of Financial Analysis*, Harcourt, Brace, and World, Inc., New York, 1966, chaps. 7, 8, and 9.

Lintner, John: "Optimal Dividends and Corporate Growth under Uncertainty," *Quarterly Journal of Economics*, vol. 88, February, 1964, pp. 49–95.

Miller, Merton H., and Franco Modigliani: "Dividend Policy, Growth, and the Valuation of Shares," *Journal of Business*, vol. 34, October, 1961, reprinted in *Foundations for Financial Management*, ed. James Van Horne, Richard D. Irwin, Inc., Homewood, Ill., 1966, pp. 481–513.

Walter, James E.: "Dividend Policies and Common Stock Prices," *Journal of Finance*, vol. 11, March, 1956, pp. 29–41.

———: "Dividend Policy: Its Influence on the Value of the Enterprise," *Journal of Finance*, vol. 18, May, 1963, reprinted in *Foundations for Financial Management*, ed. James Van Horne, Richard D. Irwin, Inc., Homewood, Ill., 1966, pp. 514–525.

Weston, Fred. J., and Eugene F. Brigham: *Managerial Finance*, Holt, Rinehart and Winston, New York, 1966, chap. 20.

Empirical Studies of Dividend Policies

A number of statistical studies have been made in order to test the validity of various theoretical propositions concerning corporate dividend policies. We shall briefly review hereunder two of these studies: one by J. A. Brittain, dealing with the major factors determining dividend policy, and the other by I. Friend and M. Puckett, concerned with the relative importance of dividends and retained earnings in determining the price-earnings ratios of common stocks.

BRITTAIN'S STUDY

J. A. Brittain[5] takes as his starting point the model proposed by Professor John Lintner, according to which dividends are determined by the firm's net profit, the long-run "target" payout ratio, and the "speed-of-adjustment" factor. Algebraically, this is expressed as

$$D - D_{-1} = a + c(rP - D_{-1}) + u$$

[5] John A. Brittain, *Corporate Dividend Policy*, The Brookings Institution, Washington, D.C., 1966.

where D is dividend, P is profit, c is the speed-of-adjustment coefficient and r is the target payout ratio. Brittain obtains statistically significant results with this model but, at the same time, finds that better results can be obtained by certain modifications and additions.

First, he substitutes the "cash-flow" (profit after taxes but including depreciation) variable, C, for the net profit variable, P. The reason for this substitution is that changes in the liberality of depreciation allowances for tax purposes invalidate reported net profits as a measure of the ability to pay dividends. Statistical tests, performed with the data for all corporations and for manufacturing corporations during the period 1942–1960, indicate that the cash flow is indeed a better explanatory variable than the reported net profit.

Next, Brittain introduces the personal income tax factor. His reasoning here is as follows: Since dividends are subject to regular income tax rates, while retained profits are taxed only if they lead to realized capital gains, to which lower rates apply, corporate payout ratios should tend to vary inversely with the differential between the tax rates on ordinary income and those on capital gains. He finds, however, that the capital gains tax, as such, does not demonstrate any significance and, consequently, the tax rate on ordinary income alone is as good an explanatory factor as the differential between this rate and the capital gains tax rate. The following regression equations have been obtained:

All corporations

$$D - D_{-1} = .47 + (.198 - .096t_{10})C - .430D_{-1} \qquad R^2 = .814$$
$$(.11) \quad (.020) \quad (.019) \qquad\quad (.042)$$

Manufacturing corporations

$$D - D_{-1} = .23 + (.188 - .097t_{25})C - .455D_{-1} \qquad R^2 = .782$$
$$(.06) \quad (.022) \quad (.030) \qquad\quad (.046)$$

The t_{10} and t_{25} variables in these equations represent the marginal tax rates paid by the stockholders in the upper 10 percent and upper 25 percent income brackets, respectively. Over the 1920–1960 period, the income tax rates showed a steep upward trend and there was a corresponding rise in the tax shelter advantage. Accordingly, this factor tended to depress the payout ratio to a considerable extent.

Finally, Brittain introduces two additional variables and finds dividends to be negatively related to interest rates (i) and to the change in sales over the previous two years (S/S_{-2}). The relevant equations are as follows:

All corporations

$$D - D_{-1} = .29 + \left(.308 - .197t_{25} - .126i - .025\frac{S}{S_{-2}}\right)C - .393D_{-1}$$

$$(.13) \quad (.036) \quad (.033) \quad\quad (.034) \quad (.016) \quad\quad\quad (.041)$$

$$R^2 = .859$$

Manufacturing corporations

$$D - D_{-1} = .18 + \left(.306 - .166t_{25} - .118i - .033\frac{S}{S_{-2}}\right)C - .436D_{-1}$$

$$(.08) \quad (.040) \quad (.041) \quad\quad (.041) \quad (.015) \quad\quad\quad (.046)$$

$$R^2 = .835$$

The S/S_{-2} variable represents the growth factor. As the rate of growth increases, so does the demand for both external and internal funds. Hence, the payout ratio tends to decline. The negative relation between dividends and interest rates indicates a tendency to shift from external to internal financing when there is a rise in the cost of borrowing.

It should be mentioned in conclusion that Brittain has also tested several models in which net profit and depreciation have been treated as separate variables. But while these models have brought out clearly the significance of the depreciation factor, their overall explanatory performance has not been found superior to that of the simpler cash-flow model.

FRIEND AND PUCKETT'S STUDY

Friend and Puckett's statistical analysis[6] was based on sample data from five industries: chemicals, electronics, electric utilities, foods, and steels, in each of two years, 1956 and 1958. They begin by using the regression equation which has been previously applied to cross-section data by other economists, viz.:

$$P_t = a + bD_t + cR_t$$

where the variables, reading from left to right, represent per share price, dividends, and retained earnings. The results of this test seem to indicate that in non-growth industries (foods and steels) there was a strong investor preference for dividends ($b > c$); while in growth industries (electronics and electric utilities) there was some preference for retained earnings ($c > b$).

[6] Irwin Friend and Marshall Puckett, "Dividends and Stock Prices," *The American Economic Review*, vol. 54, no. 5, September 1964.

The authors do not, however, accept these findings as valid because the equation used fails to take into account several important factors. First, there is the risk factor, which may impart an upward bias to the dividend coefficient. Companies which face greater uncertainty about future earnings may tend to adopt a lower payout ratio in order to reduce the risk of having to cut their dividends in the future. At the same time, greater uncertainty tends to depress the market price of the stock. Thus, there appears to be a direct relationship between the dividends and the price. But if the risk variable were included in the equation, a different dividend coefficient would probably be obtained. Secondly, there is the growth factor, which may affect the coefficient of retained earnings. If the rate of earnings retention is correlated with external financing, the value of c in the regression equation will be biased because it will reflect the effect of both factors rather than retained earnings alone.

There are other factors that should also be taken into consideration, such as random variations in income, income measurement errors, regression weighting, and least-square biases. Some of the omitted factors may be introduced by adding a lagged earnings–price ratio, E/P_{t-1}, to the regression equation. The introduction of this new variable results in a reduction of the difference between the dividend and the retained earnings coefficients. However, the application of this method runs into certain statistical complications.

Another approach has, therefore, been tried by the authors in order to eliminate random variations in income. This involves derivation of "normalized" earnings for each of the companies included in the tests. It is assumed that the dividend-price ratio is always normal, but that the earnings-price ratio is subject to short-run fluctuations. It is also assumed that the average earnings-price ratio for the sample, E/P_{kt}, is free of earnings disturbances. The normal value of a company's earnings-price ratio is then derived by using the following equation:

$$\left(\frac{E}{P}\right)_{it}^{n} = (a_i + b_{it})\left(\frac{E}{P}\right)_{kt}$$

When a normalized value of the earnings-price ratio is obtained, normalized earnings E is found by multiplying this ratio by per share price, and normalized retained earnings R_t^n is found by subtracting dividends from normalized earnings. The following regression equation is then used:

$$P_t = a + bD_t + cR_t^n + d\left(\frac{E}{P}\right)_t^n$$

and it is found that the dividend coefficient b is somewhat higher than the retained earnings coefficient c in the food and steel industries, but that the reverse is true for the chemical companies. For example, the following values have been obtained for 1958:

	b	c
Foods	13.26	8.95
Steels	13.59	12.19
Chemicals	12.18	18.62

The authors' general conclusion is stated as follows:

There is some indication that in nongrowth industries as a whole, a somewhat (but only moderately) higher investor valuation may be placed on dividends than on retained earnings within the range of pay-out experienced, but that the opposite may be true in growth industries. To the extent that this conclusion is valid, it is possible that management might be able, at least in some measure, to increase stock prices in nongrowth industries by raising dividends, and in growth industries by greater retention.[7]

[7] Ibid., p. 680.

6

Stock Valuation: The Effect of Debt Financing

In the preceding chapter we compared internal equity financing (by profit retention) with external equity financing (by new stock flotations). We shall now introduce the second component of external financing, viz., debt financing, into our analysis. We shall not differentiate here between particular types of debt: short-term and long-term, secured and unsecured, etc. It will be assumed that there is only one class of loans and that each loan is, in effect, a perpetual obligation: it can always be renewed at maturity, so that repayment of the principal can be postponed indefinitely. With respect to the interest rate, we shall at first assume that it remains constant and, later on, that it is a function of the debt-to-equity ratio.

FINANCIAL LEVERAGE: ADVANTAGES AND LIMITATIONS

To take a simple case, consider two nonexpanding firms, each operating with the same invested capital, K, and each realizing the same average internal rate of return, r, which remains constant over time.[1] Firm I operates with equity funds only ($E_1 = K$) and its total profit is, therefore, available to its stockholders ($rK = P_t = P_{e_1}$). In contrast, Firm II uses both equity and debt funds, so that

$$E_2 + D_2 = E_1 = K \tag{6-1}$$

Total profit before interest of Firm II is also equal to $rK = P_t$, but the profit accruing to its stockholders is equal to

$$P_{e_2} = rK - iD_2 = rE_2 + (r - i)D_2 \tag{6-2}$$

where i is the interest rate paid on borrowed funds. The rate of return on equity funds, which is equal to r for Firm I, must be written as

$$r_{e_2} = \frac{P_{e_2}}{E_2} = r + (r - i)\frac{D_2}{E_2} \tag{6-3}$$

for Firm II. It is clear that $r_{e_2} > r$ if $r > i$, as it is normally expected to be. It is also clear that, with given values of r and i, the difference between r_{e_2} and r will increase as the ratio of debt to equity, D_2/E_2, becomes greater. This, in essence, is the principle of "financial leverage" or "trading on the equity."

To illustrate, suppose that $K = 100$ and $r = .1$ for both firms. Then, for Firm I (which uses no debt), $P_t = P_{e_1} = 10$ and $r_{e_1} = .1$. If for Firm II we have $E_2 = 50$, $D_2 = 50$, and $i = .05$, then its profit after interest is equal to

$$P_{e_2} = (.1 \times 50) + (.1 - .05)50 = 7.5$$

and the rate of return on equity funds is

$$r_{e_2} = \frac{7.5}{50} = .15$$

Suppose now that the invested capital of Firm II consists of $D_2 = 75$ plus $E_2 = 25$. In this case we have

$$P_{e2} = (.1 \times 25) + (.1 - .05)75 = 6.25$$

[1] A firm's invested capital is defined here as the total amount of funds, whether debt or equity, used to acquire its assets. It is assumed that there are no accounting revaluations and that the book value of the firm—the sum of the book values of its debts, capital stock, and surplus—remains equal to its invested capital at all times. In contrast, the market value of the firm—the sum of the market values of all debt and equity securities—may deviate from the invested capital to a considerable extent.

and

$$r_{e_2} = \frac{6.25}{25} = .25$$

Now, if a rise in the debt-to-equity ratio can continually increase the rate of return on equity funds, will it make the firm's stock continually more attractive to the investors? If this were true, business firms would generally be under pressure to increase the D/E ratio without limit. Obviously, this is not so in the actual world, and a moment's reflection will show that there is a second important factor which must be taken into account: the financial risk inherent in contractual debt commitments. It must be realized that r represents the *expected* rate of return, which may or may not be actually realized; whereas i represents the interest rate agreed upon in the loan contract, which must be paid irrespective of any fluctuations in the firm's realized profit. As D increases relative to E, the firm's total fixed charges, iD, will also increase in relation to its total expected profit, rK, and this will tend to raise the degree of financial risk involved. Being aware of this tendency, the creditors usually require a risk premium in the form of a higher interest rate as the amount of debt increases If the firm belongs to an industry in which profits fluctuate widely, a steep rise in i may occur and the initial difference between r and i may be wiped out before the expansion of debt financing proceeds very far.

Moreover, from the stockholder's standpoint, the advantage of borrowing may disappear even before the interest rate is raised to the level of the firm's expected internal rate of return.[2] For a rise in the firm's D/E ratio, which involves a significantly greater degree of risk, may increase the capitalization factor used by investors for the determination of the stock's market value. Since the firms in this case are not expected to expand, the present value formulas for their respective stocks may be written as

$$V_{e_1} = \frac{rE_1}{k_1} \tag{6-4}$$

---

[2] J. M. Keynes, in discussing the factors affecting the volume of investment, pointed out the importance of distinguishing between the borrower's risk and the lender's risk. He wrote:

> . . . if a venture is a risky one, the borrower will require a wider margin between his expectation of yield and the rate of interest at which he will think it worth his while to borrow; whilst the very same reason will lead the lender to require a wider margin between what he charges and the pure rate of interest to induce him to lend (except where the borrower is so strong and wealthy that he is in a position to offer an exceptional margin of security).

(J. M. Keynes, *The General Theory of Employment Interest and Money*, Macmillan & Co., London, 1936, p. 145.)

$$V_{e_2} = \frac{rE_2 + (r - i)D_2}{k_2} \qquad\qquad (6\text{-}5)$$

If the capitalization factor, k_1, applicable to Firm I, is equal to the internal rate of return, r, it follows that

$$V_{e_1} = E_1 = K$$

which means that the market value of this firm's stock is equal to its book value (and, in this case, to the firm's total invested capital). Now, if the same discount rate were applied to the stock of Firm II ($k_2 = k_1$), the market value of this stock would, of course, be higher than its book value ($V_{e_2} > E_2$) with any positive value of D_2. And the greater the ratio of D_2 to E_2, the greater would be the difference between V_{e_2} and E_2. But if k_2 increases with D_2, the results may be different.

To go back to our numerical illustration, suppose that $k_1 = r = .1$. Then, the market value of the stock of Firm I is

$$V_{e_1} = \frac{.1 \times 100}{.1} = 100$$

which is the same as its book value.

If $k_2 = k_1$, the following market values could be obtained for Firm II:

1. With $D_2 = 50$ and $E_2 = 50$, the market value of its stock would be

$$V_{e_2} = \frac{(.1 \times 50) + (.05 \times 50)}{.1} = 75$$

which is 50 percent higher than the book value of its equity.

2. With $D_2 = 75$ and $E_2 = 25$, we would have

$$V_{e_2} = \frac{(.1 \times 25) + (.05 \times 75)}{.1} = 62.50$$

which is 2.5 times as high as the book value of its equity.

It may be noted that, with the capitalization factor k being constant, the market value of the leveraged firm's stock, V_{e_2}, increases relative to its book value in the same proportion as the rate of return on equity, r_{e_2}, increases relative to the rate of return on invested capital, r. Suppose, however, that k_2 increases from .1 to .13 when the D/E ratio is raised from 0 to 1. The market value of Firm II is then found to be

$$V_{e_2} = \frac{(.1 \times 50) + (.05 \times 50)}{.13} = 57.69$$

which is higher than the book value ($E_2 = 50$), but the rise is less than proportionate to the rise in r_{e_2}. Suppose, further, that $k_2 = .3$ when $D/E = 3$. In this case, we have

$$V_{e_2} = \frac{(.1 \times 25) + (.05 \times 75)}{.3} = 20.83$$

which is less than the book value ($E_2 = 25$), despite the further rise in r_{e_2}.

It may be observed that if k_2 always increased in the same proportion as r_{e_2}, the market value of the firm's stock would remain equal to the book value of its equity, irrespective of changes in the D/E ratio. And since, with a constant interest rate, the market value of the firm's debt securities is not expected to deviate from the book value, it follows that the total market value of the firm (the sum of its equity and debt) could not be affected, under these conditions, by any substitution of debt funds for equity funds, or vice versa. Professors Modigliani and Miller have argued that, given certain assumptions, the process of arbitrage in a competitive market would indeed tend to equalize market values of firms with different capital structures. Their propositions will be considered in the next section.

Before concluding this section, however, we must consider the effect of corporate income taxation on corporate profits and the value of corporate stocks when debt financing is available. Suppose that all corporate profits are taxed at the same flat rate t. If r represents pretax average rate of return, it follows that the net profit of a company which does not use any debt funds will be reduced from rK to $(1 - t)rK$. The value of its stock—assuming again that no expansion is expected—is then equal to

$$V_e = \frac{(1 - t)rK}{k_1} \tag{6-6}$$

As t increases, V_e must decline if the value of k_1 remains unaffected. However, since the assumption is that all corporations are taxed at the same rate and the investors cannot, therefore, gain by shifting from one stock to another, it is not likely that k_1 will remain constant. In the short run, an increase in the tax rate will probably depress all stock values, but in the long run, after the investors have become accustomed to lower posttax profits, the stock values may be expected to go up again (which is equivalent to saying that the capitalization factor will be adjusted downward). This does not mean, of course, that V_e will necessarily be restored to its previous level. Changes in t and k need not be proportionate, but a change in the former should be expected in the long run to have some effect on the latter.[3]

Consider now a firm that has debt in its capital structure. If the tax were imposed on the total amount of profit before interest charges, the posttax profit accruing to the stockholders would be

$$P_{e_{at}} = (1 - t)rK - iD = (1 - t)rE + [(1 - t)r - i]D \qquad (6\text{-}7)$$

In this case, the use of debt funds could increase the posttax rate of return on equity, P_e/E, only as long as the posttax rate of return on invested capital, $(1 - t)r$, remained above the interest rate i.

But if the tax is imposed on net profit after interest—and this is the actual procedure in the United States—then the posttax profit accruing to the stockholders is

$$P_{e_{at}} = (1 - t)(rK - iD) = (1 - t)rE + (1 - t)(r - i)D \qquad (6\text{-}8)$$

It is clear that, under these conditions, the use of debt financing will increase the posttax rate of return on equity as long as the pretax average rate of return on invested capital, r, exceeds the interest rate i, assuming that $t < 1$ (the tax rate is less than 100 percent). For example, suppose that

$K = 100$

$r = .1$

$i = .05$

$t = .6$

If the firm uses no debt funds, its profit after tax is $4 and the posttax rate of return on equity is .04. If the firm's capital is composed of $D = 50$ and $E = 50$, and if the tax is imposed on profit before interest, then the posttax profit on equity is $1.50 and the posttax rate of return on equity is .03. But if the tax is imposed on profit after interest, then the stockholder's post-tax profit is $3 and his posttax rate of return is .06.

Since the present value of a firm's stock is equal to

$$V_e = \frac{P_{e_{at}}}{k}$$

---

[3] A change in the tax rate may also affect, in the long run, the value of r, because of changes in the product prices.

it can be readily seen that while an increase in t will reduce $P_{e_{at}}$ in both of the above cases, the change in V_e need not be proportionate to the change in $P_{e_{at}}$ because of the possibility of variation in the value of k.

THE MODIGLIANI–MILLER HYPOTHESIS

Professors Modigliani and Miller, who will hereafter be referred to as MM, develop their propositions as follows.[4] In a system where all companies are debt-free, the market value of each firm, V_t, must be equal to its expected profit P_t, capitalized at the rate appropriate to its risk class k_n. Thus, we may write

$$V_t = \frac{P_t}{k_n} \tag{6-9}$$

When debt financing is introduced, it is argued that the market value of any firm, irrespective of its capital structure, must still be equal in an equilibrium to its total profit before interest capitalized at the rate applicable to the debt-free firms in its class. This is MM's Proposition I, which may be written algebraically as follows:

$$V_t = V_e + D = \frac{P_t}{k_n} \tag{6-10}$$

It is clear that in the above formula any increase (or decrease) in D, accompanied by an equal decrease (or increase) in V_e, would leave the value of V_t unchanged.[5]

From Proposition I we may easily derive Proposition II, which concerns the capitalization rate applicable to the stock of a firm operating with both equity and debt funds. Consider two firms each earning the same annual amount of profit before interest, P_t. Firm I is unlevered (debt-free) and the capitalization factor applicable to its class is k_1. Its value is, therefore, equal to $P_t/k_1 = V_{t_1}$. Firm II is levered and its total value is the sum of its equity and debt: $V_{e_2} + D_2 = V_{t_2}$. Profit after interest, available to the

---

[4] Franco Modigliani and Merton H. Miller, "The Cost of Capital, Corporation Finance, and the Theory of Investment," *The American Economic Review*, vol. 48, no. 3, June, 1958.

[5] For the sake of consistency, we continue to use our own algebraic symbols. In MM's article, Proposition I is expressed as

$$V_j = S_j + D_j = \frac{\overline{X}_j}{p_k}$$

where V_j is equal to our V_t, $S_j = V_e$, $\overline{X}_j = P_t$, and $p_k = k_n$.

stockholders of Firm II, is equal to $P_{e_2} = P_t - iD_2$ and V_{e_2} is equal to P_{e_2}/k_2. Since, according to Proposition I, $V_{t_1} = V_{t_2}$, we may write

$$P_{e_2} = k_1(V_{e_2} + D_2) - iD_2 \qquad (6\text{-}11)$$

and

$$\frac{P_{e_2}}{V_{e_2}} = k_2 = k_1 + (k_1 - i)\frac{D_2}{V_{e_2}} \qquad (6\text{-}12)$$

Thus, the capitalization rate for the stock of a levered company is equal to the rate applicable to the stock of an unlevered firm in the same class, plus a risk premium which is equal to the debt-to-equity ratio times the spread between k_1 and i. (See footnote 6.) As the debt-to-equity ratio increases, the value of k_2 rises continually even though k_1 and i remain unchanged. The combined effect of the increased earnings per share, resulting from leverage, and the rise in k_2 is such that the value of the levered firm's stock, P_{e_2}/k_2, plus its debt, D_2, is always equal to the value of the unlevered firm's stock, $P_{e_1}/k_1 = V_{t_1}$.

The above propositions, as MM themselves recognize, would hold precisely only in a system in which (a) the corporate income tax were either absent or levied on the entire amount of profit *before* interest and (b) certain arbitrage procedures were available which permitted individual investors to use debt financing on exactly the same terms as those that apply to business corporations. It is the arbitrage transactions that would bring the value of any firm's stock back to the equilibrium level if any deviation should temporarily occur. They are supposed to work as follows.

Consider first the case in which the value of the levered firm temporarily exceeds that of the unlevered firm $(V_{t_2} > V_{t_1})$. Suppose an investor owns a fraction α of the stock of Firm II (levered). The market value of his holdings is then equal to αV_{e_2} and his share of the firm's profit is $\alpha(P_t - iD_2)$. If he sells these shares and invests the proceeds plus an amount equal to αD_2, which he borrows personally, in the stock of Firm I (unlevered), he can acquire a fraction of the latter company's stock equal to

$$\frac{\alpha(V_{e_2} + D_2)}{V_{t_1}} = \alpha\frac{V_{t_2}}{V_{t_1}}$$

---

[6] It may be noted that the relation between k_2 and k_1, as shown above, is similar to the relation between r_{e_2} and r, as discussed in the preceding section (Equation 6-3). It should be kept in mind basically that $r_{e_2} = P_{e_2}/E_2$, where E_2 is the book value of equity, whereas $k_2 = P_{e_2}/V_{e_2}$, where V_{e_2} is the market value of equity. If we set $k_1 = r$, then $V_{t_1} = E_{t_1} = K$, i.e., the market value of Firm I is equal to its book value. According to MM, the same must be true in this case for Firm II. Thus, we have $V_{t_2} = K = E_2 + D_2$, from which it follows that $V_{e_2} = E_2$ and $k_2 = r_{e_2}$.

His share of the total profit of Firm I will then be equal to $\alpha(V_{t_2}/V_t)P_{t_1}$. However, he must pay interest amounting to αiD_2 on his personal loan, which means that his *net* income from the new investment is equal to

$$\alpha\frac{V_{t_2}}{V_{t_1}}P_{t_1} - \alpha iD_2$$

which is greater than $\alpha(P_{t_1} - iD_2)$ if $V_{t_2} > V_{t_1}$. Therefore, as long as $V_{t_2} > V_{t_1}$, the investors will gain by selling shares of Firm II and buying shares of Firm I, which will tend to depress the price of the former and raise the price of the latter. The equilibrium will be restored only when $V_{t_2} = V_{t_1}$.

Consider now the case in which the value of the unlevered firm is initially higher than the value of the levered firm. Suppose that an investor holds a fraction α of the stock of Firm I. The market value of his holdings is αV_{t_1} and his share of the firm's profit is αP_{t_1}.

Suppose now that he sells these shares and buys a portfolio consisting of both shares and bonds of Firm II as follows:

The amount invested in the firm's stock $= \alpha V_{t_1}\dfrac{V_{e2}}{V_{t_2}}$

The amount invested in the firm's bonds $= \alpha V_{t_1}\dfrac{D_2}{V_{t_2}}$

His share of the net profit after interest of Firm II is then

$$\alpha\frac{V_{t_1}}{V_{t_2}}(P_t - iD_2)$$

and his share of the total interest paid by Firm II is

$$\alpha\frac{V_{t_1}}{V_{t_2}}iD_2$$

Consequently, his combined income from the new portfolio is

$$\alpha\frac{V_{t_1}}{V_{t_2}}(P_t - iD_2 + iD_2) = \alpha\frac{V_{t_1}}{V_{t_2}}P_t$$

If $V_{t_1} > V_{t_2}$, investors can gain by selling shares of Firm I and buying shares (and bonds) of Firm II, which will depress the price of the former and raise the price of the latter. Once again, the equilibrium will be restored when $V_{t_1} = V_{t_2}$.

A numerical example should help clarify the relationship involved. Consider two firms, each of which has an annual profit of $1,000. Firm I is debt-free and its capital stock consists of 100 common stock shares. Its profit per share is then $10. If the capitalization rate for its class is equal to .1, its market value is $10,000, or $100 per share. Firm II has $5,000 of bonds outstanding on which it pays interest at the rate of 5 percent. Consequently, its profit after interest is $1,000 − $250 = $750. Let the capital stock of this firm consist of 50 common shares, which means that its profit per share is $15. Now, if the same capitalization rate were applied to the stock of Firm II, its market value would be $7,500, or $150 per share. Total value of this firm would then be $7,500 + $5,000 = $12,500.

Under the above conditions, an investor who owns 10 shares of Firm II can sell them for $1,500. If he can borrow $1,000 at 5 percent, he will be in a position to invest $2,500 in 25 shares of Firm I. His share of the profit of Firm I will be $250 and the interest on his personal debt will be $50, which means that the net income on his new investment in Firm I is $200, as compared with $150 on his shareholdings in Firm II. As these arbitrage possibilities are discovered, there will be an increase in the demand for the shares of Firm I and in the supply of the shares of Firm II in the market. This will lead to a change in their market prices.

Suppose that after a while the capitalization rate of the shares of Firm I drops to .09 and the rate for the shares of Firm II increases to .122. Then the market value of Firm I is $11,111.11, or $111.11 per share. The market value of the stock of Firm II is $6,111.11, or $122.22 per share, and the total market value of Firm II (stock plus bonds) is likewise $11,111.11. Under these conditions, an investor who owns 10 shares of Firm II can sell them for $1,222.22. By borrowing $1,000 at 5 percent he can invest $2,222.22 in 20 shares of Firm I. His profit on these shares will be $200 and his net income after interest will be $150, which is the same as the income he can have by holding 10 shares of Firm II. An increase in profit through arbitrage is no longer possible and the market is in an equilibrium.

THE MM HYPOTHESIS (CONTINUED)

Let us now consider the modifications in the MM hypothesis that must be made when the assumptions with respect to the interest rate and the tax factors are changed. As will be recalled, it was assumed that individual investors can procure debt funds and thus engage in "homemade" leverage on the same terms as corporations. Suppose, however, that a higher interest rate is charged in the capital market on personal loans than on corporate bonds, at comparable debt-to-equity ratio. It can be shown that, under these circumstances, the arbitrage procedures described by MM would not tend to equalize the market values of levered and unlevered firms.

Assume once more that a stockholder owns a fraction α of the stock of Firm II, which means that his share of the firm's profit after interest is equal to $\alpha(P_t - iD_2)$. Assume further that, if he sells these shares and invests in Firm I the amount realized through this sale plus an amount equal to αD_2, which he borrows personally, the interest rate charged on this loan will be j, which is higher than the interest paid by Firm II, i. The investor's net income on his new stock holdings in Firm I will then be equal to

$$\alpha \frac{V_{t_2}}{V_{t_1}} P_t - \alpha(iD_2)$$

In an equilibrium, this income must be equal to that realized by being a stockholder of Firm II. Thus, we have

$$\alpha \frac{V_{t_2}}{V_{t_1}} P_t - \alpha(jD_2) = \alpha P_t - \alpha(iD_2)$$

or

$$\alpha P_t \left(\frac{V_{t_2}}{V_{t_1}} - 1 \right) = \alpha D_2(j - i)$$

It is clear that if $j > i$, V_{t_2} must be higher than V_{t_1} to maintain the required equality of income.

Going back to our numerical example, suppose that $i = .05$ but $j = .08$. If $k_1 = .1$, $k_2 = .15$, and $V_{t_1} = V_{t_2} = \$10,000$, then an investor who owns 10 shares of Firm II and has a net income of \$150 would not remain in the same position if he sold these shares for \$1,000, borrowed \$1,000 at 8 percent, and invested \$2,000 in shares of Firm II. In the latter case, his income before interest would be \$200, but his net income after interest would drop to \$120. He would be able to realize net income of \$150 only if the price of a share of Firm II rose from \$100 to \$130, which would raise V_{t_2} from \$10,000 to \$11,500.

The existence of transaction costs also interferes with the working of the MM arbitrage, because a greater amount must be invested in the shares of an unlevered firm than in the shares of a levered one in order to realize the same net income after interest. Assume that $i = j = .05$, $k_1 = .1$, and $k_2 = .15$. Assume further that the transaction costs are a flat 5 percent of the total value of the shares purchased. Then in order to buy 10 shares of Firm II at \$100 each an investor must pay a total of \$1,050, which will make his net rate of return equal to $150/1,050 = .143$. But if he decides to buy 20 shares of Firm I at \$100 each, his total outlay will have to be \$2,100. If he spends \$1,050 of his own funds and borrows \$1,050 at 5 per cent, his annual interest will amount to \$52.50. Thus, his net income after interest

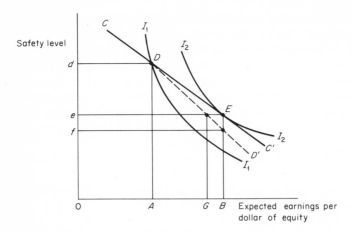

Figure 6-1   The effect of transaction costs on the individual investor's leverage opportunities.

will be $200 - 52.50 = 147.50$, which will make his net rate of return equal to $147.50/1,050 = .14$. Here again, then, homemade leverage would enable him to realize net income of \$150 only if the price of Firm II shares rose above \$100.

The effect of transaction costs is demonstrated graphically in Figure 6-1.[7] The line CC' represents the opportunities open to firms in a particular risk class: in deciding on an appropriate capital structure, each of them can raise the expected earnings per dollar of equity by increasing the degree of leverage, but this will necessarily reduce the safety level of their shares.[8]

Suppose that Firm I selects point D and Firm II selects point E on the CC' line. For an investor, whose personal preferences are indicated by indifference curves I_1, I_2, and I_3, point E is clearly preferable to point D. However, in the absence of transaction costs (and taxes), he can reach point E by purchasing shares of either firm. If he decides to buy shares of Firm I, all he has to do is use borrowed funds in addition to his own (assuming that the interest rate is the same for personal and corporate loans). But if there are

---

[7] This figure is a slightly modified version of one of the charts presented in W. Baumol and B. G. Malkiel's article, "The Firm's Optimal Debt-Equity Combination and the Cost of Capital," *Quarterly Journal of Economics*, vol. 81, no. 4, November, 1967.

[8] The equation for the opportunity line CC' is: $y = f(i)$, where y represents safety level and i represents expected earnings. Baumol and Malkiel suggest two alternative ways of measuring safety level. One way is to assume that safety level is measured by expected earnings less some fixed number of standard deviations of earnings: $y_1 = i - k\sigma$. The other way is to assume that there is some plausible range of earnings before interest and that earnings outside this range are so improbable that they can be ignored. The lower bound of this range may then be defined as $i_{min} = X_{min} - rD$, where X_{min} represents minimum earnings before interest and rD is equal to the interest charges. The safety level is then measured by $y_2 = X_{min} - rD$.

significant transaction costs, the opportunities open to an individual investor by means of homemade leverage are no longer indicated by the solid CC' line, but rather by the dotted SS' line which lies below it. Thus, if the investor wishes to invest in shares of Firm I and to realize earnings per dollar of investment equal to OB, he will have to accept the level of safety measured by Of, which is lower than Oe obtainable by purchasing shares of Firm II. Or, if he should insist on the level of safety measured by Oe, he would have to accept earnings equal to OG—again lower than OB, realizable by purchasing shares of Firm II.

Finally, let us consider the effect of a corporate income tax imposed on profits net of interest charges. MM originally argued that the value of any company would, in this case, be equal to its total income net of taxes (i.e., the sum of interest paid to the creditors and posttax profit accruing to the stockholders), capitalized at the rate applicable to a debt-free company in its class. If t_c is the corporate tax rate and P_t is profit before interest and tax, the value of an unlevered company is

$$V_{t_1} = \frac{P_t(1 - t_c)}{k_1^*}$$

where k_1^* is the posttax capitalization rate. With the same tax rate, the value of a levered company is equal to

$$V_{t_2} = V_{e_2} + D_2 = \frac{(1 - t_c)(P_t - iD_2) + iD_2}{k_1^*}$$

which is greater than V_{t_1}. Thus, when interest is deductible in computing taxable profit, the market value of a firm is no longer independent of its capital structure. The relation between V_{t_1} and V_{t_2} is given by the following equation:

$$V_{t_2} = V_{t_1} + \frac{i}{k_1^*} t_c D_2 \tag{6-13}$$

and the posttax capitalization rate for the net profit on equity of Firm II, k_2^*, is equal to

$$k_2^* = k_1^* + (k_1^* - i)\frac{D_2}{V_{e_2}} \tag{6-14}$$

Consider the following numerical example. Let profit before interest and tax be equal to \$2,000 for both firms and let the tax rate be a flat

50 percent. Profit after tax of Firm I (unlevered) is then equal to $1,000, or $10 per share (assuming that 100 shares are outstanding). If the posttax capitalization rate for this firm is $k_1^* = .1$, then its market value, V_{t_1}, is equal to $10,000, or $100 per share.

If Firm II has $5,000 of debt in its structure and the interest rate is 5 percent, then its taxable income is $2,000 - $250 = $1,750$ and the tax is $875. Its net profit after interest and after tax is $875 and its total posttax income, accruing to both the stockholders and the bondholders, is equal to $875 + $250 = $1,125$.

From Equation 6-13 it follows that the total market value of Firm II is equal to

$$V_{t_2} = 10,000 + \frac{.05}{.1}(.5 \times 5,000) = 11,250$$

Consequently, the market value of its equity is $6,250, or $125 per share (assuming that 50 shares are outstanding). The stockholders' net profit per share is $875 \div 50 = 17.50.

Now, if an investor owns 10 shares of Firm II, he can sell them for $1,250, borrow $1,000, and invest $2,250 in 22.5 shares of Firm I. The income from this investment (after the corporate tax) is equal to $225 less $50 of interest payable on his personal loan, or $175. Since this is exactly the same as the income on 10 shares of Firm II, there is no profit in arbitrage and the market seems to be in an equilibrium.

A closer look at the situation reveals, however, that the degree of risk involved for the stockholder in holding 10 shares of Firm II is not necessarily the same as that involved in holding 22.5 shares of Firm I (partly with his own and partly with borrowed funds). Once more, it must be recalled that P_{t_1} represents *expected* profit, which may or may not be realized, while iD_2 represents a fixed charge that must be paid irrespective of profit fluctuations. Suppose that actual profit before interest and taxes drops to $1,000 from the expected $2,000 level. Then, an investor who owns 10 shares of Firm II will realize $7.50 per share, or a total of $75. On the other hand, an investor who owns 22.5 shares of Firm I, but also has a personal debt of $1,000 at 5 percent, will realize $5 per share, which amounts to $112.50 before interest or $62.50 after interest.

Thus, even though the two portfolios may initially look equivalent to each other, a subsequent contraction of pretax profit would make the holding of 22.5 shares of Firm I less profitable than the holding of 10 shares of Firm II. The reverse situation would occur if pretax profit rose above the initially expected level. In general, then, the ownership of the shares of a levered firm (with no personal debt) implies less risk of income fluctuation than the ownership of the shares of an unlevered firm (which involves personal debt). Assuming that investors generally expect a premium for additional risk taking, it follows that the market value of the levered firm's equity should be somewhat higher relative to the market value of the unlevered firm's equity than Equation 6-13 indicates.

In connection with the difference in risk, one additional factor merits a brief comment. If two firms have the same expected earnings before interest with the same probability distribution and variance, the levered firm incurs a greater risk of being forced into liquidation as a result of temporary losses. Suppose the expected earnings are $1,000 per year for both firms and the interest charges of the levered firm amount to $500 annually. If a depression period should ensue and the actual earnings before interest drop below $500 for several years in a row, the levered firm could be forced into bankruptcy should the reduction in cash inflow make it impossible to meet interest obligations. If bankruptcy proceedings follow, additional costs will be incurred in the form of trustee's fees and other legal expenses. Even if efforts are made to reorganize the firm, its net earnings during the reorganization period will be reduced because of these additional costs and also because of the probable adverse effect of the bad publicity on its credit standing and the volume of sales. And should liquidation become unavoidable, the additional costs incurred would result in a further decline in the net value of the firm's assets available to the owners after the creditors have been paid off. Thus, a high degree of leverage, associated with increased probability of bankruptcy, should be expected to have a negative effect on the valuation of the firm's stock and, consequently, the total value of the firm.[9] Furthermore, it should tend to raise the interest rate required by the firm's creditors.

In a later article,[10] MM have revised their original formula as follows. They point out that, from the investor's point of view, the long-run average stream of after-tax returns appears as a sum of two components: (1) an uncertain stream $(1 - t)P_t Z$ (where P_t is the expected pretax profit and Z is a random variable having the same value for all firms in a given risk class); and (2) a sure stream tR (which represents the tax saving per period on the interest payments, R). Capitalizing the first component at the rate k_1^* and the second component at the rate equal to the interest rate i gives the value of the levered firm as follows:

$$V_{t_2} = \frac{(1 - t)P_t}{k_1^*} + \frac{tR}{i} = V_{t_1} + tD_2 \qquad (6\text{-}15)$$

[9] This factor was mentioned briefly in MM's original article (see the footnote on p. 274), and was elaborated on by Nevins D. Baxter in his article, "Leverage, Risk of Ruin and the Cost of Capital," *The Journal of Finance*, vol. 22, no. 3, September, 1967, pp. 395–403.

[10] "Taxes and the Cost of Capital: A Correction," *The American Economic Review*, vol. 53, No. 3, June, 1963.

When this formula is used, the equilibrium value of Firm II in the above example is found to be equal to

$$V_{t_2} = 10,000 + .5(5,000) = 12,500$$

which means that the value of the firm's equity is $7,500, or $150 per share, as compared with $125 per share obtained above on the basis of Equation 6-13.

If an investor holding 10 shares of Firm II sold them for $1,500, borrowed $1,000 at 5 percent, and invested $2,500 in 25 shares of Firm I, his share of the firm's profit before interest would be $250 and his net income after interest on his personal loan would be $200. This is more than the profit accruing to 10 shares of Firm II, but the risk involved in holding this alternative portfolio would also be greater. According to MM's revised statement, the amount that the investor should borrow if he wishes to switch from the stock of Firm II to the stock of Firm I with no change in risk is given by the formula

$$B = \frac{m(1 - t)D_2}{V_{e_2}} \qquad (6\text{-}16)$$

where m is the amount of his investment in the stock of Firm II. If $m = 1,500$, B is found to be equal to 500. Thus, the total amount that he should invest in the stock of Firm I is $2,000, which will yield a profit of $200 before interest. The interest on $500 of borrowed funds will amount to $25 and net income after interest will be $175, which is exactly the same as the profit accruing to 10 shares of Firm II.

THE CASE OF AN EXPANDING FIRM

In the preceding sections we considered the case of nonexpanding firms and assumed that the average and marginal internal rates of return, r, remained constant over time. We shall now consider the case of an expanding firm, in which both the marginal rate r_m and the average rate r_a vary as the firm's invested capital is increased. This model may be most conveniently discussed with the help of a set of diagrams.

We shall assume at first that the amount of equity funds is fixed and that the firm may expand only by using debt funds. In Figure 6-2 a and b, the amount of equity is equal to OA. Profit before interest is a nonlinear function of invested capital represented by the curve OP_{bi} in Figure 6-2a. Given this function, the average rate of return ($r_a = P/K$) and the marginal rate of return ($r_m = dP/dK$) curves take on the shapes shown in Figure 6-2b.

If the firm uses no debt financing, its invested capital (book value) is equal to OA and its profit is equal to Aa in Figure 6-2a. The marginal rate of return is represented by Ae and the average rate of return by Ad in Figure 6-2b. The market value of the firm's stock is equal to

$$V_e = \frac{P}{k}$$

where k is the appropriate capitalization factor. This value is assumed to be equal to Aa' in Figure 6-2a.

Now, if the firm increases its invested capital by borrowing additional funds, it has to pay interest, which must be deducted from total profit to arrive at the net profit available to its stockholders. The curve hi_m in Figure 6-2b, represents the marginal interest rate and the curve aP_{ai} in Figure 6-2a portrays net profit after interest.[11] The vertical distance between OP_{bi} and OP_{ai} is, of course, equal to the total amount of interest paid on a given amount of debt. Looking at Figure 6-2b, we see that the interest rate curve

---

[11] Two interpretations of the marginal interest rate are possible. First, we may assume that, as additional amounts are borrowed, a higher rate is charged on each successive increment of debt, while the rates on all the previous loans remain unchanged. In this case, i_m in Figure 6-2b represents both the rate charged on the marginal loan and the total cost of the marginal increment of debt.

But since all loans are assumed to be alike (with respect to security, etc.), it is not realistic to assume that the creditors who have made the previous loans would in the long run be satisfied with lower interest rates irrespective of the total volume of debt. Therefore, a more realistic assumption is that, as additional loans are obtained, a higher rate is charged (in the long run) on the entire amount of debt outstanding. In this case, the marginal cost of borrowing, c_m, is higher than the interest paid on the marginal increment of debt, i_m^*. The relation between c_m and i_m^* is given by the familiar formula

$$c_m = \frac{d(i_m^* D)}{dD} = i_m^* + D\frac{di_m^*}{dD}$$

Graphically, the relation may be shown as follows:

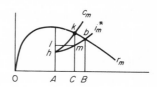

It is clear that the firm's profit on equity will be maximized at the point k, where the curve c_m intersects the curve r_m, and not at the point b, where the curves i_m^* and r_m intersect. And the total interest charges will be represented by the rectangle $AlmC$ rather than the area $AhbB$.

In this case, the marginal interest rate i_m, as shown in Figure 6-2b, must be interpreted as being equal to c_m and not to i_m^* in the above graph.

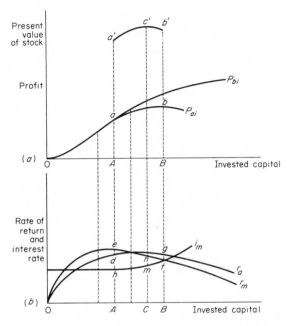

Figure 6-2   Optimal amount of debt at a fixed equity level.

crosses the marginal rate of return curve at point f when debt is equal to AB and total invested capital is equal to OB. With this amount of capital, net profit after interest is at its maximum (as represented by Bb in Figure 6-2a).

Now, if the capitalization factor k remained constant, the market value of the firm's stock would also reach its maximum when invested capital is equal to OB. The value curve V_e would in this case rise (or fall) at the same rate as the profit curve P_{ai}. But if k increases as the debt-to-equity ratio is raised, the V_e curve will rise less rapidly than the P_{ai} curve and will reach its maximum sooner. This is assumed to be the case in Figure 6-2a, where the V_e curve reaches its maximum at point c', with invested capital being equal to OC instead of OB. Thus, the stockholders will find it preferable to limit the amount of borrowing to AC, even though the marginal interest rate, Cm, at that point is still lower than the marginal rate of return, Cn.

The relation between the marginal interest rate and the marginal rate of return at the point of maximum stock value may be expressed mathematically as follows. We know that

$$V_e = \frac{P_{ai}}{k}$$

Since equity is assumed to remain constant, both P_{ai} and k may be expressed as functions of debt D. We may, therefore, write

$$V_e = \frac{P_{ai}(D)}{k(D)}$$

and

$$\frac{dV_e}{dD} = \frac{k(D)P'_{ai}(D) - P_{ai}(D)k'(D)}{k(D)^2}$$

The maximum value of V_e is obtained when $dV_e/dD = 0$. This condition is satisfied when

$$k(D)P'_{ai}(D) - P_{ai}(D)k'(D) = 0$$

We may rewrite this as

$$k\frac{\partial P_{ai}}{\partial D} = P_{ai}\frac{\partial k}{\partial D}$$

or

$$V_e\frac{\partial k}{\partial D} = \frac{\partial P_{ai}}{\partial D} = \frac{\partial P_{bi}}{\partial D} - \frac{\partial(iD)}{\partial D} = r_m - i_m$$

Solving for r_m gives

$$r_m = i_m + V_e\frac{\partial k}{\partial D}$$

It is clear that a firm wishing to maximize the value of its stock could continue borrowing and expanding operations to the point at which $r_m = i_m$ only if the rate of capitalization remained constant ($dk/dD = 0$). But if $dk/dD > 0$, then borrowing must stop at the point when r_m exceeds i_m by an amount equal to $V_e(dk/dD)$.

Let us now remove the constraint that the amount of equity capital is fixed. The firm is then free to optimize its total invested capital by varying both equity and debt components. The problem and its solution may again be demonstrated by means of diagrams. In Figure 6-3, the curve Or_m once more represents the marginal rate of return on total invested capital, r_m.

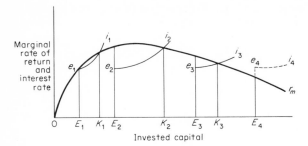

Figure 6-3 Optimal amount of debt at different equity levels.

The distances OE_1, OE_2, OE_3, and OE_4 represent, respectively, four different amounts of equity.

The curves e_1i_1, e_2i_2, e_3i_3, and e_4i_4 represent the marginal interest rates which the firm has to pay on debt funds. It is assumed that the firm can always begin borrowing at the same interest rate, irrespective of the amount of equity ($E_1e_1 = E_2e_2 = E_3e_3 = \cdots$). It is further assumed that the marginal interest rate increases as a function of the debt-to-equity ratio, from which it follows that, as the firm's equity increases, it will be paying a smaller marginal rate for any given *absolute* amount of debt. Accordingly, the slope of the interest curve decreases as the curve is shifted to the right.

The diagram shows that, when the firm's equity is equal to OE_1, its profit on equity is maximized by borrowing an amount equal to E_1K_1 (i.e., by making its total invested capital equal to OK_1). Similarly, when the firm's equity is equal to OE_2, its profit on equity is maximized by borrowing an amount equal to E_2K_2. We may thus obtain the maximum amount of profit and, therefore, the maximum rate of return on the firm's stock for any amount of equity capital it may decide to use.

The relation between the amount of equity and the average rate of return on equity, which is implicit in Figure 6-3, is depicted explicitly in Figure 6-4. The shape of the r_{ae} curve is similar to, but not identical with, the r_a curve in Figure 6-2b, for it is determined not only by productivity but also by the leverage factor. At the initial stage an increase in equity is accompanied by a rise in the optimal debt-to-equity ratio, but at a later stage the opposite is true. If the capitalization factor used for the evaluation of the firm's stock remained constant, the value of one unit of equity would rise as long as the average rate of return per unit of equity increased, would reach its maximum at the same point (e_2) at which r_{ae} is highest, and would decline thereafter.[12] This situation is represented by the curve V_{ue}. But if

[12] A *unit of equity* may be defined as $1 of the owners' capital. If the company issues one share for each dollar paid in by the owners, a unit of equity becomes equal to one share, and the value of one unit of equity is then equal to the paid-in value per share.

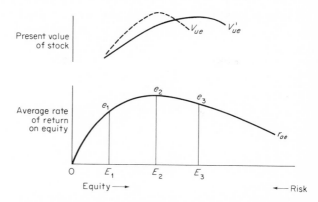

Figure 6-4 The rate of return on equity and the value of stock.

the capitalization factor changes, reflecting the degree of financial risk involved, the value curve assumes a different shape. When the firm's equity is increased beyond the E_2 point, the optimal debt-to-equity ratio declines, and the risk associated with using an optimal amount of debt is reduced. Consequently, the capitalization factor may be expected to become smaller, and this may more than counterbalance the decline in r_{ae}. The maximum market value per unit of equity may, therefore, be reached to the right of the maximum r_{ae} point (when total equity is equal to E_3 rather than E_2). This situation is represented by the curve V'_{ue}.

Suppose that OE_2 is equal to \$100 and that the firm has 100 shares outstanding. Suppose further that with this amount of equity (plus the optimum amount of debt) profit after interest is \$10. The average internal rate of return on equity is then 10 cents per share, or 10 percent. If the capitalization rate is also 10 percent, the market value of the firm's equity is then \$100, or \$1 per share—the same as the book value. Suppose now that $OE_3 = \$150$ and that there are 150 shares outstanding. Let P_{ai} be equal to \$13.50, or 9 cents per share, at this level. However, if the capitalization rate is now only 8 percent (because of a lower degree of risk), the market value of the firm's equity is \$168, or \$1.12 per share.

Of course, in a competitive market with a free entry this situation could not prevail in the long run. New firms would be organized with the optimum volume of equity funds and the market value of their equity would gradually be brought down to the level of the book value (which is assumed to correspond to the actual cost of their assets). But the market value of the firms, operating with a non-optimum volume of equity, would also decline (the entire V'_{ue} curve would shift downward) so that the market value of their equity would be below the book value.

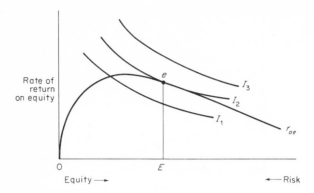

Figure 6-5 Optimal combination of financial risk and return on equity.

The relationship discussed above may be further clarified with the help of the concept of the marginal rate of substitution.[13] In Figure 6-5, the curves I_1, I_2, and I_3 are market indifference curves, whose slopes indicate the minimum marginal increase in safety (decrease in risk) acceptable to the investors as a substitute for the marginal decrease in profitability. Any movement along a given I curve leaves the market value of the company's shares unchanged, while a shift from a lower to a higher I curve results in a higher market value. The maximum market value per share is reached at point E, where the indifference curve I_2 is tangent to the r_{ae} curve. It is only at this point that the firm's marginal rate of substitution between profit and risk coincides with the investor's marginal preference.

In conclusion, let us consider the effect of the corporate income tax factor. Figure 6-6 is drawn on the assumption that a 50 percent tax is imposed on profit before interest. The amount of equity is assumed to be fixed and equal to OE_1. In Figure 6-6a, the P_{bti} curve shows total profit before tax, the P_{at} curve profit after tax, and the P_{ati} curve profit after tax and interest. In Figure 6-6b, the r_m curve depicts the pretax marginal rate of return, the r_{mt} curve the posttax marginal rate of return, and the i_m curve the marginal interest rate. As can be seen, with the 50 percent tax, net profit on equity is maximized at the point of intersection of r_{mt} and i_m, the amount of debt being equal to E_1K_1. If there were no tax, on the other hand, net profit on equity would be maximized at the point of intersection of r_m and i_m, and the amount of debt would be equal to E_1K_2. Thus, the imposition of such a tax would tend to reduce not only the amount of net profit but also the optimum amount of debt.

[13] This approach has been developed by Professor Eli Schwartz in "The Theory of the Capital Structure of the Firm," *The Journal of Finance*, vol. 14, no. 1, March, 1959.

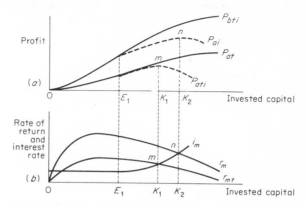

Figure 6-6 The effect of corporate income tax when interest is not tax deductible.

Figure 6-7 portrays the case in which a 50 percent tax is imposed on profit after interest. In Figure 6-7a, the P_{bit} curve shows profit before interest and tax, the P_{ai} curve profit after interest but before tax, and the P_{ait} curve profit after interest and after tax. It may be seen that the P_{ai} and P_{ait} curves both reach their highest points when debt is equal to $E_1 K_2$ and the marginal rate of return before interest and tax is equal to the marginal interest rate. Thus, while the imposition of a tax on profit after interest reduces the amount of net profit, it does not change the optimum amount of debt.

These conclusions concerning the effect of the tax factor are, of course, similar to those reached in the section entitled "Financial Leverage: Advantages and Limitations." Consider again Equations 6-7 and 6-8. The former is based on the assumption that corporate income tax is imposed on profit before interest. If we assume that the pretax average rate of return, r, and the average interest rate, i, are both functions of the amount borrowed, D, then by differentiating with respect to D and setting the derivative equal to zero we obtain

$$(1 - t)\left(\frac{dr}{dD}K + r\right) = \frac{di}{dD}D + i$$

The left-hand side of this equation represents the posttax marginal rate of return and the right-hand side the marginal interest rate. Profit is maximized when they are equal to each other.

But if we use Equation 6-8, we obtain

$$\frac{dr}{dD}K + r = \frac{di}{dD}D + i$$

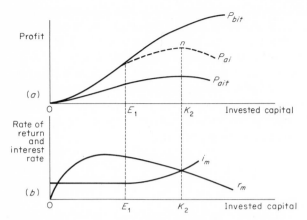

Figure 6-7   The effect of corporate income tax when interest is tax deductible.

which means that profit is maximized when the pretax marginal rate of return is equal to the marginal interest rate. Once again, the reader must be reminded that the amount of debt leading to the maximization of net profit after interest and tax should not be expected to coincide with the amount of debt resulting in the maximization of the market value of the firm's stock. If the capitalization factor, k, is an increasing function of the debt-to-equity ratio, the maximum market value will be obtained with a smaller amount of debt than that required for the maximization of net profit.

THE CASE OF CONTINUAL EXPANSION

Finally, let us consider the case of a firm which is expanding continually, year after year, at a constant rate g. This means that at the end of year 0 it wishes to add to its invested capital an amount equal to $gK_0 = I_0$; at the end of year 1, an amount equal to $gK_1 = g(K_0 + I_0) = I_1$, etc.

We assume that the firm does not plan to make any profit retentions ($b = 0$) and must, therefore, rely on external financing exclusively. But it has a choice of securing either new equity funds by selling additional shares of stock or new debt funds by selling bonds. If it decides to finance its expansion continually with new equity funds, the present value of the shares outstanding at the beginning of year 0 is given by the formula

$$V_0 = \frac{rK_0}{k} + \frac{(r - k)I_0}{(1 + k)k} + \frac{(r - k)I_1}{(1 + k)^2 k} + \cdots$$

as already explained in Chapter 5 (Equation 5-3). It will be recalled that r is the internal rate of return, assumed to remain constant, and k is the discount factor, assumed to be equal to the prevailing market rate of return on common stocks of debt-free firms in the same risk class.

If the firm decides to use debt financing continually, it will have to pay an increasing annual amount of interest on bonds instead of an increasing annual amount of dividends on the newly issued shares. If the interest is paid at the rate i, then the firm's dividends, which are assumed to be equal to its profit after interest, will be equal to

$$D_0 = rK_0$$

$$D_1 = rK_0 + rI_0 - iI_0$$

$$D_2 = rK_0 + rI_0 + rI_1 - iI_0 - iI_1$$

$$\cdots \cdots \cdots \cdots \cdots \cdots \cdots \cdots$$

Since there are no new stock issues in this case, the entire amount of dividends in all future years will be available to the holders of the shares outstanding in year 0. The present value of these shares must, therefore, be equal to

$$V_0^* = \frac{rK_0}{k'} + \frac{(r-i)I_0}{(1+k')k'} + \frac{(r-i)I_1}{(1+k')^2 k'} + \cdots$$

Now, if the interest rate i is lower than the market dividend rate k applicable to the stock of unlevered companies, then obviously $(r-i)I_0 > (r-k)I_0$; $(r-i)I_1 > (r-y)I_1$; etc. It does not follow, however, that the present value of the stock of the levered company, V_0^*, will necessarily be greater than that of the stock of the unlevered company, V_0. As already explained above, an increase in the debt-to-equity ratio tends to raise the degree of the financial risk incurred by the firm's stockholders, and this should normally lead to an increase in the capitalization factor applicable to its shares. Therefore, V_0^* may be greater than, equal to, or smaller than V_0, depending on how fast k increases as the firm continues to use debt financing.

When a corporate tax is imposed on profit after interest, another factor favorable to debt financing is brought into play. In Table 6-1 a comparison is made between two dividend streams accruing to the firm's initial shares, one of which is derived on the assumption that new financing is obtained by additional stock issues and the other on the assumption that this is done by new bond issues. In both cases, the annual amount of new financing is equal to I_0, I_1, I_2, etc. In order to isolate the effect of the tax factor, it is assumed that the interest rate on bonds is equal to the dividend yield on new shares $(i = k)$.

Table 6-1 The effect of corporate income tax on the initial stockholders' dividend stream

(a) Financing by New Stock Issues

Year	Profit after tax	New funds	Dividend on new stock	Dividend on initial stock
0	$P_0 = (1 - t_c)rK_0$	I_0		$(1 - t_c)rK_0$
1	$P_1 = (1 - t_c)(rK_0 + rI_0)$	I_1	kI_0	$(1 - t_c)(rK_0 + rI_0) - kI_0 = (1 - t_c)rK_0 + (1 - t_c)rI_0 - kI_0$
2	$P_2 = (1 - t_c)(rK_0 + rI_0 + rI_1)$	I_2	kI_1	$(1 - t_c)(rK_0 + rI_0 + rI_1) - kI_0 - kI_1$
				$= (1 - t_c)rK_0 + (1 - t_c)(I_0 + I_1)r - (I_0 + I_1)k$
$\cdots$				

(b) Financing by New Bond Issues

Year	Profit after interest and tax	New funds	Interest on bonds	Dividend on stock
0	$P_0 = (1 - t_c)rK_0$	I_0		$(1 - t_c)rK_0$
1	$P_1 = (1 - t_c)(rK_0 + rI_0 - iI_0)$	I_1	iI_0	$(1 - t_c)(rK_0 + rI_0 - iI_0) = (1 - t_c)rK_0 + (1 - t_c)rI_0 - (1 - t_c)iI_0$
2	$P_2 = (1 - t_c)(rK_0 + rI_0 + rI_1 - iI_0 - iI_1)$	I_2	iI_1	$(1 - t_c)(rK_0 + rI_0 + rI_1 - iI_0 - iI_1)$
				$= (1 - t_c)rK_0 + (1 - t_c)(I_0 + I_1)r - (1 - t_c)(I_0 + I_1)i$
$\cdots$				

As the table shows, bond financing results in tax savings amounting to $it_c I_0$ in year 1, $it_c I_1$ in year 2, etc. The present value of the entire stream of tax savings is equal to

$$S_t = t_c\left[\frac{i I_0}{1 + k} + \frac{i I_1}{(1 + k)^2} + \cdots\right]$$

It follows that, other things being equal, continual bond financing should increase the present value of the firm's initial stock by S_t, as compared with continual stock financing. But "other things" should not, of course, be expected to remain constant. The effect of the tax factor must be considered in conjunction with the other factors mentioned above. If the interest rate is considerably below the dividend rate, and if the tax rate is substantial, the advantages of bond financing should be relatively strong. But if the risk associated with continuous borrowing is considered to be high and this is reflected in the capitalization rate, a strong counterbalancing factor will emerge.

SUMMARY

If a firm can obtain debt funds at an interest rate lower than its internal rate of return, this should tend to increase the rate of return on its equity capital. This is known as the principle of "financial leverage" or "trading on equity."

An increase in the rate of return on equity should not, however, be expected to result in a corresponding rise in the value of the firm's stock, because of the risk factor involved. As the debt-to-equity ratio is raised, the financial risk associated with holding the firm's shares tends to become greater and investors are likely to use a higher capitalization rate in determining the present value of the expected revenue stream.

Professors Modigliani and Miller have argued that, under certain simplifying assumptions (most importantly, absence of taxation and of any difference in the availability and cost of credit for individuals and corporations), the market value of all firms belonging in the same risk class and having the same profit before interest would be equal irrespective of their capital structure (debt-to-equity ratio). This means that, as debt funds are substituted for equity funds, the capitalization rate applicable to the firm's stock will rise so as to completely offset the gain in earnings accruing to the stockholders as a result of the difference between the interest rate and the firm's internal rate of return.

If any difference between the market value of a leveraged firm and that of an unleveraged firm should temporarily arise, it will be eliminated in a competitive capital market by arbitrage transactions. It is assumed by

MM that an individual investor always has a choice of (1) investing a given amount in a leveraged firm's shares or (2) investing a larger amount, consisting of his own funds plus a personal loan, in an unleveraged firm's shares. In the latter case, he would be employing "homemade" leverage, and this would give him the same net amount of earnings and the same degree of risk as those involved in acquiring the leveraged firm's shares.

The assumption that "homemade" individual leverage is available on the same terms as corporate leverage is, of course, questionable. The interest rate on personal loans may be higher than the rate on corporate debt, and this will tend to restrain the tendency toward equalization of the market values of leveraged and unleveraged firms. The existence of transaction costs incurred in buying and selling securities in the market is another factor having a similar restraining effect.

The imposition of a corporate income tax on profits after interest tends to raise the value of a leveraged firm relative to that of an unleveraged firm because of the deductibility of interest charges and the resulting reduction in the amount of tax paid by the former firm. It was originally argued by MM that the value of a leveraged firm should, under these conditions, be equal to its total income net of taxes (i.e., the sum of the interest paid on all debts plus the posttax profit accruing to the stockholders), capitalized at the rate applicable to the posttax profit of a debt-free firm in the same risk class. Later on, having further analyzed the nature and degree of the financial risks involved, they offered a revised formula which allowed for a somewhat wider range of value variations in response to changes in the use of debt.

In discussing problems of capital expansion, we considered first the case of a firm which held its equity constant and absorbed new funds only by means of borrowing. As the firm's debt and, therefore, total invested capital are increased, the marginal internal rate of return will eventually begin to decline while the marginal interest rate will begin to rise. The firm will maximize its total profit on equity by extending borrowing to the point at which these two marginal rates are equal to each other. However, if the firm's objective is to maximize the value of its equity, it will probably have to stop borrowing at an earlier point where the marginal rate of return is still above the marginal interest rate. This is so because of the risk factor, which will tend to raise the capitalization rate applicable to the firm's stock as the amount of debt increases.

When a firm's equity and debt are both variable, it must make separate decisions as to the total amount of invested capital and the degree of leverage to be employed. At each level of equity, the stockholder's profit may be increased by extending debt up to the point where the marginal interest rate equals the marginal rate of return. However, as the amount of equity is raised, the profit-maximizing debt-to-equity ratio will change, and so will the financial risk involved. At some particular equity level (with the optimal debt), the highest possible profit per unit of equity will be obtained. But here again, this point may not coincide with the point of the maximum value of one unit of equity. The maximum value will result from the optimal combination of profitability and risk.

SELECTED REFERENCES

See Chapter 7.

appendix to chapter 6

Empirical Studies
of the Leverage Effect

The Modigliani and Miller propositions have been tested empirically by
several researchers. In this appendix we shall briefly review the work
done by Alexander Barges, Ronald F. Wippern, L. V. N. Sarma and
K. S. Hanumanta Rao, and MM themselves.

BARGES' STUDY

A. Barges made an extensive analysis of the data for 61 Class I railroads over
the period 1954 through 1956.[14] Two approaches were employed to test
empirically the validity of the MM hypothesis. First, the relation between
the average cost of capital and the degree of leverage employed was analyzed.
Secondly, the relation between the stock yields and the debt-to-equity ratio
was studied.

The results of the yield tests made with the railroad sample were not
too conclusive. Over the entire range of the observed debt/equity ratios a

[14] A. Barges, *The Effect of Capital Structure on the Cost of Capital*, Prentice-Hall, Inc., Englewood Cliffs, N.J., 1963.

significant linear relationship was found between the yield and the leverage. While the degree of correlation was not very great, the result was not inconsistent with the MM hypothesis. On the other hand, within the range of moderate debt/equity ratios (up to 82 percent), correlation was found to be close to zero.

The results of the average-cost tests were, however, more conclusive. A significant relation was found between the average cost of capital and the financial structure by fitting a second-degree (U-shaped) curve to the data. In other words, the tests indicated that the average costs at first tended to decline and then tended to rise as the leverage was increased. For all 61 Class I railroads the following regression equation was obtained:

$$Y = 12.39 - 0.244X + 0.00258X^2$$

where Y is the average cost and X is the ratio of long-term debt to total permanent capital, at book values. Barges argued that the use of market values of securities introduced a bias into the tests, and, therefore, he preferred to measure capital at book values. However, he also tested the relation between the average cost and the financial structure on the basis of market values and obtained results similar to the above. Barges' statistical tests also included sample data for department stores and cement companies in 1956. These data showed no significant correlation between common stock yields and debt-to-equity ratio in the moderate debt range. In summing up the results of his analysis, he concluded that the MM hypothesis appeared to be untenable.

WIPPERN'S FINDINGS

R. F. Wippern's statistical analysis was based on sample data for 50 firms from seven manufacturing industries in the years 1956, 1958, 1961, and 1963.[15] He used the following multiple regression equation:

$$\frac{\text{Earnings}}{\text{Price}} = a + b_1 \text{ leverage} + b_2 \text{ growth} + b_3 \text{ payout}$$

$$+ b_4 \log \text{size} + b_5 \cdots b_{10} \text{ industry dummy variables}$$

Professor Wippern argues that the usual measure of leverage, viz., the debt-to-equity ratio, contains important conceptual biases, whether the book value or the market value of equity is used. Consequently, he employs

[15] R. F. Wippern, "Financial Structure and the Value of the Firm," *The Journal of Finance*, vol. 21, no. 4, December, 1966.

a different measure, which is expressed as follows:

$$\text{Leverage} = \frac{i}{\bar{E} - 2s}$$

where i is the current level of fixed charges, $\bar{E}$ is the most recent year's cash flow of operating income determined from a logarithmic regression of income on time over a ten-year period, and $2s$ is equal to two standard errors around the regression line.[16]

The results of his empirical analysis indicate a linearly increasing relationship between equity yields and leverage. However, the rate of increase in the yield is not as great as that required to support the Modigliani and Miller hypothesis. When leverage is measured by the debt-to-equity ratio, the coefficient of the leverage variable should, according to MM, be equal to $k - r$ in a tax-free situation or to $(k - r)(1 - t)$ when the corporate income tax is introduced.[17] Since Wippern uses a different measure of leverage, the coefficient b_1 in his regression equation must, of course, be adjusted so as to make it comparable to the value one would expect to obtain if the MM hypothesis were valid. Having made such an adjustment, he finds that the actual values of b_1 are generally lower than the values that would support the MM propositions. For example, the following results are given for the food industry:

	1956	1958	1961	1963
The actual value of b	.0126	.0148	.0066	.0204
The value of b computed in accordance with the MM hypothesis	.0545	.0296	.0273	.0211

Professor Wippern's general conclusion is that his results favor the intermediate or traditional view of capital-structure effects: the stockholders' wealth can be enhanced by the firm's judicious use of debt financing.

THE WORK OF MODIGLIANI AND MILLER

Modigliani and Miller analyzed sample data for 63 electric utility firms in the years 1954, 1956, and 1957.[18] As discussed earlier, MM expect, on

[16] The cash flow of net operating income is defined as earnings before financing charges and taxes plus non-fund charges, such as depreciation.

[17] In these expressions, k = the equity capitalization rate for nonlevered firms in a given risk class; r = the interest rate on debt obligations; t = the marginal income tax rate.

[18] M. H. Miller and Franco Modigliani, "Cost of Capital to Electric Utility Industry," *The American Economic Review*, vol. 56, no. 3, June, 1966.

theoretical grounds, that the value of a levered firm will be equal to

$$V_{\text{lev}} = \frac{\overline{X}(1 - t)}{k_{un}} + tD = V_{un} + tD$$

where $\overline{X}(1 - t)$ is the unlevered firm's earnings after taxes and k_{un} is the capitalization rate applicable to the equity on the unlevered firm. The term tD indicates the tax advantage resulting from the introduction of debt into the capital structure. In order to test whether there are also non-tax advantages of leverage, MM fitted a regression equation in which the firm's value, adjusted for the tax advantage of leverage, was the dependent variable and earnings, size, growth, debt, and preferred stock were the independent variables.

In connection with the earnings variable, MM point out that theoretically one should use *expected* future earnings which are not directly measurable. If actually reported earnings are substituted for expected earnings, certain biases arise which may distort statistical results. In an attempt to avoid such biases, MM resort to a "two-stage instrumental" variable approach. First, a regression of reported earnings on several selected instrumental variables (size, growth, debt, preferred stock, and dividends) is obtained. Secondly, the earnings computed from this regression equation are substituted for the reported earnings.

When the direct least-square estimates using reported earnings are made, the coefficients of the debt and preferred stock variables are found to be significantly different from zero. This would seem to indicate that increases in leverage (by using either bonds or preferred stocks) result in a significant rise in the value of the levered firm. However, when the two-stage estimates are obtained, the debt and the preferred stock coefficients are substantially reduced and become so small in relation to their standard errors that they cannot be considered significant. MM conclude that these findings are in agreement with their hypothesis that the leverage factor is significant only because of the tax advantage involved.

MM also tested the significance of dividends as a factor in the valuation of the firm's stock. Their assumption was that the true, as opposed to the purely informational, effect of dividends on market value was small enough in the utilities industry to be safely ignored.

The regression equation used included the value of the firm adjusted for the leverage factor as the dependent variable and earnings, size, growth, and dividend policy as the independent variables. The dividend variable was derived by taking the difference between the actual amount of dividends paid by the firm and the amount it would have paid if it had adhered to the average payout ratio for the sample as a whole.

Here again, two sets of results were obtained. The direct least-square estimates produced significant coefficients of the dividend variable. This seemed to indicate that high dividend payouts increased the value of the firm. But the two-stage estimates resulted in coefficients of the dividend variable which lacked significance. Accordingly, MM's conclusion was that the dividend effect on the value of the firm was sufficiently small and uncertain to be safely neglected.

THE FINDINGS OF SARMA AND RAO

L. V. N. Sarma and K. S. Hanumanta Rao tested the MM hypothesis by taking a sample of thirty companies from the Indian engineering industry in the years 1962, 1964, and 1965.[19] They followed, with minor modifications, the MM two-stage least-square technique but obtained different results from those reported by MM for the electric utility firms in the United States. The coefficients of the leverage variable were found by Sarma and Rao to be significantly greater than they could be on the strength of the tax advantage of debt alone. The authors concluded that their analysis showed evidence in support of the proposition that the value of the firm can be raised by a judicious use of leverage.

[19] L. V. N. Sarma and K. S. Hanumanta Rao, "Leverage and the Value of the Firm," *Journal of Finance*, vol. 24, no. 4, September, 1969, pp. 673–677.

7
The Cost of Capital

In economic theory *costs* are defined as the values of the input quantities used in the production of various quantities of output.[1] As discussed in Chapter 2, one of the basic characteristics of capital as a factor of production is that it makes time an important variable in the productive process. When capital inputs are used, it becomes necessary, in calculating the costs, to take account not only of the initial outlay but also of the length of the period between the time when this outlay is made and the time (or times) when the revenues attributable to it are realized. Furthermore, account must be taken of the risk element involved in making capital inputs. In this chapter we shall examine the concepts and measures of the cost of different types of capital: debt funds, external equity funds, and internal funds.

THE COST OF DEBT CAPITAL

To elucidate the basic concepts and definitions employed, let us consider a simple investment project which involves an initial capital outlay C_0,

---

[1] Cf. K. E. Boulding, *Economic Analysis*, 3d ed., Harper & Brothers, New York, 1955, p. 529.

made at the beginning of time period t, and a revenue R_t, expected to be received in one lump sum at the end of this period. We may then write

$$C_0 = R_t(1 + r)^{-t}$$

where r is the average internal rate of return. If the project is to be financed with borrowed funds and the interest rate is equal to i, we may also write

$$V_0 = R_t(1 + i)^{-t}$$

where V_0 is the present value of the expected future revenue R_t. The present value of the expected profit, P_0, is equal to $V_0 - C_0$. It is clear that P_0 can be positive only if r is greater than i.

When computed at the end of the period, total cost C_t will include interest and will be equal to $C_0(1 + i)^t$. Profit P_t will then be equal to $R_t - C_0(1 + i)^t$. It follows, of course, that $P_t(1 + i)^{-t} = P_0$.

Suppose now that the firm decides to continue operations in the next period by renewing the loan and reinvesting the same amount C_0. It will not then be necessary to repay the principal amount of the loan; only the interest will have to be paid at the end of the period. Under these conditions, the management of the firm may be primarily concerned with the interest component of total cost in relation to profit before interest. We may write:

Profit before interest $= R_t - C_0 = C_0(1 + r)^t - C_0$

Interest cost $= C_0(1 + i)^t - C_0$

Profit after interest $= C_0(1 + r)^t - C_0(1 + i)^t$

Thus, profit after interest is equal to P_t as defined above.

To take a very simple numerical example, assume that a firm borrows $1,000 for one year at 5 percent and invests the funds in a project which will result in a revenue of $1,100 at the end of the year. The present value of this revenue, discounted at 5 percent, is

$$1,100(1.05)^{-1} = 1,047.50$$

and profit, measured at the beginning of the year, is $1,047.50 - 1,000 = 47.50$. The internal rate of return is equal to the value of r in the expression

$$1,000 = 1,100(1 + r)^{-1}$$

which is .1. Profit before interest at the end of the year is $1,000(1.1) - 1,000 =$ 100; the interest cost is 50, and profit after interest is $100 - 50 = 50$. The present value of profit after interest, at the beginning of the year, is $50(1.05)^{-1}$ $= 47.50$.

If the loan could be obtained interest-free, the initial cost of the project would still be $1,000, but the interest cost would be zero, and in this sense, the financing would be costless. With a positive interest rate, the minimum internal rate of return on the investment, required to avoid a financial loss, is equal to the rate of interest charged for the loan (5 percent in the above example). The cost of debt funds is sometimes defined as such a minimum required rate of return.[2]

In the above discussion we ignored the effect of borrowing on the degree of risk incurred by the firm. When the risk factor is present, the value of the firm's stock may be different at any given revenue level. To examine the effect of this factor, suppose that a firm initially operates with a capital of $1,000, consisting of equity funds only, and its expected revenues are $100 per annum. If the capitalization factor, applicable to unlevered firms in the industry in question is .1, then the market value of the firm's stock is also $1,000 (equal to the book value). Suppose now that the firm increases its capital to $2,000 by borrowing $1,000 at 5 percent per annum, as a result of which its annual revenue is expected to rise from $100 to $200 (the internal rate of return remains unchanged at .1).

The revenue increment is then equal to $100 per annum while the interest charges amount to only $50 per annum. However, let us assume that the capitalization factor goes up from .1 to .12 as a result of the additional risk associated with the debt financing. The market value of the stock is now

$$V_e = \frac{150}{.12} = 1,250$$

In analyzing the financial result of borrowing we must distinguish between the following elements:

1. The present value of the stream of the revenue increments attributable to the new funds ($100 per annum), discounted at the new capitalization rate of .12, is equal to

$$\frac{100}{.12} = 833.33$$

---

[2] See, for example, J. F. Weston and E. F. Brigham, *Managerial Finance*, 2d ed., Holt, Rinehart & Winston, New York, 1962, p. 282.

2. The present value of the stream of interest payments of $50 per year, discounted at .12, is

$$\frac{50}{.12} = 416.67$$

3. The difference between the present value of the initial revenue stream of $100 per year (prior to borrowing), discounted at .1, and the same revenue stream discounted at .12 is

$$\frac{100}{.1} - \frac{100}{.12} = 1,000 - 833.33 = 166.66$$

Thus, the *gross* gain from the new investment is $833.33, whereas the total cost of borrowing is equal to $416.67 + 166.66 = 583.33$. The *net* gain for the stockholders—reflected in the increased present value of their shares—is therefore equal to $833.33 - 583.33 = 250$. This is exactly the amount by which the value of the firm's stock has increased.

To put it in algebraic terms, let E denote the firm's equity, r its internal rate of return, and k the capitalization rate applicable to its stock when there is no debt outstanding. We may then write

$$P_{e_1} = rE \qquad \text{and} \qquad \frac{P_{e_1}}{k_1} = V_{e_1}$$

If the firm borrows an amount equal to D at an interest rate equal to i, its total profit will be

$$P_t = r(E + D)$$

and its profit on equity will be

$$P_{e_2} = r(E + D) - iD = rE + (r - i)D$$

If the capitalization rate is now k_2, the value of the firm's stock becomes

$$V_{e_2} = \frac{P_{e_2}}{k_2}$$

and the gross gain from borrowing is equal to

$$\frac{r(E + D) - rE}{k_2} = \frac{rD}{k_2} = G_g$$

The interest cost is equal to

$$\frac{iD}{k_2}$$

and the risk cost is equal to

$$\frac{rE}{k_1} - \frac{rE}{k_2}$$

Consequently, the net gain is

$$\frac{rD - iD}{k_2} + \frac{rE}{k_2} - \frac{rE}{k_1} = \frac{(r - i)D}{k_2} - \frac{rE(k_2 - k_1)}{k_1 k_2} = G_n$$

It is clear that the risk cost becomes zero if $k_2 = k_1$, and the net gain is then equal to

$$\frac{(r - i)D}{k_2}$$

Going back to our numerical example, we may note that if the annual revenue increment resulting from the new investment amounted to only $50 per year (the same as the annual interest payment), the operation would result in a financial loss for the firm's stockholders. The present value of the incremental revenue stream would then be equal to

$$\frac{50}{.12} = 416.67$$

whereas the total cost of the debt financing would still be equal to $583.33. The market value of the firm's stock would decline from $1,000 to

$$\frac{100}{.12} = 833.33$$

and the stockholders' net loss would be equal to $166.66.

It can also be easily seen that the minimum internal rate of return (before interest) on the new investment must, under the conditions assumed, be equal to .07 in order to avoid a reduction in the present value of the firm's stock. At this rate, the annual revenue increment would be equal

to $70 before interest and $20 after interest. The gross gain from the investment would be equal to

$$\frac{70}{.12} = 583.33$$

which is equal to the total cost of the debt financing.

Let us now consider the effect of the tax factor. Assume that the firm's
initial capital is $1,000 (all equity), the expected revenues are $200 before the
tax, and the tax rate is 50 percent. If the capitalization rate, applicable to
the firm's net profit after the tax, is .1, the market value of its stock is $1,000—
the same as the book value.

Assume now that the firm borrows $1,000 at 5 percent and its profit
before interest and tax increases from $200 to $400. The posttax profit on
equity is then equal to

$$
\begin{array}{ll}
400 & \\
-\ 50 & \text{Interest} \\
\hline
350 & \\
-175 & \text{50 percent tax} \\
\hline
175 &
\end{array}
$$

If the capitalization rate goes up to .12 as a result of this borrowing,
the new market value of the firm's stock will be

$$V_e = \frac{175}{.12} = 1,458.33$$

The gross gain from the new investment is

$$\frac{200}{.12} = 1,666.67$$

the interest cost is

$$\frac{50}{.12} = 416.67$$

the tax cost (the present value of the additional tax stream) is

$$\frac{75}{.12} = 625.00$$

and the risk cost is equal to

$$\frac{100}{.1} - \frac{100}{.12} = 166.67$$

Consequently, net gain accruing to the stockholders as a result of the new investment is

$$1,667.67 - (416.67 + 625.00 + 166.67) = 458.33$$

If the risk cost was zero, the minimum required rate of return (before interest and tax) on the new investment would be equal to the interest rate. But if there is a positive risk cost, the internal rate must be kept above the interest rate, to avoid a net loss for the stockholders. In our example, net gain would be reduced to zero if the internal rate on the new investment were equal to .09. In this case the posttax profit on equity would be

$$
\begin{array}{rl}
290 & \\
-\ 50 & \text{Interest} \\
\hline
240 & \\
-120 & \text{Tax} \\
\hline
120 &
\end{array}
$$

The present value of the firm's equity, capitalized at .12, would then be $1,000—the same as it was prior to the use of debt funds. There would be a gross gain from the new investment amounting to

$$\frac{90}{.12} = 750$$

But it would be completely offset by the total cost incurred:

$$\text{Interest cost:} \quad \frac{50}{.12} = 416.67$$

$$\text{Tax cost:} \quad \frac{20}{.12} = 166.66$$

$$\text{Risk cost:} \quad \frac{100}{.1} - \frac{100}{.12} = \underline{166.67}$$

$$\text{Total cost} \quad = 750.00$$

Thus, net gain would be zero.

THE COST OF EXTERNAL EQUITY

The same concept of cost as that described above may be applied to new external equity financing. From the standpoint of the existing stockholders, the sale of additional shares is worthwhile only if it is expected to raise the value of the stock that they now own. The following elements must be distinguished in connection with this form of new financing:

1. On the one hand, investment of new funds should produce a stream of revenue increments which, in itself, will tend to increase the present value of the stock outstanding prior to the new issue.

2. On the other hand, new shareholders will have a claim on the firm's earnings (and assets) equal on a per share basis to the claim of the old stockholders. This factor, in itself, will tend to diminish the value of the initial stock outstanding.

3. There may be additional risk involved in the investment of the new funds. Since the additional dividends to be paid on the new shares do not represent a fixed charge, the risk factor in this case is not, of course, the same as in the case of new debt financing. However, if the new project to be financed with external equity funds involves more risk than the firm's previous operations did, the additional risk factor must be taken into consideration in determining the full effect of the new investment on the value of the stockholders' shares.[3]

From the standpoint of the old stockholders, then, the cost of new equity financing may be defined as the combined negative effect of the last two factors—the new stockholders' claim on earnings and the change (if any) in the risk involved—on the present value of their shares. The financing would be costless only in the unlikely event of this combined effect being nil. Ordinarily, there is a significant cost, and the new investment must be considered worthwhile only if the gross gain resulting from the incremental revenue stream is expected to exceed this cost.

Suppose a firm is initially operating with an invested capital of $1,000 (all equity) and an annual profit of $100. If the market capitalizes its stock at the rate of .1, the market value of the stock is also $1,000—equal to the book value. Assuming that there are 100 shares outstanding, profit per share is $1 and the market value of one share is $10.

Suppose now that the firm is considering a new project for which an additional $1,000 of capital is required. The expected stream of revenues

---

[3] New equity financing may in some cases have a *negative* incremental risk effect. If the new investment results in strengthening the firm's market position and in stabilizing as well as expanding its operations, the degree of risk may be lessened from the standpoint of the old as well as the new stockholders.

attributable to the new project is $140 per annum, which means that the internal rate of return on the new investment is .14. However, the new project involves a greater degree of risk than that associated with the firm's present invested capital. Therefore, even if the new project is financed by selling additional stock, it is expected that the market capitalization rate for the firm's shares will go up from .1 to .11. Would such a financing result in a net gain for the existing stockholders?

The firm's total profit after the additional investment of $1,000 will be $240 per annum. Total market value of its stock (the old and the new shares combined) will then be equal to 240/.11 = 2,181. In order to raise $1,000 of additional funds the firm will have to sell 85 shares at $11.81 per share. After that, there will be 185 shares outstanding and the new profit per share will be $1.30. Total profit accruing to the old stockholders will be equal to $1.30 × 100 = $130 and the market value of their shares will rise from $1,000 to $1,181, giving them a net gain from the new project amounting to $181.

Here again, the net gain is the result of interaction of the following factors:

1. The gross gain from the project is equal to the present value of the additional revenue stream attributable to it:

$$\frac{140}{.11} = 1,272$$

2. The present value of the new investors' claims on the firm's profit is equal to

$$\frac{85 \times 1.30}{.11} = 1,000$$

3. The difference between the present value of the initial revenue stream of $100 discounted at .1 and the same stream discounted at .11 is

$$\frac{100}{.1} - \frac{100}{.11} = 91$$

Total cost of the new equity funds is the sum of items 2 and 3; or 1,000 + 91 = 1,091. The net gain from the project accruing to the old stockholders is equal to the gross gain less the total cost, or 1,272 − 1,091 = 181.

The minimum stream of revenue on the new project required to maintain the value of the old stockholders' shares without change (at the $1,000 level) is $120 per annum. In this case, the firm's total profit would be equal to $220 and the aggregate market value of its stock (the old and the new shares combined) would be

$$\frac{220}{.11} = 2,000$$

In order to raise $1,000 of additional capital the firm would have to sell 100 new shares at $10 per share. Profit per share would rise from $1.00 to $1.10, but this would have no effect on the price of the firm's shares because the capitalization rate would rise from .10 to .11.

THE COST OF RETAINED EARNINGS

Internal financing differs from external equity or debt financing in that additional funds are provided (involuntarily) by the existing stockholders rather than new investors. In the case of externally financed expansion the old stockholders make no new capital outlay and their position is improved if there is any positive increment in the value of their shares. But in the case of internally financed expansion, the stockholders can register a net gain only if the value of their stock increases by more than the amount retained. Alternatively, we may say that internal financing is worthwhile from the stockholders' standpoint only if it results in a net addition to their total wealth, which includes not only the stock of the firm concerned but also their other assets. If the firm retains a certain portion of its net profit instead of paying out the entire amount as dividends, this action in itself represents only a redistribution of the stockholders' assets: less cash on hand and more investment in the firm's assets. A net increment in their wealth may result only if reinvestment in the same firm yields a higher return than the best return available to them in the capital market.

The cost of external financing, as discussed above, is determined by the new investors' claim on the firm's earnings and by the additional risk involved in investing new funds. When internal financing is used, the existing stockholders themselves become investors of new funds and have reason to claim a return on these funds as well as on the previously invested capital. We may say that total cost of internal financing is equal to the sum of (*a*) the opportunity cost: the present value of the earnings foregone on investments that could be made elsewhere if the funds were distributed; and (*b*) the risk cost: the change in the value of the firm's stock owing to additional risks (if any) involved in the retention policy. The stockholders' gross gain from profit retention may be defined as the present value of all profit increments expected as a result of this policy. Their net gain is, of course, equal to gross gain minus total cost involved.

Suppose that a firm's capital at the beginning of a given year is $1,000 (all equity) and its profit for the year is $200, which means that the internal rate of return, r, is equal to .2. If this is the average rate for all firms in the same risk class, the capitalization rate k will also be equal to .2 and the market value of the firm's stock will be equal to its book value:

$$V_e = \frac{200}{.2} = 1,000$$

Suppose now that at the end of the year the firm pays out $100 as dividends and retains the other $100 in the business. If r remains unchanged, the firm's profit will increase to $220 in the second year and will remain at this level in all subsequent years, provided that no further retentions are made. The market value of the firm's stock must increase by an amount equal to the present value of the expected additional revenues:

$$\Delta V_e = \frac{R}{k} = \frac{20}{.2} = 100$$

This is the gross gain resulting from the retention of $100 in the first year. The cost of the retention is equal to the present value of the additional revenues that the stockholders could receive if they invested the $100 in another firm. Since we have assumed that .2 is the average rate of return for the entire industry, it is clear that the cost is also equal to $20/.2 = 100$. It follows that the stockholders' net gain from this profit retention is equal to zero.

Suppose, however, that the firm in question has a higher than average internal rate of return. If the firm's r is .2 but the average for the industry is only .15, then the capitalization factor is also .15 and the initial market value of the firm's stock is

$$V_e = \frac{200}{.15} = 1,333.33$$

If the firm retains $100 in the first year, this will increase its profit by $20 per annum, and the present value of this additional stream of revenue will be equal to

$$\frac{20}{.15} = 133.33$$

Investment of $100 in another firm would, however, produce an additional revenue stream of only $15 per annum. Consequently, the cost of the retention is equal to $15/.15 = 100$, and the stockholders' net gain is equal to $33.33.

In the above example we assumed that the retention of $100 does not change the degree of risk involved in the firm's operations. If the firm adds $100 to its initial capital of $1,000 and keeps its capital at this level in the subsequent years, this assumption seems reasonable. On the other hand, if the firm's policy is to retain part of its profit year after year, such a continual expansion of its capital may eventually result in a significant change in the degree of risk involved. When the risk factor becomes significant, it must, of course, be taken into account in computing the total cost of new internal as well as external financing.

We have also disregarded the effect of the tax factor in the above example. As already discussed above, the distributed part of corporate profit is immediately subject to the personal income tax, whereas the retained part does not add to the stockholders' personal tax liability as long as there is no realized capital gain. Moreover, when the gain is realized, it is subject to a lower tax rate. The additional personal income tax liability that would be incurred by the firm's stockholders if its entire profit were distributed would reduce the amount of funds available for and the amount of income realized from outside investment. It must, therefore, be taken account of as a factor reducing the opportunity cost of profit retention.

THE AVERAGE COST OF NEW CAPITAL FUNDS

An expanding firm does not, of course, have to raise the entire amount of new funds from one and the same source. A preferable procedure may be to finance the new project partly with debt funds, partly with external equity funds, and partly with internal funds. In some cases the new project may become worthwhile only if such a combination of different types of financing can be arranged.

Consider the following simple example. Let the firm's initial capital K_0 be equal to $1,000; its equity E_0, equal to $500; and its debt D_0, equal to $500. Let the internal rate of return be .1, the rate of interest .05, and the market capitalization rate for the firm's stock .15. Profit before interest is then $100, total interest charges are $25, and profit after interest is $75 per annum. The present value of the firm's stock is then equal to

$$V_e = \frac{75}{.15} = 500$$

(The market value is equal to the book value.)

Suppose now that the firm is considering a new project which requires an additional investment of $1,000 and is expected to raise its profit before interest by $110 per annum (to a total of $210). In other words, the internal rate of return on the new investment is expected to be .11. If the new funds are raised by borrowing, the firm's debt-to-equity ratio will increase from 1 to 3, and this will involve a rise in both the interest rate i and the stock capitalization rate k, because of a greater degree of risk. Suppose that i will increase to .08 and k to .25. The annual amount of interest will then be $120 and the value of the firm's stock will be equal to

$$V_e = \frac{210 - 120}{.25} = \frac{90}{.25} = 360$$

It would clearly not be in the stockholders' interest to finance the new project in this manner.

Assume now that the firm decides to obtain the additional $1,000 by selling new shares of stock. In this case, the debt-to-equity ratio will decline from 1 to $\frac{1}{3}$, and both i and k may be expected to decrease. If i drops from .05 to .04 and k drops from .15 to .13, the total value of the firm's stock (the old and the new shares combined) will be equal to

$$V_{et} = \frac{210 - 20}{.13} = \frac{190}{.13} = 1,461$$

and the value of the old stockholders' shares, V_{e0}, will be equal to $1,461 - 1,000 = 461$. This form of financing is, then, also unattractive from the old stockholders' standpoint.

Suppose, however, that the firm decides to keep its debt-to-equity ratio unchanged, which requires that $500 of new funds be raised by borrowing and $500 by selling new shares. We may assume that, in this case, both the interest rate and the capitalization rate remain unchanged. The total value of the firm's stock will then be

$$V_{et} = \frac{210 - 50}{.15} = \frac{160}{.15} = 1,066$$

and the value of the old shares will be $1,066 - 500 = 566$. This combination of new debt and new equity funds will, then, make the new project worthwhile from the old stockholders' standpoint.

Here again it may be shown that the net gain accruing to the old stockholders is equal to the gross gain from the new financing less its total cost. The gross gain is the additional revenue stream of $110 per annum, the present value of which is equal to

$$\frac{110}{.15} = 733.33$$

The interest cost of the new debt funds is equal to $25 per annum. The present value of this stream of payments is equal to

$$\frac{25}{.15} = 166.66$$

The new stockholders' claim on the firm's profit is equal to $75 per annum, and the present value of this revenue stream is equal to

$$\frac{75}{.15} = 500$$

Thus, total cost of the new debt and new equity financing is $166.66 + 500 = 666.66$. The net gain for the old stockholders is $733.33 - 666.66 = 66.67$.†

What is the minimum internal rate of return on the new investment required to keep the value of the old stockholders' shares unchanged?

In our first example, in which the new financing was done entirely with debt funds, the minimum required rate is found to be .145. The additional profit would then be equal to $145 and the firm's total profit would rise to $245. The new profit on equity would then be equal to $245 - 120 = 125$, and the latter amount capitalized at .25 would make the value of the firm's stock equal to $500—the same as before.

In our second example, in which the new financing is done entirely with equity funds, the required rate is found to be .12. The additional profit would then be $120 and total profit would be $220. Capitalized at .13, this would give us $1,500 as the total value of the firm's equity. Since the new stockholders' investment is equal to $1,000, it follows that the value of the old shares remains at $500.

Finally, in our third example, in which the firm absorbs $500 of equity funds and $500 of debt funds, the minimum required rate is .1. It would make the additional profit equal $100 and the firm's total profit equal $200. Net profit on equity would be $150 and the market value of the firm's total stock outstanding (capitalized at the rate of .15) would be $1,000. Since the new stockholders' investment is $500, the value of the old shares would also be $500—the same as before.

---

†To consider the situation on a *per share* basis, assume that the firm originally has 100 shares outstanding. The price of one share is then $5 and net profit per share is $.75. We have assumed above that an inflow of $500 in equity funds and $500 in debt funds raises the firm's total profit to $210 and its net profit on equity to $160 a year. If the new equity funds are obtained by selling 88 new shares at $5.66 each, the total number of shares outstanding will rise to 188 and the net profit per share will be $.85. The rate of return on the new stockholders' investment will be .15, which corresponds to the assumed stock capitalization rate. The old stockholders still own 100 shares; but with the higher profit per share, the rate of return on their original investment ($500) will rise from .15 to .17. However, the rate will still be .15 when computed on the basis of the new market value of their stock ($566).

The required internal rate of return (.1) may be derived by averaging the interest rate on debt (.05) and the capitalization rate on stock (.15). It may, therefore, be referred to as the average cost of the capital funds employed in financing the new project. Since in our example the amounts of new debt financing and new equity financing are equal ($500 each), the problem of weighting does not arise in averaging, and the simple (unweighted) arithmetic mean gives the correct figure:

$$\frac{.05 + .15}{2} = .1$$

In general, however, the interest rate and the capitalization rate must be given weights proportionate to the amounts of new debt and new equity funds used. The general formula for deriving the average cost of new capital funds, C_a, must be written as

$$C_a = \frac{i\alpha + k\beta}{\alpha + \beta}$$

where α and β are the weights which must be such that $\alpha/\beta = D/E$.

THE AVERAGE COST OF THE FIRM'S TOTAL CAPITAL

The average cost of a firm's total capital is determined by the opportunity costs of all of its investors (both owners and creditors). In other words, it is measured by the income which the investors could earn by investing their funds elsewhere. If the internal rate of return rises above the level of the average cost of capital, this will tend to raise the firm's total market value; if it drops below this level, the firm's market value will tend to decline. The minimum rate of return required to prevent the market value from dropping below the amount actually invested by the owners and the creditors must be equal to the average cost of capital.

Consider a firm that wishes to maintain its total invested capital at a given level but is willing to substitute debt for equity funds (or vice versa) so as to attain an optimum capital structure. With the amount of capital (and all other inputs) held constant and the market conditions unchanged, the firm's average internal rate of return will also remain constant. But the cost of debt and of equity capital will be affected by changes in the debt-to-equity ratio. A numerical example is given in Table 7-1 and Figure 7-1. The firm's total investment capital, K, is maintained at the $1,000 level and the internal rate of return, r, is .1.† There is no corporate income tax in this

† *Total investment capital* is defined as the total amount of funds actually invested in the firm's assets. Assuming no accounting revaluations, this is equal to the book value of the firm's equity plus debt.

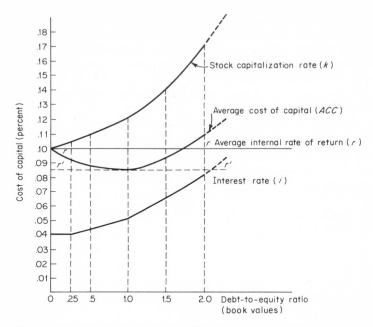

Figure 7-1   The average cost of capital with no corporate income tax.

Table 7-1   Market value of the firm and the average cost of capital (without corporate income tax)

	Book value of Debt (1)	Equity (2)	D/E ratio (book values) (3)	Interest rate (i) (4)	Stock capitaliz- ation rate (k) (5)	Market value of equity (V_e) (6)	D/E ratio (market values) (7)	Total market value of the firm (V_t) (Col. 1 + Col. 6) (8)	Average cost of capital (P_t/V_t) (9)
1.	0	1,000	0	0	.1	1,000	0	1,000	.100
2.	200	800	.25	.04	.105	876.19	.23	1,076.19	.093
3.	333	667	.5	.045	.1095	772.72	.43	1,106.05	.090
4.	500	500	1.0	.05	.12	625.00	.8	1,125.00	.088
5.	600	400	1.5	.065	.14	435.71	1.38	1,035.71	.097
6.	667	333	2.0	.08	.17	274.53	2.4	941.20	.106

Invested capital $K = 1,000$; internal rate of return $r = .1$; profit before interest $P = 100$.

example. With no debt in the capital structure, the market capitalization rate applicable to the firm's stock, k, is also assumed to be .1, which means that the market value of the firm's equity is equal to its book value. As the firm begins to borrow (and to substitute debt for equity funds), the interest rate i is initially equal to .04, but higher rates must be paid as the amount of debt increases. The stock capitalization rate also moves upward as the debt-to-equity ratio becomes greater. The table and the figure indicate changes in the market value of the firm's equity, the total market value of the firm, and the average cost of its capital that result from the assumed variations in i and k.

It can be seen that the average cost of capital is lowest, and the stock-holder's gain is greatest, when debt is equal to $500. If the firm borrows $500 and repays an equivalent amount to its stockholders by redeeming some of its shares, the aggregate book value of the remaining shares is $500, but their aggregate market value is now

$$V_e = \frac{100 - (.05 \times 500)}{.12} = \frac{75}{.12} = 625$$

Thus, the stockholders (as a group) receive $500 in cash, but the aggregate market value of their stock declines by only $1,000 - 625 = 375$. Their total wealth is now equal to $625 + 500 = 1,125$, or 12.5 percent more than it was prior to the change in the capital structure.

The average cost of capital can be measured by the ratio of total profit to total market value of the firm, which is equal to the weighted average of the interest rate and the stock capitalization rate when the weights are proportionate to the market values of the debt and equity, respectively: $(500/625 = .8/1.0)$.†

Cost of debt   .05 × .8 = .04
Cost of equity .12 × 1.0 = .12
$$\overline{\hspace{2.5cm}}$$
                            .16 : 1.8 = .0889

The rate of .0889 represents the minimum internal rate of return that would be required to maintain the total market value of the firm at the initial $1,000 level, with the debt-to-equity ratio being equal to .8 (based on market values). If profit before interest dropped to $88.89, while the amount of debt was $445 and the interest rate was 5 percent, then net profit after

---

† This equality may be easily demonstrated algebraically. Since we know that $P_t = rK$, $P_e = rK - iD$, $V_e = (rK - iD)/k$, and $V_t = V_e + D$, it follows that

$$P_t = (rK - iD) + iD = kV_e + iD$$

and

$$\frac{P_t}{V_t} = \frac{kV_e + iD}{V_e + D}$$

interest would be $66.64. The market value of the firm's stock, capitalized at .12, would be $555 and the total value of the firm would be equal to 555 + 445 = 1,000.

As long as the internal rate of return remains at .1, while the minimum required rate is only .088, there will be an incentive to expand the firm's total capital. To illustrate, suppose that a firm whose initial capital is $1,000, consisting of $500 debt and $500 equity (book values), decides to increase it to $1,200 by selling $100 worth of bonds and $100 worth of stock. Prior to the expansion, as stated above, the firm's net profit after interest is $75 and the market value of its stock is $625, or $6.25 per share if there are 100 shares outstanding. Assuming that the internal rate of return remains unchanged, the firm's profit before interest will now be $120 and its net profit after interest will be $120 - 30 = 90$. If the capitalization factor is still .12, the aggregate market value of the firm's equity will now be

$$\frac{90}{.12} = 750$$

Since the aggregate market value of the new shares is, by assumption, equal to $100, it follows that the aggregate market value of the old shares is now $650, or $6.50 per share. Thus, the old stockholders will again register a capital gain, even though there is no further change in the debt-to-equity ratio.

If the new price is $6.50 per share, the firm will have to sell 15.38 shares in order to raise $100 of new equity funds. The total number of shares will then be 115.38 and the net profit per share will be $.78. The rate of return on the new shares will be $.78/6.50 = .12$, which is equal to the assumed market capitalization rate. The price of $6.50 should therefore be acceptable to the new stockholders. However, if other firms in the industry also find it advantageous to expand, such a general expansion may lead to an excess supply of the industry's products and a decline in prices, total revenues, and profits. In other words, there may be a general decline in the internal rate of return. Assuming that the capitalization rate remains unchanged, an equilibrium condition in our example will be reached when the internal rate of return for the firms with the optimum debt-to-equity ratio drops to .089. Any firm which fails to maintain an optimum D/E ratio will be faced with the average cost of capital higher than its internal rate of return. This can be seen in Figure 7-1 by comparing the dotted line $r'r'$ with the ACC curve.

But there may also be a general rise in the capitalization rates applicable to the stocks in the industry concerned if the inflow of new capital and the resulting expansion of operations increases the financial risks incurred by the firms in this industry. A rise in the stock capitalization rates will depress the market values of the firms' equities and, thus, reduce the old stockholders' gains resulting from the inflow of new funds. An equilibrium condition will be reached when the possibility of making further gains is eliminated.

THE EFFECT OF CORPORATE INCOME TAX ON CAPITAL COST

We shall now consider the effect of the tax factor on the average cost of capital. Assume once more that the firm's invested capital remains unchanged, but that the firm is free to vary the debt-to-equity ratio by substituting debt for equity funds (or vice versa). Let the invested capital be $1,000, the pretax internal rate of return .2, and the tax rate .5. Let the interest rate and the stock capitalization rate vary with the amount of debt, as shown in Table 7-2 and Figure 7-2. When a tax is in effect, the firm's total profit is divided among the creditors, the government, and the stockholders. The pretax cost of capital is measured by the ratio of total profit to total market value of the firm,

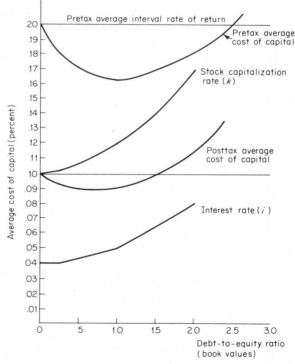

Figure 7-2 The average cost of capital with corporate income tax.

Table 7-2 Market value of the firm and the average cost of capital (with corporate income tax)

Book values of		D/E ratio (book values) (3)	Interest rate (i) (4)	Stock capitalization rate (k) (5)	Market value of equity (V_e) (6)	D/E ratio (market values) (7)	Total market value of the firm (V_t) (Col. 1 + Col. 6) (8)	Average cost of capital	
Debt (1)	Equity (2)							Pretax P/V_t (9)	Posttax $(P-T)/V_t$ (10)
1.	0	1,000	0	0	.1	1,000	0	1,000	.2	.1
2.	200	800	.25	.04	.105	914.28	.22	1,114.28	.1794	.0933
3.	333	667	.5	.045	.11	840.91	.40	1,174.24	.1703	.0915
4.	500	500	1.0	.05	.12	729.16	.69	1,229.16	.1627	.0915
5.	600	400	1.5	.065	.14	575.00	1.04	1,175.00	.1702	.1017
6.	666	333	2.0	.08	.17	431.35	1.54	1,098.02	.1821	.1153
7.	800	200	4.0	.15	.25	160.00	5.00	960.00	.2083	.1666

Invested capital $K = 1,000$; internal rate of return before tax $r = .2$; profit before tax $P = 200$; corporate income tax rate $t = .5$.

while the posttax cost is measured by the ratio of the sum of the creditors' and the stockholders' shares of total profit to total market value of the firm. It should be noticed that, owing to the tax-exempt status of interest on debt, the amount of the tax decreases as the amount of the debt is raised. Consequently, the combined amount of profit available to the owners and the creditors increases, even though total profit remains unchanged.

Figure 7-2 indicates that both the pretax and the posttax cost curves are U shaped, although their slopes are not the same. At first, while the slopes are negative, the posttax cost shows a smaller rate of decline than the pretax cost. Subsequently, when the slopes become positive, the posttax cost shows a greater rate of increase. As a result, the difference between the two cost figures is continually reduced as the debt-to-equity ratio is increased.

Under the conditions assumed, the average cost of capital is lowest and the stockholders' gain is greatest when debt is equal to $500. The market value of the firm's equity at that point is $729, as compared with the book value of $500. The D/E ratio based on the book values is 1.0 and the ratio based on the market values is .69. The pretax average cost of capital is equal to $200/1,229 = .163$. This indicates the minimum pretax internal rate of return required to maintain the total value of the firm at the $1,000 level (with the D/E ratio of .69). If the pretax profit dropped from $200 to $162.29, the firm's financial position would be as follows:

Pretax profit	$162.29
Interest at 5% on $409	20.45
	141.84
C.I. tax at 50%	70.92
Posttax profit on equity	70.92

Capitalizing the posttax profit on equity at the rate of .12, we find that the market value of the stock is $591. The total value of the firm is then equal to $591 + 409 = 1,000$.

The posttax cost of capital, when the debt is $500, is .091. This is equal to the weighted average of the interest rate and the stock capitalization rate:

$$.05 \times .69 = .0345$$
$$.12 \times 1.00 = .12$$
$$\overline{.1545} \div 1.69 = .091$$

This indicates that the minimum amount of profit that must be available to the creditors and owners in order to maintain the value of the firm at $1,000 is equal to $91.

In the examples given above, the average cost of capital curves have a distinct U shape, with a clear minimum point at one particular debt-to-equity ratio. These examples were presented, of course, for purposes of illustration only. Differently shaped curves can be obtained on the basis of different assumptions as to how the interest rate and the stock capitalization rate respond to changes in the D/E ratio.

For comparison purposes, let us consider briefly the average capital cost curves derived on the assumptions made by Modigliani and Miller. In the MM model, when no corporate income tax is imposed, total market value of the firm is independent of the D/E ratio, and the average cost of capital curve is, therefore, a straight line, as shown in Figure 7-3a.

If the firm's annual profit before interest is \$100 and the capitalization rate is $k_0 = .1$, when $D/E = 0$, the market value of the firm is \$1,000 and the

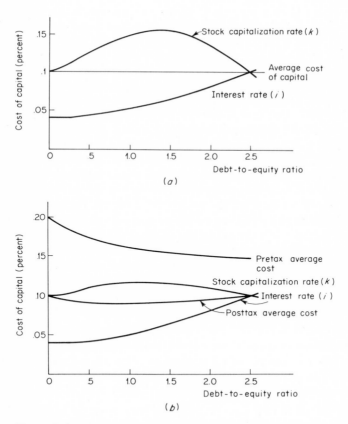

Figure 7-3 The average cost of capital: MM models. (*a*) With no corporate income tax; (*b*) with corporate income tax.

average cost of capital is $100/1{,}000 = .1$. Now, if the firm borrows \$200 at 4 percent, the new capitalization rate k is equal to

$$k = k_0 + (k_0 - i)\frac{D}{E} = .1 + (.1 - .04)\frac{200}{800} = .115$$

Profit on equity is now equal to $100 - 8 = 92$. Capitalized at .115, the latter amount gives us \$800 as the market value of the firm's stock. Thus, the total value of the firm remains unchanged, and so does the average cost of capital. The lower cost of debt funds is exactly offset by the rise in the cost of equity funds, and the weighted average of the two is still equal to .1:

Cost of debt $.04 \times 1 = .04$

Cost of equity $.115 \times 4 = \underline{.46}$

$.50 \div 5 = .1$

The reader can easily verify that the average cost of capital remains constant with any other D/E ratio.

An interesting characteristic of this model is that an increase in the D/E ratio is accompanied by a rise in the stock capitalization rate, k, only up to a certain point. Thereafter, increases in the D/E ratio (and presumably in the risk incurred by the stockholders) are associated with a reduction in the value of k. As Figure 7-3a indicates, the highest value of k is reached when $D/E = 1.5$. When $D/E = 2.4$, k drops back to the .1 level. MM tried to explain this strange phenomenon by the activities of arbitrage operators, who may find it attractive to hold a combined portfolio of the firm's shares and bonds so that the lower yield on the stock is offset by the higher return on the bonds.[4] But this explanation can hardly be accepted as realistic.

When the tax factor is introduced, in the original MM model a rise in the D/E ratio causes a decline in the pretax cost but has no effect on the post-tax cost. This is so because the total value of the firm increases in exactly the same proportion as the share of total value accruing to the stockholders and the creditors. In the revised MM model, on the other hand, an increase in the D/E ratio affects both the pretax and the posttax cost. The former declines continually, while the latter at first declines but then begins to rise. In other words, the pretax cost curve has a consistently negative slope while the posttax curve has a U shape, with a minimum point associated with a specific value of D/E.

A numerical example, based on MM's revised model, is given in Table 7-3 and shown graphically in Figure 7-3b. The values of i in this table are the

---

[4] Franco Modigliani and Merton H. Miller, "The Cost of Capital, Corporation Finance and the Theory of Investment," *The American Economic Review*, June, 1958.

Table 7-3 The average cost of capital—MM's revised model

	Book values of		D/E ratio (book values) (3)	Interest rate (i) (4)	Stock capitalization rate (k) (5)	Market value of equity (V_e) (6)	D/E ratio (market values) (7)	Total market value of the firm (V_t) (Col. 1 + Col. 6) (8)	Average cost of capital	
	Debt (1)	Equity (2)							Pretax P/V_t (9)	Posttax $(P-T)/V_t$ (10)
1.	0	1,000	0	0	.1	1,000	0	1,000	.2	.1
2.	200	800	.25	.04	.1067	900	.22	1,100	.1818	.0945
3.	333	667	.5	.045	.1109	834	.40	1,167	.1714	.0921
4.	500	500	1.0	.05	.1167	750	.67	1,250	.1600	.0900
5.	600	400	1.5	.065	.1150	700	.86	1,300	.1538	.0919
6.	666	333	2.0	.08	.1100	666	1.00	1,333	.1500	.0950
7.	715	285	2.5	.1	.1000	643	1.11	1,358	.1472	.1000
8.	800	200	4.0	.15	.0667	600	1.33	1,400	.1428	.1143

Invested capital $K = 1,000$; internal rate of return before tax $r = .2$; profit before tax $P = 200$; corporate income tax rate $t = .5$.

same as those in Table 7-2. The values of k are computed according to the formula:

$$k = k_0 + (1 - t)(k_0 - i)\frac{D}{E}$$

It will be noticed that here again, as in the no-tax case, the value of k increases up to a certain point, but then reverses its trend even though the D/E ratio (and the risk associated with it) continues to rise. With no debt at all, k is .1; when debt amounts to $500, k is .1167; but when debt goes up to $715, k drops back to .1. The posttax cost of capital reaches its minimum value, .09, when $D/E = 1$, but the pretax cost declines continually. The total value of the firm continues to rise and the stockholders can improve their financial position by substituting debt for equity funds until equity is reduced to the last dollar—clearly an unrealistic situation.

SUMMARY

We have previously defined profit derived from an investment project as the difference between the present value of expected revenues and the initial capital expenditure. Capital expenditure may, however, be financed in a variety of ways. If it is financed with debt funds, the project must generate sufficient revenues to cover the interest payments and the principal amount payable when the loan matures. But if the loan is renewed at maturity and repayment of the principal is postponed while interest must be paid at the end of the initial period, the borrower may regard the interest charge as the cost of the loan during this period. Profit before interest less the interest cost will represent net profit for the period in question. There are, however, other factors that must be taken into account in this connection.

If borrowing results in an increased financial risk, the risk must be taken into account in addition to the interest factor. Furthermore, if an increase in profit after interest is accompanied by an increase in the tax liability, the tax factor must also be taken into consideration. Thus, in analyzing the financial results of borrowing, we must distinguish between the following elements: (1) the gross gain, which is equal to the present value of all expected increments in profit before interest and taxes, (2) the interest cost, i.e., the present value of all interest payments, (3) the tax cost, i.e., the present value of all expected tax increments, and (4) the risk cost, which is measured by the difference in the present value of the firm's stock resulting from the change in the capitalization rate as a result of borrowing. The stockholders' net gain resulting from the new investment is obtained by deducting the interest, tax, and risk costs from the gross gain. The present value of the stock may be expected to increase by the amount of net gain.

When capital expenditures are financed with new stock issues, the net gain accruing to the old stockholders is equal to the difference between the gross gain, i.e., the present value of all expected profit increments after taxes, and the cost, consisting of two components: (1) the present value of the new stockholders' claims on the firm's profits, and (2) the effect of a change in financial risk (if any) on the value of the old stockholders' shares.

In the case of internal financing, the gross gain resulting from new investment must be compared with the opportunity cost incurred by the stockholders, i.e., the present value of the income stream they could earn if the funds were distributed and invested elsewhere. There may also be a risk cost, however, if the new project increases the degree of financial risk involved in the firm's operations.

If the firm's expansion is financed with a combination of equity and debt funds, the cost of new financing may be obtained by summing up the costs of both components. The minimum internal rate of return required to prevent net gain from dropping below zero is equal to the weighted average cost of the new funds.

The cost of the firm's total capital is determined by the opportunity costs of its owners and creditors, i.e., by the income they could earn if the funds were invested elsewhere. Here again, the minimum required rate of return is equal to the weighted average cost of the equity and debt components. The stockholders will obtain a net gain if the average cost of capital can be reduced by a change in the capital structure.

SELECTED REFERENCES

Barges, Alexander: *The Effect of Capital Structure on the Cost of Capital*, Prentice-Hall, Inc., Englewood Cliffs, N.J., 1963.
Baumol, W., and B. Malkiel: "The Firm's Optimal Debt-Equity Combination and the Cost of Capital," *Quarterly Journal of Economics*, November, 1967, pp. 547–578.
Baxter, Nevins D.: "Leverage, Risk of Ruin, and the Cost of Capital," *Journal of Finance*, vol. 22, September, 1967, pp. 395–404.
Durand, David: "Cost of Debt and Equity Funds for Business: Trends and Problems of Measurement," reprinted in *The Management of Corporate Capital*, Ezra Solomon, ed., The Free Press of Glencoe, Inc., New York, 1959, pp. 91–116.
Gordon, Myron J.: *The Investment, Financing and Valuation of the Corporation*, Richard D. Irwin, Inc., Homewood, Ill., 1962.
Lerner, Eugene M., and Willard T. Carleton: *A Theory of Financial Analysis*, Harcourt, Brace & World, Inc., New York, 1966, chap. 10.
Malkiel, Burton G.: "Equity Yields, Growth, and the Structure of Share Prices," *American Economic Review*, vol. 53, December, 1963, pp. 467–494.
Miller, M. H., and Franco Modigliani: "Cost of Capital to Electric Utility Industry," *American Economic Review*, vol. 56, June, 1966, pp. 333–391.
Modigliani, Franco, and Merton H. Miller: "The Cost of Capital, Corporation Finance and the Theory of Investment," *The American Economic Review*, vol. 48, June, 1958, pp. 261–297.

———— and ————: "Corporate Income Taxes and the Cost of Capital: A Correction," *The American Economic Review*, vol. 53, no. 3, June, 1963, pp. 433–443.

Schwartz, Eli: "Theory of the Capital Structure of the Firm," *Journal of Finance*, vol. 14, March, 1959, reprinted in *Foundations for Financial Management*, ed. James Van Horne, Richard D. Irwin, Inc., Homewood, Ill., 1966, pp. 413–433.

Solomon, Ezra: "Leverage and the Cost of Capital," *Journal of Finance*, vol. 18, May, 1963, reprinted in *Foundations for Financial Management*, ed. James Van Horne, Richard D. Irwin, Inc., Homewood, Ill., 1966, pp. 406–412.

————: "Measuring a Company's Cost of Capital," *Journal of Business*, vol. 28, October, 1955, pp. 240–252.

Weston, J. Fred, and Eugene F. Brigham: *Managerial Finance*, Holt, Rinehart and Winston, Inc., New York, 1966, chap. 12.

Wippern, Ronald F.: "Financial Structure and the Value of the Firm," *Journal of Finance*, vol. 21, December, 1966, pp. 615–634.

8
Depreciation as a
Source of Funds

As has already been stated in Chapter 1, gross internal financing consists of two components: retained profit and depreciation allowances.[1] But in discussing the significance of internal funds, our attention up to this point has been focused on net profit retention. In this chapter we shall examine in some detail the financial significance of depreciation.

BASIC CONCEPTS AND DEFINITIONS

While the entire amount of gross internal financing represents a portion of the firm's gross revenue stream, the difference between its two components may, in general, be stated as follows: the retained part of net profits represents the funds available for asset expansion (i.e., the funds which constitute a net addition to the firm's capital); the depreciation allowance, on the other

---

[1] In the mining industry, gross internal financing includes depletion as well as depreciation allowances. In some respects these two types of allowances are similar to each other, but there are also important differences between them. In this chapter the discussion will be confined to depreciation.

hand, represents the funds available for asset replacement (i.e., the funds required to maintain the firm's capital at a given level). In a simplified situation, in which all input and output prices remained constant over time and in which no technological changes took place, an accurate measurement of the replacement requirements would present no serious problem. In the real world, on the other hand, continuous price fluctuations and technological innovations frequently make it impossible to draw a clear dividing line between the expansion and the replacement of assets. Some of the problems arising in this connection will be considered in the latter part of this chapter.

From the above it should be clear that we intend to concentrate here on one particular aspect of depreciation: its significance as a source of funds. There are, of course, other aspects which one may wish to examine. Thus, from the standpoint of cost accounting depreciation may be regarded primarily as a device for allocating the cost of durable assets over time; while from the standpoint of asset valuation it may be considered as a device for adjusting the book values of durable items in successive accounting periods.

These different viewpoints are not actually in conflict with one another. A firm which is a going concern must allocate its costs over time; it must also adjust the book values of its durable assets as time goes on; and it must also generate and allocate capital funds for the replacement of assets which wear out and have to be scrapped. But suppose a firm remains inactive for a whole year, in which case its total revenue stream is zero and there can obviously be no accumulation of internal funds. Even in this case, annual depreciation charges would still have to be made, to take account of the decline in the value of the firm's durable assets (which would be caused in this situation mainly by obsolescence rather than physical wear and tear). If the firm incurred no other costs during the year, it would report a net loss equal to the depreciation charge. Thus, the net component of internal financing would be negative, the depreciation component would still be positive, and the gross amount of internal financing would be zero.

To take a less extreme example, suppose that a firm is active but its total revenue stream falls short of its total costs including the annual depreciation allowance. Let total revenue for the year be $1,000, total cost other than depreciation be $900, and the depreciation allowance be $150. In accounting parlance, depreciation in this case is only partially "earned." The firm will report a net loss of $50, which is equal to the unearned part of depreciation. Net internal financing is thus negative but gross internal financing is positive (150 − 50 = 100) and equal to the earned portion of depreciation.

The importance of depreciation allowances and of the funds they represent varies from one industry to another, depending on how large a part of their operating assets consists of items which are durable but not infinitely so. A *durable asset* is defined as an asset which contributes to the production process over a span of time longer than the standard accounting period (1 year). Thus, the materials which are purchased and used up in production within the same year are not a durable asset and do not require any depreciation provisions. At the other extreme, an infinitely durable asset, such as land—which is defined as an indestructible natural resource—does not require any depreciation provisions either. But a piece of equipment which is expected to remain in operation for 10 years has to be depreciated within this period. In the absence of important technical innovations, the length of an asset's useful lifetime is mainly determined by the physical process of wear and tear. On the other hand, when important innovations occur, the obsolescence factor may exert a major influence and an asset may be discarded long before the time when its physical productive capacity is exhausted.

FINANCIAL EFFECTS OF DIFFERENT DEPRECIATION METHODS: SINGLE INVESTMENT

In arranging an appropriate depreciation procedure for durable assets with a finite lifetime, the following two questions must be answered: (1) What is the total amount to be depreciated? and (2) What is the proper time distribution of depreciation allowances? As to the first question, the prevailing accounting practice is to base depreciation charges on the actual (historical) cost of each item. It has been argued, however, that during inflationary periods it would be more appropriate to use the replacement cost basis for depreciation. This problem will be considered in the section entitled "Financing of Continual Asset Expansion." As to the second question, there are several accounting depreciation methods which are relatively simple and are widely used, and there is also the economic depreciation method, which is logically faultless but not in actual use because of practical difficulties.

The simplest procedure is to make the annual depreciation a fixed amount equal to the original cost of the asset divided by the number of years in its expected lifetime. This is the "straight-line" method, which has until recently been the most widely used one. Two other methods, which are widely used by accountants and are acceptable to the Internal Revenue Service, are the declining-balance and the sum-of-the-year's-digits methods. In both cases, the annual depreciation charge does not remain constant but declines gradually as the asset becomes older.

When the declining-balance method is used, a constant rate (usually twice the straight-line rate) is applied to the unrecovered value of the asset. Thus, if the original cost is $1,000 and the expected lifetime is 10 years, the rate may be fixed at 20 percent and the amount of depreciation will be $200 in the first year, $160 in the second year, $128 in the third year, etc.

When the sum-of-the-year's-digits method is used, the annual depreciation amount is computed by multiplying the original cost of the asset by a fraction the numerator of which is the number of remaining years of the asset's lifetime and the denominator of which is the sum of the numbers representing all the years of the asset's lifetime. Thus, if the original cost is $1,000 and the expected lifetime is 10 years, the amount of depreciation will be $1,000 \times 10/55 = 181$ in the first year; $1,000 \times 9/55 = 163$ in the second year, etc.

From the standpoint of economic analysis, all of the above accounting methods are deficient in that they do not make the book value of an asset after depreciation decline at the same rate at which its economic value declines with the passage of time. As we know, the present value of an asset is equal to the sum of the discounted future revenues attributable to it. This sum becomes smaller each year because the remaining revenue stream becomes shorter. The economic depreciation in a given year is defined as the difference between the value of the revenue stream computed at the beginning of the year and the value of the remaining revenue stream computed at the end of the year.

Let the expected revenues in year $1, 2, \ldots, n$ be denoted as $R_1 \ldots R_n$. Then at the beginning of year 1 the present value of the asset is equal to

$$V_0 = \frac{R_1}{1+k} + \frac{R_2}{(1+k)^2} + \cdots + \frac{R_n}{(1+k)^n}$$

where k is the appropriate capitalization rate.

At the end of year 1, after the first annual revenue R_1 has already been received, the present value of the asset is

$$V_1 = \frac{R_2}{1+k} + \frac{R_3}{(1+k)^2} + \cdots + \frac{R_n}{(1+k)^{n-1}}$$

The economic depreciation for year 1 is, therefore, equal to

$$V_0 - V_1 = \frac{R_1}{1+k} + \left[\frac{R_2}{(1+k)^2} - \frac{R_2}{1+k} \right] + \cdots$$

$$+ \left[\frac{R_n}{(1+k)^n} - \frac{R_n}{(1+k)^{n-1}} \right]$$

To take a simple numerical example, suppose that a firm acquires a new asset with an expected lifetime of 5 years. The expected annual revenue, net of labor and material costs but gross of depreciation, is $26.38. (For simplicity's sake it is assumed at first that the asset's efficiency and the annual revenue attributable to it remain constant over its entire lifetime. It is also assumed that at the end of its life the asset has zero salvage value.)

If the capitalization rate applicable to this class of assets is .1, its present value is equal to

$$\frac{26.38}{1.1} + \frac{26.38}{1.1^2} + \frac{26.38}{1.1^3} + \frac{26.38}{1.1^4} + \frac{26.38}{1.1^5} = 100$$

Let us assume that $100 is the actual price paid by the firm for this asset at the beginning of year 1. If the straight-line depreciation method is used, the annual allowance will be $20 and the annual net profit attributable to the asset will be $6.38. The net book value of the asset will decline by $20 and the reserve for depreciation will increase by the same amount each year. At the end of 5 years, the asset will be scrapped, but the firm will have accumulated $100 for its replacement.

If the economic depreciation method is used, the annual depreciation allowance and the annual net profit will vary, as shown in Table 8-1, Panel A. The allowance for the first year is equal to the difference between the present value of the revenue stream consisting of five annual amounts of $26.38 each and the present value of the revenue stream consisting of four annual

Table 8-1   The economic depreciation method

Year	Present value of asset	Revenue before depreciation	Depreciation allowance	Net profit
A. Constant Annual Revenue				
Begn. 1	100.00			
End 1	83.62	26.38	16.38	10.00
End 2	65.60	26.38	18.02	8.36
End 3	45.78	26.38	19.82	6.56
End 4	23.98	26.38	21.80	4.58
End 5	0	26.38	23.98	2.40
B. Declining Annual Revenue				
Begn. 1	100.00			
End 1	73.21	36.79	26.79	10.00
End 2	50.53	30.00	22.68	7.32
End 3	30.58	25.00	19.95	5.05
End 4	13.64	20.00	16.94	3.06
End 5	0	15.00	13.64	1.36

amounts of $26.38 each. The allowances for the following years are derived by a similar procedure. It will be noticed that in this case depreciation increases from $16.38 in the first year to $23.98 in the fifth year, while net profit declines from $10 in the first year to $2.40 in the fifth year.

One should not, however, infer from the above that economic depreciation must always show an upward trend. If the annual revenue before depreciation is expected to decline, the annual depreciation allowance may show a downward trend. Such a case is presented in Table 8-1, Panel B, where the revenue is assumed to decline from $36.79 in the first year to $15 in the fifth year. As can be seen, the depreciation allowance in this case drops from $26.79 to $13.64 over the five-year period.

FINANCIAL EFFECTS OF DIFFERENT DEPRECIATION METHODS: CONTINUAL REINVESTMENT

In Table 8-1, the use of the economic depreciation method makes net profit for each year equal to exactly 10 percent of the *remaining net* value of the asset at the beginning of that year. But taken in relation to the *full initial* cost of the asset, the annual net profit indicates a declining rate of return. This is so because in the above examples the possibility of reinvesting accrued depreciation funds prior to the end of the fifth year, when the asset must be replaced, was left out of consideration. In actual practice, however, business firms do not keep depreciation funds idle for long periods of time. Even if a firm should not need new operating assets in the year concerned, it could always invest free funds in interest-bearing securities. But in a going concern new operating assets are, as a rule, acquired continuously, and the depreciation funds—along with the funds obtained from other sources—are continuously used to finance these acquisitions.

To illustrate the process of depreciation reinvestment, suppose that a new firm begins operations with $100 worth of durable assets, all of which have a five-year lifetime. The annual revenue before depreciation, attributable to every asset unit, is once again assumed to be 26.38 percent. The first year's revenue is then equal to $26.38. If the straight-line method is used, the depreciation allowance for the first year is $20 and net profit is $6.38. But we now assume that the depreciation funds accrued at the end of the first year are invested in additional durable assets at the beginning of the second year.[2] Consequently, total durable assets in operation during the second year amount to $120 and the revenue is 120 × .2638 = 32.18, of which $24 will be recorded as depreciation and $8.18 as net profit.

The figures for the following years are given in Table 8-2. It will be noticed that the gross amount of durable assets (GFA) increases until the

[2] This implies, of course, that the assets in question are always available in units of any desirable size.

Table 8-2   Continuous reinvestment of depreciation funds—straight-line method

Year	Gross fixed assets	Depreciation allowance	Depreciation reserve	Net fixed assets	Revenue before depreciation	Net revenue
Begn. 1	100.00			100.00		
End 1	100.00	20.00	20.00	80.00	26.38	6.38
Begn. 2	120.00		20.00	100.00		
End 2	120.00	24.00	44.00	76.00	32.18	8.18
Begn. 3	144.00		44.00	100.00		
End 3	144.00	28.80	72.80	71.20	37.99	9.19
Begn.4	172.80		72.80	100.00		
End 4	172.80	34.56	107.36	65.44	45.58	11.02
Begn. 5	207.36		107.36	100.00		
End 5	107.36	41.47	48.83	58.53	54.70	13.23
Begn. 6	148.83		48.83	100.00		
End 6	128.83	29.77	58.60	70.23	39.26	9.49
Begn. 7	158.60		58.60	100.00		
End 7	134.60	31.72	66.32	68.28	41.84	10.12
Begn. 8	166.32		66.32	100.00		
End 8	137.52	33.26	70.78	66.74	43.88	10.62
Begn. 9	170.78		70.78	100.00		
End 9	136.22	34.16	70.38	65.84	45.05	10.89
Begn. 10	170.38		70.38	100.00		
End 10	128.91	34.08	62.99	65.92	44.95	10.87

end of the fifth year, when the assets initially acquired are discarded. However, since the reserve for depreciation increases correspondingly, the net amount of durable assets (NFA) remains the same ($100) in every year. The annual amounts of revenue, both before and after depreciation, also show an upward trend during the first five years. Beginning with the sixth year, some assets are removed and new ones are acquired annually. The amounts of GFA and of depreciation reserve show only minor fluctuations and at the beginning of each year gradually approach the values of $167 and $67, respectively. The amount of NFA remains at $100 in all years. The annual revenues before and after depreciation gradually approach the values of $43 and $10, respectively.

When the economic depreciation method is used, the annual values are different, but the long-run trends are found to be generally similar to the above—see Table 8-3. Again we find that the annual values of GFA, depreciation reserve, and the revenue before depreciation increase steadily during the first 5-year period, but drop at the beginning of the sixth year because of the removal of the initial $100 worth of assets. Thereafter, the extent of variation in all of these values is relatively small. The NFA amount remains constant in all the years.

Table 8-3 Continuous reinvestment of depreciation funds—economic depreciation method

Year	Gross fixed assets	Depreciation allowance	Depreciation reserve	Net fixed assets	Revenue before depreciation	Net revenue
Begn. 1	100.00			100.00		
End 1	100.00	16.38	16.38	83.62	26.38	10.00
Begn. 2	116.38		16.38	100.00		
End 2	116.38	20.70	37.08	79.30	30.70	10.00
Begn. 3	137.08		37.08	100.00		
End 3	137.08	26.16	63.24	73.84	36.16	10.00
Begn. 4	163.24		63.24	100.00		
End 4	163.24	33.06	96.30	66.94	43.06	10.00
Begn. 5	196.30		96.30	100.00		
End 5	96.30	41.78	38.08	58.22	51.78	10.00
Begn. 6	138.08		38.08	100.00		
End 6	121.70	26.42	48.12	73.58	36.42	10.00
Begn. 7	148.12		48.12	100.00		
End 7	127.42	29.07	56.49	70.93	39.07	10.00
Begn. 8	156.49		56.49	100.00		
End 8	130.33	31.28	61.61	68.72	41.28	10.00
Begn. 9	161.61		61.61	100.00		
End 9	128.55	32.63	61.18	67.37	42.63	10.00
Begn. 10	161.18		61.18	100.00		
End 10	119.40	32.52	51.92	67.48	42.52	10.00

The main difference between Tables 8-2 and 8-3 is found in the net profit column. While the use of the straight-line method yields a widely fluctuating amount of net profit during the first 5 years and an amount approximating $10 in the subsequent years, the use of the economic depreciation method results in a net profit of exactly $10 in each year, right from the beginning of the firm's operations. In the long run, however, both methods give essentially the same results: the revenue before depreciation being equal to 26.38 percent of GFA in each year, an initial investment of $100 plus a continual reinvestment of depreciation funds yields a continual net return of 10 percent.

How does reinvestment of depreciation funds affect the physical productive capacity of the firm? Assume that the durable assets in the above example initially consist of ten identical physical units of equipment, each valued at $10. Let N denote the physical output of one unit of equipment (in combination with the other required inputs) per year. The output in the first year is equal to $10N$. Since all units have a lifetime of 5 years, total output that can be obtained by using the initial equipment as long as it lasts is equal to $50N$.

Now, if the straight-line method is used, the depreciation allowance in the first year is $20, which enables the firm to acquire two more units of equipment. Consequently, it begins operations in the second year with twelve units, and its physical output in the second year is equal to $12N$. However, the lifetime of the initial ten units has now been shortened by 1 year. Total output that can be produced by using these ten units over the remaining 4 years is equal to $40N$. Since total output of the two new units over their entire lifetime is equal to $10N$, it follows that total output obtainable from all twelve units, with which the firm begins its second year, is still $50N$—the same as it was at the beginning of the first year.

We may say, then, that while the current productive capacity (the maximum output realizable during the current year) of the firm is greater in the second year than in the first one, because more units of equipment are in operation, the total productive capacity of the firm (the sum of the maximum realizable outputs of all units of equipment currently in use over their respective life spans) is still the same because the average lifetime of the firm's equipment is now shorter. To give a simple illustration, consider the output of services obtainable from transportation vehicles, e.g., automobiles. Two used cars have twice as much current capacity to transport passengers as does one brand-new car. But if each of the used cars is so old that its remaining lifetime is less than one-half of the lifetime of the new car, then the latter's total capacity, in terms of passenger-miles, is greater than that of both used cars combined.

At the beginning of each of the third, fourth, and fifth years additional units of equipment are installed and the current productive capacity of the firm continues to expand. But at the end of the fifth year the initial ten units have to be scrapped and the current capacity is reduced substantially. In general, changes in the current capacity of the firm are indicated by changes in the gross amount of its fixed assets. This is so because all units of equipment currently in operation are included in the gross amount at their full initial cost.[3]

When changes in the total productive capacity of the firm occur, this is reflected in the net amount of its fixed assets, which includes the values of all units currently in use, adjusted for the shortening of their respective time spans. In our example, total productive capacity remains constant in every year, and so does the net fixed asset amount.[4]

---

[3] This statement is entirely correct, however, only on the assumption that the productivity of each unit remains the same in every year until the end of its useful lifetime (the "one-horse-shay" principle).

[4] The question arises in this connection as to whether the depreciation funds invested in the second, third, and fourth years represent net investment or replacement investment. In the short run, these capital expenditures increase the firm's productive capacity and may, therefore, be considered as a net addition to its capital. From the long-run standpoint, however, these expenditures offset the gradual decline in the total productive capacity (the remaining output stream of assets previously installed) and should, therefore, be considered replacement investment.

FINANCING OF CONTINUAL ASSET EXPANSION

In the situations considered above, depreciation was the only source of funds available for the firm's annual capital expenditures. Let us now consider a situation in which other funds (either internal or external) are available so that the firm's annual investment may exceed its depreciation allowance.[5]

Suppose that the firm wishes to expand its total annual expenditure on durable assets (which covers both replacement and expansion needs) at a constant rate r. Then, if the current expenditure is I_t, the expenditure a years earlier must have been equal to

$$I_{t-a} = I_t(1 + r)^{-a}$$

Furthermore, if all items of capital equipment have a lifetime equal to a years, then replacement requirements in year t, R_t, must be equal to I_{t-a}. On the other hand, depreciation allowance in year t is equal to

$$D_t = \frac{I_{t-1} + I_{t-2} + \cdots + I_{t-a}}{a} = \frac{I_t}{a} \sum_{n=1}^{a} (1 + r)^{-n}$$

$$= I_t \frac{1 - (1 + r)^{-a}}{ar}$$

The difference between depreciation allowance and replacement requirements in year t may be written as

$$D_t - R_t = I_t \left[\frac{1}{a} \sum_{n=1}^{a} (1 + r)^{-n} - (1 + r)^{-a} \right]$$

This expression is equal to zero only if $r = 0$, i.e., if there is no growth in annual investment. With any positive growth rate, the value of $D_t - R_t$ will also be positive. The ratio by which the depreciation allowance exceeds replacement requirements may be expressed as

$$E_t = \frac{(1 + r)^a - 1}{ar} - 1$$

A numerical example of continually expanding capital expenditures is given in Table 8-4. It is assumed that all items of capital equipment have

---

[5] The following discussion is based largely on Professor Robert Eisner's article, "Depreciation Allowances, Replacement Requirements and Growth," *The American Economic Review*, vol. 42, no. 5, December, 1952.

Table 8-4   Continuous expansion of capital expenditures at the rate of 10 percent per year

Year (1)	Gross fixed assets† (2)	Capital expend- iture (3)	Deprecia- tion allowance (4)	Deprec. reserve (5)	Net fixed assets (Col. 2 − Col. 5) (6)	Replace- ment require- ment (7)	Deprec. less replac. (Col. 4 − Col. 7) (8)	External funds (9)
Beg. 1	500.00	119.90		200.00	300.00			
End 1	418.10		100.00	218.10	200.00	81.90	18.10	31.90
Beg. 2	550.00	131.90		218.10	331.90			
End 2	459.91		110.00	238.01	221.90	90.09	19.91	35.09
Beg. 3	605.00	145.09		238.01	366.99			
End 3	505.90		121.00	259.91	267.89	99.10	21.90	38.60
Beg. 4	665.50	159.60		259.91	405.59			
End 4	556.49		133.10	284.00	272.49	109.01	24.09	42.46
Beg. 5	732.05	175.56		284.00	448.05			
End 5	612.15		146.41	310.51	301.64	119.91	26.50	46.70
Beg. 6	805.26	193.11		310.51	494.75			
End 6	673.36		161.03	339.64	333.72	131.90	29.13	51.39

† Beginning-of-year amounts include capital expenditure shown on the same line.

a lifetime of 5 years. The firm is pursuing a policy of increasing its capital expenditures by 10 percent each year ($r = .1$), which requires regular re-investment of the depreciation funds plus a certain amount of external funds.[6]

At the beginning of year 1, the firm's gross fixed assets are $500. This is the sum of the following items:

$119.90—The cost of the equipment which has just been acquired (as shown in column 3)

109.01—The cost of the equipment acquired one year ago

99.10—The cost of the equipment acquired two years ago

90.09—The cost of the equipment acquired three years ago

81.90—The cost of the equipment acquired four years ago
_____
$500.00

The depreciation reserve is $200 and net fixed assets are $300. The depreciation allowance made at the end of year 1 is $100, and this amount

[6] Similar results could be obtained by assuming that depreciation funds are supplemented each year by an adequate amount of net profit retention. It is simpler to assume, however, that the firm does not retain any part of its net profit but uses external funds.

of internal funds is available for new capital expenditures at the beginning of year 2. The firm also obtains at the end of year 1 external funds amounting to $31.90, which enables it to invest a total of $131.90 at the beginning of year 2 (10 percent more than the amount of $119.90 invested a year earlier). Of this total, $81.90 is used to replace the units of equipment which are worn out and scrapped at the end of year 1, while the balance of $50.00 is used to acquire additional units. Thus, the depreciation funds contribute $18.10, in addition to the $31.90 obtained from external sources, toward the purchase of new equipment over and above the replacement requirements.

As the table indicates, the firm's investment policy results in a steady 10 percent annual increase in both the gross and the net amounts of its fixed assets. The amounts of depreciation and the external funds also increase 10 percent each year. The depreciation allowance exceeds the replacement requirement by 22 percent, and the external funds represent only 63 percent of the total funds required for the purchase of new equipment in excess of replacement requirements.

THE EFFECT OF PRICE CHANGES

In the previous sections it was assumed that the prices of the durable assets used by the firm remained constant over time. The relationships involved may change considerably, however, when this assumption is removed.

Suppose that the asset prices are rising continually at a constant rate i per year. Then the rate of physical expansion of the firm's assets, r, will clearly be less than the rate at which the monetary value of its capital expenditures, r', is increased. The relationship between these variables is given by the expression

$$1 + r' = (1 + r)(1 + i)$$

The annual amount of straight-line depreciation is then equal to

$$D'_t = I'_t \frac{1 - (1 + r')^{-a}}{ar'}$$

the annual replacement requirements are equal to

$$R'_t = I'_t \left(\frac{1 + i}{1 + r'} \right)^a$$

and the ratio by which depreciation exceeds replacement requirements is

$$E'_t = \frac{(1 + r')^a - 1}{ar'(1 + i)^a} - 1$$

Under these conditions, the depreciation funds may fall short of the replacement requirements even though the capital expenditures (in current dollars) are increasing year after year. For example, if the firm's capital expenditures are increased 10 percent per year ($r' = .1$) but the prices rise 6 percent each year ($i = .06$), and if $a = 5$ and $I_t = 100$, then we have

$$D'_t = 100 \frac{[1 - (1.1)^{-5}]}{5 \times .1} = 76$$

$$R'_t = 100 \left(\frac{1.06}{1.10}\right)^5 = 81$$

$$E'_t = \frac{(1.1)^5 - 1}{(5 \times .1)(1.06)^5} - 1 = -.0877$$

Thus, the depreciation falls short of the replacement requirements by about 9 percent. If the prices increased only 4 percent per year, the price rise and the expenditure rise factors would cancel out and we would have $D'_t = R'_t$ and $E'_t = 0$. A price rise of less than 4 percent would weaken but not completely offset the effect of the expenditure rise, and we would have $D'_t > R'_t$ and $E_t > 0$.

When prices are rising and the depreciation allowance does not meet replacement requirements, the question arises as to whether the original cost of a durable asset is the appropriate basis for computing the allowance. It has been argued by a number of writers that, under such conditions, depreciation should be computed with reference to the asset's replacement cost. The basic underlying question here is whether a firm's sound financial policy requires, as a minimum, the maintenance of the dollar value of its assets, irrespective of changes in the dollar's purchasing power, or whether it requires the preservation of the assets' physical capacity. On theoretical grounds, there is much to be said for the latter proposition. Clearly, in times of severe inflation, a firm could simply be driven out of existence if it did not pay any attention to the fall in the real purchasing power of the money funds allocated for capital expenditures. However, since future price fluctuations and therefore future replacement costs cannot be accurately foreseen at the time when assets are acquired, attempts to set up practicable accounting procedures for depreciation on the replacement cost basis meet with serious

Table 8-5   Depreciation under increasing price conditions

Year	Price of new assets at the end of year	Straight-line depreciation	Depreciation based on 20 percent of current asset price	Depreciation based on n/m of asset's current price
0	100			
1	110	20	22	22
2	121	20	24	26
3	133	20	26	32
4	146	20	28	37
5	161	20	32	44
		100	132	161

n = number of years the asset has been used.
m = number of years in the asset's entire lifetime.

difficulties. This method is not allowed by the Internal Revenue Service for income tax purposes and apparently is not used by business firms to any significant extent even for their internal accounting purposes.[7]

As an illustration, suppose that a firm acquires, for $100, an asset whose expected lifetime is 5 years. Suppose further that the prices are rising steadily at the rate of 10 percent per year. Then the value of an identical new asset will be $110 one year later, $121 two years later, and so on, as shown in Table 8-5. If it were known in advance that the amount required to replace the asset at the end of the fifth year would be $161, the simplest procedure to secure adequate replacement funds would be to set the annual depreciation allowance at $32.20. But such advance information is not available in real life. Under the usual straight-line depreciation method, without regard to the price changes, the annual allowance would be $20 and the total amount of funds accrued over the 5-year period would be $100, as compared with $161 required to replace the worn-out asset with an identical new unit.

If the method were modified so as to make the annual allowance equal to 20 percent of the price of an identical new asset in each subsequent year, the total amount over the 5-year period would be only $132—still short of the amount required for the asset's replacement. In order to accumulate $161 over 5 years, the firm would have to set the annual allowance so that the accumulated depreciation reserve at the end of each year would be equal to n/m of the current price of an identical new asset, where n is the number of years the asset has been used and m is the number of years in its entire lifetime. Thus, at the end of year 1, the depreciation allowance and

[7] Some firms during and after World War II set up special reserves, in addition to the regular depreciation reserve, in order to facilitate the maintenance of real assets under inflationary conditions. This may be the simplest and most practicable device to secure adequate funds for replacement, within the existing depreciation tax framework.

total reserve would equal $(\frac{1}{5})110 = 22$; at the end of year 2 the total reserve should equal $(\frac{2}{5})121 = 48$ and the second-year allowance should, therefore, be $48 - 22 = 26$. The amounts for the other years can be seen in Table 8-5.

Of course, our assumption that prices rise at a steady rate of 10 percent per year is not realistic. With prices moving at a variable rate, the depreciation method just described would result in an even greater range of variations in the annual depreciation allowance. For example, if the asset price remained at $121 in the third year, the depreciation allowance for that year would be only $24 (less than the allowance for the second year). But if the asset price rose to $146 in the fourth year, the allowance for that year would jump to $44.

It should be noted, however, that the above example takes no account of the possibility of annual reinvestment of depreciation funds in profit-earning assets. As already explained above, such reinvestment is required in order to maintain a stable rate of return on the original investment. If the firm's durable assets are completely divisible, it should be possible to invest the entire depreciation allowance at the end of each year in additional physical units of equipment at the prices prevailing at that time. It should not, therefore, be necessary to postpone all replacement expenditures until the end of the fifth year, when prices have gone up 61 percent as compared with the initial cost. And even if the firm's assets are not completely divisible, so that additional capital expenditures must be made in amounts exceeding 1 year's depreciation allowance, it should be possible to invest depreciation funds in suitable securities. If all physical units installed in year 1 must be replaced at the end of year 5, the firm's policy should be to set the annual depreciation rate so that the amounts accrued annually plus the interest earned on them accumulate to $161 by the end of the 5-year period.

Finally, it should be pointed out that the new asset acquired at the end of the fifth year may not be technically identical with the old asset which it replaces. Actually, new assets usually incorporate some technical improvements, and their higher price must, in part, be attributed to this factor. If replacement requirements are defined as the requirements to maintain the physical productivity of the firm's durable assets intact, it may be argued that the installation of improved and more productive new units of equipment represents more than just replacement, and that depreciation reserves should not be expected to cover the cost of such installations completely. The problem of clearly defining and precisely calculating the replacement cost to be taken as a basis for depreciation becomes then very complex.

THE EFFECT OF THE TAX FACTOR

In the absence of corporate income taxation, a rise in the depreciation allowance in a given year by a given amount will, other things being equal, lower the firm's net profit in that year by exactly the same amount. If dividends remain constant, the firm's gross internal financing (the sum of depreciation and retained profit) will also remain constant. But when a corporate income tax is imposed, an increase in depreciation by an amount ΔD will reduce net profit after tax by $(1 - t)\Delta D$, t being the tax rate. Therefore, if dividends remain unchanged, the firm's gross internal financing will rise by $\Delta D - \Delta D(1 - t) = t\Delta D$. For example,

	Case I	Case II
Profit before depreciation and taxes	1,000	1,000
Depreciation	200	400
	800	600
Tax, at 40 percent	320	240
Profit after tax	480	360
Dividends	200	200
Retained profit	280	160
Gross internal financing	480	560

Since depreciation charges are fully deductible for tax purposes, an increase of $200 in these charges results, in effect, in a government contribution to the firm's gross internal financing to the extent of $.40 \times 200 = 80$. But it must be borne in mind that the government does not allow the total amount of depreciation taken over an asset's entire lifetime to exceed its original cost. Consequently, if the depreciation allowances are increased in the earlier years, they must be correspondingly reduced in the later years. The question then is whether such a redistribution of depreciation charges, without a change in the total amount allowed, can result in appreciable advantages for the firm.

Let R be the annual revenue before depreciation and taxes, attributable to an asset with a lifetime of n years. Let D be the annual straight-line depreciation allowance, t_r the corporate tax rate, and i the appropriate discount rate. The present value of the asset is then equal to

$$V_1 = \sum_{t=1}^{n} [R_t - (R_t - D_t)t_r](1 + i)^{-t}$$

where t_r is the corporate income tax rate, which is assumed to remain constant over the entire period of n years. If an accelerated depreciation method is used, there will be an annual depreciation increment equal to ΔD_t during the first k years, and an annual depreciation decrement equal to $\Delta D_t'$ during the remaining $n - k$ years, and we may write

$$V_2 = \sum_{t=1}^{k} \{R_t - [R_t - (D_t + \Delta D_t)]t_r\}(1 + i)^{-t}$$

$$+ \sum_{t=k+1}^{n} \{R_t - [R_t - (D_t - \Delta D_t')]t_r\}(1 + i)^{-t}$$

It will be noted that, with accelerated depreciation, the sum of the un-discounted revenues is increased by an amount equal to

$$\sum_{1}^{k} \Delta D_t t_r$$

during the initial period of k years, which represents the sum of all the tax savings during that period. In the subsequent period of $n - k$ years the sum of the undiscounted revenues is reduced by an amount equal to

$$\sum_{k+1}^{n} \Delta D' t_r$$

which represents the sum of the additional taxes paid. Since the total amount of depreciation allowed during the entire lifetime of the asset must be the same, it is clear that

$$\sum_{1}^{k} \Delta Dt_r - \sum_{k+1}^{n} \Delta D' t_r = 0$$

However, since the tax savings take place earlier and the additional tax payments are made later, the present value of the revenue stream is increased by this redistribution of tax payments over time. We may write

$$V_2 - V_1 = \sum_{1}^{k} \Delta Dt_r(1 + i)^{-t} - \sum_{k+1}^{n} \Delta D' t_r(1 + i)^{-t}$$

which is greater than zero as long as i remains positive. If the discount rate is relatively low and the assets' lifetime is relatively short, the advantage of such a redistribution is correspondingly small. On the other hand, when the assets' lifetime is relatively long and the discount rate is relatively high, such a redistribution may result in sizable gains.

There are two other factors which may tend to increase the advantages derived from accelerated depreciation. First, the degree of uncertainty associated with the expected revenue stream usually increases as the stream is lengthened. Therefore, the discount rate applicable to revenues in the later years may be greater than the rate applicable to revenues in the earlier years. This factor would, of course, tend to increase the difference between V_2 and V_1, as the depreciation allowances are increased in the 1 to k period and are correspondingly reduced in the $k + 1$ to n period.

Secondly, the expected annual revenue in many, if not most, situations declines as the asset becomes older. Therefore, with a given range of probable income variations, the probability of incurring a deficit is greater in the later years than in the earlier years. In the absence of loss carry-over provisions, a deficit in a given year would reduce the tax liability to zero, but there would be no tax refund. Consequently, if the revenue after depreciation in a given year is negative, a reduction in the depreciation allowance in that year and a corresponding increase in the depreciation allowance in another year in which the revenue after depreciation is positive would reduce the combined amount of tax liability for both years.

Suppose that $R_1 = 100$ in year 1 and $R_2 = -10$ in year 2, the depreciation allowance is $40 in both years, and the tax rate is 40 percent. Then the firm will report a taxable income of $60 and a tax liability of $24 in year 1. In year 2, the firm will report a net deficit of $50, and the tax liability will be zero. Now, if the depreciation allowance is increased to $60 in the first year, the taxable income will be only $40 and the tax will drop to $16. In the second year, the depreciation allowance will be $20, and net deficit will be reduced to $30, but the tax liability will still be zero. Under these conditions, the accelerated depreciation method is likely to reduce the total amount of taxes payable over the asset's entire lifetime, because it involves a partial transfer of charges from the latter period, in which deficits are more probable, to the earlier period in which they are less probable.

The situation would be different, however, if unlimited loss carry-over provisions were in effect. In this case, the firm would receive tax refunds in the deficit years and the net sum of all tax payments and tax refunds over the asset's entire lifetime would be the same irrespective of the depreciation method used. In the above example, the tax refund in the second year would be $20 if the depreciation allowance were $40, but it would be reduced to $12 if the depreciation allowance were $20. The difference in the refund would, however, exactly counterbalance the difference in the tax paid in the first year, so that the net amount of the tax paid over the two-year period would be $4 in either case. Under these conditions, the only advantage of the accelerated depreciation would lie in the more favorable time distribution of the tax payments and tax refunds.

The United States tax laws allow loss carry-overs, but only on a limited scale. At this writing, a net operating loss may be carried back to each of the three preceding years, and forward to each of the five following years. With these provisions in effect, the differences in the net tax liability over the asset's entire life span which may result from the use of different depreciation methods are bound to be reduced but not necessarily eliminated in full. The use of the accelerated method may, therefore, prove advantageous to the firm in terms of both the total amount of taxes paid and the time distribution of payments.

SUMMARY

Gross internal financing has been defined as the sum of retained profit and the depreciation allowance. In principle, depreciation allowances represent funds available for asset replacement, while retained profit represents funds available for asset expansion. However, depreciation allowances can be a source of funds only if they are "earned," i.e., if they do not exceed the amount of revenue remaining after all other costs have been met. Furthermore, in actual practice, it is often difficult to distinguish clearly between the replacement and the expansion requirements, especially in periods of significant price and/or technological changes.

The simplest—and until recently the most widespread—accounting procedure is the "straight-line" depreciation method, which keeps the annual allowance constant over the asset's entire lifetime. Other accounting methods make the annual allowance decline continually, in accordance with a formula selected at the beginning and adhered to during the asset's entire lifetime.

From the economic standpoint, the depreciation allowance should reflect the decline in the present value of the remaining revenue stream attributable to the asset as it becomes older. If the annual revenue is expected to remain constant over the asset's lifetime, the annual amount of "economic" depreciation will rise continually. But this need not be the case if the annual revenue is expected to decline as the asset grows older.

In a large firm some durable assets are discarded and replaced by new ones every year. If the firm maintains its capital at a constant level and if the asset prices do not change, the annual amounts of depreciation allowances and of capital expenditures will also remain constant and equal to each other. But if the firm's capital is expanding, capital expenditures will exceed the depreciation allowance in a given year, and the depreciation allowances will exceed current replacement requirements. In a period when asset prices show an upward trend, however, depreciation allowances based on "historical" cost may fall below the amounts required to replace worn-out physical assets.

The existence of a substantial corporate income tax makes accelerated depreciation methods preferable to the straight-line method. Even though total amounts of the allowable depreciation and of the tax liability over the asset's lifetime remain the same, accelerated depreciation writeoffs result in an advantageous time redistribution of tax payments. Consequently, the present value of the posttax revenues is increased.

SELECTED REFERENCES

Depreciation and Taxes, Symposium Conducted by the Tax Institute, November 20–21, 1958, The Tax Institute, Princeton, N.J., 1959.

Dobrovolsky, S. P.: "Depreciation Policies and Investment Decisions," *The American Economic Review,* vol. 41, no. 5, December, 1951, pp. 906–914.

Edwards, Edgar O.: "Depreciation Policy under Changing Price Levels," *The Accounting Review,* vol. 29, no. 2, April, 1954, pp. 267–280.

Eisner, Robert: "Depreciation Allowances, Replacement Requirements, and Growth," *The American Economic Review,* vol. 42, no. 3, December, 1952, pp. 820–831.

———: "Rejoinder to M. J. Gordon's Comment" [see the following item, a comment on the preceding article], *The American Economic Review,* vol. 43, no. 4, September, 1953, pp. 614–621.

Gordon, M. J.: "Depreciation Allowances, Replacement Requirements, and Growth: A Comment," *The American Economic Review,* vol. 43, no. 4, September, 1953, pp. 609–614.

Lerner, Eugene M., and Willard T. Carleton: *A Theory of Financial Analysis,* Harcourt, Brace and World, Inc., New York, 1966, chap. 4.

Morrissey, L. E.: "The Many Sides of Depreciation," *Tuck Bulletin 23,* Dartmouth College, February, 1960.

9
Alternative Valuation and Investment Criteria

In the preceding chapters it was assumed that (*a*) the value of a firm's stock is determined by the expected dividend stream and the capitalization rate applicable to its risk class, and (*b*) the firm's policies are directed so as to maximize the value of its present owners' equity. In this chapter we shall first consider an alternative approach to the stock-valuation problem, based on profit rather than on dividend capitalization. Following that, we shall discuss some of the factors that may cause the firm's financial policy to deviate from the goal of stock value maximization.

PROFIT OR DIVIDEND MAXIMIZATION?

Suppose that an investor buys the entire stock of a firm and becomes its sole owner. Since he can select any dividend policy he wishes, it would seem that his valuation of the stock in this case should be determined by the entire expected profit stream, capitalized at an appropriate rate. If there is no external financing and the entire amount of profit is distributed each year, then the invested capital K and the annual profit $rK = P$ will remain constant. The present value of the profit stream will then be equal to

$$V_0 = \frac{P}{k}$$

where k is the capitalization rate. But if a certain part of profit is retained and the retention ratio b remains constant over time, then we may write

$$V_0 = \frac{P_0}{1+k} + \frac{P_0(1+rb)}{(1+k)^2} + \cdots = \frac{P_0}{k-rb}$$

The higher the retention ratio, the faster will the annual profit grow. If the average internal rate of return, r, is constant, the maximum present value of the rising profit stream will be obtained when

$$\frac{\partial V_0}{\partial b} = \frac{P_0 r}{(k-rb)^2} = 0 \tag{9-1}$$

But this condition is satisfied only if $r = 0$. As long as r is positive, no matter how small, the value of the stock can always be increased by raising the retention ratio until the upper limit of $b = 1$ is reached.

On the other hand, if we assume that r is a function of b, the profit-maximizing condition becomes

$$\frac{\partial V_0}{\partial b} = \frac{P_0}{(k-rb)^2}\left(r + \frac{\partial r}{\partial b}b\right) = 0 \tag{9-2}$$

This condition is satisfied only if the expression in parentheses is equal to zero. As long as $r + (\partial r/\partial b)b$, which represents the marginal internal rate of return, is positive, no matter how small, the value of the stock can be increased by making the retention ratio higher.

It should be noticed that in both cases described above the derivative $\partial V/\partial b$ remains positive irrespective of whether the capitalization rate k, which is equal to the rate of return available in the market on securities in the same risk class, is smaller than, equal to, or greater than the internal rate of return, r. This is, of course, unrealistic. If the owner could add $5 per annum to his profit by retaining $100 in the business, while he could make $6 per annum by purchasing $100 worth of comparable securities in the market, the retention would obviously not be the best policy. Upon a moment's reflection, it becomes clear that a rise in the firm's profit must always be considered in relation to the concomitant rise in the cost incurred by the owner. As described earlier, the cost of retained profit is measured by the foregone opportunity to invest the funds elsewhere. If the amount bP_0 is retained in the firm at the end of year 0, this may be expected to produce an additional profit stream equal to rbP_0 per annum, beginning at the end of year 1. The present value of this stream is $rbP_0/k(1 + k)$. But the opportunity cost of this retention is kbP_0 per annum, and the present value of this series is equal to $kbP_0/k(1 + k) = bP_0/(1 + k)$. Similarly, if the amount $bP_0(1 + rb)$ is retained at the end of year 1, the opportunity cost will be $kbP_0(1 + br)$ per annum, beginning at the end of year 2. The present value of this series is equal to $bP_0(1 + br)/(1 + k)^2$. If the same retention ratio is maintained continually, year after year, the present value of the sum of all opportunity costs involved may be written as

$$C_0^* = \frac{bP_0}{1 + k} + \frac{bP_0(1 + rb)}{(1 + k)^2} + \frac{bP_0(1 + rb)^2}{(1 + k)^3} + \cdots = \frac{bP_0}{k - rb}$$

By deducting C_0^* from the present value of the profit stream we obtain

$$V_0 - C_0^* = V_0^* = \frac{P_0}{k - rb} - \frac{bP_0}{k - rb} = \frac{(1 - b)P_0}{k - rb}$$

which is identical with Equation 4-6 in Chapter 4. Thus, we find that the present value of the profit stream, adjusted for the opportunity cost, is equivalent to the present value of the dividend stream. To maximize V_0^*, we must have

$$\frac{\partial V_0^*}{\partial b} = \frac{P_0}{(k - rb)^2}\left[r - k + b(1 - b)\frac{\partial r}{\partial b}\right] = 0$$

If r exceeds k and remains constant ($\partial r/\partial b = 0$), $\partial V^*/\partial b$ will remain positive and V_0^* will continue to increase until the upper limit of $b = 1$ is reached. But if r is a declining function of b (that is, $\partial r/\partial b < 0$), the maximum value of V_0^* may be reached at a point at which b is less than 1 (and r still exceeds k).

MANAGEMENT'S ATTITUDE TOWARD PROFIT AND SALES

The objectives and policies of the large modern corporation are necessarily complex, reflecting the interests and pressures of the various groups involved: different classes of investors, management, employees, customers, and even the general public. This does not mean, of course, that each of these groups exerts an equally strong influence on corporate financial policies. In the following sections we shall confine ourselves mainly to a comparison of the interests and objectives of corporate stockholders with those of the top-level management groups (which include directors and officers).

Legally, the corporation is owned by its stockholders, who make major decisions at the general stockholders' meetings but delegate the continuing day-to-day functions of management to the board of directors and the top-level officers. This suggests that the stockholders collectively are in a position to control the company's basic policy and direct it toward the maximization of their welfare as a group, subject to the constraints arising from the pressures exerted, from time to time, by the other interested groups. There is, however, the well-known argument that the functions of ownership and control have become largely separated in the large modern corporation.[1]

[1] This thesis was originally developed by Adolph A. Berle, Jr., and Gardiner C. Means in *The Modern Corporation and Private Property*, The Macmillan Company, New York, 1933, which has since become a classic. Speaking of the large corporate organization with widely held stock, which they call a "quasi-public institution," the authors state:

> Control of physical assets has passed from the individual owner to those who direct the quasi-public institutions, while the owner retains an interest in their product and increase. We see, in fact, the surrender and regrouping of the incidence of ownership, which formerly bracketed full power of manual disposition with complete right to enjoy the use, the fruits, and the proceeds of physical assets. There has resulted the dissolution of the old atom of ownership into its component parts, control and beneficial ownership. [Pp. 7–8]

In such an organization,

> The separation of ownership from control produces a condition where the interests of owner and of ultimate manager may, and often do, diverge, and where many of the checks which formerly operated to limit the use of power disappear. [P. 6]

In his more recent study, *The Twentieth Century Capitalist Revolution*, New York, 1954, Berle reemphasized his thesis concerning the dominant power position of the corporate management. He conceded that the management's attitude had changed perceptibly during the three decades following the twenties. In his view, however, the evolution was not in the direction of making the management more responsive to and more dependent upon the stockholders' preferences, but rather toward greater recognition by the management of its responsibilities to the entire community in which the company operates.

Other writers have discussed the pros and cons of the Berle–Means thesis at considerable length. A strong statement concerning the powers of corporate directors is found in Eugene V. Rostow's essay, "To Whom and for What Ends Is Corporate Management Responsible?" in *The Corporation in Modern Society*, edited with an introduction by Edward S. Mason, Harvard University Press, Cambridge, Mass., 1966. He writes as follows:

> Corporate directors are endowed with immense discretion. In endocratic corporations, where no stockholders own more than a few per cent of the stock, the directors normally control, or come close to controlling, the electoral process from which their powers nominally derive. Where the board of directors consist largely or wholly of corporate employees, dependent upon the president for every step of their future careers, the board is simply a fictional projection of the president himself, whose power is diluted only by the possible presence on the board of bankers, representing creditors' interests, or directors representing important customers, or of an occasional so called "public" director. [P. 51]

When the stock is widely held, most stockholders remain inactive and exert little more influence on their company's policies than its bondholders do. The management group in such a company is, as a rule, well entrenched, subject to little outside pressure, and capable of conducting the company's operations with a high degree of autonomy. It may, therefore, select a policy which deviates to a considerable degree from that which the stockholders themselves would prefer if they took a more active interest in the company's affairs.

It may be reasonably assumed that corporate executives, like any other group in the economy, are strongly motivated to seek improvement in the level and security of their expected income streams. These income streams are, of course, basically dependent on the continual existence and solvency of the firm. If the latter incurred heavy deficits and failed, the executives would lose their positions. But this does not mean that profit variation is the only major determinant of executive income variation. Their basic salaries must be commensurate with the complexity of managerial duties and the scope of managerial responsibilities, which clearly increase with the firm's size, irrespective of its profitability. On the other hand, the bonuses which they receive in addition to salaries are usually related to the level of profit attained. And if the executives own any of their company's shares, their dividend income will depend on the dividend rate per share, which need not be closely correlated with the profit rate.[2]

The relative importance of these income components varies, of course, from one company to another. Some empirical tests which have been made indicate, however, that total executive incomes in large corporations are, on the average, more closely related to the firm's size than to its profit.[3] It seems plausible, therefore, that the managerial groups may be motivated to expand total volume of operations even in those situations in which a commensurate increase in the net profit accruing to the stockholders could not be expected. Professor Baumol, in pursuing this line of reasoning, has advanced the hypothesis that large oligopolistic firms typically seek to maximize, not their net profit, but rather their total revenue (sales), subject to a minimum profit constraint. The minimum profit is defined as the amount required to provide funds sufficient to pay dividends and make retentions such that the combination of dividend receipts and stock price rises can

---

[2] In addition to their monetary incomes, members of the management group of a large corporation are likely to derive considerable "psychic" income from their position as the leaders of a powerful economic organization. The psychic income may also be expected to show a closer correlation with the company's size than with its profitability. A directorship in a large, nationally known corporation would normally carry a greater prestige than a directorship in a small and relatively unknown company, even though the latter might currently be earning a higher rate of profit. And if the large corporation continues to grow, its prestige value is further advanced.

[3] See, for example, J. W. McGuire, J. S. Y. Chin, and A. O. Elbine, "Executive Incomes, Sales and Profits," *The American Economic Review*, vol. 52, no. 4, September, 1962, pp. 754–761.

remunerate the stockholders adequately.[4] In order to illustrate the range of possible differences in investment decisions, depending on which of the possible alternative objectives is pursued, let us consider the following situations.

EXPANSION WITH BORROWED FUNDS

Figure 9-1 allows us to examine the effect of debt financing on the firm's sales, cost of sales, and profits. It is assumed that initially the firm operates with equity capital alone, the amount invested being equal to OA. As Figure 9-1a indicates, total revenue (sales) is then equal to Aa, cost of sales to Am, and profit before tax to $am = Aa'$. In Figure 9-1b, the scale on the horizontal axis remains the same but the scale on the vertical axis is increased, which allows us to take a closer look at the firm's profit and its distribution. With equity capital being equal to OA and no debt at all, the amount of income tax (assumed to be levied at a flat rate of 50 percent) is measured by Aa'' and the amount of net profit after tax by $a'a''$.

Now, if the firm decides to expand by using debt funds, it will have to incur interest charges, as indicated by the curve AI. Since the interest rate is assumed to rise as the debt increases, the amount of interest—measured by the distance between the horizontal axis and the curve AI—increases more than in proportion to the amount borrowed. Profit after interest is maximized at the point at which the slopes of the profit curve and the interest curve are equal to each other. As the chart is drawn, this occurs when the amount of debt is equal to AB and the total amount of invested capital is equal to OB. Since the tax rate is a flat 50 percent on profit after interest, both the pretax and the posttax amounts of profit ($b'b'''$ and $b'b''$, respectively) are maximized at this point. It would clearly not be advantageous for the stockholders to have the firm expand its total capital beyond point B. In fact, if there is a significant degree of risk associated with borrowing, the present value of the firm's stock may be maximized by borrowing an amount smaller than AB (for example, AF).

On the other hand, if the managers' performance is evaluated and their compensation is determined primarily on the basis of total volume of operations, they will be motivated to expand the firm's capital beyond point B. In the graph, profit before interest and taxes is maximized at point c' when debt is equal to AC and total capital to OC. At this point, the stockholders' net profit after tax ($c'c''$) is greater than it is with no debt at all ($a'a''$), but not as great as it is at its maximum level ($b'b''$).

If the amount of debt is further increased until it is equal to AE, the stockholders' net profit after tax is represented by $e'e''$, which is equal to $a'a''$.

[4] William J. Baumol, *Business Behavior, Value and Growth*, rev. ed., Harcourt, Brace & World, New York, 1967.

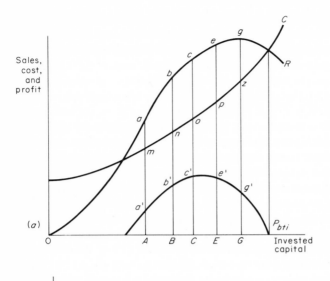

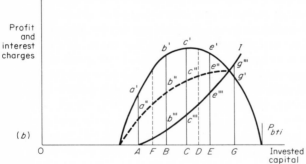

Figure 9-1 Expansion with borrowed funds.

This will allow the management to obtain a much greater volume of sales (*Ee* as compared with *Aa*) without a reduction in the stockholders' net profit or dividends. There are, however, two possible restraints. First, the greater amount of debt may lead to an increase in the capitalization rate applicable to the firm's stock, with a corresponding reduction in its present value. This may produce a serious negative reaction and a strong pressure for amelioration, in one form or another, on the part of the stockholders. Secondly, the managers themselves may feel uncomfortable having to operate with the ratio of fixed charges to profit as high as *Ee'''/Ee'*. They may therefore, decide to set the debt limit at point *D*, which will give the stockholders a greater amount of net profit than they can have without any borrowing, and at the same time will result in an acceptable fixed-charges-to-profit ratio.

As the chart is drawn, the maximum amount of total revenue is reached at point g on the OR curve, with the amount of debt being equal to AG. But with this amount of debt, the interest charges Gg''' would exceed profit before interest, Gg', and the firm would report a net deficit $g'g'''$. Clearly, under these conditions, total revenue (sales) maximization would not be an acceptable objective to either the stockholders or the management.

The above example has of course been presented only as an illustration. In the real world, different firms have different revenue and cost schedules. In some cases, net profit would decline more rapidly than our chart indicates if capital expansion were continued after the maximum profit position had been reached. In other cases, the decline would be a slower one, perhaps allowing the management to maximize total revenue and yet report a minimally acceptable amount of net profit. Furthermore, the degree of risk associated with borrowing also varies from one firm to another. In some instances the risk increases steeply, exerting a strong depressing effect on the value of the firm's shares. In other instances, the effect of this factor may be much weaker. Finally, different firms have differently composed bodies of stockholders. Some stockholders may react sharply even to small variations in the firm's net profit and in the value of its shares, while others may remain relatively passive and indifferent, unless such variations assume much greater proportions. In general, then, while an expansion-motivated management may be expected to strive for a greater increase in capital than that resulting in net profit maximization, the extent and significance of this over-expansion will vary considerably, depending on the strength of the constraining factors stated above.

EXPANSION WITH NEW EQUITY FUNDS

The effects of new equity financing are demonstrated in Figure 9-2. The curve OP represents in this case the firm's total net profit after taxes and the curve AP' the portion of this total accruing to the new stockholders. In Figure 9-2a it is assumed that new shares are sold at the same price as the old ones. Consequently, if the new shareholders invest the same amount of capital as the old stockholders did, they will receive the same number of shares and will have a claim to one-half of the firm's profit. If they invest twice as much capital, they will receive twice as many shares and have a claim to two-thirds of the firm's profit, and so on.

Since we assume that, up to a certain point, new investment increases the firm's efficiency, its net profit rises more than in proportion to capital within this range. The shaded area between the curves $abcd$ and $ab'c'd$ represents the additional profit accruing to the old stockholders as a result of the inflow of new capital. The maximum amount of this additional profit is equal to bb' and can be realized by increasing the firm's capital by an

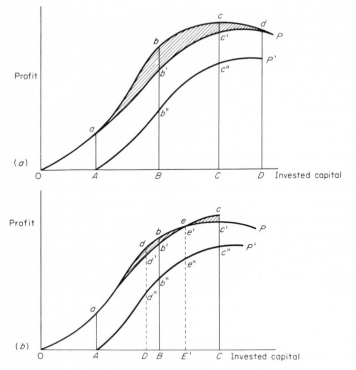

Figure 9-2 Expansion with equity funds.

amount equal to *AB*. If the management raises new equity funds in excess of *AB*, the old stockholders will still realize net profit increments, but they will be smaller than *bb'*. At the point of maximum total profit, *c*, their increment will equal *cc'*. Only if the management increases total capital beyond point *D* will the old stockholders' share of profit be less than it was prior to the expansion.

The new stockholders' profit, per share, will also be at its maximum at point *B*. An expansion of total capital beyond that point will gradually reduce it, and an expansion beyond point *D* will make it less than the old stockholders' profit per share prior to the sale of new shares.

In the case of new equity financing there need not be any significant change in the degree of risk involved in the investment.[5] We may therefore

[5] This does not mean, however, that a change in the degree of risk can never occur. As already pointed out in Chap. 3, the risk may either increase or decrease as a result of new equity financing, depending on a number of circumstances. If the new funds are used to consolidate the firm's position in the market, the risk will diminish, which will tend to raise the value of its shares. On the other hand, if the new funds are used to finance new and untried ventures, the risk may increase, which will tend to depress the value of the firm's shares.

assume that, as long as profit per share increases, the value of each share becomes greater, too. Thus, any amount of new investment, within the range AD, will improve the old stockholders' financial position. An expansion-oriented management will tend to set total invested capital as close as possible to point D. But how close they will be able to come to this point will depend on how conscious the old stockholders are of the range of possibilities open to the firm and how strongly they will oppose a decision resulting in less than the maximum possible improvement in their position.

Suppose, however, that new shares can be sold only at a lower price than that paid by the initial stockholders. In this case, for any given amount of investment the new stockholders will receive a greater number of shares and will claim a greater portion of the firm's profit than in the case considered above. This situation is portrayed in Figure 9-2b. The total profit curve OP is exactly the same in both Figure 9-2a and Figure 9-2b, but the new stockholders' profit curve AP' has a steeper slope in Figure 9-2b. Accordingly the shaded area, indicating the additional profit that may accrue to the old stockholders as a result of capital expansion, is now considerably smaller. The maximum possible additional profit is equal to dd', which is considerably less than bb' in Figure 9-2a. It may also be noted that the maximum increment is now obtained with a smaller amount of new funds than in Figure 9-2a $(AD < AB)$. At the point of maximum total profit, c, the old stockholders' increment is now negative: their share of the firm's profit at this point is smaller than their profit prior to the expansion.

We must repeat that all of the above examples have been given for illustrative purposes only. Obviously, different numerical results may be obtained by changing the functions or, in diagrammatic terms, the slopes of the curves involved. It seems clear, however, that in making investment decisions the management is usually faced with not just one but a range of possibilities, each promising to improve the stockholders' initial position, although not in the same degree. And the most attractive possibility, from the management's standpoint, is not necessarily the one yielding the maximum advantage to the stockholders, but may rather be the one resulting in the maximum expansion consistent with the minimally acceptable advantage to the stockholders. How close the corporate managements are able to get to the latter point in actual practice cannot of course be determined on a priori grounds. Further empirical studies are required in order to provide an answer to this question.

EXPANSION WITH INTERNAL FUNDS

We may also outline briefly the range of possibilities encountered when expansion is financed by profit retention. Assuming that there are no external funds involved, the rate of capital expansion is determined by the firm's rate of return on invested capital and the retention ratio. Figure 9-3*a* indicates the expansion rates which the firm would be able to maintain, on the basis of a given rate of return, by adopting different retention ratios. It is assumed that both the rate of return and the retention ratio, once selected, will remain constant over time. Figure 9-3*b* indicates the present amount of the firm's invested capital, OK, which is given, and the present market value of its stock, which is a function of the retention ratio. In this example, the market value would fall below the actual invested capital if the retention ratio were less than one-quarter of its profit. This would also be true if the ratio were more than three-quarters of its profit. On the other hand, with any retention ratio between one-quarter and three-quarters, the present value of the firm's stock would exceed its invested capital. This range is indicated by the shaded area in Figure 9-3*b*, while the corresponding range of expansion rates is shown in Figure 9-3*a*.

As the figure shows, the market value of the firm's stock reaches its maximum when the retention ratio is equal to .5. The corresponding expansion rate is indicated by C_2 in Figure 9-3*a*. While this situation would be most advantageous from the stockholders' standpoint, the management

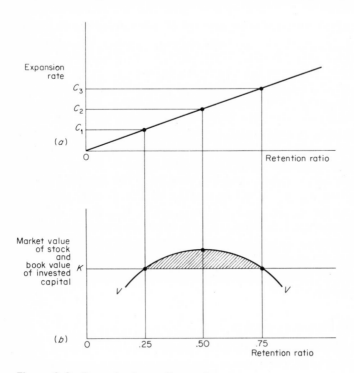

Figure 9-3 Expansion by profit retention.

may prefer a higher retention ratio which would result in a higher expansion rate. As the chart indicates, it would be possible to raise the retention ratio to .75, and thus reach the expansion rate indicated by C_3, without dropping the market value below the invested capital level. While the management may not wish to move all the way to the upper limit, it may decide, if the expansion incentives are strong, to set the retention ratio somewhere between one-half and three-quarters.

SUMMARY

In the previous chapters it was assumed that the present value of a firm's stock was determined by the expected dividend stream. An alternative approach is to assume that the present value is determined by the entire expected profit stream. This approach seems particularly applicable in the case of an investor who owns all or most of a firm's stock and can, therefore, set its dividend policy at will. It should be realized, however, that when the owner decides to retain part of the profit in the business, he incurs an opportunity cost which must be taken into account. When this is done, the present value of the profit stream is found to be equivalent to the present value of the dividend stream.

In a large modern corporation with a widely held stock, the objectives and policies are necessarily complex, reflecting the interests and pressures of the various groups involved: different classes of investors, the management, employees, customers, and even the general public. A hypothesis has been advanced that the managerial policy in such a firm is likely to be directed toward gross income (sales) maximization, subject to a minimum-profit constraint.

In its efforts to maximize the total volume of business, the management may carry the expansion beyond the optimal level from the stockholders' standpoint. This may be true, whether the new funds are obtained by borrowing, new stock issues, or profit retention. In deciding on the appropriate total volume and "mix" of new financing, the management is likely to be faced with a range of possibilities, each promising to improve the stockholders' initial position, although not in the same degree. And the most attractive possibility from the management's standpoint may not be the one yielding the maximum advantage to the owners, but rather the one resulting in the maximum sales expansion consistent with the minimally acceptable advantage to the owners.

SELECTED REFERENCES

Baumol, William J.: *Business Behavior, Value and Growth*, rev. ed., Harcourt, Brace & World, New York, 1967.

Berle, Adolph A., Jr., and Gardiner C. Means: *The Modern Corporation and Private Property*, The Macmillan Company, New York, 1933.

————: *The Twentieth Century Capitalist Revolution*, New York, 1954.

Mason, Edward S., ed.: *The Corporation in Modern Society*, Harvard University Press, Cambridge, Mass., 1966.

McGuire, J. W., J. S. Y. Chin, and A. O. Elbine: "Executive Incomes, Sales, and Profits," *The American Economic Review*, vol. 52, no. 4, September, 1962.

Miller, Merton H., and F. Modigliani: "Dividend Policy, Growth, and the Valuation of Shares," *The Journal of Business of the University of Chicago*, vol. 34, no. 4, October, 1961, pp. 411–433.

part two

The Financial System: Capital Market, Interest, and the Flow of Funds

10

Basic Financial Flows
and Institutions

In Part One we were concerned with the financial operations, policies, and problems of the firm. This area is generally referred to as the "microfinance." In Part Two we shall move into the area of "macrofinance" and examine the financial processes and problems of the business sector of our national economy as a whole. Our definition of *business financing* as the flow of funds required for the maintenance and expansion of business assets remains basically the same. But it may be useful to change the wording somewhat, so as to conform to the established macroeconomic terminology.

In macroeconomics, *real capital* of an economic system is defined as the sum of all its physical assets used for productive purposes. And *real capital formation*, or *real investment*, is defined as the sum of additions to physical assets made over a given period of time. The full value of these additions, prior to an adjustment for capital consumption, is referred to as *gross investment*, while the remaining value after such an adjustment is called *net investment*. In the national income accounting, the following items are included in the computation of gross private domestic investment: producers' durable equipment, changes in business inventories, and new business and residential construction. The accumulation of assets other than houses in the household sector and of any assets in the government sector is not included in the investment figures.

Accordingly, the financing of the business sector of our economy consists of all capital fund flows required for gross capital formation (or gross investment) purposes. It includes all internal funds—depreciation allowances as well as retained net profits—and all external funds—equity as well as debt. It should be clear, of course, that capital fund flows in the business sector cannot be studied in isolation. The business sector is only a part of the total economic system. All parts—and all fund flows throughout the system—are interrelated, and this fact must always be kept in mind.

BASIC FINANCIAL FLOWS

To clarify the concepts and relationships involved, let us begin by considering some highly simplified economic systems. First, let us examine a stationary system consisting of the business and household sectors only. It is assumed that the quantities of capital and labor remain constant, there are no technological changes, and, therefore, the national product in real terms also remains constant year after year. It is further assumed that the amount of money in the system and all factor and product prices remain unchanged, so that the money value of GNP is also constant. Since the capital stock is not expanding, it is clear that there is no net saving in either the household or the business sector. However, the business sector must make provisions for replacement of capital goods which have only a finite durability. Thus, the gross national product, even in this simple system, consists of both consumer and capital goods. Although net capital formation is zero, gross capital formation is still positive.

Such a system is presented diagrammatically in Figure 10-1a. Gross national product is equal to $140 billion, of which $120 billion represents the value of consumer goods and $20 billion the value of capital goods required for replacement purposes.

Net national product, which in this case is equal to national income and also to personal income, is $120 billion, and this entire amount is spent on consumption goods. The consumption goods industry receives $120 billion from the household sector. Of this amount $100 billion is paid out as wages to the workers and as dividends to the owners of this industry (the profits are assumed to be entirely distributed). The remaining $20 billion is used to purchase new equipment from the capital goods industry. *This is the only capital fund flow in this system.* The capital goods industry uses the $20 billion it receives to pay wages to its workers and dividends to its owners.[1] Thus, gross capital formation is $20 billion, while net capital

---

[1] For simplicity's sake the asset replacement requirements of the capital goods industry are ignored in this example.

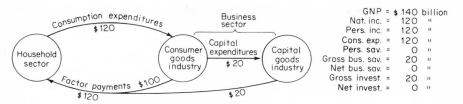

(a) Nonexpanding system, with replacement investment

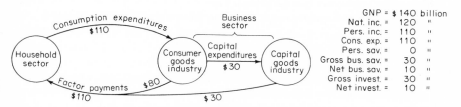

(b) Expansion financed by profit retention

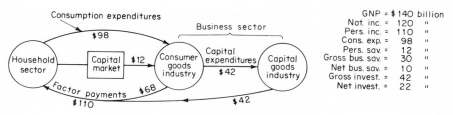

(c) Expansion financed by internal and external funds

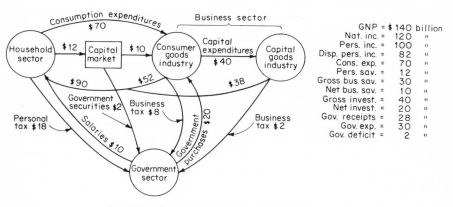

(d) Expanding system with a government sector

Figure 10-1   Basic financial flows.

formation is zero in this case. Correspondingly, gross saving (equal to depreciation allowances) of the business sector is equal to $20 billion, while its net saving is zero. There is no saving at all in the household sector.

Let us introduce net internal financing in the business sector. This situation is illustrated in Figure 10-1b. Gross national product is still $140 billion and national income is still $120 billion, as in Figure 10-1a, but personal income has now dropped to $110 billion because $10 billion of profit is retained in the business sector.[2] Personal saving is still zero, and the household sector spends its entire income of $110 billion on consumer goods. The consumer goods industry now pays only $80 billion in wages and dividends and spends the remaining $30 billion on new capital equipment. This enables it to replace the worn-out machinery and, in addition, expand its capital facilities by $10 billion. The capital fund flows are again found in the business sector only. Business gross saving, which is equal to gross capital formation, is now $30 billion. Business net saving, which equals net capital formation, is now positive, amounting to $10 billion.

Of course, the system is no longer a static one under these conditions. Since there is net capital expansion, one should expect the system to be able to produce a greater output in the next period. And if profit retention becomes a continuous policy, the system's capital and national product should also expand continually. But while the figures will change, the direction of the fund flows will remain unchanged as long as the expansion is financed by business internal funds only.

Our next step is to introduce personal saving and external business financing into the system. This is illustrated in Figure 10-1c. We now assume that of the $110 billion received by the household sector only $98 billion is spent on consumption while the remaining $12 billion is saved. We further assume that the funds saved are not held in cash (hoarded) but are channeled into the business sector by purchases of securities (broadly defined so as to include all long-term and short-term financial instruments). We thus have an additional flow of funds in our system which requires additional facilities in the form of some sort of capital market where individuals supplying funds can meet with businessmen demanding funds and determine by negotiation the prices of different kinds of securities and the amounts issued. In the real world, this is an extremely complex process, involving a great variety of financial instruments and institutions. We shall examine the structure of our actual capital market in some detail in the following sections. At this point, we wish only to indicate, in a very general way, the relation of external financial flows to other fund flows in a simplified economic system.

---

[2] Again, for simplicity's sake, we assume that retentions are made only by the consumer goods industry.

As Figure 10-1c indicates, the consumer goods industry now receives from the household sector $98 billion in the consumer goods market and $12 billion in the capital market. It pays the household sector, in the form of wages and dividends, $68 billion and uses $42 billion for new capital expenditures. The latter amount represents gross capital formation, while net capital formation is now equal to $22 billion. The system's net expansion is now financed partly by internal business financing ($10 billion) and partly by external financing ($12 billion). Again, the system is not a static one: a continual capital expansion will result in a continual national product expansion and the amounts involved will change in each succeeding year.

Finally, to move one more step closer to reality, let us introduce the government sector into the system. We assume that the government's revenue is received partly in the form of personal income tax, paid by the household sector, and partly in the form of corporate profits tax, paid by the business sector. The government expenditures fall into two classes: salaries of government employees and payments for goods purchased from the business sector. It is assumed in this example that the goods required by the government are all produced by the consumer goods industries.

The flow of funds in this situation are illustrated in Figure 10-1d. As can be seen, the household sector's total income is $100 billion, which is the sum of $90 billion received from the business sector and $10 billion received from the government sector. The personal income tax is $18 billion, which makes the disposable personal income equal to $82 billion. Consumption expenditures amount to $70 billion and personal saving to $12 billion.

The consumer goods industry sells $70 billion worth of goods to the consumers and $20 billion worth of goods to the government. It also received $10 billion of external funds by selling securities. Its profit tax amounts to $8 billion. The capital goods industry sells $40 billion worth of goods to the consumer goods industry, of which $20 billion represents replacement investment and $20 billion net capital formation. This industry's profits tax is $2 billion and its payments to the household sector amount to $38 billion.

The government sector collects $18 billion in personal taxes and $10 billion in business profit taxes, a total of $28 billion. Its expenditures, however, total $30 billion: $10 billion paid in salaries and $20 billion paid for the goods purchased. The deficit is covered by selling $2 billion worth of government securities in the capital market. It is assumed in this illustration that all government securities are purchased by individuals and none by business firms.

Thus, the system must now have a capital market in which both corporate and government securities are traded. Such a market could be organized in a variety of ways. One could conceive of a very simple organization not involving any specific financial institutions. Business firms and government agencies wishing to obtain external funds from the household sector would simply make public announcements to this effect (by using newspapers and other advertising media) and then wait for interested individual investors to contact them and negotiate the terms for the transfer of funds.

In a large economy with a multitude of firms, there would presumably be a fairly large number of companies in the market for external funds every day, and their security offerings would have to be competitive. There would also be a large number of individual suppliers of funds who would be acting in competition with one another. Thus, there would be a competitive market for new security issues, and the prices and quantities of the various types of securities sold would be determined by the aggregate supply and demand schedules.

The individuals wishing to convert previously purchased securities into cash and the individuals wishing to purchase previously issued securities would also contact each other by means of newspapers and other advertising media. Since each day there would presumably be large numbers of buyers and sellers, a competitive resale market for most securities could be established and maintained. However, such a system, while conceptually possible, would not, of course, be an efficient one. Since individual firms float new security issues rather infrequently, they would find it burdensome to establish and maintain security selling departments. And individual investors would also find it burdensome if they had to "shop" for suitable securities by contacting various prospective issuers directly. Clearly, then, both sellers and buyers of securities would prefer to operate through intermediaries who specialize in the securities business.

FINANCIAL INTERMEDIARIES: INVESTMENT BANKERS AND BROKERS

In the primary securities market, in which new issues are sold, the role of intermediaries is performed by investment bankers, who enter into underwriting agreements with security-issuing corporations. Such an agreement stipulates that the banker (or the group of bankers who have formed a syndicate) will purchase the entire amount of new securities issued, at an agreed price, with the intention of reselling the issue to the public at a higher price. There is, of course, no assurance that the public will purchase the securities at the anticipated price. Should the public demand fall short of the bankers' anticipations, which would necessitate a price reduction, the bankers and not the issuing company would have to absorb the loss. The main advantages of such an agreement to the company are found in (a) the expert advice received from the bankers during the preparation of the new issue for sale, (b) the services of an efficient professional distributor network, and (c) the assurance of receiving the stipulated amount of funds irrespective of market fluctuations. There are certain advantages in this arrangement from the investor's standpoint, too. More information is available and, if the bankers offering the issue are well known, there is a certain degree of confidence that the company has been professionally evaluated and found reasonably strong and secure.

The price of the investment bankers' services is the spread between the purchase and the resale price of the securities they handle. In a strongly competitive market, the spread would be narrowed down so as to allow the bankers to cover their costs and earn a minimally acceptable rate of profit. In a strongly oligopolistic situation, on the other hand, the bankers may succeed in maintaining a much wider spread resulting in a much higher profit rate. Our investment banking industry actually has distinct oligopolistic characteristics. How much extra profit this enables it to make has been the subject of considerable debate, but no conclusive evidence has been produced yet.

A public offering is not, however, the only available method of selling corporate securities. The issuing corporation may be able to contact a single large investor, or a small group of large investors, and sell the entire issue privately and in one transaction. Such private placements have become important mainly in the corporate bond market during the last three decades, the life insurance companies being the main users of this method of acquisition. The elimination of the middleman and his compensation in a private placement should, other things being equal, prove advantageous to both the seller and the buyer.[3] But some misgivings have been expressed by those who feel that the use of this method allows large investors to remove the top-quality issues from the market altogether, thus depriving the general public of an opportunity to participate in the most attractive investments.

In the secondary (resale) market, the function of intermediaries is performed by investment brokers and dealers. The transactions in this market fall into two classes: those performed on one of the stock exchanges and those made "over-the-counter." The members of the stock exchange meet personally and transact business "on the floor" by the auction method. They may act as brokers, buying and selling securities for the account of their customers; or they may operate as dealers, buying and selling for their own account. They serve as intermediaries, of course, only when they perform as brokers.

In general, the exchange transactions are confined to the securities (both stocks and bonds) listed on the exchange. In order to have its securities listed, a corporation must conform to certain minimum requirements concerning its size, financial condition, and stock ownership (the stock must be widely held and have an active market).

[3] In some cases investment bankers participate also in private placements, but their role is then limited to being advisers. There is no need for an underwriting contract.

Business procedures on the stock exchanges are efficiently organized and transactions are speedily executed. The operations are closely supervised by the exchange administration within the framework established by government regulation. Since the brokers' commission rates are set by the exchange, there is, generally speaking, no price competition among the brokers.[4] They can compete in attracting customers' business only in terms of the scope and quality of the services performed (non-price competition). The larger brokerage firms usually supply their customers, free of charge, with periodic reports on the general business conditions as well as the conditions and prospects of individual industries and firms. Moreover, a customer may ask for a critical appraisal of his own investment portfolio, with recommendations for improvement in the light of his individual financial goals. And he may also ask the brokerage firm to keep the shares purchased, collect dividends, and credit them to his account.

Although there is no explicit charge for these supplementary services, they are not, of course, actually free. The customers must pay for them indirectly, since the brokers would not remain in business in the long run unless the commissions received covered the cost of all services rendered plus an acceptable profit margin. On the other hand, since entry into the industry is not free (the number of seats of the exchanges is limited), an influx of new firms cannot be relied upon to bring about a downward adjustment when profit rates rise above the average level.

---

[4] Price competition has, however, developed in special situations, despite the generally restrictive regulations. During the hearings before the Securities and Exchange Commission on stock exchange brokerage commission rates, held in June–July, 1968, the practice of "give-ups" was brought to light. It transpired that the brokers competing for the lucrative business of trading for the mutual funds had been willing to give up 40 to 80 percent of their commissions either to the fund managers themselves or to other parties designated by the managers.

Thus, the brokers were, in effect, competing with each other through volume discounts on large orders, which reduced the net price received for their services. This practice was found objectionable on two counts. First, it violated the NYSE minimum commission rate regulations. Secondly, since the money given up by the brokers was rarely returned to the funds, the funds' shareholders were, in effect, paying the full commission rates, while other parties were receiving the benefit of the "give-ups." Some representatives of the funds' managements argued that the funds' shareholders were deriving indirect benefits from this practice, because the "give-ups" enabled the managers to reduce their fees and/or increase promotional efforts. But, of course, the extent of such indirect benefits could never be reliably measured. All things considered, the SEC staff felt that although the "give-up" practice probably could not be stopped entirely, mandatory measures should be taken to ensure the return of the money given up by the brokers to the funds. (See: Business Week, July 27, 1968, p. 97.)

The president of the New York Stock Exchange recently suggested that the Exchange should reconsider its commission structure and move toward complete abandonment of fixed minimum rates in favor of negotiated rates, as the ultimate objective. Such a reform, if adopted, would allow effective price competition among the Exchange members. (See The New York Times, Nov. 18, 1970.)

The "over-the-counter" market comprises all securities transactions performed outside of the organized exchanges. The number of stock issues listed on the exchanges is only a small fraction of the total number of stocks in existence. But since the listed stocks represent almost all of the largest corporations, the dollar value of stock sales on the exchanges far exceeds the dollar value of stocks sold over-the-counter. On the other hand, the major part of corporate bond sales and all of the government bond sales take place on the over-the-counter market. Consequently, the total dollar value of all stocks and bonds traded over-the-counter is several times as large as that of securities traded on all the exchanges combined.

The over-the-counter market provides no physical facilities—such as the "floor" of an exchange—where brokers and dealers could meet and trade with each other. However, a well-organized communication network has been developed by means of telephone, telegraph, and teletype, and transactions are, as a rule, executed easily and efficiently. Uniform procedures and commission rates have been prescribed by the National Association of Security Dealers, which is registered with and subject to regulation by the Securities and Exchange Commission.

The firms operating over-the-counter may act as brokers on the commission basis or as dealers who acquire an inventory of securities in which they are interested (take a "position" in them) and then offer these securities for sale. In the latter case, their revenue results from the "spread" between the purchase and the sale price. The firms specializing in government securities usually operate as dealers: they purchase large amounts of different types and maturities either directly from the Treasury or from other investors and then resell them to customers.

In concluding this brief review of the securities markets, we must mention the activities of the dealers who buy and sell securities on their own account for speculative purposes. It has been argued that they perform a useful social function by helping to stabilize the market in periods of erratic price movements caused by unwarranted swings in the public mood and preferences. This implies, of course, that professional speculators are generally able to discern the "real" value of a stock and then take advantage of temporary market deviations from it. When a temporary buying wave occurs and drives the stock prices up, they will sell while the stocks are overvalued. Contrariwise, during a temporary selling wave which brings the stock prices down, they will buy as long as the stocks are undervalued.[5] The argument has some plausibility on general grounds, but no conclusive evidence exists as to how strong an effect the dealers' transactions actually have on the market as a whole.

---

[5] Members of the stock exchanges who operate as specialists in particular stocks are actually required to act in support of the weaker side of the market.

OTHER TYPES OF FINANCIAL INTERMEDIARIES

The function of investment bankers is to facilitate the process of distribution of new corporate securities, while the function of investment brokers consists in facilitating the process of redistribution of the previously issued securities. To put it differently, we may say that the bankers assist in transferring capital funds from the household to the business sector, while the brokers are mainly helpful in transferring funds within the household sector from those who decide to invest in securities to those who decide to disinvest.[6]

These processes do not involve a substitution of one type of financial claims (liabilities) for another type. Thus, the newly issued shares remain exactly the same, whether they are sold to the investors directly or through investment bankers. And once issued, the shares retain exactly the same financial characteristics irrespective of how many times they change hands and whether or not investment brokers are involved in the process.

But there are financial institutions which engage in claim substitution while transferring capital funds. In other words, they not only *transfer* but also *transform* capital funds in the process. For example, when a savings institution receives funds from the public in the form of new deposits and then invests these funds in bonds or mortgages, the claims it acquires on the issuers of these securities are clearly of a different type from that of the claims acquired by its depositors.

Before reviewing the various types of institutions in this class, let us consider briefly the main types of capital funds (or financial instruments representing them) in our economy. The following classification will suffice for our purposes:

1. Money, defined as currency plus demand deposits, is the most liquid form of capital funds. Currency (paper bills and subsidiary coins) is, in principle, a claim on (liability of) the government, although it is not at present redeemable in gold or any other kind of full-bodied money.

Demand deposits are claims on commercial banks, which may be presented for payment at any time without notice. Payment will have to be made either in currency or by a check on a Federal Reserve Bank.

2. Savings and time deposits are claims on commercial banks or savings institutions which are payable either on demand or at short notice.

3. Short-term promissory notes represent funds transferred for a

---

[6] Of course, the brokers may also assist in transferring funds within the business sector, when one firm wishes to sell securities from its portfolio and another firm wishes to buy these particular securities. And they may also assist in intersector fund transfers when business firms increase or decrease their securities portfolios by purchases from or sales to individual investors.

specified period of time within one year. They may be claims on (liability of) individuals, business firms, or the government.

4. Bonds represent long-term fund transfers, usually for periods longer than 10 years. They may be of the unsecured (debenture) type, or they may be secured by a lien on some specified assets owned by the debtor.

5. Mortgages are another type of long-term claim secured by a lien on real estate.

6. Corporate stocks are residual claims on corporate assets (junior to the creditors' claims) with no specific maturity term. No repayment of the principal is generally expected until the time of a voluntary or involuntary liquidation of the company.

We shall now outline briefly the main types of financial intermediaries involved in both transferring and transforming capital funds.[7]

COMMERCIAL BANKS

The assets of commercial banks consist mainly of short-term loans to business firms and households and of long-term securities (mainly government bonds) and mortgages. Their liabilities are mainly in the form of demand deposits, which constitute the major part of the money in circulation in the United States, and of time deposits.

When the household sector makes a direct transfer of funds to the business sector through purchase of new securities, the immediate result is a reduction in the amount of household demand deposits and a corresponding increase in the amount of business demand deposits. At the same time, there is a rise in the household sector's direct claims on the business sector (securities) and a corresponding rise in the latter's liabilities. The total amount of financial assets in the household sector remains the same but their composition is changed. In contrast, the business sector will record a rise in both financial assets (demand deposits) and liabilities.

Suppose now that instead of buying securities directly from business firms, individuals transfer funds from their demand deposit accounts into time deposit (savings) accounts with the banks, which pay interest and may, therefore, be considered an alternative form of investment. This transfer will create excess reserves for the banks and enable them to make additional

[7] Professor R. W. Goldsmith, the author of several studies of financial institutions, applied the term *financial intermediaries* only to the institutions of this type. On this definition, security brokers act as financial intermediaries only to the extent that they finance purchases of securities by their customers through collateral loans out of funds which they borrow from commercial banks. While the distinction between a mere transfer of funds and a transfer involving a transformation is, of course, an important one, we prefer to apply the term *intermediary* to both types of financial institutions, since they both perform a middleman's function. We shall, however, always make it clear in the text which type of intermediation we are referring to.

loans to the business sector.[8] But the banks' new claims on the business firms, arising from the loan agreements, will not have the same financial characteristics as the individuals' new claims on the banks arising from the time deposit agreements.

In this case also there will be no change in the total amount of financial assets held by the individuals: the decrease in their demand deposits will be fully offset by the increase in their time deposits. On the other hand, the banking sector and the business sector will both register increases in financial assets and liabilities.[9]

MUTUAL SAVINGS BANKS AND SAVINGS AND LOAN ASSOCIATIONS

The assets of these institutions are mainly in the form of mortgages and, to a much smaller extent, government securities, while their liabilities are predominantly in the form of savings deposits. When funds are transferred from the household sector to these savings institutions in the form of either currency or checks drawn on commercial banks, the households' cash balances are reduced but they acquire new financial assets in the form of savings deposits. The savings institutions first deposit the funds in their checking accounts with commercial banks and then transfer them either back to the household sector or to the business sector by buying various kinds of mortgages. On balance, then, the household sector acquires deposit claims on the savings banks and associations, which, in turn, acquire mortgage claims on either individuals or business firms.

FINANCE COMPANIES

Various types of finance companies have become important suppliers of funds to both business firms and households. In dealing with the business sector, they provide loans secured by trade receivables, inventories, and other assets; they also finance equipment purchases on installment terms and arrange for wholesale or floor-plan financing. In dealing with the household sector they provide a variety of short- and medium-term personal loans. Automobile installment financing represents the largest portion of this business.

The funds used by these companies are procured partly through other financial intermediaries and, in part, from the household sector directly.

[8] New money will be created in the process, which distinguishes commercial bank lending from that performed by other financial institutions in our system.

[9] Of course, since all the banks are, in the final analysis, owned by individuals, it may be argued that there is no real difference between the two cases when the accounts of the household and banking sectors are consolidated. However, differences in the financial structure doubtless exert their own significant effect on the activity of the economic system as a whole.

Loans are obtained from commercial banks and commercial paper (short-term marketable promissory notes) is sold through specialized dealers. In addition, public offerings are made of long-term bonds and stock shares. Since some of the finance companies are very large and operate on a nation-wide scale (unlike commercial banks, they are not restricted to one state), they are able to offer a high degree of diversification to investors in their securities.

INVESTMENT COMPANIES

These institutions specialize in substituting their own securities for the stocks and bonds issued by nonfinancial business firms. The reason for this substitution, and therefore for the existence of such companies, is found in the portfolio diversification which they offer to small individual investors. An individual purchasing a few hundred dollars' worth of stock of an investment company acquires a small share of a very large portfolio consisting of the stocks—or both stocks and bonds—of a hundred or more corporations from a number of different industries. He also purchases the continuous services of professionally competent portfolio managers. While this does not, of course, guarantee that losses will never occur, it doubtless greatly diminishes the financial risks involved and removes many, if not all, of the disadvantages of the small-scale investments in common stocks. But it also virtually eliminates the chance of making a quick speculative capital gain.

The largest class of investment companies consists of open-end companies or mutual funds, which sell their shares continually and also redeem them continually on the basis of their respective asset values. The other class consists of closed-end companies, whose shares can be purchased or sold on the stock market by the same procedures as shares of other corporations.

Some investment companies pursue the policy of diversification to the fullest possible extent and invest in a great variety of stocks and bonds. Others confine their investments to common stocks, which increases the possibilities of capital gains. Still others concentrate on a relatively small number of selected industries or companies which are thought to have the greatest growth potential.

INSURANCE COMPANIES

The primary function of life insurance companies is the provision of death benefits and retirement income. In terms of fund flows, this means a transfer of funds from and a subsequent retransfer back to the household sector. But since the amounts received during a given period as premiums usually exceed the amounts paid out as benefits, there are, as a result, large fund accumulations available for transfer to the business and government sectors.

Most of the funds accumulated by the life insurance companies are invested in bonds (both corporate and government) and real estate mortgages. As has already been mentioned, these companies are the principal buyers of corporate bonds by the private placement method. However, they also invest large amounts directly in physical assets: commercial and residential buildings and various types of business equipment. Moreover, in recent times, some life insurance companies have made sizable investments in common stocks.

The other insurance companies are primarily engaged in providing coverage against various risks, such as fire, marine, accident, theft, embezzlement, etc. In the course of their operations they also accumulate substantial amounts of funds obtained from the household sector, which they transfer to the business and government sectors by purchasing corporate stocks and bonds and government obligations.

Here again, then, we find an accumulation of claims by the household sector on the financial intermediaries in one form (insurance policies) and a concomitant accumulation of claims by the intermediaries on the business and government sectors in another form (mainly bonds and mortgages).

PENSION FUNDS

These institutions differ from the other financial intermediaries in that their fund accumulations result from *compulsory* contributions by employers and employees. The funds are accumulated for the purpose of later payment of retirement benefits to participants who, in this case, cannot liquidate, or borrow upon, their contracts.

The social security funds, accumulated under the Federal Old Age and Survivors Insurance program, are invested in special issues of Treasury securities. The state and local government and private pension funds are invested partly in government securities and partly in corporate stocks and bonds.

Some of the private pension funds are administered by life insurance companies and their assets are commingled with the assets of these companies. The other private funds are administered by the trust departments of commercial banks or have their own boards of trustees. In some cases, private funds have been invested predominately in common stocks, which provides a higher rate of return and also, presumably, serves as a hedge against inflation. However, this practice raises the question of safety of the reserves required for meeting the participants' claims, in case a serious business contraction should occur.

In conclusion, we may say that, in performing their function of transferring and transforming capital funds, financial intermediaries enable individual investors to reduce financial risks by means of increased liquidity or diversification. But a price must be paid for these services, which is measured by the difference between the rate of return earned by the intermediaries on their investments and the rate of return accruing to their clients or participants.

In the case of demand deposits in commercial banks, the depositors receive no return at all, since no interest is paid. In fact, the depositor must pay a service charge to the bank if the balance of his account drops below a certain minimum set by the bank. The banks consider this charge compensation for the services performed in handling the client's deposits into and withdrawals from his account. In the case of time deposits at commercial or savings banks, interest is paid but at a lower rate than that earned by the banks on their loans and investments.

Investment companies pay out almost all of their net income to the shareholders; but in computing net income they must, of course, deduct from their total investment income all operating expenses incurred: the cost of their office facilities, as well as the wages, salaries, and fees paid to the staff, managers, and consultants. Insurance companies and pension funds also must deduct their operating costs in computing the amount of funds available for distribution as benefits and income.

The prices of the intermediaries' services cannot in the long run fall below the level at which their operating costs are covered and the lowest acceptable rate of return on their capital is earned. Otherwise, there would be a gradual withdrawal of capital from this sector of the economy. But what is to prevent the prices from rising above this minimum level? Since in most parts of the financial sector there is a substantial degree of concentration, it would seem that the leading firms should be powerful enough to set and maintain their prices so as to be able to realize a higher than minimally acceptable rate of return.

However, the policies of financial institutions have generally been constrained by a considerable amount of regulation and supervision by public authorities. The governmental policies have been aimed at maintaining and stimulating competitive processes, on the one hand, and at preserving and strengthening stability and safety factors on the other. Unfortunately, these two objectives cannot always be easily reconciled with each other.

Thus, in the area of commercial banking the government's measures taken to restrain the merger and holding company developments have tended to maintain competition. But the regulations prohibiting the banks from paying any interest on demand deposits and paying more than the prescribed maximum rate on time deposits have served to restrain interbank competition for new funds.

In the area of securities markets, measures such as the competitive-bidding requirement for public utilities have helped to strengthen competition.

But the establishment of uniform commission rates has tended to confine competition among brokerage firms to non-price methods.

The problems involved are complex, but we cannot discuss them here at greater length. In general, one should realize that two sets of factors should be considered in analyzing any industry with a high degree of concentration. On the one hand, an increase in the number of firms should tend to reduce the probability of collusive rather than competitive practices. On the other hand, a reduction in the average size of a firm may have an unfavorable effect on the efficiency and financial strength of the units concerned. The relative importance of these factors varies from one case to another. No generalizations are possible with respect to all industries in the economy or even in its financial sector alone.[10]

SUMMARY

Considered in the aggregate, the financing of the business sector of an economic system consists of all capital fund flows required for gross capital formation purposes. It includes all internal funds—depreciation allowances as well as retained net profits—and all external funds—equity as well as debt.

In a simplified system, in which all business financing was done internally, there would be no need for a capital market. But in a system which consists of a multitude of private firms using external financing, a capital market where the supply of and demand for funds are brought into equilibrium becomes a necessity. And as the system develops and becomes increasingly complex, different classes of financial institutions emerge and act as intermediaries between the suppliers and the demanders of funds.

Investment bankers with their affiliated network of dealers and brokers act as financial intermediaries in the primary securities market, in which new issues are sold. Securities exchanges and over-the-counter dealers perform the intermediation function in the secondary (resale) securities market. In performing their functions these institutions help transfer funds from one sector of the economy to another, but they do not transform funds by substituting one type of financial claim for another.

In contrast, commercial banks and other lending institutions not only transfer but also transform capital funds in the process. When an individual makes a new deposit to his bank account, which enables the bank to extend a new loan to a business firm, the individual's new claim on the bank does

[10] Recent empirical studies have indicated the existence of economies of scale in commercial banking. Unit costs appear to decline as the size of the bank increases, but the rate of change does not remain the same. The difference between small and medium-size banks is much more pronounced than the difference between medium-size and large banks. (See L. E. Gramley, *A Study of Scale Economics in Banking*, 1962, and P. M. Horwitz, *Economics of Scale in Banking*, 1963.)

not have the same financial characteristics as the bank's new claim on its client.

Aside from commercial banks, the major classes of financial intermediaries which both transfer and transform capital funds are: mutual savings banks, savings and loan associations, insurance companies, investment companies, and pension funds.

In performing their functions, financial intermediaries enable individual investors to reduce financial risks by means of increased liquidity and/or diversification. But a price must be paid for these services which is measured by the difference between the rate of return earned by the intermediaries and the rate of return accruing to their clients or participants.

SELECTED REFERENCES

Commission on Money and Credit: *Private Financial Institutions*, Prentice-Hall, Inc., Englewood Cliffs, N.J., 1963.

Friedland, Seymour: *The Economics of Corporate Finance*, Prentice-Hall, Inc., Englewood Cliffs, N.J., 1966, chaps. 11, 14, and 15.

Goldsmith, Raymond W.: *Financial Institutions*, Random House, New York, 1968.

————: *The Flow of Capital Funds in the Postwar Economy*, National Bureau of Economic Research, New York, 1965.

Husband, William H., and James C. Dockeray: *Modern Corporation Finance*, 6th ed., Richard D. Irwin, Inc., Homewood, Ill., 1966, part 4, "Sale and Regulation of Securities."

Leffler, G. L., and L. G. Farrell: *The Stock Market*, 3d ed., The Ronald Press Co., New York, 1963.

Robinson, Roland I.: *Money and Capital Markets*, McGraw-Hill Book Co., New York, 1964.

Securities and Exchange Commission: *Special Study of Securities Markets*, the Commission, Washington, D.C., 1963.

Waterman, M. H.: *Investment Banking Functions*, University of Michigan Press, Ann Arbor, Mich., 1958.

Weston, Fred J., and Eugene F. Brigham: *Managerial Finance*, 2d ed., Holt, Rinehart and Winston, New York, 1966, chaps. 23–25.

11
Flow-of-funds Accounts

The functioning of financial institutions and the interrelationships between them and the nonfinancial sectors of the economy can be examined in considerable detail within the framework provided by the flow-of-funds system of national accounts. This system has been developed by the research staff of the Board of Governors of the Federal Reserve System, on the basis of the pioneering project directed by Professor Morris A. Copeland.[1]

The flow-of-funds accounts represent an important complement of the other two national accounting systems: the national income and the input-output accounts. They encompass all transactions that involve a transfer of credit and/or money, including those representing purchases and sales of existing assets as well as those relating to purchases and sales of current output. As is stated in the Board of Governors' report:

> The boundaries of the system extend beyond the measurements of national output alone. Since flows of funds arise in transfers of existing assets as well as in purchases and sales of current production,

[1] M. A. Copeland, *A Study of Moneyflows in the United States*, National Bureau of Economic Research, New York, 1952.

the accounts include measures of transactions in land, existing homes, and used automobiles in addition to measures of purchases and sales of new homes and new automobiles. Flows of funds also arise out of shifts in composition of portfolios. Therefore, transactions in mortgages, securities, trade credit, and other financial instruments, as well as changes in cash balances, are measured in the system.[2]

In combination with the national income accounts, the flow-of-funds accounts provide a comprehensive and internally consistent body of data which enables us to gain new insights into the working of financial and nonfinancial markets and the interdependence between financial and nonfinancial processes in our economy. This should be of importance both to the economic theorists, concerned with theoretical models, and to the business economists, interested in improved forecasting techniques. Unfortunately, the potential usefulness of the flow-of-funds system has not yet been fully realized. Much further analytical work remains to be done in this area.[3]

A SIMPLIFIED TWO-SECTOR SYSTEM

In the flow-of-funds system, each transaction is recorded by at least four entries in the accounts of participating sectors. Thus, a purchase of goods for cash is entered as a purchase of goods by the buyer, as a sale of goods by the seller, as a reduction in cash for the buyer, and as an increase in cash for the seller. The purchase and sale of goods are defined as nonfinancial entries, while the reduction and the increase in cash are defined as financial entries.

A purchase of securities for cash also involves four entries—all in the financial class in this case. The buyer's account will show an increase in one type of financial assets (securities) and a decrease in another type of financial assets (cash). The reverse will be true of the seller's account if the transaction involves previously issued securities. But if the seller issues new securities, his account will show an increase in cash and a corresponding increase in financial liabilities. In describing the accounts, nonfinancial entries of the transactions recorded are usually referred to as "nonfinancial transactions," and the financial entries of the transactions concerned as "financial transactions."

Before examining the complex accounts developed by the Federal Reserve, it will be helpful to go through a couple of simplified examples which

[2] *Flow of Funds in the United States, 1939–1953*, Board of Governors of the Federal Reserve System, 1955.
[3] Cf. Lawrence S. Ritter, "The Flow of Funds Accounts: A Framework for Financial Analysis," *The Bulletin*, New York University, Institute of Finance, no. 52, August, 1968.

bring out the basic intersector relationships. Let us first consider a system consisting of two sectors only: households and business firms. The initial (beginning-of-the-year) balance sheets of these sectors are as follows:

Households			*Business*		
Cash	10		Cash	15	
Securities		Net worth 100	Inventories	20	
owned	90		Gross fixed		Securities
Total assets	100		assets	110	outstanding 90
			Depr. reserve	55	
			Net fixed		
			assets	55	
			Total assets	90	

As can be seen, the assets of the business sector consist of cash and physical properties: inventories and fixed assets (land, plant, and equipment). The household sector owns only financial assets: cash and securities representing claims on the business sector.[4] The physical goods owned by consumers are ignored in this example. Since there are no banks or any other financial institutions in this system, the total amount of money remains constant and changes in the cash balances of the household and business sectors must completely offset each other.

The following transactions take place during the period:

Wages and salaries	250
Dividends	50
Total personal income	300
Consumption expenditures	275
Personal saving	25
Securities purchased by households	23
Increase in households' cash balances	2
Real investment by business firms:	
Increase in inventories	5
Gross plant and equipment expenditures	35
	40
Capital consumption allowances	15
Net investment	25
Decrease in business cash balances	2

---

[4] The securities held may include both stocks and bonds. Both types may be broadly defined as "claims" of households on business firms, the specific differences between debt and equity instruments being of no importance at this point.

At the completion of the period, the balance sheets will be:

Householders				Business			
Cash	12			Cash	13		
Securities	113	Net worth	125	Inventories	25		
Total assets	125			Gross fixed		Securities	
				assets	145	outstanding 113	
				Depr. reserve	70		
				Net fixed			
				assets	75		
				Total assets	113		

On the basis of the above data, we can construct the following flow-of-funds statement:

Table 11-1

	Households		Business		Total	
Transactions	S	U	S	U	S	U
Nonfinancial						
Payroll	250			250	250	250
Dividends	50			50	50	50
Purchases/sales:					315	315
Consumer goods		275	275			
Capital goods			40	40		
Total	300	275	315	340	615	615
Financial						
Securities		23	23		23	23
Cash		2	2		2	2
Total	300	300	340	340	640	640

S = Source; U = Use.

In the household sector, nonfinancial transactions consist of payments received for the productive services of labor and capital (factor payments), on the one hand, and of the expenditures made on consumption goods on the other. Nonfinancial sources of funds in this sector exceed nonfinancial uses of funds, the difference being equal to personal saving. The major portion of the funds saved by the households is transferred to the business firms through financial transactions—purchases of newly issued securities—and the balance is added to the households' cash balances. The increases in the households' financial assets represent financial uses of funds. Since the households do not borrow funds in this example, their financial sources are zero.

In the business sector, nonfinancial sources are represented by the sales revenues of both the consumption goods and the capital goods industries. The nonfinancial uses of funds are equal to the sum of the factor payments and the capital goods purchases. In this sector, nonfinancial sources fall short of nonfinancial uses, and the deficit is covered by financial transactions: new securities' sales and cash balance reduction.

Total (financial and nonfinancial) sources are equal to total uses in each sector and in the system as a whole. The individual classes of sources and uses are not necessarily equal to each other in the individual sectors but must always be equal for the entire system. The total amount of fund flows in the system during a given period is, of course, much greater than the value of output produced during the period. In our example, the GNP is equal to $315 and the national income to $300 only.

If it is desired to focus attention on the financial flows and the saving-investment relationship in the system, the statement of sources and uses may be rearranged and presented in the following form:

Table 11-2

	Households		Business	
	S	U	S	U
Investment:				
Change in inventories				5
Plant and equip. expenditures				35
Gross investment				40
Saving:				
Personal saving	25			
Bus. saving (capital consumption allowances)			15	
Financial flows:				
Purchase/sale of securities		23	23	
Change in cash balance		2		−2

S = Source; U = Use.

The fund flows and the savings-investment relationship may also be presented in the form of accounting equations. Since these equations follow directly from the accepted set of definitions, they are, of course, mere identities. They provide a useful framework of analysis—as do the accounts themselves—but do not express any definite functional relationships that could be subjected to empirical testing.

The following symbols will be used:

Stock variables:

C = cash $\qquad\qquad$ GF = gross fixed assets

S = securities $\qquad\quad$ DR = depreciation reserve

IN = inventories $\qquad$ NF = net fixed assets

The superscripts H and B will indicate the household and the business sectors, respectively; the subscripts 0 and 1 will indicate the amounts at the beginning and the end of the period, respectively.

Flow variables—amounts received (paid) during the period:

WS = wages and salaries

D = dividends

CE = consumption expenditures

ΔS = new securities purchased

ΔDR = depreciation allowance

ΔC = change in cash

$GI = \Delta IN + \Delta GF$ = gross investment

We may then express the inflows and outflows of funds in each of the two sectors as follows:

$$C_0{}^H + WS + D - CE - \Delta S = C_1{}^H$$

$$C_1{}^H - C_0{}^H = \Delta C^H$$

$$C_0{}^B + CE + GI - GI - WS - D + \Delta S = C_1{}^B$$

$$C_1{}^B - C_0{}^B = \Delta C^B$$

Gross investment is both added and deducted in the business sector equation, because it represents receipts for the firms selling capital goods and expenditures for the firms purchasing them. Since in our simplified system the total amount of cash remains unchanged, we may write

$$C_0{}^H + C_0{}^B = C_1{}^H + C_1{}^B$$

and

$$\Delta C^H + \Delta C^B = 0$$

The investment-saving relationship may be expressed as follows:

$$GI = \Delta GF + \Delta IN = \Delta DR + \Delta S - \Delta C^B = \Delta DR + \Delta S + \Delta C^H$$

where ΔDR represents business saving and $\Delta S + \Delta C^H$ is equal to personal saving.

A FOUR-SECTOR SYSTEM

Let us now introduce financial institutions into the system and examine the intersector relationships arising out of their operations. We assume that there are two types of financial institutions: (1) commercial banks which carry demand deposits and make loans to business firms; (2) savings institutions which accept time deposits and invest funds in bonds issued by nonfinancial business firms. All cash balances in the business and household sectors are in the form of demand deposits with commercial banks. Commercial bank reserves are held in the form of gold.

The initial balance sheets of the four sectors are as follows:

Households				Nonfinancial business			
Cash (DD)	10	Bank loans	10	Cash (DD)	15	Bank loans	15
Time deposits	40	Net worth	90	Inventories	20	Bonds	32
Stocks owned:				G.F. assets	110		
Nonfinancial				Depr. res.	55	Cap. stock	43
business	43			N.F. assets	55		
Banks	7						
Total	100	Total	100	Total	90	Total	90

Commercial banks				Savings institutions			
Reserves	15	DD_{HH}	10	Cash (DD)	8	Time deposits	40
Loans to bus.	15	$DD_{Bus.}$	15	Bonds	32		
Loans to HH	10	DD_{SI}	8				
			33				
		Cap. stock	7				
Total	40	Total	40	Total	40	Total	40

The following transactions are assumed to have taken place during the year:

Wages and salaries	
Paid by nonfinancial business	278
Paid by commercial banks	1
Paid by savings institutions	1
	280

Dividends		
Paid by nonfinancial business to households	17	
Paid by commercial banks to households	2	
Paid by savings institutions to households	2	
	21	

Interest		
Paid by nonfinancial business to banks	2	
Paid by nonfinancial business to savings institutions	3	
Paid by households to banks	1	
	6	

Consumption expenditures	275
Real investment	
Change in inventories	5
Gross plant and equipment expenditures	35
	40

Saving	
Nonfinancial business (capital consumption allowances)	15
Household sector	25
	40

New securities	
Stocks sold by nonfinancial business to households	17
Bonds sold by nonfinancial business to savings institutions	3
	20

New loans	
By commercial banks to nonfinancial business	5
By commercial banks to households	1
	6

Disposition of personal saving	
Purchase of securities of nonfinancial business	17
Increase in time deposits with savings institutions	5
Increase in demand deposits with commercial banks	4
Less increase in consumers' loans	−1
	25

Consequently, the end-of-the-year balance sheets must be as follows:

Households				Nonfinancial business			
Cash (DD)	14	Bank loans	11	Cash (DD)	15	Bank loans	20
Time dep.	45	Net worth	115	Inventories	25	Bonds	35
Stocks owned:				G.F. assets	145	Cap. stock	60
Nonfinancial				Depr. res.	70		
bus.	60			N.F. assets	75		
Banks	7						
Total	126	Total	126	Total	115	Total	115

Commercial banks				Savings institutions			
Reserves	15	DD_{HH}	14	Cash (DD)	10	Time dep.	45
Loans to bus.	20	DD_B	15	Securities	35		
Loans to HH	11	DD_{SI}	10				
			39				
		Cap. stock	7				
Total	46	Total	46	Total	45	Total	45

The flow-of-funds statement compiled from these data (Table 11-3) is considerably more complex than the one given in our first example (Table 11-1), although still much simpler than the statements prepared by the Federal Reserve for the United States economy.

Table 11-3

Transactions	HH		Banks		S.I.		Nonfin. bus.		Total	
	S	U	S	U	S	U	S	U	S	U
Nonfinancial										
Factor payments:										
Wages and salaries	280			1		1		278	280	280
Dividends	21			2		2		17	21	21
Interest		1	3		3			5	6	6
Purchases/sales:										
Consumption goods		275					275		275	275
Capital goods								40	40	40
Financial										
Securities:										
Nonfin. bus.		17				3	20		20	20
Banks										
Sav. inst.										
Bank loans	1		6				5		6	6
Time deposits		5			5				5	5
Demand deposits		4	6			2			6	6
Total	302	302	9	9	8	8	340	340	659	659

Gross national product	= 315
Consumption expenditures	= 275
Gross investment	= 40

S = Source; U = Use.

As can be seen, the household sector is again characterized by an excess of nonfinancial sources over nonfinancial uses of funds, the difference being equal to personal saving ($25). Of the amount saved by the households, however, only \$17 is invested directly in the securities of nonfinancial business firms. The balance is invested in assets which represent claims on financial institutions: \$5 billion is deposited with the savings institutions and \$4 billion is deposited with commerical banks. The savings institutions invest \$3 billion in bonds of nonfinancial business firms and increase their demand deposits at commercial banks by \$2 billion. Commercial banks show an increase of \$6 billion in demand deposits and a corresponding increase in loans (\$5 billion to nonfinancial business and \$1 billion to households).

Once again, total sources are equal to total uses for each of the four sectors. For the system as a whole, the sources and the uses amounts are equal to each other in every class of transactions individually as well as for all classes combined.

Gross investment in real assets—all done in the nonfinancial business sector—amounts to \$40 billion (see Table 11-4). It is equal to gross savings, which consists of business depreciation allowances and personal saving (all net profits are distributed and there is no net business saving). Net investment and net saving amount to \$25 billion each.

Table 11-4

	HH		Banks		S.I.		Nonfin. bus.		Total	
	S	U	S	U	S	U	S	U	S	U
Investment:										
Change in inventories								5		5
Plant and equip. exp.								35		35
Gross investment								$\overline{40}$		
Saving:										
Personal	25								25	
Business (C.C. allowances)							15		15	
Gross saving									$\overline{40}$	
Change in fin. assets		26		6		5				37
Change in fin. liabilities	1		6		5		25		37	
Net financial investment (ΔF.A. $-$ ΔF.L.)		25		0		0	($-$25)		0	0

However, in order to finance this net investment, the system creates \$37 billion worth of new financial assets and, of course, an equal amount of new financial liabilities. Figure 11-1 should help to elucidate the relationships involved:

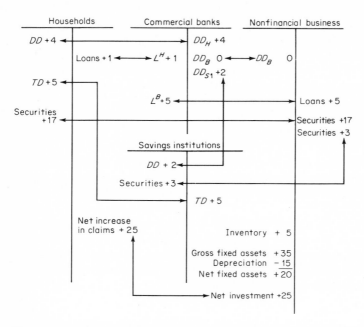

Figure 11-1   Financial intermediaries in relation to household and
business sectors.

The increase of $17 billion in the securities held by the household sector
represents a direct new claim against the nonfinancial business sector.

The increase of $5 billion in the time deposits represents a new claim
of the household sector on the savings institutions. The latter increase
their claims on the business and the banking sectors by $3 billion and $2
billion, respectively.

The $4 billion increment in the DD held by the households represents
a new claim on the banking sector. Thus the liabilities of the banks increase
by $6 billion and their claims on the other sectors rise by the same amount:
$5 billion of new loans to business firms and $1 billion of new loans to
consumers.[5] Thus, the nonfinancial business sector obtains $25 billion
in new funds and reports corresponding increases in real assets and financial
liabilities. The two financial sectors combined report new financial assets
and new liabilities amounting to $11 billion each. The household sector has
a $26 billion increase in financial assets and a $1 billion increment in liabilities.

---

[5] An increase in DD represents new-money creation in the system. Since in this example there
is no Treasury currency, only commercial banks can perform this monetary function as long as
their reserve situation permits it.

In order to express the flow of funds through each sector of the system algebraically, we must now introduce the following additional symbols:

Cash items:

DD^H = demand deposits held by households
DD^B = demand deposits held by nonfinancial firms
DD^{SI} = demand deposits held by savings institutions
BR = commercial bank reserves

Bank loans:

ΔL^H = new loans to households
ΔL^B = new loans to nonfinancial firms
ΔL^{SI} = new loans to savings institutions

Securities:

$\Delta S_H{}^B$ = new securities of business firms sold to households
$\Delta S_{SI}{}^B$ = new securities of business firms sold to savings institutions

Time deposits:

TD = time deposits with savings institutions held by households

Dividends:

$D_B{}^H$ = dividends received by households from nonfinancial firms
$D_{Bk}{}^H$ = dividends received by households from commercial banks
$D_{SI}{}^H$ = dividends received by households from savings institutions

Interest:

$I_B{}^{Bk}$ = interest received by commercial banks from business
$I_H{}^{Bk}$ = interest received by commercial banks from households
$I_{Bk}{}^{SI}$ = interest received by savings institutions from commercial banks

We may then write:

$$DD_0{}^H + WS + D_B{}^H + D_{Bk}{}^H + D_{SI}{}^H + \Delta L^H - CE - I_H{}^{Bk}$$
$$- \Delta S_H{}^B - \Delta TD = DD_1{}^H$$

$$DD_0{}^B + CE + GI - GI + \Delta S_H{}^B + \Delta S_{SI}{}^B + \Delta L^B - WS_B{}^H$$
$$- D_B{}^H - I_B{}^{SI} - I_B{}^{Bk} = DD_1{}^B$$

$$DD_0{}^{SI} + \Delta TD + I_B{}^{SI} - WS_{SI}{}^H - \Delta S_B{}^{SI} - D_{SI}{}^H = DD_1{}^{SI}$$

For the banking sector we have:

$$DD_0{}^H + DD_0{}^B + DD_0{}^{SI} + \Delta L^H + \Delta L^B + D_{Bk}{}^H - I_H{}^{Bk} - I_B{}^{Bk}$$
$$+ WS_{Bk}{}^H = DD_1{}^H + DD_1{}^B + DD_1{}^{SI}$$

Since the revenues of the banking sector are equal to its disbursements, we have:

$$I_H{}^{Bk} + I_B{}^{Bk} = D_{Bk}{}^H + WS_{Bk}{}^H$$

It follows that:

$$(DD_1{}^H + DD_1{}^B + DD_1{}^{SI}) - (DD_0{}^H + DD_0{}^B + DD_0{}^{SI}) = \Delta L^H + \Delta L^B$$

The increase in the total amount of demand deposits in the system is equal to the increase in the loans granted by the banking sector.

Finally, the investment-saving relation may be stated as follows:

$$GI = \Delta DR + (\Delta S_H{}^B + \Delta DD^H + \Delta TD - \Delta L^H)$$

where ΔDR is business saving and the sum of the terms in parentheses represents personal saving.

THE FLOW-OF-FUNDS ACCOUNTS OF THE UNITED STATES

The flow-of-funds accounts for the United States economy, published by the Federal Reserve, are prepared for 11 sectors:

1. Consumers and nonprofit organizations
2. Farms
3. Noncorporate business
4. Corporate business
5. Federal government
6. State and local governments
7. Commercial banking
8. Savings institutions
9. Insurance
10. Financial, not elsewhere covered
11. Rest of the world

The consumer sector statement is the most detailed one. It shows the entire amount of personal income and outlays, gross saving and investment, and the various financial sources and uses of funds. In an abbreviated form, the statement for 1968 is as follows:

1. Personal Income	685.8
2. Personal Taxes	96.9
3. Personal Outlays	548.2
4. Personal Saving	40.7
5. Various Adjustments	8.7
6. Consumer Durables (net)	16.9
7. Net Saving	66.4
8. Capital Consumption	75.3
9. Gross Saving	141.7
10. Capital Expenditures (on real assets)	107.9
11. Net Financial Investment	25.4
12. Gross Investment	133.3
13. Net Acquisition of Financial Assets	60.1
14. Net Increase in Liabilities	34.7
15. Net Financial Investment	25.4

The amounts shown on the first four lines are equal to those found in the national income tables. But beginning with line 5, the flow-of-funds statement is different from the national income tabulations. The amount on line 5 represents the sum of imputed saving associated with growth of government life insurance and retirement reserves and of capital-gain dividends from open-end investment companies. The amount on line 6 represents net value of consumer durables, other than residential dwellings, purchased during 1968. This item reflects a major difference in the concept of national saving and investment. In the national income and product accounts, the only type of expenditure by households that is considered investment is the outlay on residential construction. Expenditures on all other types of durables (e.g., automobiles) are considered consumption outlays. In contrast, in the flow-of-funds accounting, expenditures on consumer durables are included, along with expenditures on residential construction, in the gross amount of investment in the system, and the system's gross saving is increased correspondingly.[6] In order to derive net investment (and net saving), it is necessary to deduct capital consumption on all types of durable assets concerned. In 1968, gross residential construction amounted to $21.3 billion and gross purchases of consumer durables amounted to $82.5 billion. Capital consumption for these two items was equal to $9.7 billion and $65.6 billion, respectively.

---

[6] Conceptually, gross saving must equal gross investment, and net saving must equal net investment. But the actual amounts usually differ from one another to some extent, because of statistical discrepancies. As can be seen, in 1968 gross saving of the household sector exceeded its gross investment by $8.4 billion.

As usual, gross saving of the household sector exceeded its real capital expenditures in 1968 by a considerable amount which represented the sector's net financial investment. Net financial investment ($25.4 billion) is equal to net acquisition of financial assets ($60.1 billion) less net increase in liabilities ($34.7 billion). Net acquisition of financial assets is equal to total purchases less sales; and net increase in liabilities represents the total amount of newly contracted liabilities less the amount of liabilities redeemed.

In the actual sector statements and in the summary of flow-of-funds accounts, prepared by the Federal Reserve, financial transactions are reported in considerable detail. The summary statement for 1968 will be presented and some comments on intersector relationships in that year will be made at the end of this section. But first, the other sector accounts must be briefly discussed.

The government sectors also show total inflows and outflows of funds. The entire amount received is reported for each major source of revenue (income and other taxes, insurance and retirement program receipts, etc.), and the entire amount spent is given for each major type of expenditure (purchase of goods and services, interest on government securities, social security payments, etc.). In both the federal and the state and local government sectors, expenditures have exceeded total revenues, and gross saving (which is equal to net saving in this case) has been negative in most of the recent years.

Since capital expenditures in the government sectors are not reported separately but are included with purchases of other goods and services, gross saving is equal to net financial investment, except for statistical discrepancies. In an abbreviated form, the statement for the United States government for 1968 is as follows:

Tax receipts	135.4
Insurance receipts	41.5
Total	176.9
Net purchases of goods and services	100.0
Net interest paid	11.8
Insurance benefits paid	33.6
Other payments	38.0
Total	183.4
Gross saving	− 6.5
Net financial investment	− 4.7
Statistical discrepancy	− 1.8

The statement for state and local governments is prepared in a similar form. In 1968, total receipts in this sector were $78.7 billion and total expenditures $83.8 billion. Thus, there was a dissaving amounting to $5.2 billion.

In the nonfinancial business sectors total receipts and total outlays are not given. The corporate statement begins with profit before taxes and the noncorporate statement with the proprietors' net income, as defined in the national income accounts. An abbreviated statement for the nonfinancial corporate sector in 1968 is as follows:

Profit before taxes plus inventory valuation adjustment	73.5
Tax accruals	35.6
Dividends	19.3
Net saving	18.6
Capital consumption	45.5
Gross saving	64.1
Capital expenditures	80.2
Net financial investment	−17.5
Statistical discrepancy	1.4

The negative amount of net financial investment indicates the extent to which capital expenditures were financed from external sources. In the noncorporate sector, net income was $72.3 billion and gross saving was $18.0 billion. Capital expenditures exceeded the latter amount by $2.8 billion, thus making net financial investment negative also in this case.

The financial sectors show relatively small amounts of gross saving and gross investment. On the other hand, their role as financial intermediaries is clearly indicated by large acquisitions of financial assets accompanied by almost equally large increases in liabilities. In the case of nonbank financial institutions, net acquisition of financial assets and net increase in liabilities amounted each to approximately $46 billion in 1968. The corresponding figure for commercial banks is approximately $42 billion.

The rest-of-the-world sector comprises the residents and governments of countries outside the United States and its territories and possessions. It includes international organizations, such as the International Monetary Fund, the International Bank for Reconstruction and Development, and the United Nations. The transactions include exports and imports of goods and services, on the one hand, and acquisitions of financial assets (and corresponding increases in liabilities) on the other. On balance, net financial investment of this sector was negative in most recent years, which means that net acquisition of financial assets by foreign parties fell short of net increases in foreign liabilities to the United States. Nevertheless, there was a continuous net acquisition of gold (which is considered a financial asset in the flow-of-funds accounts) by the rest-of-the-world sector.

Table 11-5 Summary of flow of funds for year 1968

(In billions of dollars)

Sector / Transaction category	Private domestic nonfinancial sectors								U.S. govt.	
	House-holds		Busi-ness		State and local govts.		Total			
	U	S	U	S	U	S	U	S	U	S
1 Gross saving	—	141.6	—	82.2	—	−5.2	—	218.6	—	−6.5
2 Capital consumption	—	75.3	—	63.3	—	—	—	138.6	—	—
3 Net saving (1 − 2)	—	66.4	—	18.9	—	−5.2	—	80.0	—	−6.5
4 Gross investment (5 + 10)	133.3	—	80.8	—	−5.1	—	209.0	—	−4.7	—
5 Private cap. expend., net	107.9	—	101.1	—	—	—	209.0	—	—	—
6 Consumer durables	82.5	—	—	—	—	—	82.5	—	—	—
7 Residential constr.	21.3	—	8.6	—	—	—	29.9	—	—	—
8 Plant and equipment	4.0	—	84.8	—	—	—	88.8	—	—	—
9 Inventory change	—	—	7.7	—	—	—	7.7	—	—	—
10 Net financial invest. (11 − 12)	25.4	—	−20.3	—	−5.1	—	—	—	−4.7	—
11 Financial uses, net	60.2	—	30.8	—	10.9	—	101.9	—	14.2	—
12 Financial sources	—	34.7	—	51.1	—	16.0	—	101.9	—	18.8
13 Gold and off. U.S. fgn. exch.	—	—	—	—	—	—	—	—	2.0	—
14 Treasury currency	—	—	—	—	—	—	—	—	—	.4
15 Dem. dep. and currency	—	—	—	—	—	—	—	—	—	—
16 Private domestic	14.9	—	1.2	—	.6	—	16.7	—	—	—
17 U.S. Govt.	—	—	—	—	—	—	—	—	−.2	—
18 Foreign	—	—	—	—	—	—	—	—	—	—
19 Time and svgs. accounts	27.6	—	—	—	—	—	32.6	—	—	—
20 At coml. banks	14.9	—	2.5	—	2.6	—	20.0	—	.1	—
21 At svgs. instit.	12.7	—	—	—	—	—	12.7	—	—	—
22 Life insur. reserves	4.8	—	—	—	—	—	4.8	—	—	.1
23 Pension fund reserves	15.7	—	—	—	—	4.1	15.7	4.1	—	1.2
24 Consol. bank items*	—	—	—	—	—	—	—	—	—	—
25 Credit mkt. instr.	3.1	31.9	7.7	36.3	7.7	11.4	18.4	79.7	8.1	16.6
26 U.S. Govt. securities	4.1	—	1.7	—	—	2.8	8.6	—	—	16.6
27 State and local oblig.	1.4	—	.1	—	−.4	11.1	1.1	11.1	—	—
28 Corp. and foreign bonds	3.9	—	—	12.9	4.5	—	8.5	12.9	—	—
29 Corp. stocks	−6.3	—	—	−.4	—	—	−6.3	−.4	—	—
30 1- to 4-family mortgages	—	15.4	—	—	.7	—	.7	15.4	2.5	—
31 Other mortgages	—	.8	—	9.5	—	—	—	10.3	.8	—
32 Consumer credit	—	11.1	2.4	—	—	—	2.4	11.1	—	—
33 Bank loans n.e.c.	—	3.2	9.1	—	—	—	—	12.3	—	—
34 Other loans	—	1.4	3.5	5.3	—	.3	3.5	7.0	4.8	—
35 Open market paper	—	—	3.5	1.8	—	—	3.5	1.8	—	—
36 Federal loans	—	.2	—	1.3	—	.3	—	1.8	4.8	—
37 Security credit	.8	2.2	—	—	—	—	.8	2.2	—	—
38 To brkrs. and dealers	.8	—	—	—	—	—	.8	—	—	—
39 To others	—	2.2	—	—	—	—	—	2.2	—	—
40 Taxes payable	—	—	—	2.5	.1	—	—	.1	3.4	—
41 Trade credit	—	.4	14.9	12.6	—	.5	14.9	13.4	.6	—
42 Equity in noncorp. business	−8.4	—	—	−8.4	—	—	−8.4	−8.4	—	—
43 Misc. financial trans.	1.7	.3	4.6	8.1	—	—	6.3	8.4	.1	.5
44 Insurance accruals	.9	—	1.5	—	—	—	2.4	—	—	—
45 Direct fgn. inv.	—	—	.6	.4	—	—	.6	.4	—	−1.1
46 Unallocated	—	—	2.5	7.7	—	—	2.5	7.7	—	.5
47 Sector discrepancies (1 − 4)	8.3	—	1.4	—	−.1	—	9.6	—	−1.8	—

* Claims between commercial banks and monetary authorities: member bank reserves, vault cash, F.R. loans to banks. F.R. float, and stock at F.R. Banks.

SOURCE: *Federal Reserve Bulletin*, May, 1969

| | Financial sectors | | | | | | | | Rest of the world | | All sectors | | Discrepancy | Natl. saving and invest- | |
| Total | | Monetary auth. | | Coml. banks | | Nonbank finance | | | | | | | | ment | |
U	S	U	S	U	S	U	S	U	S	U	S	U		
—	2.5	—	—	—	2.8	—	-.4	—	.8	—	215.4	—	214.6	1
—	1.3	—	—	—	.7	—	.6	—	—	—	139.9	—	139.9	2
—	1.2	—	—	—	2.1	—	-1.0	—	.8	—	75.5	—	74.7	3
1.7	—	—	—	—	2.1	—	-.4	—	1.1	—	207.1	8.2	209.1	4
1.2	—	—	—	—	.6	—	.6	—	—	—	210.2	5.2	210.2	5
—	—	—	—	—	—	—	—	—	—	—	82.5	—	82.5	6
—	—	—	—	—	—	—	—	—	—	—	29.9	—	29.9	7
1.2	—	—	—	—	.6	—	.6	—	—	—	90.0	—	90.0	8
—	—	—	—	—	—	—	—	—	—	—	7.7	—	7.7	9
.5	—	—	—	—	1.5	—	-1.1	—	1.1	—	-3.1	3.1	-1.1	10
92.4	—	—	3.8	—	42.8	—	45.8	—	8.1	—	216.5	—	7.0	11
—	91.9	—	3.8	—	41.3	—	46.9	—	7.0	—	219.6	—	8.1	12
-1.2	—	-1.2	—	—	—	—	—	1.2	2.1	2.1	2.1	—	—	13
.2	—	.2	—	—	—	—	—	—	—	.2	.4	.2	—	14
—	13.2	—	1.4	—	11.9	—	—	—	—	—	18.4	13.2	—	15
1.2	13.8	—	2.4	—	11.5	1.2	—	—	—	—	17.9	13.8	-4.1	16
—	-1.3	—	-1.1	—	-.2	—	—	—	—	—	-.2	-1.3	-1.1	17
—	.7	—	.1	—	.6	—	—	—	.7	—	—	.7	—	18
-.2	32.5	—	—	—	—	—	-.2	—	—	—	—	32.5	—	19
.1	20.1	—	—	—	20.1	.1	—	-.1	—	—	—	20.1	—	20
-.3	12.4	—	—	—	—	-.3	12.4	—	—	—	—	12.4	—	21
—	4.7	—	—	—	—	—	4.7	—	—	—	—	4.8	—	22
—	10.4	—	—	—	—	—	10.4	—	—	—	—	15.7	—	23
3.2	3.2	1.0	2.2	2.2	1.0	—	—	—	—	3.2	3.2	—	—	24
83.0	12.3	3.7	—	37.1	.3	42.2	12.0	2.1	2.9	111.5	111.5	—	—	25
8.5	—	3.8	—	2.8	—	1.8	—	—	-.5	—	16.6	—	—	26
10.0	—	—	—	8.1	—	2.0	—	—	—	—	11.1	—	—	27
6.6	1.1	—	—	.3	.3	6.3	.7	—	1.1	—	15.1	—	—	28
9.7	5.7	—	—	—	-.1	9.7	5.7	2.0	.2	—	5.4	—	—	29
12.4	.2	—	—	3.5	—	8.9	.2	—	—	—	15.5	—	—	30
9.5	—	—	—	3.2	—	6.3	—	—	—	—	10.3	—	—	31
8.7	—	—	—	4.9	—	3.8	—	—	—	—	11.1	—	—	32
14.1	2.1	—	—	14.1	—	—	—	2.1	-.3	—	14.1	—	—	33
3.5	3.3	-.1	—	.2	—	3.3	3.3	.6	1.9	12.3	12.3	-.1	—	34
—	2.5	-.1	—	.2	—	-.1	2.5	.6	-.2	—	4.1	—	—	35
—	.9	—	—	—	—	—	.9	—	2.1	—	4.8	—	—	36
3.9	2.5	—	—	1.9	—	2.0	2.5	.3	.2	—	4.9	—	—	37
1.5	2.5	—	—	1.5	—	—	2.5	.3	—	—	2.5	—	—	38
2.4	—	—	—	.4	—	2.0	—	—	.2	—	2.4	—	—	39
—	.1	—	-.1	—	.1	—	.1	—	—	3.5	2.6	-.9	—	40
.3	—	—	—	—	—	—	.3	—	—	15.8	13.4	-2.3	—	41
—	—	—	—	—	—	—	—	—	—	—	-8.4	—	—	42
2.0	12.9	—	.3	1.7	8.0	.3	4.6	4.0	1.8	12.3	23.6	11.3	—	43
—	—	—	—	—	—	—	—	—	—	—	2.4	—	—	44
—	—	—	—	—	—	—	—	-1.1	.6	—	—	—	—	45
—	—	—	—	—	—	—	—	1.6	1.2	5.9	17.1	NS	—	46
.8	—	—	—	.7	—	.1	—	-.3	—	8.2	—	8.2	5.5	47

Let us now take a closer look at the summary statement for the United States economy in 1968 (Table 11-5). It can be seen that gross saving amounted to $215 billion for the national economy as a whole. Gross investment, which conceptually equals gross saving, was slightly lower in the statement because of a statistical discrepancy. For each individual sector, gross investment is equal to the sum of the capital expenditures on physical assets and net financial investment (the difference between net increase in financial assets and net increase in liabilities). But since the sum of all domestic financial assets is always equal to the sum of all domestic liabilities, it follows that net financial investment for the system as a whole must be equal to net foreign investment. As the figures show, the latter was very small in comparison with the domestic capital expenditures, and we may therefore say that national investment consisted almost entirely of additions to real capital stock (including consumer durables).

Slightly over one-half of all capital expenditures were made in the household sector and a little less than one-half in the business sector ($108 and $101 billion, respectively). The household sector had an excess of gross saving over real capital expenditures of about $34 billion, while the internal funds generated by the business sector fell short of its capital expenditures by about $20 billion. The government sectors (federal, state, and local governments combined) on balance absorbed new capital funds to the extent of almost $10 billion.

If the households had supplied new funds directly to the business and government sectors which required new financing, the amount of newly created financial assets would have also been approximately $35 billion. Actually, as the table shows, the household sector reported net acquisition of financial assets (line 11, "Financial uses") amounting to $60 billion and, at the same time, a net increase in liabilities (line 12, "financial sources") amounting to $35 billion. New financial assets were accumulated by the households mainly in the form of demand deposits and currency ($15 billion), time deposits ($27 billion), and life insurance and pension fund reserves ($19 billion). The households also acquired $5 billion of government securities and $4 billion of corporate bonds, but their holdings of corporate stocks were reduced by $6 billion. The increases in the household's liabilities were mainly in the form of mortgages ($16 billion) and consumer credit ($11 billion).

Thus, on balance, the household sector did not directly channel any new funds into the business sector. The latter's financial liabilities rose by $51 billion, but virtually all the funds, except for trade credit, were obtained through financial intermediaries. The main increases in business liabilities were in the form of corporate and foreign bonds ($13 billion), mortgages ($10 billion), bank loans ($9 billion), and trade credit ($12 billion). At the same time, the business sector's financial asset holdings increased by $30 billion, mainly in the form of trade credit ($15 billion), various loans ($3 billion), and consumer credit ($2 billion). Since all nonfinancial sectors obtained new funds predominately through financial intermediaries, the result was an enormous accumulation (over $90 billion) of financial assets, matched by an almost equal increase in liabilities in the financial sectors. As the table shows, roughly one-half of this amount was accounted for by commercial banks and the other half by nonbank financial institutions.

What is the general economic significance of this great accumulation of financial assets and liabilities in our economy? Some of the important questions arising in this connection are: What is the effect of the concentration of stock and bond holdings in financial institutions on security yields and prices? What effect does this concentration have on the rate of saving and investment in real assets? How does the growing complexity of financial asset-liability interrelationships affect the growth and stability of our economy in terms of real output and wealth? We are not as yet in a position to give definitive answers to such questions, and additional analytical work in this direction is clearly called for.

SUMMARY

The flow-of-funds accounts represent an important complement to the other two national accounting systems: the national income and the input–output accounts. They encompass all transactions that involve transfers of credit and/or money, including those representing purchase and sale of existing assets as well as those relating to purchases and sales of current output.

In combination with the national income accounts, the flow-of-funds accounts provide a comprehensive and internally consistent body of data enabling us to gain new insights into the working of and interdependence between financial markets and goods and services markets. This should be of importance both to economic theorists, concerned with theoretical models, and to business economists, interested in improved forecasting techniques. Unfortunately, the potential usefulness of the flow-of-funds system has not yet been fully realized and much additional work is required in this area.

The importance of financial transactions in our economy may be illustrated by a few figures, as follows: The household sector in 1968 had an excess of saving over capital expenditures amounting to $34 billion. The business and government sectors required external financing to the extent of $20 billion and $10 billion, respectively. But only a minor part of the households' savings was channeled into the business and government sectors directly. The predominant part was transferred via financial intermediaries, and the various financial transactions involved resulted in an asset (and liability) accumulation of over $90 billion in the financial sectors.

Some important questions arise as to the general economic significance of the enormous accumulation of financial assets and liabilities in our economic system. How does it affect the rate of growth and stability of the economy in terms of real output and wealth? What is the effect of the growing concentration of stock and bond holdings in financial institutions on security prices and yields, the rate of personal savings, and the rates of personal and business investment in real assets? We have as yet no definitive answers to such questions, and further analytical work in this direction is clearly called for.

SELECTED REFERENCES

Copeland, M. A.: *A Study of Moneyflows in the United States*, National Bureau of Economic Research, New York, 1952.

Flow of Funds in the United States, 1939–1953, Board of Governors of the Federal Reserve System, 1955.

Friedland, Seymour: *The Economics of Corporate Finance*, chap. 16, Prentice-Hall, Inc., Englewood-Cliffs, N.J., 1966.

Powelson, John P.: *National Income and Flow-of-funds Analysis*, McGraw-Hill Book Co., New York, 1960.

"Revision of Flow of Funds Accounts," *Federal Reserve Bulletin*, vol. 48, no. 1, November, 1962.

Ritter, Lawrence S.: "The Flow of Funds Accounts: A Framework for Financial Analysis," *The Bulletin*, New York University, Graduate School of Business Administration, Institute of Finance, no. 52, August, 1968.

12
Theory of Interest

In the preceding two chapters we have discussed the basic function performed by the capital market, the institutions operating in it, and a system of flow-of-funds accounts which can be used as a framework for financial analysis. Our next task is to analyze the major factors determining the volume of capital fund flows in a given period and the fluctuations in these flows from one period to another.

In general, it is clear that a competitive capital market must have some sort of pricing mechanism, similar to those found in commodity markets. A competitive market price is determined by the aggregate demand and supply functions, which are the sums of all individual demanders' and suppliers' functions, respectively. Once the market price is established, each individual transactor takes it as given and adjusts the quantity he wants to buy (or sell) accordingly. If this price is a true equilibrium price, it will "clear" the market. If it is not, an adjustment process will take place which will bring the price up (or down) to the equilibrium level.

The price of capital funds is defined as the interest rate paid for their use per unit of time. In our actual capital market, different types of funds do not, of course, command the same price. Interest rates vary according to the term to maturity and the financial risks involved. The term structure of interest rates will be discussed in Chapter 15. In this chapter, however, we shall assume that capital funds are homogeneous and that the market determines the interest rate applicable to all of them. We shall also assume here that the capital market is free of government interference.

The factors determining the demand for funds from business firms have already been discussed at considerable length in Part One. It has been shown that the expected earnings-costs relationships and the investment risk considerations play a dominant role in shaping up the demand schedules. The supply of funds to the market is generally dependent on the existence in the system of economic units which are able to save.[1] However, while the ability to save is a necessary condition, it is not a sufficient one. Once a decision to save has been made, a second decision is required: whether to hold the amount saved in liquid (monetary) form or to invest it in some profit-earning assets. The older (nonmonetary) theories tended to minimize the importance of the latter decision. It was assumed that saving, in general, was interest-elastic and that the entire amount saved, with minor exceptions, was available for investment as long as any positive rate of return could be obtained. In contrast, the newer (monetary) theories consider the liquidity-versus-earnings decisions to be of central importance. Saving, as such, is regarded as having a low (or even zero) interest elasticity, but the amount of funds the savers wish to hold liquid—and, consequently, the amount they wish to invest—is considered to be much more interest-elastic.

We shall begin our review by outlining briefly the nonmonetary theories of E. von Böhm-Bawerk and Irving Fisher.

BÖHM–BAWERK'S THEORY

According to Böhm-Bawerk, there are three basic reasons for the existence of positive interest rates which represent premiums on present goods when exchanged for future goods.

The first reason is found in the difference between present and future needs relative to the scarcity of means to meet these needs. Thus, young people whose earning capacity is expected to increase with time will value future goods less highly than present goods because of the diminishing marginal utility of income. In some cases, the value of present goods relative to future ones rises sharply because of illness, unexpected loss of property, etc. Although these factors may sometimes work in reverse, present possession of durable assets generally has the advantage of making it possible for the owner to enjoy either present or future consumption at his discretion,

---

[1] Occasionally, a unit may supply funds by reducing its previously accumulated cash balance. But a continual flow of capital funds may result only from continual saving.

whereas future possession confines him to the latter alternative. Therefore, a premium or "agio" may normally be expected in favor of presently available assets.

The second reason is the tendency to underestimate the future relative to the present (a sort of shortsightedness or myopia), which Böhm-Bawerk attributes to lack of imagination, limited willpower, and the shortness and uncertainty of life. Böhm-Bawerk was criticized by some economists for introducing this reason because it implies irrationality of behavior. This is not, however, a methodologically sound criticism: any motives significantly affecting human behavior, whether rational or not, must be taken into account by theoretical as well as empirical economics.

It has also been pointed out that the existence of myopia, which tends to put a premium on present goods, may be offset, at least partially if not fully, by the incentive to save for "the rainy day" or for the benefit of one's heirs, which tends to exert the opposite effect. While the uncertainties of the future may induce some people to discount heavily future needs and to adopt the "live it up" attitude at the present, they may, at the same time, generate in other people exaggerated fears of possible future hardships and make them redouble their efforts to build up reserves for contingencies.

The third reason for interest is found in the "technical superiority" of present over future goods. This term, as used by Böhm-Bawerk, has a specific meaning which must be clearly understood. It does not, of course, imply that present instruments of production generally have better physical qualities than future instruments are expected to have. But Böhm-Bawerk's theory of production was based on the proposition that longer (roundabout) methods of production generally lead to greater results than shorter (direct) methods. The lengthening of the period of production will generally increase total product, although the rate of increase may diminish after a certain point. It follows that a given input of goods (and labor) made now will result in a greater output at any given time in the future than an equivalent input made later. Or, to put it differently, if the input is postponed from the present into the future, an equivalent output can be realized only at a correspondingly later date.

The concept of "period of production," which may seem straightforward and clear at first glance, is actually a complex and difficult one. Suppose a new productive process is started today and the finished product is expected to be available in 90 days. If we assume that labor will be used during this process continually, it is clear that the first dose of labor—applied today—will have a "waiting period" of 90 days, the second dose—applied tomorrow—will have to wait only 89 days, etc. If we know the quantities of labor used day after day (which need not be equal to one another), we may then compute the average waiting period for the entire amount of labor involved.

But labor is not usually the only input involved. In virtually all modern productive processes some durable equipment and some raw materials are required. These materials and equipment have been produced by an earlier input of labor and material goods; and the latter have, in their turn, been produced by a still earlier input of labor and goods. Thus, in principle, the production period for most goods is of virtually infinite duration: the finished goods that become available today are the result of inputs of the primary factors (labor and land) made over a period of time going back to the dawn of our civilization.

Böhm-Bawerk proposed a rather involved and questionable procedure for measuring the average period of production or, as he calls it, the average waiting time. This gave rise to a considerable amount of criticism and countercriticism in the economic literature. Some economists (J. B. Clark and F. H. Knight) came to the conclusion that the average period cannot be meaningfully calculated and that the concept is not, therefore, an operationally useful one. Others have defended the concept and proposed various elaborations and refinements.

In recent years, the period-of-production concept has not been prominent in either theoretical or empirical economic investigations. However, a related concept—the capital-output ratio—has become an accepted and important tool of economic analysis, on both the theoretical and the empirical levels. We shall discuss it in Chapter 16.

The conceptual intricacies and the problems of actual measurement of the average production period need not concern us here in any detail. It is important to point out, however, that there is no disagreement among economists concerning the basic proposition that time is an essential element in modern production and that the adoption and financing of more time-consuming (roundabout) processes is generally considered in relation to the expected gain in productivity.[2] There would obviously be no point in lengthening the production period without any output gain, unless the consumers in the system were generally characterized by a negative time preference (i.e., a general preference for postponing consumption from the present into the future).

It is clear that in a system characterized by a positive or neutral time preference the existence of business loans at a positive rate of interest is dependent upon the greater productivity of roundabout processes. Consumer loans, on the other hand, could exist even in the absence of the productivity factor. The consumers who are willing to borrow at a positive interest rate obviously must have a positive time preference. Those who are willing to lend, on the other hand, may have a negative, neutral, or even

---

[2] In determining productivity gains, changes in quality as well as quantity of the product must, of course, be taken into account. The classical example is the process of aging, and the resulting increase in quality and value, in the production of wine.

positive time preference—of a lesser degree than that of the borrowers. If, in a given situation, the marginal rate of substitution of next year's goods for this year's goods is 1.1 for individual A and 1.05 for individual B, then any interest rate smaller than 10 percent but larger than 5 percent should induce the former to borrow and the latter to lend funds. The individual amounts demanded and supplied may, of course, vary widely, but the total amounts of borrowing and lending in the system must be equalized through interest rate adjustments.

FISHER'S THEORY

I. Fisher's theory of interest was built on the foundations laid by Böhm-Bawerk but was developed with greater precision and mathematical elegance. He presented it in both geometric and algebraic terms.

Geometrically, Fisher's theory may be expressed by drawing a set of "opportunity," "willingness," and interest rate curves. What he calls the *opportunity curve* (*PP* in Figure 12-1) is the technical-transformation curve showing net productivity of capital. It is concave to the origin owing to the diminishing returns from sacrificing part of present income to obtain greater future income. The greater the productivity of capital, the steeper is the

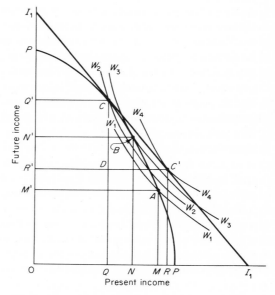

Figure 12-1   Fisher's theory: borrower's optimal position.

opportunity line. In a two-dimensional diagram, we can compare the present period with only one future period. Every individual is confronted with a single opportunity curve which indicates the range of possible combinations of his present and future incomes.

The *willingness curves* (WW in Figure 12-1) indicate an individual's (or the community's) time preference. They are convex to the origin owing to the diminishing marginal utility of income. Every individual is confronted with a family of willingness curves, each of them being an indifference curve indicating the rate of substitution of future income for present income at a particular level of satisfaction.

Suppose that initially an individual's position is represented by point A on the opportunity curve PP. His present income is then equal to OM and his future income to OM'. His total satisfaction in both periods is indicated by the willingness curve $W_1 W_1$. It is clear that the individual can improve his position by moving upward along the opportunity curve until he reaches point B, at which his present income is reduced from OM to ON but his future income is increased from OM' to ON'. He has now reached the willingness curve $W_3 W_3$, and this is the maximum satisfaction he can derive on the basis of his given opportunity curve, without the possibility of borrowing or lending.

Suppose now that external financing becomes available at the interest rate indicated by the slope of the straight line $I_1 I_1$, which is drawn so that it is tangent to the opportunity curve PP at point C. Without the possibility of borrowing, the individual concerned would not wish to move to that point, because it would put him on a lower willingness curve ($W_2 W_2$). But if he moves to point C, and then borrows an amount equal to QR, he will reach point C' on the $I_1 I_1$ curve. This will place him on the willingness curve $W_4 W_4$, which is higher than either $W_2 W_2$ or $W_3 W_3$. His present income, including the amount borrowed, is now OR, while his future income is OQ' (before repayment of the loan with interest) and OR' after the repayment. This combination is evidently preferable to the best one he could obtain without borrowing.

Let us now consider a situation which leads an individual to lending rather than borrowing. This is illustrated in Figure 12-2. Assuming again that his initial position is at point A, it is clear that he can improve it by moving upward along the PP curve until he reaches point B. At this point his opportunity curve is tangent to the willingness curve $W_3 W_3$, and this is the position of maximum satisfaction obtainable without borrowing or lending. Now, if we introduce the interest curve $I_1 I_1$, which is tangent to the opportunity curve at point C, the individual concerned may further improve his position by making his present income equal to OQ and then lending an amount represented by $CE = QR$. His future income will then be equal to OQ' plus EC' (the amount of the loan with the accrued interest), and he will

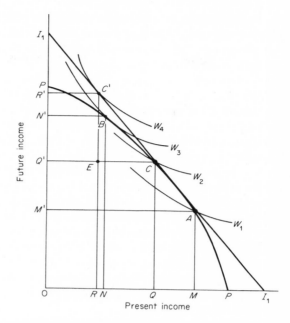

Figure 12-2 Fisher's theory: lender's optimal position.

reach point C', where the $I_1 I_1$ line is tangent to the willingness curve $W_4 W_4$, which is above the curve $W_3 W_3$.

In a closed system total amount of borrowing must equal total amount of lending. If the supply and demand for loans do not match, an equilibrium can be attained through an appropriate change in the rate of interest. Since in the above example there are only two individuals, the amount that Mr. X wishes to borrow must be equalized with the amount that Mr. Y wishes to lend. Suppose that initially the loan asked for by X ($C'D$ in Figure 12-1) exceeds the loan that Y is willing to grant (CE in Figure 12-2); this will lead to a rise in the interest rate. A higher interest rate is represented in Figure 12-3a and b by the steeper line $I_2 I_2$, which, in both cases, is tangent to the opportunity curve at a lower point than the $I_1 I_1$ line. As Figure 12-3 indicates, this will reduce the desired amount of borrowing from $C'D$ to $F'G$ and, at the same time, will increase the desired amount of lending from CE to FH. If $F'G = FH$, the system has reached an equilibrium position. If this is not so, there will be further adjustments in the interest rate until an equilibrium is attained.

The above presentation of Fisher's theory was based on the assumption of perfect foresight. When a significant risk factor is present, it must, of course, be taken into account. The model then becomes considerably more

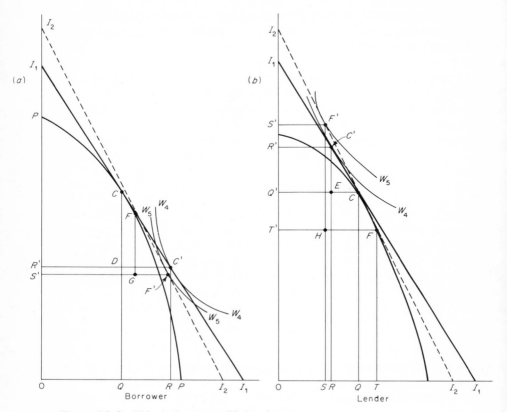

Figure 12-3 Fisher's theory: equilibrium interest rate.

complex, and we shall not discuss it here. However, it may be pointed out very briefly that, under conditions of uncertainty, an investor will not necessarily select the opportunity with the highest anticipated return. Each opportunity will have to be adjusted for the risk associated with it. One could then interpret an opportunity curve, such as that drawn in Figure 12-1, as the locus of points representing certainty equivalents of uncertain income streams.

    An investor's willingness curve would also be affected by the risk associated with substituting future income for the present one. Obviously, the higher the risk associated with this substitution, the greater must be the rate at which future income is discounted.[3]

    Let us now turn to an algebraic presentation of Fisher's theory which

---

[3] Fisher himself recognized the importance of the uncertainty factor. Further work in this area has been done by other economists, notably J. Hirshleifer (see the selected references at the end of this chapter).

has the advantage of being able to demonstrate his basic propositions in a system consisting of many instead of just two individuals. The basic elements of the system are as follows:[4]

1. Definition of income streams. Let $y_1', y_1'', y_1''', \ldots, y_1{}^m$ denote the annual amounts in the income stream of Individual 1 during the years 1 to m, prior to borrowing or lending, and let $x_1', x_1'', \ldots, x_1{}^m$ represent the annual receipts or payments resulting from borrowing, lending, or repayment of loans (including interest). His complete income stream may then be written as

$$(y_1' + x_1'), (y_1'' + x_1''), \ldots, (y_1{}^m + x_1{}^m)$$

The same notation can be applied to Individuals 2, 3, $\ldots$, n by appropriate changes in the subscript.

2. Impatience Principle A states that individual time preferences (marginal rates of substitution between income of one year and that of another) are functions of the prospective income streams during the current and all future years:

$$f_i{}^j = F_i{}^j[(y_i{}^j + x_i{}^j), (y_i{}^{j+1} + x_i{}^{j+1}), \ldots, (y_i{}^m + x_i{}^m)]$$

The symbol $f_i{}^j$ represents individual i's marginal rate of substitution between income of the year j and the year $j + 1$. If there are n individuals in the system, the total number of equations for the system as a whole is $n(m - 1)$.

3. Impatience Principle B states that the marginal rates of time preference must be equal to the corresponding rates of interest:

$$f_i{}^j = r^i$$

where r^i represents the rate of interest for one year: from j to $j + 1$.

The number of such equations in the system is also equal to $n(m - 1)$.

4. Market Principle A states that the total amount of borrowing must equal the total amount of lending (including payment and receipt of interest) in each year. Or, in other words, the market for loans must always be cleared:

$$x_1{}^j + x_2{}^j + x_3{}^j + \cdots + x_n{}^j = 0$$

There are m such equations in the system: one for each year.

---

[4] Our brief presentation is based on Fisher's original statement in *The Theory of Interest* and some minor modifications made by J. W. Conard in his *Introduction to the Theory of Interest*. (Irving Fisher, *The Theory of Interest*, The Macmillan Co., New York, 1930; Joseph W. Conard, *An Introduction to the Theory of Interest*, University of California Press, Berkeley and Los Angeles, 1963.)

5. *Market Principle B* expresses the equivalence of loans and discounted repayments. In other words, it states that the sum of all changes in the present value of an individual's income resulting from all future borrowing and repayments must equal zero:

$$x'_1 + \frac{x''_1}{1 + r'} + \frac{x'''_1}{(1 + r')(1 + r'')} + \cdots$$

$$+ \frac{x_1{}^m}{(1 + r')(1 + r'') \cdots (1 + r^{m-1})} = 0$$

There are n such equations in the system: one for each individual.

6. *Opportunity Principle A* relates to the range of possible combinations of different years' income streams available to each individual. It is assumed that, in considering appropriate income combinations for any two years, an individual will always move along his opportunity curve for these years, the shape of which is determined by technical conditions. The choices available to each individual over the entire period of m years may be represented by an equation of the following form:

$$\phi_i(y'_i, y''_i, \ldots, y_i{}^m) = 0$$

Since there are n individuals, there are n such equations in the system.

7. *Opportunity Principle B* states that the present value of each individual's income stream is maximized when the marginal rate of return between any one year and the succeeding year is equal to the rate of interest between the same two years:

$$S_i{}^j = r^j$$

For each individual there are $m - 1$ such equations, and the total number of equations in the system is $n(m - 1)$.

The marginal rate of return over cost, S, is defined as

$$S_i{}^j = -\frac{\partial y_i{}^{j+1}}{\partial y_i{}^j} - 1$$

and there are $n(m - 1)$ such equations for the system as a whole.

The sum of all the equations stated above is:

Impatience Principle A	$n(m-1)$
Impatience Principle B	$n(m-1)$
Market Principle A	m
Market Principle B	n
Opportunity Principle A	n
Opportunity Principle B	$2n(m-1)$
Total	$4mn + m - 2n$

It can be shown, however, that one equation is not independent but can be derived from the others. Thus, if we add together the n equations representing Market Principle B, we obtain

$$x'_1 + x'_2 + \cdots + x'_n + \frac{x''_1 + x''_2 + x''_3 + \cdots + x''_n}{1 + r'} + \cdots$$
$$+ \frac{x_1{}^m + x_2{}^m + \cdots + x_n{}^m}{(1 + r')(1 + r'') \cdots (1 + r^{m-1})} = 0$$

But since the numerator of each fraction is equal to zero (according to Market Principle A), the above equation reduces to

$$x'_1 + x'_2 + \cdots + x'_n = 0$$

which is precisely the first equation in the set representing Market Principle A. Consequently, one equation in the combined set of equations expressing Market Principles A and B is redundant.

We may thus state that the number of *independent* equations in the system is equal to:

$$4mn + m - 2n - 1$$

The number of unknowns in the system is:

The annual income of each individual before borrowing (lending), $y_i{}^j$	mn unknowns
The additional receipts from borrowing (lending), $x_i{}^j$	mn unknowns
The marginal rate of substitution, $f_i{}^j$	$n(m-1)$ unknowns
The interest rate between each pair of successive years	$m-1$ unknowns
The marginal rate of return over cost, $S_i{}^j$	$n(m-1)$ unknowns
Total	$4mn + m - 2n - 1$

Thus, the number of unknowns is equal to the number of independent equations, and this suggests that the system may have a determinate solution if certain other conditions are satisfied.

A SIMPLE KEYNESIAN MODEL

The theories considered above are referred to as nonmonetary theories because they do not specifically include the quantity of money and its velocity among the factors determining the interest rate. Essentially, they are concerned with real-income streams and their redistribution over time. When an individual abstains from present consumption (saves), he is assumed to make an investment which will increase his consumption at some future time. There is no accumulation of money (hoarding) to any significant extent.

In contrast, the theories which we shall review in this and the following sections consider monetary factors to be of major importance in the determination of interest rates. Monetary theories of interest are not new. In fact, their roots are found in the writings of early preclassical economists. On the other hand, the classical doctrine developed during the nineteenth century focused attention on "real" rather than "monetary" factors. The modern revival of monetary theories has taken place independently in Sweden and Great Britain, and has developed into three different approaches or schools. The Swedish approach was initiated by Kurt Wicksell and developed further by B. Ohlin, E. Lindahl, and others. In England, the theory was given its most novel and challenging form by John M. Keynes. A different approach, closer to that taken by the Swedish economists, was developed by D. H. Robertson.

We shall first review the Keynesian theory, which has become known as the *liquidity-preference theory.*

In launching his vigorous attack on what he called the "classical" theory of interest, Keynes argued as follows:

> The psychological time-preferences of an individual require two distinct sets of decisions to carry them out completely. The first is concerned with that aspect of time-preference which I have called the propensity to consume, which, operating under the influence of the various motives set forth in Book III, determines for each individual how much of his income he will consume and how much he will reserve in some form of command over future consumption.
>
> But this decision having been made, there is a further decision which awaits him, namely, in what form he will hold the command over future consumption which he has reserved, whether out of his current income or from previous savings. Does he want to hold it in the form of

immediate liquid command (i.e., in money or its equivalent)? Or is he prepared to part with immediate command for a specified or indefinite period, leaving it to future market conditions to determine on what terms he can, if necessary, convert deferred command over specific goods into immediate command over goods in general? In other words, what is the degree of his liquidity-preference—where an individual's liquidity-preference is given by a schedule of the amounts of his resources, valued in terms of money or of wage-units, which he will wish to retain in the form of money in different sets of circumstances?

   We shall find that the mistake in the accepted theories of the rate of interest lies in their attempting to derive the rate of interest from the first of these two constituents of psychological time-preference to the neglect of the second; and it is this neglect which we must endeavor to repair.[5]

Keynes considered it obvious that the rate of interest cannot be a return on saving or waiting as such, because a man who saves and hoards the entire amount earns no interest at all. In order to receive interest, the saver must take the second step and part with liquidity in exchange for a debt to be repaid at a specified future time. Thus, the interest rate is determined by the liquidity preference and the available quantity of money. Given the interest rate and the schedule of the marginal efficiency of capital, the amount of investment may be derived. And once the amount of investment has been determined, the equilibrium level of national income may be found, if the propensity to consume is known.

   The most peculiar characteristic of this theory, which has provoked a long controversy, is that it seemingly runs counter to the usual conception of the interest rate as the price of loanable funds determined by the supply and demand factors in the capital market. It appears as though in the Keynesian system a change in the business demand for funds (because of a shift in the marginal efficiency of capital schedule) would affect only the volume of investment but not the interest rate. The latter would have to be considered by business firms as given. It will be seen, however, that in the complete Keynesian system the interest rate is not determined by the supply and demand for money alone—in isolation from all the other factors. The model consists of a number of equations (functions), which must be solved simultaneously in order to find the equilibrium values of all the variables concerned. Both the supply and the demand for loanable funds are implicitly included in such a model. But before we describe it, let us examine the factors which determine the liquidity-preference function. Keynes has classified the motives for holding cash as follows:

[5] *The General Theory of Employment, Interest and Money*, Macmillan & Co., Ltd., London, 1936, pp. 166–167.

1. The transactions motive arises because of differences in the time distributions of payments and receipts, in the case of both households and business firms. With a given velocity of money, the transactions demand for cash increases proportionately with income.

2. The precautionary motive relates to the need of holding cash as a reserve against unforeseen decline in receipts or increase in expenditures. The precautionary demand varies directly with the degree of uncertainty about the future felt by households and firms. But it is also related to income, because, with a given degree of uncertainty, a greater reserve is needed as the flow of receipts and payments becomes larger.

3. The speculative motive relates to the desire to hold cash in order to be able to take advantage of the expected future variations in interest rates and security prices. The speculative demand is a function of the interest rate: if the rate drops, the desire to hold cash increases because the reward for investment is reduced and, at the same time, the probability of a future rise in the rate (and a corresponding decline in security prices) is increased. If the rate rises, the reverse tendency is likely to develop.

4. The finance motive represents the desire to have a "revolving fund" from which money can flow out into actual investments. If the interest rate falls, business firms are likely to demand more funds at present in order to accumulate resources needed to finance the expected future projects. This demand, then, also varies inversely with the interest rate.

Total demand for cash is, of course, the sum of the four components listed above. It depends on the amount of income, the degree of uncertainty regarding future business conditions, and the expectations concerning the future rate of variations. In a simple Keynesian model it has become customary to combine the transactions and precautionary motives into one function, and the speculative and the finance motives into a second function. Thus, we may write

$$L = L_1(Y) + L_2(i)$$

where Y is income and i is the interest rate.

The supply of money in the economy, M, is determined by the banking system (including the central bank authorities). In the simplest model it may be taken as given. We then have:

$$M = L_1(Y) + L_2(i)$$

$$M = \text{given}$$

In a slightly more complex model it may be assumed that M is also a function of i: the banking system is willing and able to extend more loans and thus create more deposits when the interest rate is higher. We may then write:

$$M = M(i)$$

The other equations in the system are as follows:

$$Y = C + I$$

This is an accounting identity: income must be equal to the sum of consumption and private investment expenditures, since government is excluded from this simple system.

$$C = C(Y)$$

This is a simplified consumption function: the amount consumed is dependent on current income alone.

$$I = I(i)$$

This is a simplified business investment function: the amount invested is dependent on the interest rate alone.

Thus, we have six equations and six unknowns: L, M, i, Y, C, and I. If the parameter values in the equations describing the liquidity preference, the supply of money, the consumption function, and the investment function are known, a simultaneous solution will yield the numerical values of all the variables concerned. As presented above, the system does not explicitly include saving. But since saving is defined as $Y - C$, it is clear that it must always be equal to I. (See footnote 6.) It should also be clear that if the consumption function is known, the savings function can easily be derived, since the following relation must always hold:

$$C(Y) + S(Y) = Y$$

This simple model may be conveniently illustrated by a diagram, such as Figure 12-4, which consists of four quadrants. The MEC curve in Quadrant I represents the investment function; the S line in Quadrant II is the saving function; the L_1 line in Quadrant III shows the transaction demand for money; and the L_2 curve in Quadrant IV indicates the speculative demand for money. Total supply of money is equal to OD and is invariant to interest

---

6 This model is concerned only with the realized values of saving and investment. The concepts of planned saving and planned investment, which may differ from each other, are discussed later.

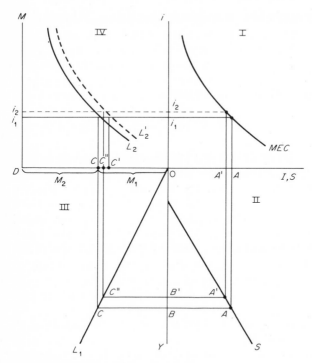

Figure 12-4 Simple Keynesian model.

rate, as indicated by the vertical line DM in Quadrant IV. If the interest rate is equal to Oi_1, investment is measured by OA and saving by BA (which is equal to OA). National income is then equal to OB, the transaction cash balances are measured by OC and the desired speculative cash balances are represented by CD. The system is in an equilibrium position.

Suppose now that, as the result of a change in expectations, the liquidity preference becomes stronger and the curve L_2 moves to a higher position, as indicated by the dotted line L_2'. At the current interest rate Oi_1, the people would wish to hold a larger amount of speculative cash DC'. But since the total amount of cash is fixed, this could be done only by reducing the transaction balances, which would throw the system into a disequilibrium. As the figure indicates, a new equilibrium position can be attained only at a higher rate of interest Oi_2, which will reduce investment and saving to $OA' = B'A'$, national income to OB', and the transaction cash balances to OC''. The speculative balances will now be equal to DC'', which is larger than DC but smaller than DC'.

Neither the chart nor the underlying equations, however, show us the process by which a new equilibrium can be reached. Since the system is a static one, it can yield only the equilibrium values of the variables for any given set of parameters. When one or more of the parameters are changed, new equilibrium values can be derived, but no light is thrown on the "equilibrium path." In order to elucidate the chain of events that will lead to a new equilibrium, following an initial change in the people's liquidity preference, let us consider the following example. Assume that initially gross national product is $200 million and gross saving is $30 million. Since the system is in an equilibrium position and the amount of money remains constant, it follows that both the speculative and the transaction cash balances also remain constant and the entire amount saved is made available to industry for investment purposes. Suppose that the total amount of money is $100 million, of which $60 million represents the transaction cash and $40 million the speculative balances. Suppose also that business internal financing consists only of depreciation allowances, amounting to $10 million, and that the net investment ($20 million) is financed by a sale of perpetual bonds which are all alike, each paying $1 annually as interest. Then, if the interest rate is 5 percent, the price of each bond is $20 and the industry has to sell 1,000,000 bonds in order to raise the required amount of external funds.

Now, a rise in the liquidity preference (the L_2 curve in the figure) means that people are no longer willing to buy $20 million worth of bonds annually at the 5 percent interest rate. At this rate, they prefer to increase their speculative cash balances and reduce bond purchases correspondingly.

Assume that they are now willing to purchase only 750,000 bonds at $20 each, thus investing a total of $15 million and adding $5 million to the cash balances. Since the industry's investment function has not changed and it still wishes to borrow $20 million at the 5 percent rate, it is clear that there is now an excess supply of bonds in the capital market and this must lead to a fall in bond prices or, to put it differently, a rise in the interest rate. As the price of the bonds declines, the incentive to borrow is weakened, while the incentive to lend is strengthened. Suppose that at the price of $16.67 (which makes the interest rate 6 percent) the industry is willing to sell 959,000 bonds, thus borrowing a total of $16 million, and that this is equal to the amount which the lenders are willing to loan at 6 percent. At this rate, then, the equilibrium in the capital market is reestablished.[7]

---

[7] Of course, when the interest rate begins to rise there must be a drop not only in the price of the new bonds offered by industry but also in the price of the old bonds already owned by the public. Suppose that 10,000,000 bonds were outstanding at the beginning of the period. At 5 percent their total value is $200 million, but at 6 percent it is reduced to $166.67 million. This may induce some old bondholders, who expect a further drop in the price, to convert their holdings into cash. But at the same time other individuals may decide to convert their previously accumulated cash balances into bonds when the price has dropped to $16.67. If, on balance, there is an excess supply of old bonds, this must lead to a further decline in the price of both the old and the new bonds or, in other words, to a further rise in the interest rate. In our example, we assume, however, that at 6 percent the old bondholders, on balance, do not wish to either invest or disinvest and that the amount available for investment out of current savings is invested in newly issued bonds.

But investment is now reduced from $20 million to $16 million per year, and so is saving. The GNP must also decline, and this will reduce the need for transaction cash balances. Suppose that income drops from $200 million to $180 million and the required transaction cash from $60 to $56 million. The speculative balances are increased from $40 million to $44 million. If the system's new position is an equilibrium one, the entire amount of saving must again be fully invested in securities and the speculative and transaction cash balances must remain at the new levels as long as the interest rate remains unchanged.

We have thus been able to describe the process of transition from one equilibrium position to another in the familiar terms of supply and demand adjustments in the capital market. But we may also describe the same process in different terms, without changing the substance of our story in any way. Instead of saying that an increase in the liquidity preference creates an excess supply of bonds in the securities market, we may say that it creates an excess demand for cash. And instead of saying that the excess supply of bonds leads to a fall in their price (in terms of money), we may say that the excess demand for cash leads to a rise in the price of cash in terms of bonds (i.e., the price of immediate command over goods in terms of deferred command).

Thus, at the interest rate of 5 percent the price of $1 in cash available now in terms of cash available a year from now is $1.05. If the interest rate rises to 6 percent, the price of presently available cash becomes $1.06 in terms of cash deferred for one year. It should be clear, of course, that the interest rate which eliminates the excess supply of bonds must also eliminate the excess demand for cash. In other words, an equilibrium position in the securities market implies an equilibrium cash position, and vice versa.[8]

THE LOANABLE FUND THEORY

Let us now consider the loanable-fund variant of the monetary interest theory. The sources of loanable funds are (1) personal saving, S_P, (2) business saving (depreciation allowances and retained profits), S_b, and (3) new credit money created by commercial banks, ΔM. Total supply is the sum of these three components less the amount H which the households and firms wish to add to their cash balances for either transaction or speculative purposes. We may therefore write:

$$S_L = S_p + S_b + \Delta M - H$$

---

[8] It is customary to refer to the process of exchanging cash for securities as a "securities market," i.e., the market in which securities are bought and sold for money. Logically, however, one could describe the same process as a "cash market," in which money is "bought" and "sold" for securities.

Total demand for capital funds is the sum of the amounts demanded by (1) business firms engaged in new investment D_b, (2) households using consumer credit D_c, and (3) the government when it sells new securities D_g. We may write:

$$D_L = D_b + D_c + D_g$$

In an equilibrium, we must have $D_L = S_L$, or

$$S_p + S_b + \Delta M - H = D_b + D_c + D_g$$

By subtracting consumer loans from personal saving we may, however, obtain the amount of *net* personal saving, S_{pn}, and rewrite the last equation as follows:

$$S_{pn} + S_b + \Delta M - H = D_b + D_g$$

Furthermore, if we assume that net business demand for loanable funds, D_{bn}, is equal to total investment less the available amount of internal funds (business saving), we may write:

$$S_{pn} - H + \Delta M = D_{bn} + D_g$$

or

$$S_{pn} = D_{bn} + D_g + H - \Delta M$$

Now, the basic definitional equations in national income accounting are:

$$Y = C + I + G$$

and

$$Y = C + S_{pn} + S_b + T$$

where G represents government purchases of goods and services and T stands for taxes (net of transfer payments). It follows that:

$$I + G = S_{pn} + S_b + T$$
$$S_{pn} + S_b = I + G - T$$
$$S_{pn} = (I - S_b) + (G - T)$$

The amount $I - S_b$ is equal to net business demand for loanable funds, as defined above. The amount $G - T$ represents government deficit which must be covered by borrowing, i.e., selling securities. We may, therefore, write:

$$S_{pn} = D_{bn} + D_g$$

But we have shown above that in an equilibrium net personal saving is also equal to

$$S_{pn} = D_{bn} + D_g + H - \Delta M$$

It follows that in an equilibrium we must have $H - \Delta M = 0$ or $H = \Delta M$. The amount of the desired increase in cash balances must be equal to the amount of new money which the banks are willing to create.

The loanable funds theory is presented in diagrammatic terms in Figure 12-5. The curve D_{bn} represents net business demand and the curve $D_{bn} + D_g$ the sum of net business and government demands for loanable funds. The vertical line S_{pn} represents net personal saving (which is assumed to be invariant to the interest rate), and the curve $S_{pn} - H$ indicates the amounts of loanable funds which can be obtained from the personal sector at various interest rates. As the figure indicates, the entire amount of net personal saving would be available to the capital market if the rate of interest were equal to i_1. But at this rate the banks would be willing to extend new credit amounting to ΔM and the total supply of loanable funds from the

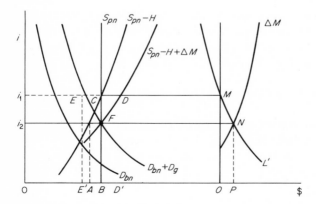

Figure 12-5 Loanable fund theory.

household and banking sectors $(S_{pn} - H + \Delta M)$ would substantially exceed total demand for loanable funds by the industrial and government sectors $(D_{bn} + D_g)$. Clearly, then, i_1 is not an equilibrium rate. The total supply and total demand curves cross at point F, with the interest rate being equal to i_2. At this rate the household sector wishes to lend an amount equal to OA and add to its cash balances an amount equal to AB. But the new lending—and new money—supplied by the banks is also equal to AB, which brings the loanable fund market to an equilibrium and, at the same time, balances the desire to hold cash with the available supply of money.

The right-hand part of the diagram demonstrates explicitly the equality between the supply and demand for new money. It should be noted that in this case the liquidity-preference curve L' represents not the total amount of cash that the households wish to hold, but only the *additional* amounts desired at different interest rates. Correspondingly, the ΔM curve represents not the total stock of money, but only the amounts that the banks are willing to add to the existing stock at varying interest rates.

THE GENERAL EQUILIBRIUM APPROACH

In a general equilibrium analysis the markets for all goods, services, and financial instruments are considered to be interrelated parts of an integrated economic system. The demand for and supply of any particular good in such a system are determined not only by its own price but by the prices of all other goods, too. Interest, as the price of capital funds, must also be included in the demand and supply functions for every good, and all goods prices must be included in the demand and supply functions for capital funds.

In order to expound the general equilibrium approach, we shall consider a highly simplified model of an exchange economy, in which there is no production at all but in which each individual is "endowed" with certain quantities of goods and money at the beginning of each period and is free to adjust his stocks by sales to or purchases from other individuals during the period. Initially, we assume that there are no loanable funds and no interest in the system. We also assume that:

1. There are n goods in the system, whose prices, in terms of money, are $p_1, p_2, \ldots, p_n$, respectively.
2. There is a stock of money, M, the price of money in terms of itself being, of course, equal to $1 : p_m = 1$.
3. There are k individuals in the system, the initial stocks of goods held by the jth individual being $\bar{x}_{j1}, \bar{x}_{j2}, \ldots, \bar{x}_{jn}$, and his initial stock of money being $\bar{m}_j$.
4. The jth individual's demand for each good (the quantity he wishes to retain) is $x_{j1}, x_{j2}, \ldots, x_{jn}$, and his demand for money is m_j.

5. The individual's demand for each good is a function of all n prices:

$$x_{j1} = f_1(p_1 \cdots p_n)$$
$$x_{j2} = f_2(p_1 \cdots p_n)$$
$$\cdots \cdots \cdots \cdots$$
$$x_{jn} = f_n(p_1 \cdots p_n)$$

6. The quantity $x_{j1} - \bar{x}_{j1} = z_{j1}$, if positive, represents the jth individual's excess demand for good 1. If negative, it represents his excess supply of good 1.

Total initial stock of good 1 in the system is equal to the sum of all individual holdings:

$$\bar{X}_1 = \sum_{j=1}^{k} \bar{x}_{j1}$$

and total demand for good 1 is equal to the sum of all individual demands:

$$X_1 = \sum_{j=1}^{k} x_{j1}$$

Total stock of money is equal to the sum of individual cash balances, and total demand for money is equal to the sum of individual demands:

$$\bar{M} = \sum_{j=1}^{k} \bar{m}_j \qquad \text{and} \qquad M = \sum_{j=1}^{k} m_j$$

Since there is no production in this system, it is clear that in an equilibrium we must have

$$X_1 = \bar{X}_1 \qquad \text{and} \qquad Z_1 = 0$$
$$\vdots$$
$$X_n = \bar{X}_n \qquad \text{and} \qquad Z_n = 0$$
$$M = \bar{M} \qquad \text{and} \qquad Z_m = 0$$

We thus have $n + 1$ equations but only n unknowns: $P_1 \cdots P_n$. However, it can be easily shown that one of the equations follows from the rest and is not, therefore an independent function.

An individual's demand for money must be equal to his initial cash balance plus (minus) the amount by which his desired sales of goods exceed (fall short of) his desired purchases of goods. In other words, it must equal his initial money stock plus the net algebraic sum of his excess demands for and excess supplies of various goods:

$$m_j = \overline{m}_j - \sum_{i=1}^{n} z_{ji} p_i$$

An individual's excess demand for money is equal to:

$$z_{jm} = -\sum_{i=1}^{n} z_i p_i$$

For the system as a whole, we have:

$$M = \overline{M} - \sum_{i=1}^{n} Z_i p_i$$

But we know that in an equilibrium the sum of all excess demands and supplies of goods must be equal to zero. It follows that in an equilibrium we must also have:

$$M = \overline{M} \qquad \text{and} \qquad Z_m = 0$$

To put it differently, when the n goods equations are solved for n goods' prices, this set of prices will necessarily equilibrate not only the demand and supply of every good but in addition the demand and supply of money.

It is interesting to note that an identical solution can be obtained by using $n - 1$ goods equations plus the money equation, i.e., by leaving one of the goods equations out. The amount of money that an individual is prepared to spend on good 1, for example, must be equal to his initial money balance, plus the algebraic sum of his receipts and expenditures resulting from selling and buying other goods, minus his demand for money:

$$z_{j1} p_1 = \overline{m}_j - \sum_{i=2}^{n} z_{ji} p_i - m_j = -\left(z_{jm} + \sum_{i=2}^{n} z_{ji} p_i \right)$$

For the system as a whole, in an equilibrium position, we must have

$$Z_1 p_1 = -\left(Z_m + \sum_{i=2}^{n-1} Z_i p_i \right) = 0$$

Thus, if the equilibrium prices are found by solving the equations for goods 2 to n and the money equation, this set of prices must make $X_1 = \overline{X}_1$ and $Z_1 = 0$.

Let us now introduce loanable funds and interest into this model. We shall assume that all loans are obtained by selling bonds, and that each bond represents a promise to pay \$1 at the end of the period. If the interest rate is equal to r, the price of each bond sold at the beginning of the period is equal to $1/(1 + r)$.

The jth individual's demand for each of the n goods is a function of all goods' prices and the interest rate:

$$x_{ji} = f_i(p_1 \; \cdots \; p_n, r)$$

His demand for bonds, if he is a lender, or his supply of bonds, if he is a borrower, are also functions of all goods' prices and the interest rate:

$$x_{jb} = f_b(p_1 \; \cdots \; p_n, r)$$

Since all bonds are redeemed at the end of the period, there is no initial stock outstanding at the beginning of the period. Consequently, an individual's demand for bonds is equal to his excess demand. For the system as a whole, in an equilibrium, total demand for bonds (D_b) must equal total supply of bonds (S_b), and the excess demand must equal zero. We thus have the following system of equations:

$$X_1 = \overline{X}_1 \qquad Z_1 = 0$$
$$\vdots$$
$$X_n = \overline{X}_n \qquad Z_n = 0$$
$$D_b = S_b \qquad Z_b = 0$$
$$M = \overline{M} \qquad Z_m = 0$$

There are $n + 2$ equations, but only $n + 1$ unknowns: $p_1, \ldots, p_n$ and r. However, here again one equation follows from the rest.

An individual's demand for money must be equal to his initial cash balance plus (minus) the amount by which his desired sales of goods exceed (fall short of) his desired purchases of goods, plus (minus) the amount of bonds he wishes to sell (buy).

$$m_j = \overline{m}_j - \sum_{i=1}^{n} z_{ji} p_i - x_{jb} p_b$$

For the system as a whole we have

$$M = \overline{M} - \sum_{i=1}^{n} Z_i P_i - Z_b P_b$$

or

$$M = \overline{M}$$

because the second and third terms on the right-hand side are each equal to zero. Thus, the equilibrium may be determined by leaving the money equation out and solving n goods equations and the bonds equation for the $n + 1$ variables involved.

Alternatively, one can leave the bonds equation out and solve n goods equations and the money equation for the $n + 1$ variables concerned. An individual's demand for securities is equal to his initial cash balance plus (minus) the amount by which his desired sales of goods exceed (fall short of) his desired purchase of goods minus the amount of cash he wishes to retain.

$$x_{jb} = \overline{m}_j - \sum_{i=1}^{n} z_{ji} p_i - m_j = -\left(\sum_{i=1}^{n} z_{ji} p_i + z_{jm} \right)$$

For the system as a whole we may write

$$\sum_{j=1}^{k} x_{jb} = -\left(\sum_{i=1}^{n} Z_i p_i + Z_m \right)$$

In an equilibrium, the right-hand side of this equation must equal zero. Consequently, the algebraic sum of all the individual demands for and supplies of bonds must also equal zero. In other words, total demand for bonds must equal total supply of bonds. Thus, if we solve n goods equations and the money equation, the resulting set of goods' prices and the interest rate must satisfy the bonds equation, too.

Identical results could also be obtained by solving $n - 1$ goods equations, the money equation, and the bond equation. The remaining goods equation would then also necessarily be satisfied.

While the general equilibrium approach is useful in demonstrating the interrelationships of different markets and prices, two points should be made very clear. First, its use is not limited to a system in which the demand for each good is significantly related to the price of every other good. Such a system would, of course, be unrealistic. In the actual world, the cross elasticities of demand are relatively high between some goods (positive if they are substitutes for each other and negative if they are complementary to each other) but negligibly low between many other goods.

Thus a considerable change in the price of butter, other things being equal, would probably have a significant effect on the quantity of margarine demanded but not on the quantity of toothpaste. And a change in the price of either butter or margarine, other things being equal, could hardly be expected to produce a perceptible effect on the market demand for loanable funds. On the other hand, a simultaneous change in the prices of a substantial number of important commodities would most probably be felt in the capital market.

Secondly, the fact that one of the equations may be derived from the others does not, of course, mean that the function omitted in solving the system is in itself of no importance. If we know an individual's total resources, his expenditures on all goods other than beef, and the amount of cash he wishes to retain, we may derive his expenditures on beef. But this does not mean, of course, that he will buy beef simply because he has some money left after all other allocations have been made. He will buy beef only if he likes it, and the quantity purchased must be commensurate with its utility.[9] Similarly, an individual will lend funds to others not simply because he has some money left after all other expenditures have been determined, but because his time-preference function warrants reallocation of his income over time.

SUMMARY

In this chapter we have examined the major factors involved in interest rate determination. For simplicity's sake it has been assumed that there is only one interest rate in the system at any given time. In the first two sections, the nonmonetary theories of Böhm-Bawerk and I. Fisher are outlined. In the next two sections, the liquidity-preference and the loanable-fund variants of the modern monetary theory are discussed.

According to Böhm-Bawerk, there are three basic reasons for the existence of a positive interest rate: (1) the difference between present and future needs relative to the scarcity of means to meet these needs; (2) the tendency to underestimate future needs (consumer's myopia); and (3) the "technical superiority" of longer (roundabout) method of production.

On the foundations laid by Böhm-Bawerk, I. Fisher developed a much more elaborate theory, which can be expressed in either geometric or algebraic terms. Essentially, Fisher shows how the interest rate may be

---

[9] In the language of economic theory the purchases of beef will be made up to the point at which the ratio of its marginal utility to its price is equal to similar ratios for other goods.

derived from a set of opportunity (technical transformation) curves, willingness (time-preference) curves, and the existence of borrowing-lending facilities.

Keynes argued that the rate of interest is not a return on saving or waiting as such, but rather a return for parting with liquidity by exchanging present cash for a promise to repay cash at a specific future time. Consequently, the interest rate is determined by the liquidity preference and the available quantity of money. This seems to run counter to the usual conception of the interest rate as the price of loanable funds determined by the supply and demand factors in the capital market. It has been shown, however, that in the complete Keynesian system the supply of and demand for loanable funds are implicitly included.

The loanable fund theory brings out explicitly the process whereby the supply of capital funds, as determined by the saving propensity, the liquidity preference, and the new bank credit facilities, is equated with the demand for funds, as determined by the external-financing requirements of business and government. Although this is a different approach from that developed by Keynes, these two variants of the monetary theory are reconcilable with each other.

We have also outlined briefly the general equilibrium approach, which brings out the interdependence of all markets and prices (including the interest rate) in the economic system. It has been shown that a system in which n goods, money, and bonds of one specified type are exchanged may be represented by a set of $n + 2$ equations, one of which may, however, be derived from the others. Thus, we may leave the bond equation out and solve n goods equations and the money equation for the $n + 1$ variables concerned. This will give us a set of goods' prices and an interest rate which must satisfy the bond equation, too. Alternatively, we may include the bond equation but leave out one of the goods equations, and this will produce the same results. In either case, the interdependence between the bond market and the other markets is clearly revealed.

SELECTED REFERENCES

Blaug: *Economic Theory in Retrospect*, rev. ed., Richard D. Irwin, Inc., Homewood, Ill., 1968.
Conard, Joseph W.: *An Introduction to the Theory of Interest*, University of California Press, Berkeley and Los Angeles, 1963.
Fisher, Irving: *The Theory of Interest*, The Macmillan Company, New York, 1930.
Hahn, F. H., and F. P. R. Brechling, eds.: *The Theory of Interest Rates*, Macmillan & Co., London, 1965.
Hirshleifer, J.: "Investment Decision under Uncertainty: Choice-Theoretic Approaches," *The Quarterly Journal of Economics*, vol. 79, no. 4, November, 1965.
————: "Risk, the Discount Rate, and Investment Decisions," *American Economic Review*, vol. 51, May, 1961.

Keynes, John Maynard: *The General Theory of Employment, Interest, and Money*, Macmillan
    & Co., London, 1936.
Lutz, Friedrich A.: *The Theory of Interest*, Aldine Publishing Co., Chicago, 1968.
Patinkin, D.: *Money, Interest, and Prices*, 2d ed., Harper & Row, New York, 1965.
Smith, Warren L.: "Monetary Theories of the Rate of Interest: A Dynamic Analysis," *Review
    of Economics and Statistics*, vol. 40, February, 1958.
Tsiang, S. C.: "Liquidity Preference and Loanable Funds Theories, Multiplier and Velocity
    Analysis: A Synthesis," *The American Economic Review*, vol. 46, no. 4, September, 1956.

A Dynamic Model

The models described in Chapter 12 are static: they can be used to determine the equilibrium values of the variables concerned, i.e., the values which will enable the system to operate continually at the same level. If one or more of the parameters in the system are changed (because of exogenous factors), a static model will yield new equilibrium values; but it will not describe the "equilibrium path," i.e., the process by which the new level of activity can be reached.

In order to describe the process of change over time, the models must be "dynamized" by explicitly introducing the time factor into them: all the variables must be dated and at least some of the functional relations must involve two or more periods of time. The mathematical method most frequently employed in the construction of dynamic models is that of difference equations. This method permits one to determine the numerical values of the variables involved during consecutive *finite* periods of time.

We shall consider here only one simple dynamic model in order to show the basic characteristics of dynamic analysis as used in the economic theory in general and the theory of interest in particular.[10] Our model is as follows:

$$Y_t = C_t + I_t + G_t \tag{12-1}$$

$$C_t = a + b(Y_{t-1} - T_t) - dR_t \tag{12-2}$$

$$T_t = wY_{t-1} \tag{12-3}$$

$$I_t = e + gY_{t-1} - hR_t \tag{12-4}$$

$$L_{1_t} = kY_t \tag{12-5}$$

$$L_{2_t} = n - mR_t \tag{12-6}$$

$$L_{1_t} + L_{2_t} = M_t \tag{12-7}$$

$$M_t = p + qR_t \tag{12-8}$$

$$S_t = Y_{t-1} - C_t - T_t \tag{12-9}$$

The variables are: Y = income, C = consumption, I = investment, G = government expenditures (assumed to be given), T = the amount of taxes (imposed at a flat rate, w), R = interest rate, L_1 = transaction cash balances, L_2 = speculative cash balances, M = money supply, and S = saving.

The letters a, b, d, e, g, h, k, n, m, p, q, and w represent the parameters which are assumed to remain constant.

As can be seen, both consumption and investment in a given year are assumed here to be functions of the preceding year's income. The amount

---

[10] A very simple illustration should help to understand the nature of the "dynamics" involved. Consider first the following static model:

$$Y = C + I \qquad C = 50 + .5Y \qquad I = 20$$

Solving for Y, we find that $Y = 140$. Income will remain at this level as long as the parameters are unchanged. Now, if we change I from 20 to 40, Y will change from 140 to 180. But how will the system reach the new equilibrium position? In order to answer this question we shall "dynamize" the model by assuming that consumption responds to changes in income with a one-year lag: $C = 50 + .5(Y_{t-1})$. If $I = 20$ and $Y_{t-1} = 140$, then income will remain constant: $Y_{t-1} = Y_t = Y_{t+1} = \cdots$. But if we change I to 40 in year t and hold it constant thereafter, we shall have:

$Y_t = 50 + .5(140) + 40 = 160$	$S_t = 140 - 120 = 20$
$Y_{t+1} = 50 + .5(160) + 40 = 170$	$S_{t+1} = 160 - 130 = 30$
$Y_{t+2} = 50 + .5(170) + 40 = 175$	$S_{t+2} = 170 - 135 = 35$
. . . .	. . . .
$Y_n = 50 + .5(180) + 40 = 180$	as n approaches infinity

Thus, income will rise by 20 in year t, by an additional 10 in year $t + 1$, by an additional 5 in year $t + 2$, etc. In other words, it will move toward the new equilibrium level of 180 continually, year after year, but at a decreasing rate.

of taxes paid in a given year is also a function of last year's income. These three equations (12-2, 12-3, and 12-4) give the model its dynamic characteristics. By substituting from Equations 12-1 to 12-6 into Equation 12-7 we obtain:

$$k(a + bY_{t-1} - bwY_{t-1} - dR_t + e + gY_{t-1} - hR_t + G_t)$$
$$+ n - mR_t = p + qR_t \quad (12\text{-}10)$$

Since the value of Y_{t-1} is known, and since G_t is an exogenous variable (determined outside of the system), Equation 12-10 can be solved for R_t as follows:

$$R_t = Y_{t-1} \frac{gk + bk - bwk}{kd + kh + m + q} + \frac{k}{hd + kh + m + q} G_t$$
$$+ \frac{ak + ek + n - p}{kd + kh + m + q} \quad (12\text{-}11)$$

Equation 12-11 indicates that the interest rate in a given period depends on the previous period's income, current government expenditures, and all the parameters of the model.

A graphic illustration of the interest rate determination in a given year is presented in Figure 12-6. The straight vertical lines Y_{t-1} and M_{t-1} represent the previous year's income and the money stock at the end of the previous year, respectively. These magnitudes are given data. The

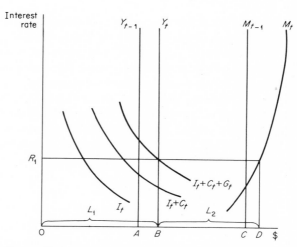

Figure 12-6 Interest rate determination in a given year (t).

curves I_t, $I_t + C_t$, and $I_t + C_t + G_t$ represent, respectively, current investment, the sum of current investment and consumption, and the sum of
investment, consumption, and government expenditure at various interest
rates. The curve M_t represents the sum of the previous year's money stock
and the additions to it which the banks are willing to make in the current
year at different interest rates. In other words, it represents total money
stock at the end of the current year.

As the figure indicates, the current year's interest rate must be equal
to OR_1 and the current year's income (Y_t) must be equal to OB. Total
money stock at the end of year t is represented by OD, the transaction cash
balances amounting to OB (which is the same as income because the value
of k in Equation 12-5 is assumed to be equal to 1) and the speculative balances
adding up to BD. As can be seen, income in year t is greater than income in
year Y_{t-1} by AB, and the money stock at the end of year t is greater than
that at the end of year $t - 1$ by CD.

If stability conditions are satisfied, the system will gradually move
toward an equilibrium position, which is characterized by constant values
of income and the other variables year after year. By setting $Y_t = Y_{t-1} = \bar{Y}$
and $R_t = R_{t-1} = \bar{R}$ in Equations 12-1 to 12-8 and solving for $\bar{Y}$ and $\bar{R}$, we
obtain:

$$\bar{Y} = \frac{(q + m)(a + e + G) - (d + h)(n - p)}{(q + m)[1 + bw - g - b + (d + h)k/(q + m)]} \tag{12-12}$$

$$\bar{R} = \frac{k(a + e + G) + (n - p)(1 + bw - b - g)}{(q + m)[1 + bw - b - g + (d + h)k/(q + m)]} \tag{12-13}$$

These are the equilibrium values of income and interest rate. The equilibrium
values of M, I, and C may then be easily obtained.

In Figure 12-6, the distance between the Y_t and Y_{t-1} lines will become
smaller as the system moves toward the equilibrium position. When this
position is reached, the two lines will coincide.

Our dynamic model can also be used to demonstrate that the interest
rate will be set each year so as to bring into balance the supply of and demand
for loanable funds. In a static model considered in the section entitled
"The Loanable Fund Theory" we have shown that the supply of funds is
equal to:

$$S_L = S_P + S_b + \Delta M - H$$

and the demand is equal to

$$D_L = D_b + D_c + D_g$$

If we assume that the net supply of funds by the household sector is equal to $S_P - D_c = S_{pn}$, and that the net demand for funds by the business sector is equal to $I - S_b = D_{bn}$, we may write:

$$S_{pn} + \Delta M - H = D_{bn} + D_g \qquad (12\text{-}14)$$

We shall now develop a corresponding equation for the dynamic model. Each year, total supply of and total demand for money must, of course, be balanced: $M_t = L_{1_t} + L_{2_t}$ and $M_{t-1} = L_{1_{t-1}} + L_{2_{t-1}}$. By subtracting the second equation from the first, we obtain

$$\Delta M_t = \Delta L_{1_t} + \Delta L_{2_t}$$

Assuming that the ratio of transaction cash to income, k, is constant, we must have

$$\Delta L_{1_t} = k(Y_t - Y_{t-1})$$

We know that

$$Y_t = C_t + I_t + G_t$$
$$C_t = a + b(Y_{t-1} - T_t) - dR_t$$

and

$$S_t = Y_{t-1} - T_t - C_t$$

It follows, therefore, that

$$Y_t - Y_{t-1} = (I_t - S_t) + (G_t - T_t)$$

where

$$G_t - T_t = D_{g_t}$$

By substitution we obtain

$$\Delta L_{1_t} = k(I_t - S_t + D_{g_t})$$

Since $I_t = D_{bn_t} + S_{b_t}$ and $S_t = S_{pn_t} + S_{b_t}$, we may also write

$$\Delta L_{1_t} = k(D_{bn_t} + D_{g_t} - S_{pn_t})$$

It follows that

$$\Delta M_t = k(D_{bn_t} + D_{g_t} - S_{pn_t}) + \Delta L_{2_t}$$

and

$$kS_{pn_t} + \Delta M_t - \Delta L_{2_t} = kD_{bn_t} + kD_{g_t}$$

or

$$S_{pn_t} + \frac{1}{k}(\Delta M_t - \Delta L_{2_t}) = D_{bn_t} + D_{g_t} \tag{12-15}$$

Comparing Equations 12-14 and 12-15, we find that their right-hand sides are identical but their left-hand sides are slightly different. The difference may, however, be easily explained. Equation 12-14 is part of a static system, in which income remains the same in each period. Consequently, the transaction demand for cash is also unchanged (assuming that the value of k is constant); and we have: $\Delta L_1 = 0$ and $\Delta M = H = \Delta L_2$. On balance, the supply of loanable funds is equal to net personal saving, S_{pn}. In contrast,

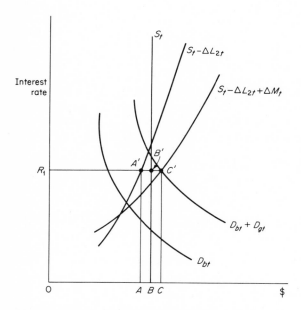

Figure 12-7 Equating of supply and demand for loanable funds in a given year.

Equation 12-15 is part of a dynamic system in which income and the transaction demand for cash increase in every period. In other words, ΔL_{1_t} is positive and $\Delta M_t > \Delta L_{2_t}$. In this situation, total supply of loanable funds is equal to net personal saving plus the additional transaction cash required to finance the increase in income.

A graphic illustration of how the supply of and demand for loanable funds are equated in a given year is given in Figure 12-7. The vertical straight line S_t represents net personal saving, which is a function of the preceding year's income. The curve $S_t - \Delta L_{2_t}$ represents the amounts which the individuals wish to lend after adjusting their speculative cash balances in response to a change in the interest rate. The curve $S_t - \Delta L_{2_t} + \Delta M_t$ indicates the total amount of loanable funds made available by the personal and banking sectors. The curves D_{bt} and $D_{bt} + D_{gt}$ represent net business demand and the combined demand from the business and government sectors, respectively. The interest rate in year t must be equal to R_1, so that total supply of and total demand for funds are balanced. The personal sector supplies funds amounting to OA and the banking sector supplies funds (new money) equal to AC. Of the total amount of new money created in year t, an amount equal to $AB = A'B'$ is added to speculative cash balances and an amount measured by $BC = B'C'$ is added to transaction cash balances.

13
Economic Significance
of Corporate Internal Financing

The models considered in the preceding two chapters were, of course, highly simplified. They do not allow us to examine the effect of certain financial factors which are of especial interest to students of business finance. In this chapter we shall analyze, in some detail, the effect of corporate income retention on capital growth, interindustry allocation of resources, and the amplitude of cyclical fluctuations. In the following chapter we shall take a closer look at the determinants of business investment. And in Chapter 15 we shall examine the factors responsible for the interest rate differentials relating to the bonds' term to maturity.

INTERNAL FINANCING AND CAPITAL GROWTH

Let us consider the case of a simplified economic system whose business sector consists of 1,000 incorporated firms, which are all alike in their financial characteristics. The initial invested capital of each firm is $1,000 and the first year's profit is $100. Total corporate profits in year 1 are then equal to $100,000. They are all distributed as dividends, and the stockholders save $20,000 and invest the entire amount in new corporate shares. Total income from other sources (wages and salaries) is $300,000 in year 1, of which $30,000 is saved and invested in new shares. We assume at first that there is no uncertainty about the future in this system: all shares are considered riskless investment and all firms are expected to earn 10 percent on invested capital in all subsequent years. We also assume initially that there are no taxes of any kind and no transaction costs in connection with buying or selling securities.

Under these conditions, it can easily be shown that replacement of external funds by an equivalent amount of internal funds would produce no significant change in the performance of the system. Suppose that each firm has 100 shares outstanding at the beginning of year 1. Profit per share in year 1 is then $1.00, and the market price may be assumed, under our simplified conditions, to be equal to the book value, which is $10 for all shares. At the end of year 1 each firm issues five new shares at $10 each, which increases its invested capital by 5 percent. Total number of new shares in the market is then 5,000. The existing stockholders, whose saving amounts to $20,000, purchase 2,000 new shares, and the wage and salary earners, whose saving is $30,000, purchase the remaining 3,000 new shares.

In year 2, total profit of each firm will rise to $105, since the rate of return is assumed to remain unchanged. However, since each firm has now 105 shares outstanding, profit per share will still be $1.00. The old stockholders now hold 102,000 shares and their dividends in year 2 amount to $102,000. The new stockholders hold 3,000 shares and receive $3,000 in dividends.

Suppose now that all firms decide to retain one-half of their profits instead of raising external funds. Each firm will now pay $50 in dividends instead of $100 in year 1. The number of shares will remain unchanged, but the stockholders' investment in the firm's assets will rise from $1,000 to $1,050. The price of one share will rise to $10.50 at the end of year 1. If the stockholders still wish to spend $80 on consumption, they can sell 2.85 shares in the market for $30 in order to obtain the additional cash required. After that, their investment in the firm's assets will be equal to 97.15 shares at $10.50 each, or $1,020. Thus, their saving in year 1 amounts to $20— exactly the same as in the external-financing case.

For the economy as a whole, at the end of year 1, the existing stockholders now hold 97,150 shares valued at $1,020,000, while new stockholders acquire 2,850 shares valued at $30,000, which corresponds to the full amount of their saving. The total number of shares outstanding remains unchanged in this case, but the dollar amounts of the assets held and the savings made are equivalent to those in the previous case.

The results would remain essentially the same if the firms decided to retain less than one-half of their profits and to supplement internal funds with external financing. Thus, if 20 percent of profit was retained, the existing stockholders' dividends would correspond to their desired consumption expenditures and they would not have to either sell or buy shares. The price of one share would go up to $10.20 at the end of year 1. Total number of new shares issued by all firms at the end of that year would be 2,941, and they would all be sold to new stockholders for $30,000—the amount equal to their total savings.

The results would be different, however, if all firms decided to retain more than one-half of their profits, since the total amount retained would in this case exceed the total desired amount of personal saving. Suppose that each firm retains 70 percent of its profit and pays out only 30 percent as dividends at the end of year 1. The total amount of dividends paid by all firms would then be $30,000. If the existing stockholders attempted to maintain their consumption expenditures at the $80,000 level, they would have to sell $50,000 worth of shares at the end of year 1. But this would result in an oversupply of shares in the market, since the total saving of the wage and salary earners is assumed to be only $30,000. Consequently, the market price of the shares would have to fall. A fall in share prices means, of course, an increase in their yields, and this may induce some members of the wage- and salary-earning class to increase their savings. However, personal saving is generally considered to have a low interest elasticity.

At the same time, an increase in business investment, resulting from higher retentions, should have an effect on the volume of production and the national income. If there is less than full employment at the beginning of year 1, national income, consumption, and saving may all rise in real terms. On the other hand, if we start from a position of full employment, inflationary tendencies may develop in the economy.

Another factor to be considered in a situation of this kind is the stockholders' pressure on corporate managements to increase the rate of dividend payments. Although the stockholders have no right to vote for an increase in dividends directly, they may, of course, attempt to change the firm's policy by voting the present directors out of office. The effectiveness of such pressure will depend on the prevailing size and structure of corporate enterprise. If a typical corporation in the system is relatively small and its stock is not widely held, the stockholders should be in a relatively strong position vis-à-vis the management. In contrast, if a typical company is a large organization with a widely distributed stock ownership, the stockholders may generally find it rather difficult to influence the management's policies to a significant extent.

THE EFFECT OF UNCERTAINTY

How would the situation change if we dropped the assumption that there is no uncertainty about future profits? Suppose that while business firms, on the average, are expected to earn 10 percent on invested capital, some individual firms may actually perform better and some worse than the average, so that there is always a certain amount of risk involved in investing funds in any single firm. Obviously, most investors would prefer, under such conditions, to diversify their portfolios as much as possible.

If all firms retained a large part of their profits, the existing stockholders of any particular company would wish to convert part of the retained profit into cash by selling some of their shares in the market, and then invest the funds in shares of other companies. At the same time, however, some stockholders of other firms, wishing to diversify their portfolios, would be willing to buy shares of the company in question. On balance, then, the supply of and demand for different shares should not be thrown out of balance by these additional transactions, unless a general feeling developed in the market that some firms were in a more risky class than others. In the absence of such a consensus, the stockholders should still be able to maintain equivalent earnings and assets, irrespective of whether the firms financed their expansion with internal or external funds.

On the other hand, under conditions of uncertainty, corporate management could be expected to show a general preference for internal over external financing because of liquidity considerations. Since the use of external funds involves an increase in the number of shares outstanding, it also involves a rise in the total amount of dividends, if dividends per share are to remain the same. In our example above, the number of shares for each firm was increased from 100 to 105 at the end of year 1 and the profit in year 2 rose to $105, so that dividends remained at $1 per share. Suppose, however, that the profit realized by a given firm in year 2 is only $102—lower than expected. If the management wanted to maintain the $1 dividend rate, it would have to either reduce its liquid resources or resort to borrowing. But if the firm was financed in the first year by retaining one-half of its profits, the dividends per share would be only $.50, and this rate could probably be maintained, or even raised, in the second year without creating a liquidity problem. Of course, if the company paid out more than one-half of its lower-than-expected profit in the second year, this would slow down its capital expansion and tend to retard future earnings growth. Yet, the stockholders' immediate reaction to a drop in retained profit would probably not be as strong as it would be in the case of an equivalent dividend cut. Therefore, the management's position vis-à-vis the stockholders during a period of reduced profitability would probably be less disadvantageous in a firm which had previously maintained a low payout ratio than in a firm which had previously established a high payout ratio.

THE EFFECT OF TRANSACTION COSTS AND INCOME TAXES

Let us now drop the assumptions that there are no transaction costs and no taxes in the system. The effect of these factors on stock valuation has already been discussed in Chapter 5. We shall now make only a few brief remarks concerning their effect on the financial processes in a growing economy as a whole.

First, we shall consider briefly the effect of transaction costs involved in selling corporate shares. Suppose that resale of shares by the existing stockholders involves a flat 5 percent transaction cost. Then, if the stockholders' average propensity to save is 20 percent, but the company retains 50 percent of its profit, they will not be able to obtain an additional $30 in cash by selling 2.85 shares in the market. The net amount realized by such a sale would be only $28.50 and the stockholders' total cash income would be only $78.50, as compared with $80 that would be received if the company's retention ratio were dropped to 20 percent. However, if the company retained only 20 percent of its profit, while the optimum capital expansion rate was 5 percent, it would have to resort to external financing by issuing new shares, and this would also involve transaction costs in the form of underwriting fees and various selling expenses. Consequently, the company's net return on investment capital would drop below the 10 percent level in the following years. Thus, the stockholders' net return on their investment would in the long run be unfavorably affected by the transaction costs in either case.

In the real world, of course, the stockholders do not all have the same saving propensity. Different classes of stockholders may therefore be expected to prefer different retention ratios. If there were in our system a group of stockholders who wished to save 50 percent of their income and were not especially concerned about diversification, they would prefer to invest in a company retaining one-half of its profit. This would enable them to avoid the transaction costs involved in selling any of their shares, and it would also enable the firm to avoid the transaction costs involved in new-share issues (assuming that the optimum rate of growth is 5 percent per year). It does not follow, however, that the stockholders with the average propensity to save of 20 percent would necessarily find it best to invest in a company retaining one-fifth of its profit. The optimal retention ratio for this group would have to be determined by considering also the other factors involved: the relative magnitudes of the transaction costs for newly issued and old shares, the stockholders' diversification preferences, and the company's optimal rate of growth.

Suppose now that dividends are subject to a personal income tax, imposed at a flat rate of 25 percent, while retained profit is free from this tax. To begin with, assume that there is no tax on realized capital gains and no transaction costs.

If all profits were distributed, each firm in our example would pay out $100, and total dividends in the system would amount to $100,000. However, the stockholders' disposable (posttax) income would be only $75,000 and their desired saving—assuming the average propensity to consume to be 80 percent—would amount to $15,000. If total pretax income of wage and salary earners is $300,000, their disposable income must be $225,000. And since their average propensity to save is assumed to be 10 percent, their desired saving is equal to $22,500. Thus, total saving in the system, available for investment in corporate shares, in now $37,500, which will enable the firms to expand their investment capital by only 3.7 instead of 5 percent in the year concerned.

But suppose that all companies retain one-half of their profits. Total dividends would amount in this case to $50,000 before tax and $37,500 after tax. But the stockholders will also register a $50,000 increment in the value of their shares. Their total posttax income, including the capital gains, will be $87,500 and their desired saving will be $17,500. Since the companies have retained $50,000, the stockholders will want to sell $32,500 worth of stock to the wage and salary earners. But since the latter group's saving amounts to only $22,500, disequilibrium will result in the capital market and share prices will tend to decline.

An equilibrium position could be attained, however, if all companies retained 39.5 percent and distributed 60.5 percent of their profits. The total dividend would then be $60,500 before tax and $45,375 after tax. The stockholders' total posttax income, including capital gains, would be $84,875 and their desired saving would be $17,000. They would offer for sale 2,163 shares at $10.40 each, for a total of $22,500, which corresponds to the amount of saving by the wage- and salary-earning class.[1] The internal funds available to the firms in this case will enable them to expand their capital at the rate of 3.95 percent.

It is clear that, under the conditions assumed, every additional dollar retained increases the stockholders' total posttax income (inclusive of capital increment) by 25 cents. And since the capital gains tax as well as the transaction costs are ignored, conversion of shares into cash does not reduce the amount of this gain.

Suppose, however, that a flat 12.5 percent realized capital gains tax is imposed and there are transaction costs amounting to 2 percent of the amount of the shares sold. If corporations retain 39.5 percent of their profits, the price of one share will rise from $10 to $10.40. Therefore, when the stockholders sell 2,163 shares for $22,500, their realized capital gain will be $870. This is, however, gross of the transaction costs, which amount to $550. Their net gain will therefore be $320, and the tax on this net amount at 12.5 percent will be $40. Thus, the stockholders' total income would, in this case, be reduced by a total of $15,715:

[1] Our example does not represent a complete model because no information is given on government expenditures and their effect on national income. A complete, though highly simplified, algebraic model is presented in the last section of this chapter.

Personal income tax on dividends	$15,125
Personal capital gains tax	40
Transaction costs	550
	$15,715

On the other hand, if all profits were distributed, the personal income tax on dividends alone would amount to $25,000.

INTERNAL FINANCING AND CAPITAL ALLOCATION

In the preceding sections it was assumed that all firms in all industries were growing continually at the same uniform rate. This is, of course, unrealistic. In a dynamic system, new technological developments and changes in consumers' tastes and preferences are bound to accelerate the rate of growth in some industries and retard it in other industries, during most periods of time. Also, if the economy as a whole is subject to cyclical fluctuations, their amplitude is likely to be wider in some industries than in the others.

It may be shown that an internally financed system will not react to such disturbances in the same manner as an externally financed system. In this section we shall examine the effects of a shift in consumer demand from the product of one industry to the product of another. To simplify the discussion, we assume once again that there are no taxes and no transaction costs. An industry confronted with a relatively large increase in demand will then be able to earn extra profit during the period of time required to reallocate productive resources so as to reestablish the equilibrium conditions under which the rate of return is the same in all industries. Conversely, an industry confronted with a relatively small increase—or no increase at all—in demand will earn lower than normal profit over a similar transition period. In the industries in which the demand grows at the "normal" rate— corresponding to the overall rate of the growth of the economy—the rate of profit will remain unchanged in the immediate as well as the more distant future.

For a firm belonging to an industry which grows at an equilibrium rate we may write

$$\frac{P_1}{K_1} = \frac{P_2}{K_2} = \frac{P_3}{K_3} = \cdots = r_e$$

where P_1, P_2, etc., are the amounts of profit earned in years 1, 2, etc.; K_1, K_2, etc., are the amounts of capital invested in years 1, 2, etc.; and r_e is the equilibrium rate of return. But for a firm operating in an industry confronted with a sudden shift in demand we have a different set of relationships. Suppose there is an unusually large increase in the demand for the industry's products in year 1, followed by continual normal increases in the subsequent years. Suppose further that it will take n years to reallocate productive resources and reestablish the equilibrium situation in this industry. For a firm belonging to this industry we may then write:

$$\frac{P_1}{K_1} = r_1 > \frac{P_2}{K_2} = r_2 > \cdots > \frac{P_n}{K_n} = \frac{P_{n+1}}{K_{n+1}} = r_e$$

The annual rate of profit will rise abruptly in year 1 and will then diminish gradually—owing to the inflow of new resources—until the equilibrium rate of return (r_e) is reached in year n.

The opposite will be true, of course, of an industry confronted with a relative decline in the demand for its products. The immediate result will be a decline in the rate of return on invested capital. In the subsequent periods, however, the industry's capital will gradually be adjusted to the new demand schedule and the rate of return will return to the equilibrium level. In this case, we may write:

$$\frac{P_1}{K_1} = r_1 < \frac{P_2}{K_2} = r_2 < \cdots < \frac{P_n}{K_n} = r_e$$

The speed with which capital adjustments can be made depends in large measure on how quickly new funds can be reallocated between different industries. In the absence of external financing, the rate of capital expansion would depend solely on the rate of profit reinvestment. If the demand for an industry's products rose and an increase in output was desired, additional funds for capital expansion would have to be obtained through either a reduction in dividends or a rise in profits or both. A cut in dividends would mean that additional financing was, in effect, provided by the industry's stockholders. A rise in profits resulting from higher product prices would mean that new funds were, in effect, contributed by the consumers of the industry's products.

On the other hand, when external funds are available, rapidly expanding industries have access to the general pool of funds in the capital market, accumulated by inflows from all sectors of the economy. An industry confronted with a substantial increase in demand for its products should therefore be able to obtain a larger amount of new funds within a shorter period of time than it could do through profit reinvestment alone.

Let total corporate profits in year 1 be P_1 and profits in Industry A be a fraction n of P_1. If the payout ratio is α for all firms in the economy, total corporate dividends are equal to αP_1 and total retained profits to $(1 - \alpha)P_1$. The corresponding amounts for Industry A are $\alpha n P_1$ and $(1 - \alpha)n P_1$.

Suppose now that in year 2 there is a more than average increase in the demand for Industry A's products, as a result of which its share of total profits rises from n to $n + m$. Its retained profit in year 2 amounts then to $(1 - \alpha)(n + m)P_2$. In the absence of external financing, this is the maximum amount that Industry A can add to its capital in year 2, as long as it maintains the payout ratio of α. If it could discontinue paying out dividends altogether ($\alpha = 0$), the maximum amount of its capital expansion would be equal to $(n + m)P_2$.

But if the entire amount of corporate profit was distributed and capital expansion was financed by external funds, the expansion possibilities for Industry A would be different. Assume that the total amount of external funds is equal to the total retained profit in the previous case: $(1 - \alpha)P_1$ in year 1 and $(1 - \alpha)P_2$ in year 2. In year 1, this industry reports average profit and is able to secure its proportionate share of new funds, $(1 - \alpha)nP_1$. But in year 2 its profits are above the average level, and it should be able to obtain a larger share of the total external funds available. If this share is now equal to $n + k$, the inflow of new funds into the industry concerned must be equal to $(1 - \alpha)(n + k)P_2$.

Thus, the difference between the amount of new funds available to Industry A in the internal-financing case, $(1 - \alpha)(n + m)P_2$, and the amount available to it in the external-financing case, $(1 - \alpha)(n + k)P_2$, depends on the relative values of m and k. Since in a highly competitive capital market, even a relatively small rise in an industry's profit should result in a relatively large increase in the inflow of external funds, one could expect, under such conditions, to find that k is generally greater than m.

The situation would change to some extent if Industry A was able to lower, or even suspend temporarily, payment of dividends. As stated above, its retained fund in year 2 would amount to $(n + m)P_2$, if it paid no dividends at all. In this case, it could expand faster with external than with internal funds only if the value of k exceeded the value of $(m + \alpha n)/(1 - \alpha)$. This would probably be true for an industry which represented only a small fraction of the total economy, for both n and m could then be expected to be much smaller than k. (See footnote 2.) But an industry which represented a large sector of the total economy could find itself in a position to expand faster by retaining its entire profits than by using external funds.

A simple numerical example is given in Table 13-1. Business economy is divided into five sectors: A, B, C, D, and E. Sectors A and B represent industries confronted with an increase in the demand for their products, while sectors C and D represent industries in which the demand decreases. Sector E includes all other industries, which are unaffected by the demand shifts concerned.

[2] The maximum possible value of k is equal to $1 - n$, in which case the industry concerned would receive all external funds available in the market.

Table 13-1   Allocation of new funds in an internally financed and externally financed system (dollar amounts in thousands)

	Sectors					
	A	B	C	D	E	Total
No. of firms	100	100	100	100	600	1,000
Capital	100	100	100	100	600	1,000
Part I						
Profit	10	10	10	10	60	100
Dividends	5	5	5	5	30	50
Retained profit	5	5	5	5	30	50
Expansion rate	5%	5%	5%	5%	5%	5%
Part II						
Profit	20	15	5	0	60	100
Dividends	10	7.5	2.5	0	30	50
Retained profit	10	7.5	2.5	0	30	50
Expansion rate	10%	7.5%	2.5%	0	5%	5%
Part III						
Profit	20	15	5	0	60	100
Dividends	5	5	5	5	30	50
Retained profit	15	10	0	−5	30	50
Expansion rate	15%	10%	0	−5%	5%	5%
Part IV						
Profit	20	15	5	0	60	100
Dividends	20	15	5	0	60	100
External funds	35	15	0	0	0	50
Expansion rate	35%	15%	0	0	0	5%

Initially (Part I), the rate of return is 10 percent for all sectors. If they all retain 50 percent of their profits and finance their expansion internally, the rate of expansion also is 5 percent for each sector. If they distribute the entire profits, the rate of expansion is still a uniform 5 percent, because it is assumed that the total amount of external funds is equal to the total amount retained in the previous case, and each sector receives its proportionate share of new funds.

Suppose now that a shift in demand has occurred (Part II), as a result of which profits in Sectors A and B temporarily rise, while profits in Sectors C and D temporarily fall. If the payout ratio for all sectors is still 50 percent, the expansion rate for Sector A will rise from 5 percent to 10 percent and the rate for Sector B will rise from 5 percent to 7.5 percent in the year concerned. In contrast, the expansion rate for Sector C will drop from 5 percent to 2.5 percent and the rate for Sector D will fall from 5 percent to zero. In all the other industries, which are unaffected by these shifts in demand, the expansion rate remains at 5 percent.

If the firms in Sectors A and B can manage to avoid an immediate increase in dividends, thus retaining their entire profit increments, their expansion rates will increase to 15 percent and 10 percent, respectively (as shown in Part III of the table). These rates, however, are still much lower than the rates that could be obtained in a system in which all profits were distributed and all new financing was made by means of external funds. For, in the latter case, the entire amount of new funds available in the capital market could be channeled into Sectors A and B, if the market was sufficiently competitive and sensitive to profit changes. In Part IV it is assumed that Sector A is able to obtain $35,000, which increases its expansion rate to 35 percent while Sector B obtains $15,000, which raises its expansion rate to 15 percent in the year concerned. All the other industries—not only those confronted with a decline in demand, but also those in which the demand has remained unchanged—temporarily receive no new funds and show no capital expansion at all. Obviously, the reallocation of capital resources, required to expand the capacity of Sectors A and B up to the level commensurate with the rise in the demand for their products, can be attained much faster in this way than by means of profit retention.[3]

It should be realized, of course, that other factors, which are ignored in our example, may interfere and bring about significant changes in the pattern of interindustry allocation of new funds. We have assumed that Sectors A and B begin to attract additional amounts of external funds only *after* the shift in demand has already taken place and their profits have already increased. In some cases, however, demand shifts may be anticipated by both managements and investors, and new funds may begin to flow in increasing amounts to an industry whose current profit is only average but whose future profits are expected to rise. Under such conditions, an externally financed system would show an even greater flexibility as compared with an internally financed one: the flow of internal funds can obviously increase only concurrently with, but not in advance of, a profit rise (assuming no reduction in dividends).

On the other hand, it may be argued that an internally financed system may actually have a considerably greater flexibility than our example indicates. If there is a shift in demand toward the products of Sectors A and B, some firms in other sectors may decide to use their internal funds so as to open up new divisions and begin manufacturing the products for which the demand has increased. In doing so they will, in effect, enter Sectors A and B and help increase their outputs. If this process became widespread, the

---

[3] If dividends are subject to personal income tax, the total amount of external funds available in the capital market will probably be less than $50,000. Suppose that it is only $40,000, of which $28,000 is allocated to Sector A and $12,000 to Sector B. In this case, the expansion ratio for these two sectors would be 28 percent and 12 percent, still considerably higher than the rates attainable by internal financing.

output of the products in question might be increased just as rapidly in an internally financed system as in an externally financed one.

However, the probability of such a widespread adoption of new production lines by firms in other industries does not appear to be high. Industries which have in the past been manufacturing products generally similar to those for which the demand has increased may be able to make the required adjustments with relative ease. But other industries may find it difficult and undesirable to expand operations by entering new areas in which they have had no previous experience or technical know-how. Generally speaking, business firms clearly cannot shift their manufacturing processes from one product to another as easily as individual investors can shift their preferences from one industry to another in selecting new securities for their portfolios.[4]

THE EFFECT OF CYCLICAL FLUCTUATIONS

Consider a business economy consisting of two distinct classes of industries: cyclical and noncyclical. Both classes begin the cycle with the same aggregate amount of capital and both earn the same amount of profit over the entire cycle, which is assumed to be of a five-year duration. But in the noncyclical Class A, profits grow at a steady annual rate g, while in the cyclical Class B the annual rate of change is variable. Suppose that the years 1 and 5 are recession years in which profits in Class B fall short of those in Class A by the amounts C_1 and C_5, respectively. In contrast the years 2, 3, and 4 are cyclical expansion years, in which profits in Class B exceed those in Class A by the amounts C_2, C_3, and C_4, respectively. We may then write:

	Annual profit	
Year	Class A	Class B
1	P	$P - C_1$
2	$(1 + g)P$	$(1 + g)P + C_2$
3	$(1 + g)^2 P$	$(1 + g)^2 P + C_3$
4	$(1 + g)^3 P$	$(1 + g)^3 P + C_4$
5	$(1 + g)^4 P$	$(1 + g)^4 P - C_5$

Assume at first that the system is financed with internal funds only and that the following dividend policies are pursued: The firms in the non-

[4] It would probably be easier for firms in other industries to loan their internal funds to firms in Sector A rather than begin producing new products in their own plants. But if such loans were made, they would represent external financing from the standpoint of the borrowing units and the system would no longer be, strictly speaking, an internally financed one. If such interfirm loans became common practice, some sort of capital market would probably have to be developed.

cyclical class maintain the same payout ratio, α, in all years, so that their dividends and retained profits both grow at the same steady rate g. The firms in the cyclical class for competitive reasons pay exactly the same dividend each year as do the firms in the other class, which means of course that their payout ratio varies from year to year. Profits retained—and reinvested—by the two classes may then be written as:

	Retained profit		
Year	Class A	Class B	A + B
1	$(1 - \alpha)P$	$(1 - \alpha)P - C_1$	$2(1 - \alpha)P - C_1$
2	$(1 - \alpha)(1 + g)P$	$(1 - \alpha)(1 + g)P + C_2$	$2(1 - \alpha)(1 + g)P + C_2$
3	$(1 - \alpha)(1 + g)^2 P$	$(1 - \alpha)(1 + g)^2 P + C_3$	$2(1 - \alpha)(1 + g)^2 P + C_3$
4	$(1 - \alpha)(1 + g)^3 P$	$(1 - \alpha)(1 + g)^3 P + C_4$	$2(1 - \alpha)(1 + g)^3 P + C_4$
5	$(1 - \alpha)(1 + g)^4 P$	$(1 - \alpha)(1 + g)^4 P - C_5$	$2(1 - \alpha)(1 + g)^4 P - C_5$

It may be seen that the cyclical pattern of retained profit in Class B is similar to that of its total profit. But since dividends are assumed to be growing at a steady rate, the *relative* year-to-year change in retained profit is greater than the relative year-to-year change in total profit.

Suppose now that all profits are distributed as dividends and that capital expansion is financed by external funds only. To simplify matters, we may assume that total amount of external funds available in the capital market is equal each year to the total amount of profits retained by all firms in the internal-financing case. The question we have to consider then is the allocation of new funds between the cyclical and noncyclical classes in each year of the cycle. In general, this allocation will depend on the expected profitability of both classes, as viewed by the suppliers of funds (buyers of securities). If the suppliers' investment horizon was limited to one year, all external funds available in a given year would flow into that class of firms whose profits were expected to be higher in that particular year. Thus, Class A would receive all of the funds in the years 1 and 5, while Class B would absorb all funds in the years 2, 3, and 4. Consequently, capital expansion in Class A would not proceed at a steady rate but would assume a countercyclical pattern in this case. In contrast, capital expansion in Class B would show an even more pronounced cyclical pattern.

On the other hand, if the suppliers' investment horizon extended over the entire cycle, and if they were able to make accurate profit forecasts for both classes, investment in either one of them would appear to be equally attractive.[5] Consequently, both classes would be able to obtain equal

[5] We ignore here the difference in the time distribution of profits during the cycle.

amounts of funds each year, as follows:

Year 1: $(1 - \alpha)P - \frac{1}{2}C_1$

Year 2: $(1 - \alpha)(1 + g)P + \frac{1}{2}C_2$

Year 3: $(1 - \alpha)(1 + g)^2P + \frac{1}{2}C_3$

Year 4: $(1 - \alpha)(1 + g)^3P + \frac{1}{2}C_4$

Year 5: $(1 - \alpha)(1 + g)^4P - \frac{1}{2}C_5$

Here again, then, Class A would not be expanding at a steady rate, but would show a cyclical pattern of expansion. Class B would have the same cyclical pattern, which is much less pronounced than that obtained for this class in the previous case.

It should, of course, be realized that we have examined highly simplified situations. In the real world there are different classes of investors with a wide range of investment horizons and forecast capabilities. The actual allocation of external funds could not, therefore, be expected to adhere to either one of the simplified patterns derived above, but would probably follow a path lying between these two extremes. It seems clear, however, that in a system in which noncyclical industries must rely to a large extent on external funds, they cannot remain insulated from the cyclical fluctuations experienced by other industries. The amount of funds they can raise is bound to be affected by the impact of cyclical factors on the capital market.

A MODEL WITH SEPARATE CORPORATE
AND PERSONAL SAVING FUNCTIONS

To conclude our discussion of the economic effects of alternative methods of financing capital expansion, an algebraic model is presented below which includes corporate retained profits as a separate variable. While this model is not comprehensive enough to bring out the effect of each of the factors discussed above, it is nevertheless useful in demonstrating some of the basic interrelationships between profit retention, investment, and income. Our model includes the following variables:

Y = national income
C = consumption expenditures
I = investment expenditures
G = government expenditures (assumed given)
S_p = personal saving
S_c = corporate retained profit
P = corporate profit before corporate income tax

W = wages and salaries before personal income tax
t_p = personal income tax rate (given)
T_p = total amount of personal income tax
t_c = corporate income tax rate (given)
T_c = total amount of corporate income tax
R = interest rate
M = money stock (assumed given)

The model consists of the following equations:

Accounting identities

1. $Y = C + I + G$
2. $Y = C + S_p + S_c + T_p + T_c$
3. $Y = W + P$

Profit equation

4. $P = nY$
   It is assumed that profit is a constant fraction of national income, which is determined by exogenous factors (e.g., union-management collective bargaining). It follows, of course, that $W = (1 - n)Y$.

Retained profit equation

5. $S_c = m(P - T_c)$
   It is assumed that the retention ratio m is also determined by exogenous factors. The same retention ratio is supposed to hold for all firms.

Tax equations

6. $T_c = t_c P = t_c nY$
   The corporate income tax is imposed on all firm's profits at the same flat rate t_c.
7. $T_p = t_p(W + P - S_c)$
   The personal income tax is imposed on all wages and salaries and all profits distributed as dividends at the same flat rate t_p. Retained profits are not subject to this tax, and there is no tax on realized capital gains.

Consumption function

8A. $C = a + b_1[(1 - t_p)(1 - n)Y] + b_2[(1 - t_p)(nY - T_c - S_c) + S_c]$
8B. $C = a + b_1[(1 - t_p)(1 - n)Y] + b_2[(1 - t_p)(nY - T_c - S_c)] + b_3 S_c$

The expression $(1 - t_p)(1 - n)Y$ represents the posttax income from wages and salaries, and b_1 is the marginal propensity to consume of the wage and salary earners.

In Equation 8A the expression $(1 - t_p)(nY - T_c - S_c) + S_c$ represents the amount of dividends after personal income tax plus the amount of retained profit after corporate income tax. In other words, it represents the stockholders' total income, including capital increment, after the corporate and personal income taxes. We assume here that the stockholders' consumption (and saving) is determined by this total amount and by the value of b_2, which stands for the marginal propensity to consume.

In Equation 8B, on the other hand, the stockholders' propensity to spend out of their dividend income (b_2) is assumed to be different from their propensity to spend by converting retained profit into cash by selling shares (b_3). In the extreme case in which the stockholders simply disregard capital increments, we have $b_3 = 0$.

Investment function

9. $I = d + gS_c - hR$

> We assume that corporations always invest a fixed proportion, g, of their retained profits. The amount of external funds used $(d - hR)$ is, however, inversely related to the interest rate, R.

The money equation

10. $M = kY + v - wR$

from which it follows that

$$R = \frac{k}{w}Y + \frac{v}{w} - \frac{M}{w} = xY + z$$

By substituting and solving for Y, we obtain

$$Y = \frac{a + d - hz + G}{1 - b_1 + b_1 t_p + b_1 n - b_1 n t_p - b_2 n + b_2 n t_c + b_2 n t_p}$$

$$- b_2 n t_c t_p - b_2 mn t_p + b_2 mn t_c t_p - gmn + gmn t_c + hx$$

$$= \frac{U}{Z_A} \qquad \text{(Equation 11A)}$$

if we use the consumption function specified in Equation 8A. Alternatively we obtain

$$Y = \frac{a + d - hz + G}{1 - b_1 + b_1 t_p + b_1 n - b_1 n t_p - b_2 n + b_2 n t_c + b_2 mn}$$
$$- b_2 mn t_c + b_2 n t_p - b_2 n t_c t_p - b_2 mn t_p + b_2 mn t_c t_p$$
$$- b_3 mn + b_3 mn t_c - gmn + gmn t_c + hx$$

$$= \frac{U}{Z_B} \qquad \text{(Equation 11B)}$$

if we use the consumption function specified in Equation 8B.

Let us first consider Equation 11A. What effect will an increase in the retention ratio have on national income in this system? To determine this, we must take the first derivative of Y with respect to m. This gives us

$$\frac{dY}{dm} = \frac{-U[b_2 n(t_c t_p - t_p) - gn(1 - t_c)]}{Z_A{}^2}$$

Since both t_c and t_p are fractions, the expression $t_c t_p - t_p$ must be negative, while the expression $1 - t_p$ must be positive. Consequently, the entire numerator is positive. Since the denominator, being a square, is also positive, it follows that $dY/dm > 0$. In other words, an increase in the retention ratio must result in a rise in the national income.

This result follows, of course, from the assumptions made. An increase in retained profit and an equivalent decline in dividends will reduce the amount of the stockholders' personal income tax. Therefore, there will be a rise in their total posttax income, inclusive of the capital increment, and in their consumption expenditures. At the same time, an increase in profit retention will be accompanied by a rise in the corporate investment expenditures. Both of these factors will have an expanding effect on national income.

Consider now Equation 11B. The first derivative of Y with respect to m is now found to be

$$\frac{dY}{dm} = \frac{-U[b_2 n(1 - t_c - t_p + t_c t_p) - b_3 n(1 - t_c) - gn(1 - t_c)]}{Z_B{}^2}$$

In this case, dY/dm may be either positive or negative, depending on the relative magnitudes of b_2, b_3, and g. If retained profit is increased, while dividends are reduced, consumption expenditures may decline despite the smaller amount of personal income tax liability, if b_3 is much lower than b_2. Investment expenditures will rise, but the combined effect on national income may still be negative, if consumption expenditures are curtailed substantially.

We may also examine the effect on national income of a change in the relative shares accruing to stockholders, on the one hand, and to wage and salary earners on the other. Suppose, for example, that the employees manage to secure a larger share of "the pie," as a result of successful collective bargaining. In other words, there is a decrease in n and a corresponding increase in $1 - n$. How will this affect Y in our system? By taking the first derivative of Y with respect to n, we obtain

$$\frac{dY}{dn} = \frac{-U[b_1(1 - t_p) - b_2(1 - t_c - t_p + t_c t_p + m t_p - m t_c t_p) - g(m - m t_c)]}{Z_A^2}$$

if we use Equation 11A, and

$$\frac{dY}{dn} = \frac{-U[b_1(1 - t_p) - b_2(1 - t_c + m + m t_c - t_p + t_c t_p + m t_p - m t_c t_p) - b_3(m - m t_c) - g(m - m t_c)]}{Z_B^2}$$

if we use Equation 11B.

It may be seen that, in either case, dY/dn may be positive or negative, depending on the relative values of b_1, b_2, b_3, and g. If the employees' marginal propensity to consume is large in relation to the stockholders' marginal propensity to consume and to the corporations' marginal propensity to invest, the derivative will be negative, which means that a drop in n will tend to raise Y. An increase in the employees' share of income will, in this case, result in additional consumption expenditures on their part which will more than offset the effect of lower profits on the stockholders' consumption expenditures and in the companies' investment expenditures. Contrariwise, if b_1 is relatively small as compared with b_2, b_3, and g, the derivative will be positive and a drop in n will then tend to reduce Y. On a priori grounds, we are unable to determine the relative strength of the factors involved. Comprehensive empirical studies are required to provide definitive answers.

SUMMARY

Under simplified conditions (no uncertainty, no income taxes, and no transaction costs) the rate of growth of an economic system would not be affected by a shift from external to internal financing, or vice versa. Neither stockholders nor corporate managements would have strong reasons to prefer either one of these methods of financing.

When there is uncertainty as to the future profit trends, stockholders may prefer to have profits distributed rather than retained for reasons of diversification. Managements, on the other hand, may prefer profit retention for reasons of liquidity.

When an income tax is imposed on dividends, a significant factor favoring profit retention is introduced. If corporations were forced to distribute their entire profits, the rate of economic growth could be unfavorably affected.

When reallocation of capital resources in the economic system is required because of new technological developments or shifts in consumer preferences, an externally financed system may be expected to have a greater flexibility than an internally financed one. This is so because the general pool of external funds available in the capital market may be directed, with relative ease and efficiency, into the industries in which the need for expansion is greatest.

If the system consists of both cyclical and noncyclical industries, the prevalent method of financing may have a significant influence on the cyclical pattern of capital expansion in both sectors. If corporations generally finance their expansion by profit retention, the noncyclical sector may remain largely insulated from the fluctuations experienced by the cyclical sector. But if external financing is generally used, the noncyclical industries are likely to be affected by cyclical swings via the capital market.

The relation between corporate saving, business investment, and national income may be brought into sharper focus by means of a simple algebraic model which includes corporate and personal saving as separate variables. A general change in the retention ratio may be expected to affect both consumption and investment expenditures in the system. The net effect will depend on the interrelationship between the marginal tax rates on dividends and capital gains, stockholders' and wage earners' marginal propensities to consume, and business firm's marginal propensities to invest. On a priori grounds, it is impossible to determine whether this net effect will be positive or negative. Comprehensive empirical studies are required to provide a definitive answer.

SELECTED REFERENCES

See Chapter 14.

14
Determinants of
Business Investment

In the algebraic models considered in Chapters 12 and 13 very simple investment functions were used. Actually, of course, the determination of the aggregate volume of business investment in our economy is a much more complex process. A variety of factors are at work and they differ from one another not only in relative strength but also in the time lags involved in their operation. In this chapter we shall first discuss several factors which are considered to be important on theoretical grounds, and then review some recent empirical studies of business investment behavior.

Keynes argued that the volume of investment is determined by the "marginal efficiency of capital" schedule and the interest rate. If the interest rate is lowered, other things remaining constant, more investment will be undertaken. Some economists have pointed out, however, that an increase in the demand for capital goods must result, in the short run, in a rise in their prices, and this will cause the short-run "marginal efficiency of investment" schedule to deviate from the long-run "marginal efficiency of capital" schedule. We shall consider this problem in the first section of this chapter.

Other economists have pointed out that one must distinguish between the initial (autonomous) and the subsequent (induced) changes in investment. An initial rise in investment expenditures will result in a multiple increase in national income and product; but a greater volume of production will require further additions to capital equipment and, therefore, necessitate further investment expenditures. The latter relation is known in the economic literature as the "acceleration principle." We shall examine it in the second section.

In the third and fourth sections, the results of several empirical investigations will be briefly summarized.

THE MARGINAL EFFICIENCY OF CAPITAL AND OF INVESTMENT

Keynes defined the marginal efficiency of capital as follows:

> The relation between the prospective yield of a capital-asset and its supply price or replacement cost, i.e., the relation between the prospective yield of one more unit of that type of capital and the cost of producing that unit, furnishes us with the marginal efficiency of capital of that type. More precisely, I define the marginal efficiency of capital as being equal to that rate of discount which would make the present value of the series of annuities given by the returns expected from the capital asset during its lifetime just equal to its supply price. This gives us the marginal efficiencies of particular types of capital assets. The greatest of these marginal efficiencies can then be regarded as the marginal efficiency of capital in general.[1]

An increase in investment in any given type of capital assets will reduce its marginal efficiency partly because of a fall in the expected revenues and partly because of a rise in the supply price. Thus, for each type of capital assets we may build up a schedule showing the relation between the amount invested and the marginal efficiency. We may then aggregate the schedules for all types of capital assets and construct a schedule relating total investment in the economy to the marginal efficiency of capital in general. Keynes calls this aggregate schedule the *investment demand schedule*, because it shows the amount of new investment desired, in a given period, by all business firms combined, at any given interest rate.

In diagrammatic terms the Keynesian theory of investment is portrayed in Figure 14-1. In this figure, the amount of capital (and of investment, which is defined as addition to capital stock) is measured horizontally, while the marginal efficiency of capital and the interest rate are measured vertically.

[1] J. M. Keynes, *The General Theory of Employment, Interest and Money*, Harcourt Brace, New York, 1936, p. 135.

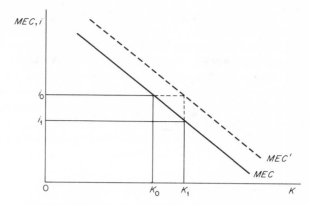

Figure 14-1   Investment determination in a simple Keynesian model.

Assume that the initial amount of capital is equal to OK_0, the rate of interest is equal to i_0, and the marginal efficiency of the capital schedule is represented by the solid line MEC. The system is then in an equilibrium position, since $MEC = i_0$ and there is no incentive to expand the capital stock. Net investment is zero, but replacement investment (not shown in the graph) must of course be made continually, if the capital stock is to be maintained at its present level.

Suppose now that the market interest rate declines from i_0 to i_1. If the marginal efficiency schedule remains unchanged, the equilibrium capital stock is now measured by OK_1, and the system may be expected to generate net investment equal to K_0K_1. The incentive to undertake new investment may also arise because of a shift in the marginal efficiency schedule to the right, while the interest rate remains unchanged. Thus, if the new MEC schedule corresponds to the dotted line in the chart, while the interest rate is still equal to i_0, the equilibrium capital stock is again found to be equal to OK_1 and new investment to K_0K_1. It must be emphasized in this connection that the marginal efficiency of capital is based not on the currently realized revenues, but on the expected future revenues. Under conditions of uncertainty, business expectations are subject to continual fluctuations. When they are revised upward, the MEC schedule shifts to the right; a downward revision produces the opposite result.

The theory, as sketched above, is obviously oversimplified. One important question that is left unanswered is that of the time period required to bring the capital stock up to the new equilibrium level. Keynes himself did not go into this question, but it has been considered in some detail by several other economists. We shall briefly outline their conclusions as to the probable time path of new investment during the adjustment process.

Since the capacity of an economic system to produce new capital goods is always limited, an increase in the demand for these goods (because of a fall in the interest rate or an upward revision of revenue expectations) will cause their prices, in the short run, to rise. But when such a price rise occurs, the *MEC* schedule must be revised downward. It will not, therefore, be possible for the system to reach the new long-term equilibrium point (point K_1 in Figure 14-1) until the prices of the capital goods are lowered again.

The three parts of Figure 14-2 should help to clarify the process of adjustment. Figure 14-2a depicts the long-term marginal efficiency of capital

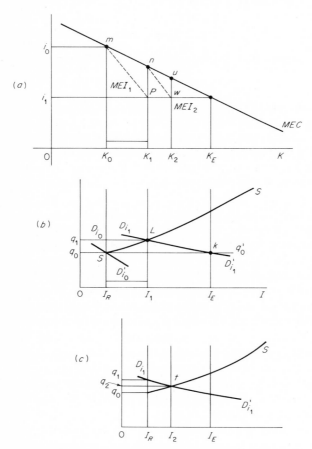

Figure 14-2 Investment determination in successive time periods.(*Source:* This chart is a slightly modified version of the one found in Per M. Wijkman's article, "The Marginal Efficiency of Capital and of Investment: A Didactic Exercise," *The Swedish Journal of Economics,* vol. 67, no. 4, December, 1965.)

as a function of the amount of capital. It is drawn on the assumption that the prices of capital goods remain constant over time. Suppose that initially (in year 0) the amount of capital is equal to OK_0 and the interest rate is equal to Oi_0. The system is then in an equilibrium position and there is no net investment. Replacement investment is measured by OI_R, and the price level of capital goods by Oq_0, as shown in Figure 14-2b. The negatively sloped line $D_{i_0}D'_{i_0}$ in Figure 14-2b represents the demand for capital goods as a function of their price, on the assumption that the interest rate remains fixed at the Oi_0 level (in Figure 14-2a).

Suppose now that the interest rate falls from Oi_0 to Oi_1. Other things remaining equal, the equilibrium amount of capital will then change from OK_0 to OK_E. (See footnote 2.) If the capital goods industry could increase the output of capital goods from OI_R (replacement requirements) to OI_E in the next period *without* a rise in the prices of its products, then the process of adjustment would be relatively uncomplicated. As a result of the fall in the interest rate, the demand curve for capital goods would shift from $D_{i_0}D'_{i_0}$ to $D_{i_1}D'_{i_1}$, while the supply curve would be represented by a horizontal line $q_0q'_0$. The demand and supply curves would intersect at point k; new capital goods ordered and produced during the period would amount to OI_E (including replacement requirements); and total capital stock would increase from OK_0 to OK_E by the end of the period.

But such an assumption concerning the supply schedule is unrealistic. Actually, the cost of producing capital goods and their prices must rise in the short run, as their output is expanded. Accordingly, the short-run supply curve is represented in Figure 14-2b by the rising curve SS. On this assumption, the demand and supply curve will intersect at point L; gross investment in period 1 will be equal to OI_1, and net investment to I_RI_1; and total capital stock will increase at the end of that period from OK_0 to OK_1 only.

Looking at Figure 14-2a we see that, with capital being equal to OK_1 at the end of period 1, the long-term marginal efficiency of capital (which assumes constant capital good prices) is still above the new interest rate ($nK_1 > pK_1$). But the marginal efficiency of investment (the dotted line MEI_1), which reflects the effect of the price rise, intersects the interest line exactly at point p, and the system is therefore in a state of short-term equilibrium.[3] This equilibrium cannot, however, last long. If the price of the capital goods remains at the q_1 level at the beginning of period 2, no further capital expansion will be undertaken, and investment will fall back to the replacement volume, OI_R. But in a competitive market this must result in

---

[2] Both interest and capital changes have been made unrealistically large in order to enable the reader to follow the shifts in the curves more easily. This does not change the essence of the argument.

[3] The MEI line actually is the locus of all points of intersection between the SS curve and different D_i curves that could be drawn by varying the interest rate in the Oi_0 to Oi_1 range.

price reductions. The new short-term equilibrium position (for period 2) is shown in Figure 14-2c, which is similar to Figure 14-2b except that the origin has been moved to the right so that new investment now begins at the point corresponding to point K_1 in Figure 14-2a. As can be seen, the demand and supply curves now cross at point t, which means that the new equilibrium price is equal to Oq_2, gross investment is measured by OI_2, and net investment is measured by $I_R I_2$. Thus, at the end of the second period total capital will equal OK_2. The marginal efficiency of capital will again be higher than the interest rate ($uK_2 > wK_2$), but the marginal efficiency of investment (indicated by the dotted line MEI_2) will equal the interest rate at point w.

By similar reasoning, one can find the amounts of net investment that will take place in periods 3, 4, etc. The capital stock will gradually move (at a declining rate) toward the long-run equilibrium point K_E.

"ACCELERATION" THEORIES OF INVESTMENT

It is clear that no firm could continually expand its output without increasing its operating assets. If the ratio of capital—defined as the sum of operating assets—to output remained constant at all times, we could write

$$K = \alpha O \qquad \text{and} \qquad \Delta K = \alpha(\Delta O)$$

where K and O denote capital stock (net of retirements) and output, respectively, and α is a constant coefficient.

The increment of capital, ΔK, represents net investment, which would be zero if output did not change. However, even if output remained at a constant level, capital goods production would still be required for replacement purposes. Assuming that a constant fraction m of the capital stock must be replaced every year, annual replacement investment must be equal to mK.

Gross investment, which is the sum of replacement and net investment, must in any given year be equal to

$$I_{g_t} = I_{r_t} + I_{n_t} = mK_{t-1} + \alpha(O_t - O_{t-1})$$

Since K_{t-1} and O_{t-1} are given, it is clear that the amounts of both net and gross investment are determined by the difference between the current year's output and the preceding year's output.

A simple numerical example is presented in Table 14-1. It is assumed that (1) the required amount of capital in each year is twice the value of that year's output ($\alpha = 2$) and (2) the average lifetime of capital equipment is 10 years, so that the annual amount of replacement investment is equal to $.1K_1$. (Replacement investment remains constant during the period covered

Table 14-1   An illustration of the acceleration principle

Year	Output O	Change i output ΔO	Capital net of retirement K	Net investment I_n	Replacement investment. I_r	Gross investment	Percent change in O	Percent change in I_g
1	50		100					
2	50	0	100	0	10	10		
3	55	5	110	10	10	20	10	100
4	65	10	130	20	10	30	18	50
5	85	20	170	40	10	50	31	66
6	100	15	200	30	10	40	18	−20
7	110	10	220	20	10	30	10	−25
8	95	−15	210	0	0	0	−14	−100
9	95	0	200	0	0	0	−5	0
10	95	0	190	0	0	0	−5	0

by the table, because new equipment installed in year 2 does not have to be replaced until year 12; new equipment installed in year 3 will have to be replaced in year 13; and so on.) It can be seen that while output increases continually from year 3 through year 7, investment (both net and gross) rises through year 5 only and declines thereafter. This is so, of course, because the increments of output (the ΔO's) increase in years 3 to 5 but decrease in years 6 and 7. It should also be observed that while output rises from 50 to 85, or by 70 percent, during the first five years, gross investment rises from 10 to 50, or by 400 percent, during the same period.

In year 8, the output declines to 95, which makes the required amount of capital equal to 190. However, the firm could not be expected to reduce its capital to that level in one year. Even if it did not make any replacements during that year, the capital would still be equal to 210 at the end of the year. As the table shows, it would take two more years to reduce the capital to 190, assuming that no replacements were made at all during that period. Actually, the firm may find it impossible not to replace at least some units of equipment which are essential for keeping its technical facilities in working order, in which case the process of downward capital adjustment would be further prolonged.[4]

The proposition that investment depends on the rate of change in output rather than the absolute level of output is known in the economic literature as the "acceleration principle." This is an important tool of economic analysis because it helps to explain the amplitude and timing of

---

[4] In some cases, a firm could accelerate the process of downward capital adjustment by selling its excess assets to other firms. But this would probably involve financial losses and would not be considered an appropriate policy unless the production decline was expected to be permanent.

cyclical fluctuations in different sectors of our economy.[5] It has actually been observed that the capital goods industries have generally been subject to a greater degree of cyclical fluctuations than the consumer goods industries. It has also been observed that the turning points in the capital goods output have tended to precede those in the consumer goods industries.

However, actual cyclical fluctuations have not generally followed the pattern that would be in strict accordance with the acceleration principle. This is not surprising, because the principle, as outlined above, involves some assumptions which are not generally realistic. First, it is clear that an increase in output during a given period will require an immediate increase in the capital stock only if the firm is already working at full capacity at the beginning of the period. If this is not the case, and initial excess capacity exists, output may be raised without any net investment during the period concerned. Furthermore, even if the firm is already operating close to capacity at the beginning of the period, arrangements can usually be made to increase output to a certain extent by such means as drawing down inventories, working overtime, introducing extra shifts, etc.

Secondly, when additional equipment is required, it cannot of course be purchased, installed, and put into operation without any loss of time. In other words, when output is increasing, investment should be expected to respond with a certain time lag. In the case of a simple one-period lag, the investment equation may be rewritten as follows:

$$I_{g_t} = mK_{t-1} + \alpha(0_{t-1} - 0_{t-2})$$

In the case of a more complex lag, spreading over several periods, the equation may be given the following form:

$$I_{g_t} = mK_{t-1} + \alpha_1(0_{t-1} - 0_{t-2}) + \alpha_2(0_{t-2} - 0_{t-3}) + \cdots$$
$$+ \alpha_n(0_{t-n+1} - 0_{t-n})$$

Another device, which can be used to take into account the time factor involved, is to make the coefficient α represent the relation between output

[5] More elaborate models, based on a combination of the accelerator and investment multiplier principles, have been developed by several economists in order to investigate further the nature of cyclical fluctuations in an economic system. For an early model of this type see Paul Samuelson's article "Interaction between the Multiplier Analysis and the Principle of Acceleration," *The Review of Economic Statistics*, vol. 21, no. 2, May, 1939, pp. 75–78. Samuelson's findings are discussed in A. H. Hansen's books *Fiscal Policy and Business Cycles*, 1941, and *Business Cycles and National Income*, 1951.

A later version of this type of model was developed by J. R. Hicks in his book *A Contribution to the Theory of the Trade Cycle*, 1950. For a critical evaluation of Hicks' analysis, see James Duesenberry, "Hicks on the Trade Cycle," *Quarterly Journal of Economics*, vol. 64, August, 1950, and A. F. Burns, *The Frontiers of Economic Knowledge*, 1954.

and the desired or optimal amount of capital. We may then write:

$$K_t^* = \alpha O_t$$

and

$$I_{g_t}^* = mK_{t-1} + \alpha(O_t - O_{t-1})$$

where K^* is the desired capital and I_g^* is the gross investment that would raise K_{t-1} to the level desired in year t. The actual amount of investment that can be achieved in year t may, however, fall considerably short of I_g^*. The equation for I_g may then be written as

$$I_{g_t} = mK_{t-1} + \alpha\beta(O_t - O_{t-1})$$

where β represents the fraction of the desired net investment that can be completed in year t.

In the following sections we shall see how the acceleration principle was tested in some empirical studies.

INSTITUTIONAL FACTORS

As already discussed in Chapter 9, investment policies of large corporations are, as a rule, directed by professional salaried managements, whose stockholdings, if any, are not important enough to ensure that the maximization of dividends or of stock values will invariably be their prime policy objective.

To be sure, the managements are in some cases subject to a strong stockholders' pressure for higher dividends and stock appreciation. But they are also subject, from time to time, to pressures exerted by other groups in the society. The management of a large company does not make a major investment decision without considering its effect not only on the stockholders' equity, but also on the welfare of the communities involved, the level and pattern of employment and the probable reaction of the labor groups concerned, the attitude of various governmental agencies on the federal, state, and local levels, and the entire range of the firm's public relations or its public "image" generally.

In a growing economy, most firms make plans for expansion. In fact, as has already been discussed, an expansion-oriented management may be tempted to pursue expansion policy beyond the point that would be most advantageous from the present stockholders' standpoint. However, if the expansion is to be financed with external funds, the management may be constrained by the fact that an additional cash outflow in the form of increased interest or dividend payments must be provided for almost immediately.

On the other hand, if the expansion can be financed with internal funds, this constraint does not arise; dividends may have to be increased in the future, but there is no definite schedule or deadline that the management must meet. There is, therefore, a natural preference for using internal financing first and resorting to external funds only when the internal source has already been fully tapped.

As has been pointed out by some writers, even within the internal fund category, managements tend to differentiate between the depreciation and the net profit components.[6] In a going concern, the need to maintain productive capacity at least at the present level is usually taken for granted, and depreciation funds are reinvested in a more or less routine, "semi-automatic" manner. Even in periods of depression, when current operations are curtailed, many firms prefer not to impair capacity by reducing replacement investment, but rather to be prepared for the next recovery period. On the other hand, investment of retained profits in additional assets may be temporarily postponed. The only factor that may seriously interfere with the process of routine reinvestment is a liquidity crisis. If a firm's cash inflow becomes so low as to make it difficult to meet currently maturing obligations, it may, of course, be forced to suspend all investment expenditures—replacement as well as new ones.

MEYER AND GLAUBER'S STUDY

Professors Meyer and Glauber developed and tested a hypothesis which attempts to explain investment by combining the accelerator factor with what they call the "residual funds" factor.[7] The *residual funds* are defined as the total net flow of funds realized from current operations (i.e., net profit plus depreciation) less dividend payments. In other words, the residual funds are equivalent to what we previously defined as gross internal funds.

According to this hypothesis, under conditions of less than full-capacity utilization, a firm's investment is limited to a level not in excess of the funds internally available after conventional dividends have been met. On the other hand, under conditions of fully utilized capacity, investment is primarily determined by the sales trend and the optimal capital-output ratio.

In testing their hypothesis, Meyer and Glauber used both cross-section and time-series data. The cross-section samples, compiled for

[6] See Edgar M. Hoover, "Some Institutional Factors in Business Investment Decisions," *American Economic Review*, vol. 44, May, 1954.

[7] John R. Meyer and Robert R. Glauber, *Investment Decisions, Economic Forecasting, and Public Policy*, Harvard University, Boston, 1964.

This is an extension of an earlier investigation by J. R. Meyer and Edwin Kuh published under the title: *The Investment Decision: An Empirical Study*, Harvard University Press, Cambridge, Mass., 1959.

each year during the 1951–1954 period, were composed primarily of large manufacturing corporations. The relationships were tested by means of multiple regression equations, which included the following independent variables: capacity utilization, sales, change in sales, residual funds (measured by retained profit or retained profit less working capital needs), and investment in the previous period.

As was to be expected, different results were obtained for different industries and years. The author's general conclusions from their cross-section analysis were stated as follows:

> Specifically, the pattern of year-to-year results of the cross-section study lends confirmation, but only mild confirmation, to the accelerator-residual funds hypothesis. That is, accelerator-type variables—capacity, change in sales, and sales—all do better than the measure of residual funds in the buoyant year of 1951; however, these accelerator variables also perform comparatively well in 1954 which along with 1953 must be ranked as the most depressed year in the sample. Similarly, residual fund variables perform reasonably adequately on the whole in 1953 but only provide a semi-adequate explanation of investment in 1954.[8]

In their time-series analysis, Meyer and Glauber used quarterly data on manufacturing, both total and for component industries, for the period 1948–1958. Several equations were tried, and the best results were obtained by using the following independent variables: (1) the residual funds $T - V$; capacity utilization C^M, measured by the ratio of the Federal Reserve Board's production index to the McGraw-Hill capacity series; the interest rate r, measured by the quarterly average of Moody's AAA industrial bond rates; percentage change in the stock prices, ΔSP, computed from the quarterly average of Standard and Poor's index of 425 industrial stocks; and investment expenditures I incurred in a previous period.

All variables were lagged for one, two, or three quarters, and the following regression equation was obtained for all manufacturing combined:

$$I_t = -3,051.6 + .243(T - V)_{t-1} + 3,500.6C_{t-1}{}^M + 107.1r_{t-3}$$
$$+ 14.9\Delta SP_{t-1} + .793I_{t-2} + \text{seasonal dummies} \qquad R^2 = .995$$

All coefficients, except the one for the interest rate, were found significant at the 5 percent level. The interest rate coefficient not only lacked significance, but also showed the wrong sign (in theory, it should be negative and not positive).

[8] *Op. cit.*, p. 134.

As in the case of cross-section analysis, here again the coefficients obtained for individual industries in the manufacturing class showed a considerable degree of variation. For most industries the residual fund variable was found to perform considerably better than the capacity utilization variable. Also, in almost all individual cases, the interest rate coefficient was negative, as one would expect on theoretical grounds.

Meyer and Glauber also made separate tests of investment behavior during the upswing and the downswing periods. Since it was found that capacity utilization was generally higher during the upswings than during the downswings, the capacity variable was included in the equation for the former periods but excluded from the equation for the latter periods.

Contrariwise, the residual fund variable was included during the downswings but excluded during the upswings. The results obtained are stated below:

Upswings (last three quarters of 1950, all of 1951, 1952, and 1953, the last three quarters of 1955, and the first quarter of 1956):

$$I_t = 747.7 + 2,563.3C_{t-1}{}^M + 19.2SP_{t-1} - 935.0r_{t-3} + .868I_{t-2}$$

$$(700.6) \qquad (3.4) \qquad (274.1) \qquad (.094)$$

$$+ \text{(seasonal corrections)} \qquad R^2 = .977$$

Downswings (last two quarters of 1949, the first quarter of 1950, all of 1954, and the first quarter of 1955):

$$I_t = 490.7 + .409(T - V)_{t-1} - 433.3r_{t-3} + 877I_{t-2}$$

$$(.126) \qquad\qquad (199.3) \qquad (.217)$$

$$+ \text{(seasonal corrections)} \qquad R^2 = .900$$

It should be pointed out that Meyer and Glauber themselves considered their findings as only tentative and suggestive. While their study succeeded in establishing some interesting and statistically significant relations for the industries included in their samples and for the particular periods concerned, their models are not entirely adequate because of certain theoretical and statistical difficulties involved. Attempts to use their equations for forecasting purposes yielded rather disappointing results.

Professors Meyer and Glauber also tried to test the relation between liquid assets and investment. On a priori grounds, liquidity considerations should be an important factor in forming business investment decisions. Maintaining a continually adequate liquidity position requires an appropriate scheduling of cash inflows and outflows for all periods within the firm's planning horizon. Moreover, under conditions of uncertainty it also requires holding at all times adequate stocks of liquid assets (cash and near-cash items, such as marketable securities) as a reserve against contingencies. Attempts to correlate total liquid stocks with investment have yielded relatively poor results.[9] This is not surprising, because the desired level of liquid reserves varies widely from one industry to another and even from one firm to another in the same industry. What is of importance in connection with investment expenditures is not the absolute amount, but the difference, if any, between the actual and the desired stocks of liquid assets.

Better results were obtained when *changes* in liquid stocks were correlated with investment. Significant negative relations were established in many cases over the 1951–1954 period, indicating that an increase in investment was often accompanied by a reduction in liquid stocks. This finding in itself does not, however, answer the question whether the reduction in liquidity was the cause or the effect of increased investment. Was additional investment undertaken because the existing liquid assets were in excess of the desired long-term levels? Or was the incentive to invest so strong as to make many firms reduce their liquid stocks temporarily below the desired long-term proportions? Further studies in this area are clearly desirable, but unfortunately the available data are less than adequate for this type of analysis.

OTHER EMPIRICAL STUDIES

Professor John Lintner developed and tested a model in which investment determinants include the accelerator, financial leverage, and interest rate factors.[10] Quarterly data for all United States manufacturing corporations over the period 1953–1963 were used. The following equation was fitted to the data:

$$\frac{I_{t+1}}{K_{t-1}} = SD + b_1 + b_2 X_i + b_3 \frac{LTD - RF}{SP} + b_4 r + b_5 [tr(\Delta r)_{t-1}]$$

$$+ b_6 T$$

where I_{t+1} = value of plant and equipment outlays of manufacturing companies for the quarter following the reference date

K_{t-1} = value of manufacturers' stocks of real capital at the beginning of the reference quarter

[9] *Op. cit.*, pp. 91–93.

[10] John Lintner, "Corporation Finance: Risk and Investment," in Determinants of Investment Behavior, Universities—National Bureau Conference Series, vol. 18, 1967.

SD = three seasonal dummies

X_i = accelerator-capacity variable

LTD = long-term debt, measured by all debt due in more than one year to banks and the lenders

RF = retained funds, measured by net profits after taxes, less cash dividends, plus depreciation and depletion

SP = market value of equity computed from the Standard and Poor index of the market prices of 425 industrial securities

r = interest rate, measured by the average of the monthly Baa rates (Moody's) during the quarter

$tr(\Delta r)_{t-1}$ = trend in the Baa rates

T = time

Several variants of the accelerator-capacity variable were used, the simplest one being the ratio of output to capital, O_t/K_{t-1} (the output was measured by an unweighted average of the Federal Reserve Board's Index of Production). In the other variants several indexes of the utilization of manufacturing capacity were used.

Lintner also considered several variants of the financial leverage variable. He found the one indicated above, i.e., $(LTD - RF)/SP$, to be preferable on theoretical grounds for the following reason: for any given level of investment outlay, the availability of retained funds should enable the firm to have less debt outstanding at the end of the period.

As an example, we state hereunder one of the multiple regression equations obtained by Lintner:

$$\frac{I_{t+1}}{K_{t-1}} = .011 + .1396(O_t/K_{t-1}) - .3188(LTD - RF) - 1.7169r$$

$$- 10.973tr(\Delta r)_{t-1} + .0001T \qquad R^2 = .7282$$

It will be noticed that the signs of all coefficients are in agreement with what one would expect on theoretical grounds—positive for the accelerator-capacity variable but negative for the leverage and the interest rate variables.

A significant negative relation between leverage and investment and between interest and investment was indicated also by most of the other equations obtained. While Lintner considered this to be the most important finding in his study, he emphasized nevertheless the tentative character of this result and the desirability of further work in this area.

Professors Jorgenson and Siebert tested several hypotheses of business investment behavior on the basis of a sample of firms selected from the

Fortune Directory of the 500 largest United States industrial corporations for 1962.[11]

The following four theories were selected for testing:

1. *The Accelerator Theory*, in which the desired capital is assumed to be proportional to output. This is expressed algebraically as

$$K_t^* = \alpha Q_t$$

where α is the desired capital-output ratio.

2. *The Liquidity Theory*, in which the desired capital is assumed to be proportional to liquidity (which is defined as the flow of internal funds available for investment). This is expressed as:

$$K_t^* = \alpha L_t$$

3. *The Expected Profits Theory*, in which the desired capital is proportional to the market value of the firm:

$$K_t^* = \alpha V_t$$

The market value V_t is considered to be an approximation to the discounted value of expected future cash flow net of future investment expenditures.

4. *The Neoclassical Theory*, in which the desired capital is proportional to the value of the output divided by the price of capital services:

$$K_t^* = \alpha \frac{P_t Q_t}{c_t}$$

This theory is based on the following theoretical propositions concerning business firm behavior: (1) the firm will adjust its operations so as to maximize its net worth, (2) net worth is maximized when each factor of production is employed up to the point at which its marginal physical products are equal to its real marginal cost, and (3) the marginal productivity of each factor is derived from the firm's production function.[12] It follows

---

[11] Dale W. Jorgenson and Calvin D. Siebert, "A Comparison of Alternative Theories of Corporate Investment Behavior," *The American Economic Review*, vol. 58, no. 4, September, 1968.

[12] We discussed these basic propositions of economic theory in Chaps. 2 and 3. With respect to the production function, it should be noted that Jorgenson uses the Cobb–Douglas function, which may generally be stated as follows: $O = AL^\alpha K^{1-\alpha}$, where O is output, A is a constant, L is the quantity of labor, and K is the quantity of capital. Some of Jorgenson's specific assumptions have been questioned and criticized by other economists. But since our brief review of his approach and empirical findings is given only for purposes of illustration, we shall not go into this controversy here.

that the desired amount of capital is determined by the physical capital-output relationship, the price of output, and the price of capital services, the latter being defined as the "shadow" price or implicit rental of one unit of capital service per period of time.[13]

In the absence of corporate income tax and of capital gains, we would have

$$c_t = q_t(\delta + r)$$

where c_t is the price of capital services, q_t is the investment goods price index, δ is the rate of replacement, and r is the cost of capital (interest rate). When the corporate income tax is imposed at the flat rate u and when the depreciation allowed for tax purposes represents the proportion w of the "true" depreciation at replacement cost, the formula for c_t becomes much more complex:

$$c_t = \frac{q_t}{1 - u_t}[(1 - u_t w_t)\delta + r_t]$$

Finally, when capital gains are taken into account, we have:

$$c_t = \frac{q_t}{1 - u_t}\left[(1 - u_t w_t)\delta + r_t - \frac{q_t - q_{t-1}}{q_t}\right]$$

Other things being equal, the inclusion of capital gains reduces the value of c and, consequently, increases the value of K^*. The version of the neoclassical theory in which capital gains are incorporated in the price of capital services is referred to by the authors as *Neoclassical I*. The version in which capital gains are omitted is referred to as *Neoclassical II*.

On the basis of their tests, Jorgenson and Siebert have ranked the theories concerned in the following order: (1) Neoclassical I; (2) Neoclassical II; (3) Expected Profits; (4) Accelerator; and (5) Liquidity. The liquidity theory was found inadequate and was dismissed from serious consideration as an explanation of corporate investment behavior. The Expected Profits and the Accelerator models performed better, but not as well as the Neoclassical models. And of the latter two, Neoclassical I provided a somewhat better explanation of investment behavior than Neoclassical II.

In their statistical tests, Jorgenson and Siebert used distributed lag functions. To illustrate the empirical results, the multiple regression equation

---

[13] See D. W. Jorgenson, "Capital Theory and Investment Behavior," *American Economic Review*, vol. 53, no. 2, May, 1963, p. 249.

obtained for the Neoclassical I model is stated hereunder:

$$I_t = .2449 + .0160\left(\frac{p_t Q_t}{c_t} - \frac{p_{t-1}Q_{t-1}}{c_{t-1}}\right) + .0150\left(\frac{p_{t-1}Q_{t-1}}{c_{t-1}} - \frac{p_{t-2}Q_{t-2}}{c_{t-2}}\right)$$
$$ (.0063) (.0066)$$
$$+ .3444(I_{t-1} - \delta K_{t-2}) + .1794 K_{t-1}$$
$$(.2061) (.0540)$$

As can be seen, investment in a given period was found to be positively correlated with output changes in the two preceding periods, with investment made in the immediately preceding period, and with the preceding period's capital stock.

SUMMARY

The aggregate volume of investment in our economy is determined by a variety of factors which differ from one another not only in relative strength but also in the time lags involved in their operations. Since the investment functions used in the previous chapters were grossly oversimplified, we have taken in this chapter a closer look at some of the major factors involved.

In the first two sections we have discussed some relevant theoretical propositions, and in the following sections we have examined briefly the results of some empirical investigations of investment behavior.

According to Keynes, new investment expenditures will generally be undertaken as long as the marginal efficiency of capital remains above the interest rate. It has been pointed out, however, that an increase in the demand for capital goods will lead to a rise in their prices, and this will cause the short-run marginal efficiency of investment to deviate temporarily from the long-run marginal efficiency of capital. Thus, the time path toward the equilibrium position is more complicated than it was apparently assumed to be by Keynes.

It has also been pointed out that a distinction must be made between the initial (autonomous) and the subsequent (induced) changes in investment. The latter changes may be expected to be related to the rate of change in the volume of output. If output is subject to cyclical fluctuations, induced investment will display an even stronger cyclical pattern; and the turning points in the investment cycle will precede those in the output cycle (the "acceleration" principle).

Professors Meyer and Glauber have formulated and tested statistically the "accelerator-residual funds" hypothesis, according to which the available amount of internal funds is the primary factor determining investment during periods of less than full-capacity utilization, while the sales trend and the optimal capital-output ratio are the main determinants of investment during periods of fully utilized capacity. Statistical results obtained from sample data on manufacturing corporations provide some support for this hypothesis; but the authors themselves consider their conclusions to be tentative and suggestive only.

Professor Lintner developed and tested a model in which investment determinants include the accelerator, financial leverage, and interest rate factors. A significant negative relation between leverage and investment and between interest and investment was revealed by the data used. However, Lintner also emphasized the tentative character of this result and the desirability of further work in this area.

Professors Jorgenson and Siebert tested several hypotheses of investment behavior on the basis of a sample of industrial corporations. Their best results were obtained by applying the "neoclassical" theory, according to which the desired capital (*and the investment required to reach that level*) is proportional to the value of the output adjusted by the price of capital services. In deriving the investment function, based on this proposition, the authors used the distributed lag approach.

SELECTED REFERENCES

Allen, R. G. D.: *Macro-Economic Theory*, St. Martin's Press, New York, 1967, chap. 4.
Ferber, Robert, ed.: "Determinants of Investment Behavior," A Conference of the Universities, National Bureau Committee for Economic Research, Columbia University Press, New York, 1967.
Jorgenson, Dale W.: "Capital Theory and Investment Behavior," *American Economic Review*, vol. 53, no. 2, May, 1963.
————, and C. D. Siebert: "Theories of Corporate Investment Behavior," *American Economic Review*, vol. 58, no. 4, September, 1968.
Meyer, J. R., and R. R. Glauber: *Investment Decisions, Economic Forecasting, and Public Policy*, Harvard University, Boston, 1964.

15

The Term Structure
of Interest Rates

In simplified theoretical models it is assumed that there is only one interest rate in the system at any given time. We followed the practice of making this simplifying assumption in the preceding chapters. But in the real world, of course, there is a wide range of interest rates applicable to different types of credit transactions.

On the one hand, securities with the same maturity date may offer the investors considerably different rates of return or yields, depending on the market evaluation of their quality, based on such factors as credit risk, marketability, tax status, etc. On the other hand, securities of comparable quality may offer substantially different yields, depending on the length of their term to maturity. In this chapter we shall be concerned with the latter type of yield differentials. Their range and pattern over time are usually referred to as the *term structure* of interest rates.

THE YIELD CURVES

In analyzing the term structure of interest rates it is important to select securities which differ in their term to maturity but are as similar as possible

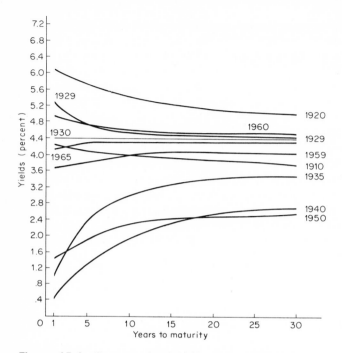

Figure 15-1 Corporate bond yield curves, selected years. (*Source:* For the earlier years, see David Durand, "Basic Yields of Corporate Bonds, 1900–1942," Technical Paper 3, National Bureau of Economic Research, 1942; and David Durand and Willis J. Winn, "Basic Yields of Bonds, 1926–1947," Technical Paper 6, National Bureau of Economic Research, 1947. For the later years, see Sidney Homer, *A History of Interest Rates,* Rutgers University Press, New Brunswick, N.J., 1963; and B. G. Malkiel, *The Term Structure of Interest Rates,* Princeton University Press, Princeton, N.J., 1966.)

in all other respects. The United States government and the top-rate corporate securities are most suitable for this analysis, because their use virtually eliminates the risk of a default factor.[1]

The data on high-grade corporate bond yields in the United States are available since 1900. Some of these data are presented graphically in Figure 15-1. It should be noticed that most of the yield curves show a marked

[1] It should be realized, however, that investment in even the highest-grade bonds (private or public) involves risks other than that of default. If an investor anticipates that he may have to sell his bonds in the market prior to maturity, he must consider the risk of sustaining a capital loss because of adverse price fluctuations. And even if he fully expects to hold the bonds to maturity, there is the risk of a loss in terms of real purchasing power in periods of general price inflation.

slope—either positive or negative—within the short- and medium-term range, but tend to flatten out as the term becomes longer. Most of the yield curves for the early part of the century (1900–1920) are negatively sloped. In contrast, most of the curves for the more recent decades (1930–1960) show a positive slope: the yields increase with the term to maturity, although the rate of increase declines rapidly for maturities longer than 10 years.

The yield curves for the United States government securities, covering the period 1958–1970, are shown in Figure 15-2. It may be observed that there was an almost continual upward shift in the yields for all maturities over that period. But there was also a significant change in the shape of the curves in the later years as compared with the earlier ones. The 1958, 1960, and 1962 curves are positively sloped: there is a continual increase in the yield as the term to maturity lengthens, although the rate of increase declines markedly as one moves to the right along the curve. The 1965 yield curve is almost horizontal: there is very little variation in the yield for different

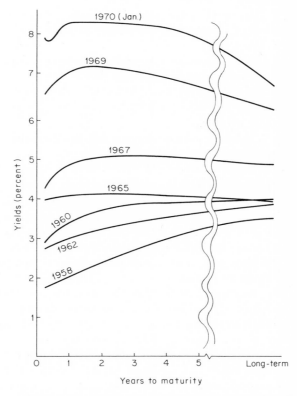

Figure 15-2 Yields of U.S. government securities, selected years. (*Source:* Federal Reserve Bulletin, various issues.)

maturities. In contrast the 1967, 1969, and 1970 curves exhibit a significant "hump": the slope is positive within the short- and medium-term range, but becomes negative for longer maturities.

We shall now turn to an analysis of the major factors responsible for the yield differentials between different maturities. Several theories of the term structure have been formulated, and they will be discussed in the following sections.

THE EXPECTATIONS THEORY

The expectations theory, the rudiments of which can be found in Irving Fisher's writings, was later developed and refined by J. R. Hicks, F. A. Lutz, and several other economists. Its basic proposition is that the yield to maturity on a long-term security will be approximately equal to an average of the short-term rates expected to be in effect over the remaining life of the security.

A simple variant of this theory can be easily demonstrated if the following assumptions are made:

1. Investors are in a position to make accurate forecasts concerning all future short-term rates of interest.
2. All securities are riskless with respect to the payment of interest and principal, and there are no differences among them with respect to taxability, convertibility, etc.
3. There are no transaction costs in connection with switches among securities of different maturities.

Suppose that the current one-year rate $_tR_1$ is 2 percent and that next year's expected one-year rate $_{t+1}R_1$ is 4 percent. Under these conditions, an investor who has funds to invest for two years may buy a one-year bond now and earn 2 percent and then reinvest the proceeds and earn 4 percent the next year. His average annual return will then be 3 percent (approximately). It follows that, in an equilibrium, the current two-year rate $_tR_2$ must also be equal to 3 percent.

Suppose now that another investor has funds at his disposal for one year only. If he buys a one-year issue, his annual return will be 2 percent. But he can also buy a two-year bond, hold it for one year, and then sell it in the market. In an equilibrium situation, the price of a 3 percent two-year bond must drop to $99 at the end of the first year. The one-year investor will then receive $3 in interest but will suffer a loss of $1 on the sale of the bond, which will make his net return equal to 2 percent—the same as the yield on the one-year bond purchased at the beginning of year 1. The new holder of the two-year bond will receive $3 in interest and realize a $1 gain when the bond is redeemed at its face value of $100 at the end of year 2, which will make his total yield equal to $4—the same as the short-term interest rate in effect in year 2.

To show how the equilibrating mechanism works, suppose that initially the two-year rate $_tR_2$ is not 3 but $3\frac{1}{2}$ percent. In this case, an investor with funds available for two years would prefer to invest in a two-year bond rather than purchase a one-year bond and then reinvest at the end of the first year. An investor with funds available for one year would also prefer to purchase a two-year bond and then sell it at the end of the first year. This is so because the price of the $3\frac{1}{2}$ percent two-year bond would have to be $99.50 at the end of the first year if the one-year rate in the second year was 4 percent. Furthermore, this situation would create opportunities for arbitrageurs to make a profit by selling short one-year bonds, on which they would pay 2 percent, and buying two-year bonds on which they would realize a net return of 3 percent ($3\frac{1}{2}$ percent interest minus $\frac{1}{2}$ percent capital loss) during the first year. Because of the preferences of all of the groups concerned, the price of two-year bonds would be bid up and the price of one-year bonds would be driven down. In other words, the yield of two-year securities would tend to decline and the yield of one-year securities would tend to rise, until all holding-period yields were equalized.

In algebraic terms, the equilibrium relation between the short-term rate in year 1, $_tR_1$, the short-term rate in year 2, $_{t+1}R_1$, and the long-term rate $_tR_2$ may be stated as follows:

$$1 + {}_tR_2 = \sqrt{(1 + {}_tR_1)(1 + {}_{t+1}R_1)}$$

And if we increase the number of years involved from 2 to n, we may write:

$$1 + {}_tR_n = [(1 + {}_tR_1)(1 + {}_{t+1}R_1) \cdots (1 + {}_{t+n-1}R_1)]^{1/n}$$

or

$$1 + {}_tR_n = [(1 + {}_tR_{n-1})^{n-1}(1 + {}_{t+n-1}R_1)]^{1/n}$$

As can be seen, the present long rates must exceed the present short rates when the future short rates are expected to rise, while the reverse will be true when the short rates are expected to fall.

In the above derivations, long-term rates were obtained on the basis of given short-term rates. It should be clear, however, that if $_tR_1$ and $_tR_2$ are given, a definite value of $_{t+1}R_1$ is implied and can be easily derived by rearranging the formula given above as follows:

$$_{t+1}R_1^* = \frac{(1 + {}_tR_2)^2}{1 + {}_tR_1} - 1$$

More generally, we may write

$$_{t+n-1}R_1^* = \frac{(1 + {}_tR_n)^n}{(1 + {}_tR_{n-1})^{n-1}} - 1$$

The value of $_{t+1}R_1^*$, implicit in the term structure, represents the "forward" short rate, as distinct from the "spot" rate which will actually be in effect in year $t + 1$. In the simple model discussed here the two must be equal under equilibrium conditions.

THE HICKSIAN LIQUIDITY PREMIUM

Professor Hicks argued that long rates depend not only on the expected future short rates but also on the lenders' and borrowers' liquidity preferences. He suggested that even if the future short rates were not expected to change from the present level, the long rates would still show a tendency to rise as the term to maturity increased because of the risks involved in longer-term lending.

The Hicksian argument is based on the following propositions. It is known that many borrowers who wish to embark on long-term projects have a strong propensity to borrow long. On the other side of the market, however, in many cases there is an opposite propensity: other things being equal, many lenders have a significant preference for short-term as opposed to long-term contracts. This tends to create a certain imbalance or "constitutional weakness" in the loanable fund market, which can be corrected only if the borrowers are prepared to offer better terms in order to persuade the lenders to switch over into the long market. More specifically, the borrowers must be willing to offer a long rate which is higher than just the average of the relevant short rates, and the premium must be large enough to offset the risk incurred—as viewed by the lenders.

Algebraically, the Hicksian variant of the theory may be expressed as follows:

$$1 + {}_tR_n = [(1 + {}_tR_1)(1 + {}_{t+1}R_1 + L_2) \cdots (1 + {}_{t+n-1}R_1 + L_n)]^{1/n}$$

where $L_2, L_3, \ldots, L_n$ are the risk (or liquidity) premiums for periods $2, 3, \ldots, n$. It is expected that

$$0 < L_2 < L_3 \cdots < L_n$$

Suppose once again that $_tR_1$ is 2 percent and $_{t+1}R_1$ is 4 percent. Then, in the absence of risk premium, the long rate $_tR_2$ must be equal to 3 percent. But suppose that there is a risk premium of 1 percent which must be paid to induce an investor to buy a two-year bond. By using the formula

$$1 + {_tR_2} = [(1 + {_tR_1})(1 + {_{t+1}R_1} + L_2)]^{\frac{1}{2}}$$

we then find that the long rate must be equal to $3\frac{1}{2}$ percent.

The forward short rate, implicit in the assumed term structure, is equal to

$$\frac{(1 + {_tR_2})^2}{1 + {_tR_1}} - 1 = .05$$

It is equal, of course, to the expected short rate in the second year plus the assumed risk premium.

B. G. MALKIEL'S REFORMULATION

Many critics have questioned the assumption that investors buying long-term securities do so on the basis of definite expectations as to what the future short rates will be over the entire period concerned. It does indeed seem unrealistic to assume that an investor buying a bond with a fifty-year term to maturity will be able to compute an acceptable long rate on the basis of the short rates expected in each of the following fifty years.[2]

It has been shown, however, that the assumptions can be modified and made much more realistic without changing the substance of the expectations theory. We shall now describe a modified alternative formulation of the expectations theory, as developed by B. G. Malkiel.[3]

Professor Malkiel's reformulation involves, first of all, a rigorous reexamination of the relationship between bond yields and bond prices. In general, the market value of a bond, V, is determined by its face value, or the principal amount to be paid at maturity, F, the coupon rate of interest, i, the number of years to maturity, n, and the prevailing market rate of return or yield to maturity, r, for this particular class of securities. Algebraically,

---

[2] To take an extreme case, as pointed out by Mrs. Joan Robinson, a buyer of perpetual bonds (such as the British consols) would have to form definite expectations of the short rates "from today until Kingdom Come." See her article "The Rate of Interest," *Econometrica*, April, 1951.

[3] B. G. Malkiel, *The Term Structure of Interest Rates, Expectations and Behavior Patterns*, Princeton University Press, Princeton, N.J., 1966.

relationships are as follows:

$$V = \frac{iF}{1+r} + \frac{iF}{(1+r)^2} + \cdots + \frac{iF}{(1+r)^n} + \frac{F}{(1+r)^n}$$

$$= \frac{iF}{r}\left[1 - \frac{1}{(1+r)^n}\right] + \frac{F}{(1+r)^n} \tag{15-1}$$

It can be seen that as n approaches infinity, V approaches the limit iF/r. Thus, the market price of a perpetual bond (consol) must be equal to its face value times the ratio of the coupon rate to the yield:

$$V_c = \frac{i}{r}F$$

If Equation 15-1 is rewritten as

$$V = \frac{iF}{r} + \frac{[F - (iF/r)]}{(1+r)^n} \tag{15-2}$$

it becomes clear that the market value of a bond with any term to maturity must be equal to its face value if $i = r$. The bond will be selling at a premium ($V > F$) if $i > r$; it will be selling at a discount ($V < F$) if $i < r$.

The following additional propositions (or theorems) may be demonstrated:

1. Bond prices move inversely to bond yields. Differentiating Equation 15-1 with respect to r, we obtain

$$\frac{\partial V}{\partial r} = -\frac{iF}{(1+r)^2} - \frac{2iF}{(1+r)^3} - \cdots - \frac{niF}{(1+r)^{n+1}} - \frac{nF}{(1+r)^{n+1}} < 0 \tag{15-3}$$

Thus, if r is increased, i being constant, V must decline, and vice versa.

2. For a given change in yield from the coupon rate, changes in bond prices are greater, the longer the term to maturity.

Differentiating Equation 15-2 with respect to n, we obtain:

$$\frac{\partial V}{\partial n} = \left(\frac{iF}{r} - F\right)(1+r)^{-n}[\ln(1+i)] \tag{15-4}$$

When $i > r$ (which means that the bond sells at a premium), $\partial V/\partial n$ must be positive. In other words, the value of the bond will be higher the longer the term to maturity (for any given values of i and r).

When $i < r$ (which means that the bond sells at a discount), $\partial V/\partial n$ must be negative. In this case the value of the bond will be lower the longer the term to maturity.

3. While the price of a bond increases (or decreases) with n, as described in the preceding paragraph, the rate of change in the price diminishes as n increases.

The second derivative of V with respect to n is

$$\frac{\partial^2 V}{\partial n^2} = \left(\frac{iF}{r} - F\right) [\ln(1 + r)]^2 (1 + r)^{-n}$$

Thus, when $i > r$, the second derivative is negative, which means that V increases at a decreasing rate. When $i < r$, the second derivative is positive, which means that V declines at a diminishing rate.

4. Equal (proportionate) increases and decreases in yield produce asymmetric results: a decrease in yields raises bond prices more than an equal increase in yields lowers prices.

By taking the second derivative of V with respect to r, we obtain:

$$\frac{\partial^2 V}{\partial r^2} = \frac{2iF}{(1 + r)^3} + \frac{2 \times 3iF}{(1 + r)^4} + \cdots + \frac{n(n + 1)iF}{(1 + r)^{n+2}} + \frac{n(n + 1)F}{(1 + r)^{n+2}} > 0$$

Since the second derivative is positive, while the first derivative is negative (see Proposition 1), it follows that the slope of the function $V = f(r)$ is negative but becomes less steep as r increases. Consequently, a decline in the price resulting from an increase in the yield by, say, 1 percent will be smaller than the rise in the price resulting from a 1 percent drop in the yield.

5. The higher the coupon rate of the bond, the smaller will be the percentage price fluctuation for a given percentage change in yield (except for one-year securities and consols).

Mathematically this proposition may be stated as:

$$\frac{\partial[(\partial V/\partial r)(r/V)]}{\partial(iF)} > 0 \qquad \text{for all finite } n \geq 2$$

Since the algebraic proof is rather lengthy, it will be omitted here.[4]

Some of the relationships stated above are portrayed graphically in

[4] The interested readers may refer to Malkiel, *op. cit.*, p. 56.

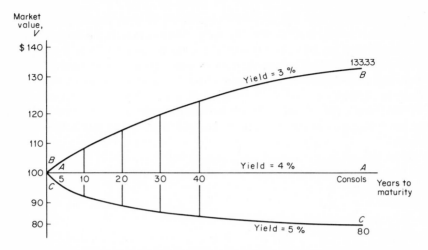

Figure 15-3 Market value of bonds with coupon rate of 4 percent, but different term to maturity.

Figure 15-3. It is assumed that the coupon rate i is 4 percent and the face value of the bonds, F, is \$100. If the yield r is also equal to 4 percent, the market value V remains at \$100 irrespective of the term to maturity, as indicated by the horizontal line AA. But if the yield drops to 3 percent while the coupon rate remains at 4 percent, the market value will rise above the face value—as indicated by the curve BB. The value of V will now depend on the term to maturity: it will be \$104.58 for a five-year bond, \$108.60 for a ten-year bond, and \$133.33 for a perpetual bond (consol). It can be seen that, as N increases, V increases, too, but at a declining rate (Propositions 2 and 3).

The reverse changes in market value are observed when the yield is raised to 5 percent while the coupon rate remains at 4 percent. This is shown by the curve CC. It will be seen that V drops to \$95.67 for a five-year bond, to \$92.28 for a ten-year bond, and to \$80 for a consol. It will also be seen that the amounts by which a 1 percent drop in the yield increases the market value are greater than the amounts by which a 1 percent rise in the yield reduces the market value (Proposition 4). In the extreme case of a consol, the increment of V is equal to \$33.33 while the decrement amounts to only \$20.

THE NORMAL RANGE OF INTEREST RATES

In developing his variant of the expectations theory, Professor Malkiel introduces the concept of "the expected normal range of interest rates." As the first approximation, all of the individuals comprising the market are assumed to believe that the historical range of interest rates will prevail in the future. Suppose that the expected normal range for government bonds, based on their past performance, is roughly between 4 and 6 percent. Suppose further that the current interest rate for one-year bonds is $4\frac{1}{2}$ percent and is not expected to change within a year. Then the one-year bonds with the coupon rate of $4\frac{1}{2}$ percent must be selling at par. But what about the longer-term bonds? Since the current rate is much closer to the lower limit of the expected normal range than it is to the upper limit, the maximum possible capital gain (from a drop in the rate from $4\frac{1}{2}$ to 4 percent) is considerably smaller than the maximum possible capital loss (from a rise in the rate from $4\frac{1}{2}$ to 6 percent). Consequently, even if the investors have formed no definite expectations as to whether the rates will actually rise or fall, they must feel that in buying longer-term bonds they have more to fear than hope, and this must tend to reduce the market prices of such bonds.

Professor Malkiel's central proposition is that definite long-term yields may be derived even if it is assumed that bond investors typically have rather short planning horizons. In fact, he provides an illustration in which the relevant horizon is limited to one year: the investors are assumed to expect no change in the interest rate during the first year but to have no definite expectations beyond that. The figures given in Table 15-1 have been derived by following Malkiel's reasoning and adhering to his one-year horizon assumption.

As can be seen, a one-year bond will sell at par, since the coupon interest rate is equal to the market interest rate and no change is expected during the year. The market price of a two-year bond, however, need not be equal to its face value, since the market interest rate may change in the second year. If the market rate should increase to 6 percent at the beginning of year 2, the price of a 4.5 percent bond would drop to

$$\frac{104.50}{1.06} = 98.56$$

and the investor would sustain a capital loss of $1.44. But if the market rate should drop to 4 percent at the beginning of year 2, the price of the bond would increase to

$$\frac{104.50}{1.04} = 100.49$$

and the investor would register a capital gain of $0.49.

Now, if the investors are ignorant of the probabilities of these two outcomes, they should be expected to treat both results as equally likely.

Table 15-1 Alternative derivations of the term structure of interest rates (coupon rate = 4.5%)

Years to maturity (1)	Market price of bond if interest rate falls to 4% (2)	Resulting capital gain (3)	Market price of bond if interest rate rises to 6% (4)	Resulting capital loss (5)	Math. expectation of loss when Col. 3 and Col. 5 are equally probable (6)	Equilibrium market price from Col. 6 (7)	Derived structure of interest rates from Col. 7 (8)	Math. expectation of loss when probability of Col. 3 is .25 and probability of Col. 5 is .75 (9)	Equilibrium market price from Col. 9 (10)	Derived structure of interest rates from Col. 10 (11)
1	100.00	—	100.00	—	—	100.00	4.50	—	100.00	4.50
2	100.49	+.49	98.56	−1.44	−.48	99.52	4.75	−.97	99.03	5.02
5	101.83	+1.83	94.74	−5.26	−1.72	98.28	4.89	−3.49	96.51	5.30
10	103.75	+3.75	89.68	−10.32	−3.29	96.71	4.92	−6.93	93.07	5.41
20	106.61	+6.61	83.13	−16.87	−5.13	94.87	4.90	−11.00	89.00	5.41
50	110.70	+10.70	76.38	−23.62	−6.46	93.54	4.84	−15.04	84.96	5.37
Consol	112.50	+12.50	75.00	−25.00	−6.25	93.75	4.80	−15.63	84.37	5.33

In other words, the probability of each result is equal to .5 and the mathematical expectation of gain is equal to

$$-1.44(.5) + .49(.5) = -.48†$$

Consequently, the market price of the two-year bond at the beginning of year 1 must be equal to \$99.52. The bond's yield to maturity can be found by solving the following equation for $_tR_2$:

$$99.52 = \frac{4.50}{1 + {}_tR_2} + \frac{104.50}{(1 + {}_tR_2)^2}$$

We find that $_tR_2$ is equal to .0475. The implied forward rate in year 2 can be determined by solving the equation:

$$_{t+1}R_1^* = \frac{(1.0475)^2}{1.045} - 1 = .05$$

The market prices and the yields to maturity of longer-term bonds, computed on the same assumptions, are given in columns 7 and 8 of the table. It can be seen that the yields rise at first and then begin to decline as the number of years increases.

Consider now a case in which investors believe that interest rate movements in one direction are more likely than movements in the other direction. Assume once more that the current one-year interest rate is equal to 4.5 percent and the expected one-year normal range is between 4 and 6 percent. However, since the current rate is closer to the bottom than to the top of the normal range, the investors feel that an upward movement is more probable than a downward one next year. Suppose that they attach the probability of .75 to the loss they would sustain if the market rate increased to 6 percent and the probability of .25 to the gain they would enjoy if the market rate fell to 4 percent.

† As Malkiel points out, while this is not the only possible hypothesis, it seems the most reasonable one in connection with the problem concerned. In the literature on decision making, different criteria are used in dealing with this type of problem. He selects the Laplace (Bayes) principle, according to which the decision maker will assign to each act X_i its expected utility index

$$\frac{U_{i1} + \cdots + U_{in}}{n}$$

and choose the act with the largest index. If the utility numbers are assumed to be equal to the gains (losses), in the above case, we have $U_{i1} = -1.44$ and $U_{i2} = .49$. Since $n = 2$, the probability of each "state of nature" is equal to .5.

In the case of a two-year bond the mathematical expectation of gain is now equal to

$$-1.44(.75) + .49(.25) = -.97$$

which means that the market price of such a bond at the beginning of year 1 must be equal to $99.03. By solving for $_tR_2$ the equation

$$99.03 = \frac{4.50}{1 + {}_tR_2} + \frac{104.50}{(1 + {}_tR_2)^2}$$

we find that the yield to maturity is .05. The implicit forward rate for year 2 is now equal to

$$_{t+1}R_1^* = \frac{(1.05)^2}{1.045} - 1 = .055$$

The yields to maturity of longer-term bonds are indicated in column 11 of Table 15-1. Once again, we find that the yields first rise and then decline as the number of years increases. For any given number of years (greater than 1), the rate in column 11 is higher than the rate in column 8. This is, of course, what one would expect: if investors attach a greater probability to a rise in the market than to a drop, they will offer a lower price for the bonds maturing in more than one year, which implies a higher yield to maturity.

The Hicksian liquidity premiums can be introduced into Malkiel's model by assuming that losses are weighted more heavily than equivalent gains by the investors. This will have the effect of raising the yields to maturity of the longer-term bonds.

For example, if we double the negative values of column 5 of Table 15-1, the mathematical expectation of gain in the case of a two-year bond will be equal to

$$-2.88(.5) + .49(.5) = -1.20$$

Thus, the market price of a two-year bond will be $98.80 instead of $99.52 and the yield to maturity will be .051 instead of .0475. In the case of consols, the price would be $81.30 instead of $93.75, and the yield would be .0553 instead of .0480.

In summary, then, Malkiel's model does not require the assumption that investors form definite expectations of a whole series of forward short-term rates. The only expectation that investors are assumed to have is that interest rates will continue to fluctuate within their normal range. He shows that with his alternative formulation he can generate a set of interest rate relationships with properties similar to those obtained by the traditional analysis.

TRANSACTION COSTS

Let us now drop the assumption that there are no transaction costs in connection with buying and selling bonds in the market. Suppose that while the purchase of a new bond from the issuing corporation involves no transaction cost, subsequent resale in the market entails a cost equal to one-half of 1 percent, and that this cost is shared equally by the seller and the new buyer. Then, if the short rate in year 1 is 2 percent and the short rate in year 2 is expected to be 4 percent, it can be easily shown that a two-year bond with the coupon rate of 3 percent cannot be sold at par but will have to be offered at a discount.

In order to compete with the one-year bonds, the two-year bond must enable an investor who buys it at the beginning of year 1 and sells it at the beginning of year 2 to earn 2 percent; and it must also enable an investor who buys it at the beginning of year 2 and holds it to maturity to earn 4 percent on his investment. The price of the bond at the beginning of year 2 must be equal to

$$\frac{103.00 - .25}{1.04} = 98.75$$

where $.25 is the transaction cost borne by the second investor. But the original investor (the seller) will realize only $98.75 - .25 = 98.50$, since he also bears one-half of the total transaction cost. Consequently, in order to make 2 percent on his investment, the original buyer must be able to acquire the 3 percent bond from the issuing corporation at $99.50.

If the issuer insisted on selling new two-year bonds at par, he would have to raise the coupon rate from 3 percent to $3\frac{1}{4}$ percent. In this case, the bond would have a market price of $99.00 at the beginning of year 2, which would enable the buyer to earn 4 percent. The seller would realize $98.75, and his rate of return would be 2 percent if the original price at the time of issue was $100.

INSTITUTIONAL RESTRAINTS

Another factor impeding the shifts from one maturity to another in the real world is the existence of certain institutional restraints. The writers emphasizing this factor point out that different types of financial institutions are forced by tradition or law to maintain fairly rigid portfolio structures and are severely limited in their freedom to choose maturities so as to take advantage of interest rate differentials.[5]

Thus, life insurance companies are predominantly long-term investors because of the long-term nature of their contractual obligations to policy-holders. In contrast, commercial banks are primarily short-term investors, also as a result of the nature of their obligations to depositors. Similarly, on the borrowing side of the market, the maturity composition of debts outstanding must be related to the debtor's asset structure and the length of time for which the funds are tied up. It would be quite unusual—and unwise, by the prevailing financial precepts—for an industrial corporation to finance plant and equipment expenditures with short-term loans that would have to be renewed at frequent intervals, even if such an arrangement could result in lower interest charges.

Consequently, according to the institutionalists, the securities market is to a large degree segmented and the interest rates for different maturities are determined more or less independently by the supply and demand interactions, without either lenders or borrowers having much freedom of intersegment movement. It is clear that under such conditions significant interest rate differentials may arise and remain in effect for considerable periods of time, even in the absence of the other factors which were examined above.

As an example, consider a simplified securities market consisting of only two segments: one-year and two-year bonds. Assume that the investors in each segment, who cannot shift from one maturity to the other, wish to buy in a given period $10 million worth of bonds, irrespective of the yield. Their demand, in each case, may then be represented by a rectangular hyperbola, as shown in Figure 15-4. Assume further that the borrowers in each sector wish to sell during the same period 100,000 bonds with a par value of $100 and a coupon rate of 4 percent. Under these conditions, both the one-year and the two-year bonds will sell at par, and the yield to maturity for both of them will be equal to the coupon rate. In the figure, the equilibrium points are A_1 and A_2, respectively.

But suppose now that the supply of one-year bonds increases to 105,000 while the supply of two-year bonds declines to 95,000. Since the investors, by assumption, still want to invest $10 million in each market, it follows that the price of the one-year bonds will decline to $95.24 and their yield will rise to 9.2 percent, while the price of the two-year bonds will rise to $105.26 and their yield to maturity will decline to 1.5 percent. In the figure the equilibrium points are now B_1 and B_2, respectively.

Of course, if investors were able to shift their funds freely from one maturity to the other, this differential could not persist. The higher yield

[5] See J. M. Culbertson, "The Term Structure of Interest Rates," *Quarterly Journal of Economics*, vol. 71, no. 4, November, 1957.

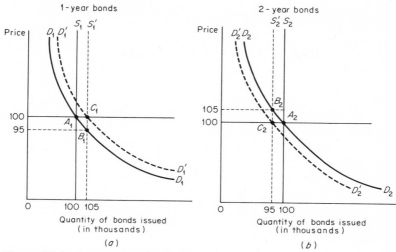

Figure 15-4 Segmented market for bonds.

of the one-year bonds would attract additional funds into the short-term segment of the market, while the lower yield of the two-year bonds would have the opposite effect in the long-term segment. In the figure, the demand curve for one-year bonds would move to the right, as indicated by the dotted line $D'_1 D'_1$, while the demand curve for two-year bonds would move to the left, as shown by the dotted line $D'_2 D'_2$. Equilibria in both segments would be reestablished when the price returned to $100 and the yield to 4 percent for both maturities.

There is no question that institutional restraints actually exist and exert considerable influence in our securities market. This does not mean, however, that different segments of the market are completely insulated from one another. Relatively small yield differentials may not be strong enough to induce maturity shifting on the part of investors with traditionally rigid portfolio structures. But there are always other investors whose position is more flexible. And if the differentials widen, even those in the relatively rigid portfolio class may find it feasible to shift at least some of their funds into more attractive maturities.

INTERACTION OF DIFFERENT FACTORS

In general, it is clear that the term structure of interest rates at any given time is the result of interaction of several factors. At a time when the current short rate is approximately in the middle of the "normal range" and there is no definite expectation of a rate change in one direction or the other, the yield curve would tend to become a straight horizontal line if there were no other influences. But if a significant Hicksian liquidity-preference factor is present, the curve will tend to be an upward-sloping one. When the liquidity factor is combined with the expectation of a rise in the short rate, the upward slope will become more pronounced. And even if the rate is expected to fall, the yield curve may still show a positive slope owing to a strong liquidity preference.[6] However, when the downward rate movement is expected to be pronounced, it will probably more than offset the liquidity factor, and the yield curve will become negatively sloped.

Of course, investors do not always expect that the short rate will either increase or decrease monotonically within their investment horizon. Sometimes they expect the rate to fluctuate, and such expectations may result in a yield curve with a "hump." When such a hump tends to develop, the existence of significant institutional constraints, hindering intersector flows of funds, is likely to make it more pronounced.

As an example of a special combination of factors producing a down-sweeping yield curve, the situation at the end of 1959 and the beginning of 1960 may be briefly reviewed. At that time the interest rates reached their highest level in approximately 30 years, and most lenders and borrowers in the capital market expected a reversal of the trend in the near future. Accordingly, many lenders endeavored to protect themselves against a drop in the yield by buying longer-term securities, while at the same time many borrowers became reluctant to make long-term commitments. Thus, the demand for long-term bonds increased but their supply diminished; their prices were bid up and the yields decreased correspondingly.

The "segmentation" of the market also played a significant role during that period. The cyclical recovery in 1959 was accompanied by a rapid accumulation of inventories. Demand for short-term funds rose sharply, pushing the short-term rates up to a considerably higher level than the long-term rates. Yet, business firms were generally unaccustomed to financing inventory accumulations with long-term funds and showed reluctance to do so. On the other side of the market, many institutional investors, accustomed to long-term lending, were reluctant to shift to short-term maturities and take advantage of the higher short rates.

SUMMARY

In contrast to the simplified theoretical models, the real economic system is characterized by a multiplicity of interest rates applicable to different types of credit transactions. Securities with the same maturity date offer different yields depending on such factors as credit risk, marketability, tax status, etc.; while securities of comparable quality offer different yields depending on

[6] Some writers have referred to the positively sloped yield curve as the "normal curve." See G. W. Woodworth, *The Money Market and Monetary Management*, Harper and Row, New York, 1965, p. 193.

their term to maturity. In this chapter we have examined the factors determining the term structure of interest rates.

According to the expectations theory, the yield to maturity on a long-term security is approximately equal to an average of the short-term rates expected to be in effect over the remaining life of the security. It has been argued by some writers, however, that even if the future short-term rates were not expected to change from the present level, the long rates would still show a tendency to rise as the term to maturity increased, because of the risks involved in longer-term lending.

Some critics have questioned the assumption that investors buying long-term securities are able to form definite expectations as to what the future short rates will be over the entire period concerned. But it has been shown that the assumptions can be modified and made more realistic without changing the substance of the expectations theory. In Professor Malkiel's model, the only expectation that investors are assumed to have is that interest rates will continue to fluctuate within the "normal" historical range. He shows that with this alternative formulation we can generate a set of interest rate relationships with properties similar to those obtained by using the traditional formulation.

The actual term structure of interest rates is bound to deviate somewhat from the theoretical models considered above owing to the transaction costs involved in switching from one maturity to another and to the institutional factors restraining the freedom of choice between maturities for many financial institutions. It has been argued by some writers that our securities market is to a large degree segmented and the interest rates for different maturities are determined more or less independently by the supply and demand interactions, without either lenders or borrowers having much freedom of intersegment movement.

SELECTED REFERENCES

Conard, J. W.: *Introduction to the Theory of Interest*, University of California Press, Berkeley and Los Angeles, 1963, chaps. 14–17.

Culbertson, J. M.: "The Term Structure of Interest Rates," *Quarterly Journal of Economics*, vol. 71, no. 4, November, 1957.

Luckett, D. G.: "Multi-Period Expectations and the Term Structure of Interest Rates," *Quarterly Journal of Economics*, November, 1967.

Malkiel, B. G.: *The Term Structure of Interest Rates, Expectations and Behavior Patterns*, Princeton University Press, Princeton, N.J., 1966.

Meiselman, David: *The Term Structure of Interest Rates*, Prentice-Hall, Inc., Englewood Cliffs, N.J., 1962.

Woodworth, G. W.: *The Money Market and Monetary Management*, Harper and Row, New York, 1965, chap. 10.

16
Historical Trends in Capital Formation and Its Financing in the United States

In this last chapter we shall review some long-term trends in the capital formation and the methods used to finance it in our national economy. A study of such trends is useful because it reveals some basic, deep-rooted propensities and tendencies in our economic system. While past events and developments should not, of course, be mechanically and uncritically projected into the future, their knowledge provides the historical perspective for a more realistic evaluation of the present capabilities and the growth potential of our economy. Our review will be based primarily on the extensive study made at the National Bureau of Economic Research by a number of researchers, under the general direction of Professor Simon Kuznets.[1]

CAPITAL FORMATION IN THE ECONOMY AS A WHOLE

The general trends in capital formation, both gross and net of capital consumption, over the period 1869–1955, are indicated by the data assembled

[1] For a comprehensive summary of this study see S. Kuznets, *Capital in the American Economy; Its Formation and Financing*, Princeton University Press, Princeton, N.J., 1961.

in Table 16-1. Capital formation in this table includes all types of construction (including residential); producers' durable goods; net changes in business inventories; and net changes in claims against foreign countries. The data in lines 1 to 5 include military construction and other military durables, while the data in lines 3a, 4a, and 5a exclude the military expenditures. As can be seen, the average annual volume of gross capital formation shows a more than ninefold increase over the 1869–1955 period when the military component is included, and more than an eightfold rise when the latter component is excluded. The average amount of capital consumption, however, shows an even greater increase over the same period. As a result,

Table 16-1   Capital formation in the United States, 1869–1955 (amounts in billions of dollars in 1929 prices)

Periods	Gross capital formation (1)	Capital consumption (2)	Net capital formation (3)	Ratio of Col. 2 to Col. 1 (4)
Total	*Volume (average per year)*			
1. 1869–1888	3.48	1.46	2.02	.42
2. 1889–1908	8.68	4.03	4.65	.46
3. 1909–1928	15.5	8.39	7.12	.54
4. 1929–1955	22.7	17.3	5.44	.76
5. 1946–1955	33.0	25.1	7.88	.76
Total excluding military				
3a. 1909–1928	15.0	8.0	7.0	.53
4a. 1929–1955	19.1	14.4	4.69	.75
5a. 1946–1955	29.7	19.3	10.5	.65
Total	*Percentage rate of growth per decade*			
6. 1869–88 to 1889–08	58.0	66.1	51.8	
7. 1889–08 to 1909–28	33.7	44.3	23.8	
8. 1909–28 to 1929–55	17.7	36.1	−10.8	
9. 1909–28 to 1946–55	26.6	40.9	3.2	
10. 1869–88 to 1946–55	36.7	48.4	20.8	
Total excluding military				
11. 1869–88 to 1889–08	58.0	66.1	51.8	
12. 1889–08 to 1909–28	31.5	40.9	22.7	
13. 1909–28 to 1929–55	10.9	28.6	−15.7	
14. 1909–28 to 1946–55	23.8	31.6	13.3	
15. 1869–88 to 1946–55	34.7	43.1	25.7	

SOURCE: This table and Tables 16-2, 16-3, 16-4, 16-6, and 16-7 represent parts of Tables 2, 3, 6, 7, 39, and 48, respectively, in *Capital in the American Economy: Its Formation and Financing*, by Simon Kuznets (copyright © 1961 by Princeton University Press), National Bureau of Economic Research. Reprinted by permission of Princeton University Press.

the upward trend in net capital formation was less pronounced than that in gross capital formation.

It may also be seen that the percentage rate of growth per decade shows a declining trend when the successive subperiods indicated in the table are compared with one another.[2] Capital formation represents additions to the existing stock of capital goods, and it is interesting to compare the growth of this stock with the growth of the total labor force and of the total population. The data needed for this comparison are presented in Table 16-2.

In column 1 capital stock is given gross of the accumulated depreciation reserves but net of retirements. It represents the sum of all capital goods that are still in operation, taken at full initial values irrespective of their age.

[2] The subperiod 1929–1955 includes, of course, the years of the Great Depression. However, the rate of growth in the postwar subperiod was also lower than those obtained for the early subperiods.

Table 16-2   Rate of growth in capital stock, population, and labor force, 1869–1955

Years	Total capital stock ($ billions, in 1929 prices) Gross* (1)	Nett (2)	Population (millions) (3)	Labor force (4)	Capital stock per capita ($ thousands) Gross (5)	Net (6)	Capital stock per member of labor force ($ thousands) Gross (7)	Net (8)
			Volumes					
1. 1869	36	27	40.0	12.8	.90	.68	2.82	2.11
2. 1879	56	42	49.7	17.0	1.12	.85	3.27	2.49
3. 1889	89	68	62.5	22.3	1.43	1.09	4.01	3.06
4. 1899	143	108	75.1	28.5	1.90	1.44	5.01	3.79
5. 1909	224	165	90.9	37.4	2.47	1.82	5.99	4.41
6. 1919	323	227	105.9	41.6	3.04	2.15	7.75	5.46
7. 1929	440	306	122.3	48.4	3.60	2.50	9.09	6.33
8. 1939	480	319	131.8	52.8	3.64	2.42	9.08	6.04
9. 1946	547	374	142.0	58.0	3.85	2.63	9.43	6.45
10. 1955	649	442	165.9	65.6	3.91	2.66	9.89	6.74
			Percentage rate of growth per decade					
1869 to 1889	57.6	58.9	25.1	32.1	26.1	27.0	19.3	20.3
1889 to 1909	58.4	55.7	20.6	29.6	31.3	29.2	22.2	20.1
1909 to 1929	40.1	36.2	16.0	13.8	20.7	17.4	23.2	19.8
1929 to 1955	16.1	15.1	12.4	12.4	3.3	2.4	3.3	2.4
1869 to 1955	40.0	38.4	18.0	21.0	18.6	17.3	15.7	14.4

* Capital stock in this column is gross of accumulated depreciation, but net of retirements.
† Capital stock in this column is net of depreciation and of retirements.
SOURCE: See Table 16-1.

In column 2, capital stock is given net of the depreciation reserves on the assets still in existence. As may be observed, capital stock, both gross and net, grew at considerably faster rates than either total population or total labor force. As a result, capital stock per capita, and per member of labor force, showed a remarkable increase over the entire period 1869 to 1955.

When the percentage rates of growth per decade are considered, both capital variants reveal a strong downward trend over the entire 1869–1955 period. The rates of population growth and of labor force growth also indicate a downward trend, although a considerably milder one. Consequently, the differences between the capital growth rates and the population (and labor force) growth rates are found to be much less pronounced during the 1929–1955 subperiod than during the earlier subperiods.

When total capital stock is compared with annual national product, the results are quite interesting. As Table 16-3 indicates, the average capital-to-output rato was generally rising during the period 1869–1939. This means, of course, that capital was growing at a faster rate than output. Thereafter, however, the trend was reversed: the ratios for the 1939–1949 and 1946–1955 periods are considerably lower than the ratios for the earlier decades. This is true when gross capital stock is related to gross national product and also when net capital stock is related to net national product.

The marginal capital-to-output ratios, i.e., the ratios of changes in the capital stock to changes in the national product are given in Table 16-4.

Table 16-3   Ratio of capital stock to average annual national product per decade, 1869–1955 (in 1929 prices)

Intervals for capital stock, geometric mean of terminal years	Periods for national product, annual averages	Ratio of gross capital to gross national product	Ratio of net capital to net national product
	Total stock and product		
1. 1869 and 1879	1869–1878	5.3	3.5
2. 1879 and 1889	1879–1888	4.5	2.9
3. 1889 and 1899	1889–1898	5.2	3.4
4. 1899 and 1909	1899–1908	5.3	3.4
5. 1909 and 1919	1909–1918	5.9	3.6
6. 1919 and 1929	1919–1928	6.0	3.5
7. 1929 and 1939	1929–1938	7.3	3.9
8. 1939 and 1949	1939–1948	5.4	2.5
9. 1946 and 1955	1946–1955	5.4	2.5

Note: The figures in this table and the following table are based on the national product estimates of the Department of Commerce beginning with 1929. The figures for the earlier years represent S. Kuznets' extrapolations.

SOURCE: See Table 16-1.

**Table 16-4   Ratio of changes in capital stock to changes in average
annual national product per decade, 1869–1955**

Interval	Ratio of changes in gross capital stock to changes in gross national product	Ratio of changes in net capital stock to changes in net national product
1. 1873–1883	3.6	2.3
2. 1883–1893	7.2	4.9
3. 1893–1903	5.4	3.2
4. 1903–1913	7.4	4.3
5. 1913–1923	6.3	3.2
6. 1923–1933	25.6	9.6
7. 1933–1943	2.8	.7
8. 1943–1952	5.3	1.8

SOURCE: See Table 16-1.

As one would expect, they show a greater degree of variation than the average ratios, but a similar reversal of the trend in the more recent decades.

These findings may seem to be surprising. One is inclined to associate industrial progress with a continual installation and use of more elaborate and costly technical equipment. Therefore, it would seem natural to expect that, as time goes on, capital stock should continually increase not only in relation to the labor force but also in relation to the annual output of finished goods.[3] How, then, can we explain the decline in the capital-to-output ratio in the more recent subperiods? While a complete explanation is, unfortunately, not available, some relevant factors may be briefly outlined.

In any given industry, as it goes through successive stages of development, certain factors come into play which tend to raise the C/O ratio in the early periods and then lower it in the later periods. In the early stages of development, construction of new capacity often results in additions geared to longer future. In the immediate future new additions are likely to be underutilized and the C/O ratio is likely to rise temporarily. But as the industry approaches maturity, the rate of capital growth diminishes and other factors, which tend to reduce the C/O ratio, come into play.

Heavy and durable construction becomes less important as a component of capital formation, while shorter-lived equipment gains in relative importance. Furthermore, the decline in the rate of growth is accompanied by a rise in capital consumption and replacement in relation to total capital formation. But the units of equipment which are scrapped are usually replaced with improved models capable of producing greater output when

[3] In Böhm-Bawerkian terms, this would mean a continual adoption of more "roundabout" productive processes or a continual lengthening of the average period of production.

used with the same quantities of other inputs. This factor also tends to reduce the C/O ratio.

The pattern outlined above is bound to change, however, when important technical innovations occur. Such innovations may be of either the capital-saving or the labor-saving variety. When they are of the former type, more capital and less labor are required to produce a given output, and the C/O ratio will tend to rise. But when they are of the latter type, the amount of capital is reduced in relation to both labor and output, and the C/O ratio will tend to fall. There are some indications that the innovations made in the more recent decades of the period studied had a considerable capital-saving effect.

Changes in the average capital-to-output ratio for the economy as a whole may also be due, to some extent, to changes in the relative importance of different industries in the successive subperiods examined. Thus, the data indicate a significant decline in the relative share of capital formation accounted for by the regulated public utility industries, in which the C/O ratio was relatively high. Concurrently, there was an increase in the relative share of capital formation accounted for by the manufacturing and mining industries, in which the C/O ratio was much lower.

Finally, it must be realized that no firm and no industry is able to operate at full capacity and maintain the technically optimal capital-to-output ratio at all times. During depression periods, when production has to be quickly and substantially curtailed, there is bound to be a temporary rise in the C/O ratio. (See the sharp rise in the C/O ratio in the early thirties, indicated in Tables 16-3 and 16-4.) When an expansion period begins, greater output requirements may at first be met by using the existing capital equipment with a greater degree of intensity. As full capacity is approached, new equipment will have to be installed, but the speed and the extent of new installations will depend not only on the technical factors but also on the economic ones: the availability and the cost of new capital funds, the management's evaluation of the future market trends, etc.

It is difficult to determine the relative importance of each of these factors even in the case of a single industry, let alone the national economy as a whole. In the following section we shall examine a little more closely the trends in the manufacturing and mining industries, which represented the fastest-growing sector of our economy.

CAPITAL FORMATION IN MANUFACTURING AND MINING

Over the long period comprising the last three decades of the last century and the first half of the present one, the manufacturing and mining sector expanded even more rapidly than the economy as a whole. During the decade of 1870–1880, income originating in manufacturing and mining was close to 16 percent of total national income. This proportion increased in nearly every subsequent decade and was close to 30 percent in 1944–1953. Valued at 1929 prices, fixed capital in this sector was roughly $3.2 billion in 1880 and rose to $42.9 billion in 1948: a more than thirteenfold increase. For the economy as a whole the comparable figures are $60.2 billion and $350.7 billion, respectively: a rise of less than sixfold.[4]

Despite its higher expansion rates, however, the manufacturing and mining sector was characterized by long-term trends similar to those observed above for the entire economy. Once again we find that the rates of expansion of both capital and output were declining over the entire period studied. And we also find that the capital-to-output ratio was rising during the earlier decades but declining during the later decades.

The general pattern of the C/O ratio variation in manufacturing during the period 1880–1953 is portrayed in Figure 16-1. The relevant figures are given in Table 16-5. The three curves in the upper part of the graph represent,

[4] Daniel Creamer, Sergei P. Dobrovolsky, and Israel Borenstein, *Capital in Manufacturing and Mining, Its Formation and Financing*, Princeton University Press, Princeton, N.J., 1960. p. 3.

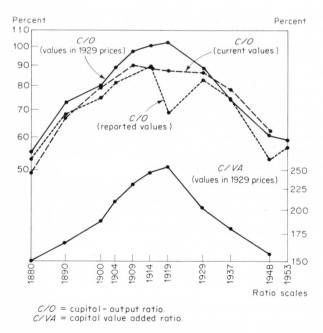

C/O = capital − output ratio.
C/VA = capital value added ratio.

Figure 16-1 Ratios of capital to output and to value added, selected valuations, all manufacturing, selected years, 1880–1953. (*Source:* See Table 16-5.)

Table 16-5 Ratios of capital to output and to value added, selected valuations, all manufacturing, selected years, 1880–1953

Benchmark years	Capital (book value) to output (current prices) (1)	Capital to output (1929 prices) (2)	Capital to output (current prices*) (3)	Capital to value added (1929 prices) (4)
		Ratio of		
1880	.528	.547	.489	1.506
1890	.679	.730	.670	1.651
1900				
Comparable with preceding years	.748	.803	.795	1.878
Comparable with following years	.743	.794	.790	1.882
1904	.815	.891	n.a.	2.093
1909	.851	.967	.900	2.309
1914	.894	1.008	n.a.	2.460
1919	.688	1.022	.873	2.555
1929	.829	.885	.867	2.020
1937	.744	.741	.787	1.809
1948	.532	.609	.621	1.550
1953†	.570	.590	n.a.	n.a.

n.a. = not available.

* Capital in current prices is equivalent to replacement costs in the given year.

† If privately operated, government-owned facilities are excluded from total capital, the respective ratios are 0.549 and 0.570.

SOURCE: D. Creamer, S. Dobrovolsky, and I. Borenstein, *Capital in Manufacturing and Mining: Its Formation and Financing*, Princeton University Press, Princeton, N.J., 1960, p. 39.

respectively, the ratio of (a) capital taken at book value to output valued at current prices, (b) capital to output when both are expressed in 1929 prices, and (c) capital valued at replacement cost to output measured in current prices. It can be seen that the general shape of the curve is the same in all three cases: there is a pronounced rise from 1880 to 1914 or 1919, followed by a substantial decline in the following period.

Of the three measures, (a) is of course the crudest. Since price changes are incorporated more rapidly into the value of output than into the book value of capital, they should be eliminated for a more accurate comparison. Variants (b) and (c) represent two alternative methods of adjustment for price changes. It can be seen that the adjusted ratios obtained by either method are very similar to each other.

The curve in the lower part of the graph represents the ratio of capital to value added, both in 1929 prices. The use of value added in the denominator of the ratio serves to eliminate interfirm transactions from the total value of output. While this increases the ratio in each year, the long-term trends clearly remain essentially the same.

Within the manufacturing sector, the capital-to-output ratios varied substantially from one industry to another. In 1880 the range was from .085 (packing house products) to 2.11 (chemicals). There was also a wide variation in the rates of growth of individual industries. The question arises, therefore, whether the trends in the C/O ratios for the sector as a whole could not be explained, at least in part, by the changing relative importance of particular industries. An analysis of the available data indicates, however, that changes in industry composition accounted for only about one-sixth of the total increase in the C/O ratio for all manufacturing between 1880 and 1919. Moreover, this factor in itself should have produced a further rise of the ratio in the subsequent decades, whereas the actual movement was downward.

There are also some indications that the capital-to-output ratio was positively related to the size of the firm. In 1947, for example, the ratio of fixed capital to output for different asset classes of manufacturing corporations was as follows.

	For firms with assets
.098	Under $100,000
.116	From $100,000 to $1 million
.154	From $1 million to $10 million
.221	$10 million and over

Again, the question arises as to the possible effect of this tendency on the observed trends in the C/O ratio. Unfortunately, there are no reliable statistics by asset size over long periods of time. But it seems plausible to assume that the trend toward larger firm size in the earlier decades was a factor contributing to the rise of the C/O ratio. As for the later decades, a fairly strong tendency toward larger establishments was observed in some of them (1929–1937) but not in the others (1919–1929 and 1937–1947). On balance, this particular factor apparently was not strong enough in the latter part of the period to prevent the C/O ratio from declining.

In general, the authors of the study on manufacturing and mining were inclined to consider the changing nature of technical innovations to be the major factor responsible for the reversal of the C/O ratio trend. Their conclusion was stated as follows: "In the earlier decades, capital innovations on balance probably served more to replace other factor inputs than to increase output. Since World War I, capital innovations serve more to increase the efficiency of capital, hence to increase output, than to replace other factor inputs."[5]

In a later study, devoted specifically to the post-World War II period, D. Creamer found that while the C/O ratio continued to decline between 1948 and 1953, it rose considerably between 1953 and 1957, reversing the downward trend of nearly four decades.[6] This reversal may be explained, at least partially, by the fact that the most significant technological innovations in the 1948–1957 period were those centering around automation. The most obvious aspect of automation is, of course, its labor-saving character, which tends to raise the C/O ratio. However, automated processes may also bring about economies in the utilization of machinery and equipment. Such economies may result, for example, from the greater speed of operations, self-regulation in combining variable proportions of materials so as to achieve optimum utilization of machinery, etc. This factor may significantly weaken the upward trend of the C/O ratio in an automated industry.

Apparently, during the 1948–1953 period, the capital-saving tendencies in the automated as well as nonautomated industries were still the prevalent factor. In the 1953–1957 period, on the other hand, other factors came into play, supplementing and strengthening the effect of the labor-saving features of automation. The rate of capital expansion rose during those years, and a significant degree of excess capacity developed in some industries by 1957. As a result, the capital-to-output ratio registered a considerable rise.

FINANCIAL TRENDS: INTERNAL VERSUS EXTERNAL FINANCING

We shall now review briefly the long-term trends in financing capital formation in the United States. Two questions are of particular interest in this connection: (1) Were there any significant changes in the relative importance of internal and external financing over long periods of time? and (2) Was there any significant variation in the relative shares of debt and equity funds? We shall consider the first of these questions in this section and the second in the next section.

The data assembled in Table 16-6 permit a comparison of internal and external financing used by all nonfinancial corporations in the United States over the period 1901–1956.[7] It can be seen that the ratio of gross internal financing (retained profit plus capital consumption allowances) to total sources (total amount of funds used) varied from .55 during the 1901–

[5] *Op. cit.*, p. 65.

[6] Daniel Creamer, *Capital Expansion and Capacity in Postwar Manufacturing*, The National Industrial Conference Board, New York, 1961.

[7] Unfortunately, the financial data, unlike the data on capital formation, are not available prior to 1900.

Table 16-6   Sources of funds, nonfinancial corporations, 1901–1956 (amounts in billions of dollars)

Period	Total sources (1)	Gross internal (2)	Capital consumption (3)	Retained profits (4)	External sources (5)	Ratio of Col. 2 to Col. 1	Ratio of Col. 4 to Col. 1	Ratio of Col. 5 to Col. 1
1901–1912*	40.0	22.1	13.4	8.7	17.9	.55	.22	.45
1913–1922	76.1	46.0	25.6	20.4	30.1	.60	.27	.40
1923–1929	86.1	47.1	32.1	15.0	39.0	.55	.17	.45
1930–1933	−.6	4.1	20.8	−16.7	−4.8			
1934–1939	28.9	28.2	31.4	−3.3	.7	.98		.02
1940–1945	75.4	60.5	36.6	23.9	14.9	.80	.32	.20
1946–1949	110.6	71.3	33.7	37.6	39.3	.64	.34	.36
1946–1956†	355.3	205.0	106.4	98.6	150.3	.58	.28	.42

* The figures for 1901–1949 are Raymond W. Goldsmith's estimates.
† The figures for 1946–1956 are Department of Commerce estimates.
SOURCE: See Table 16-1.

1912 period to .98 during the 1934–1939 period; it follows, of course, that the ratio of external financing to the total varied from .45 to .02. Thus, in all of the subperiods indicated in the table, the amount of gross internal financing exceeded that of external financing obtained by borrowing or selling equity securities.

However, no pronounced trend is observed in the relative importance of the two components over the entire period 1901–1956. The ratio of gross internal financing to total sources rose markedly from 1901–1912 to 1934–1939, but declined subsequently and was only slightly higher in 1946–1956 than in 1901–1912.

When net internal financing (retained profit alone) is considered, we find that it made a substantial contribution to total financing in all subperiods except for 1930–33 and 1934–39, when corporations showed net dissaving instead of retention. Here again, however, there is no clear trend in the ratio of this component to total sources over the entire period covered.

Capital consumption allowances were greater than retained profits in most of the subperiods. They were positive even in the 1930–1933 and 1934–1939 periods, but it must be realized, of course, that allowances made on the books represent an actual source of funds only when they are earned. Since in these two periods gross internal financing fell short of consumption allowances (because of net dissaving), the actual amount of internal funds generated by corporations was not adequate to maintain, let alone expand, their durable assets.

It should be noted that the inflow of external funds into the corporate sector, which increased the claims of other sectors on corporations, was accompanied by the expansion of financial assets held by corporations, which increased their claims on other sectors. When external financing is taken net of financial asset expansion, the resulting amount, representing net absorption of funds from other sectors, is found to be substantially smaller than retained profit—and, of course, even smaller in comparison with gross internal financing. The figures for selected periods are as follows:

	Total external financing	Financial asset expansion	Net external financing	Retained profit
		(in billions of dollars)		
1901–1922	48.0	40.6	7.4	29.1
1913–1939	65.0	58.8	6.2	15.4
1946–1956	150.3	79.4	70.9	98.6

The data for manufacturing and mining also fail to indicate a clear trend in the relative shares of internal and external financing over the first half of the twentieth century. A complete statement of sources and uses of funds for this sector is not available over the entire period, but a comparison can be made between net profit retention and net asset expansion during 1900–1953. The figures are as follows:

	Retained profit as percentage of asset change
1900–1909	41.3
1914–1919	52.5
1919–1929	26.1
1937–1948	53.5
1948–1953	49.2

As can be seen, the ratio of retained profit to asset expansion was fairly close to one-half in most subperiods.

It is also possible to compare gross internal financing (retained profit plus depreciation allowances) with gross plant and equipment expenditures. The ratio of the former to the latter is found to be as follows:

	Retained profit plus depreciation as percentage of gross plant and equipment expenditure
1900–1914	87.1
1919–1929	107.8
1936–1940	92.2
1946–1953	109.9

One is tempted to conclude from the above that plant and equipment expenditures were essentially financed with internal funds and that external funds were required only to finance relatively small investments in other assets: inventories, receivables, and marketable securities. On the basis of aggregate data, however, one cannot justifiably match individual sources with individual uses of funds. Some corporations that were engaged in substantial plant modernization or expansion programs doubtless required large amounts of external funds in addition to the funds generated internally. At the same time, other companies generated internal funds well in excess of their own expenditures on plant and equipment. Nevertheless, it is interesting to observe that, for the industry as a whole, the amount obtained from the internal source was approximately equal to the amount required to finance the most important type of expenditures.

In contrast to manufacturing and mining, the regulated industries —railroads, telephones, and electric light and power—show a pronounced upward trend in the relative importance of internal financing over the first half of our century. The trend was especially steep in the case of steam railroads: the ratio of gross retentions to total sources of funds rose from 9.5 percent during 1893–1907 to 101.6 percent during 1941–1949. For the other two regulated industries the increase in the ratio was less pronounced but nevertheless quite substantial: from 6.3 percent to 40.5 percent for the telephone companies and from 7.6 percent to 50.3 percent for the electric light and power companies. It should be borne in mind that the last subperiod included in the table combines the years of World War II, when external financing was especially low, with the postwar years, in which external financing showed a considerable resurgence. A rough calculation indicates, however, that the ratio of gross retentions to total sources of funds in the postwar period was still considerably higher than it was in the early decades.[8]

The decline in the relative importance of external financing in the regulated industries is in large measure explained by the slowing down in their rate of growth. In the early part of the century, they were expanding

[8] Kuznets, *op. cit.*, p. 254.

Table 16-7 Structure of external financing, nonfinancial corporations, 1901–1955 (amounts in billions of dollars)

Periods	New stock issues (1)	New bond issues (2)	Mortgage loans (3)	Total long-term external (4)	Total short-term external (5)	Total external (6)	Ratio of Col. 1 to Col. 4	Ratio of Col. 4 to Col. 6
1901–12*	5.6	8.2	.8	14.6	3.2	17.9	.38	.82
1913–22	8.5	6.5	2.6	17.6	12.6	30.1	.48	.58
1923–29	16.7	12.2	6.4	35.3	3.7	39.0	.47	.91
1930–39	5.4	−.3	−1.0	4.1	−8.2	−4.1	1.32	
1940–45	3.5	−3.8	0	−.3	15.3	14.9		
1946–55†	19.8	35.7	8.4	63.9	65.0	128.9	.31	.50

* 1901–1945: R. Goldsmith's estimates.
† Department of Commerce estimates.
SOURCE: See Table 16-1.

so fast that internal funds fell far short of the total financing required. In the later decades, the much lower rate of expansion reduced the need for external financing to a substantial extent.[9]

FINANCIAL TRENDS: DEBT VERSUS EQUITY FINANCING

It remains to examine briefly variations in the relative importance of the major components of external financing over the half-century period concerned. The relevant data for all nonfinancial corporations are given in Table 16-7. First, one should note that the ratio of long-term external to total external financing tended to decline, although not consistently. One factor that tended to increase the relative importance of short-term external funds was the growth of accrued tax liabilities.

Secondly, within the long-term component of external financing one finds a downward trend in the ratio of equity funds (new stock issues) to debt funds (new bond issues and mortgage loans). An increase in new debt financing in the postwar period was largely due to the deductibility of interest, as opposed to dividends, in corporate income tax computations.

Similar tendencies are observed when the data for manufacturing and mining are examined. The ratio of long-term external to total external financing for this sector was as follows:

[9] See Neville J. Ulmer, *Capital in Transportation, Communications and Public Utilities: Its Formation and Financing*, Princeton University Press, Princeton, N.J., 1960, pp. 150–153.

	Long-term external financing as a percentage of total external financing
1900–1919	57
1920–1937	98
1937–1953	34

The ratio of new bond issues to new stock issues, on the other hand, showed a steep rise in the last subperiod:

	Net bond issues as a percentage of net stock issues
1900–1919	53
1920–1937	1
1937–1953	142

As already mentioned above, an increase in short-term external financing in the more recent subperiods was, in large measure, due to a rise in tax accruals resulting from higher corporate income tax rates.

It is interesting to note that accumulation of tax accruals on the liability side was accompanied by an increase in corporate holdings of government securities on the asset side. If both of these items—representing, in effect, borrowing from and lending to the government—are excluded from the balance sheet, the rise in the debt-to-assets ratios is found to be considerably smaller. Thus, while the ratio of total debt to total assets of all manufacturing and mining corporations increased from 25 percent in 1929 to 36 percent in 1952, the ratio of total debt less tax accruals to total assets less government securities increased from 25 percent in 1929 to only 31 percent in 1952. The unadjusted ratio of current liabilities to total assets shows a rise from 17 percent to 24 percent over the same period; the adjusted ratio indicates a rise from 17 percent to 19 percent.

Finally, in the regulated industries one also finds a declining tendency in the ratio of new stock financing to total external financing. In the telephone industry the ratio declined from 0.69 in 1893–1907 to .14 in 1941–1950. In the electric light and power industry, it dropped from .51 in 1881–1912 to .37 in 1941–1950. In these industries, current liabilities represented only a minor fraction of total external financing. However, some increase in their relative importance over the period studied may be observed.

SUMMARY

Statistical data on capital formation in the United States are available for a fairly large period comprising roughly the final quarter of the last century and the first half of the present one. They indicate that our national capital stock generally grew at a much faster rate than our total population. As a result, capital stock per capita showed a remarkable increase over this period. The percentage rates of increase per decade, however, reveal a strong downward trend in both capital and population growth.

When capital stock is compared with annual national product, an interesting reversal of the trend is found to have taken place in the last two decades of the period concerned. The average capital-to-output ratio was rising during the period 1869–1939. Thereafter, however, the ratio declined markedly. A variety of factors must have been responsible for this reversal: a change in the nature of technological innovations (in the direction of capital-saving techniques), the slowing down of the rate of growth in several important sectors of the economy, the decline in the relative importance of some industries with a higher than average capital-to-output ratio, etc.

The manufacturing and mining industries represented the fastest-growing sector of the economy during the period reviewed. They were, however, characterized by long-term trends generally similar to those observed for the economy as a whole. The rates of growth in both capital and output were declining over the entire period. The capital-to-output ratio was rising during the earlier decades but began to decline in the later decades. It is interesting to note that while the ratio continued to decline during the first several years after World War II, characterized by a strong tendency toward "automation," the trend was once more reversed and a rise in the ratio was registered in the 1953–1957 period.

The amount of gross internal financing exceeded the amount of external financing used by nonfinancial corporations in all decades during the 1901–1956 period. There is, however, no clear evidence that internal financing increased in relative importance over that period.

The data for manufacturing and mining industries also fail to indicate a clear trend in the relative shares of internal and external financing over the first half of the present century. In contrast, the regulated industries—railroads, telephones, and electric light and power—show a pronounced upward trend in the relative importance of internal funds. This was probably due mainly to the slowing down in the rate of growth of these industries.

The ratio of long-term external financing to total external financing declined over the period reviewed. One factor that tended to raise the relative importance of short-term external funds was the growth of accrued tax liabilities.

Within the long-term component of external financing one finds a downward trend in the ratio of equity funds (new stock issues) to debt funds (new bond issues and mortgage loans). This was due, in large part, to the tax factor: as the corporate income tax rates became higher, the deductibility of interest for tax purposes gave debt financing an increasing measure of advantage.

SELECTED REFERENCES

Creamer, Daniel: *Capital Expansion and Capacity in Postwar Manufacturing*, National Industrial Conference Board, Inc., New York, 1961.
————, Sergei P. Dobrovolsky, and Israel Borenstein: *Capital in Manufacturing and Mining: Its Formation and Financing*, Princeton University Press, Princeton, N.J., 1960.
Kuznets, Simon: *Capital in the American Economy; Its Formation and Financing*, Princeton University Press, Princeton, N.J., 1961.
Ulmer, Neville J.: *Capital in Transportation, Communications, and Public Utilities; Its Formation and Financing*, Princeton University Press, Princeton, N.J., 1960.

Index